Die Warhait ist vntödtlich.

The truth is indestructible.

— Balthasar Hubmaier (ca. 1480–1528)

FOR GOD'S TRUTH

A Hutterite History Reader

JESSE HOFER & KENNY WOLLMANN, *editors*

2024

Softcover ISBN: 978-1-998141-07-4
Hardcover ISBN: 978-1-998141-08-1
eBook ISBN: 978-1-998141-25-8

Library and Archives Canada Cataloguing in Publication
Title: For God's truth : a Hutterite history reader / Jesse Hofer & Kenny
Wollmann, editors.
Names: Hofer, Jesse, editor. | Wollmann, Kenny, editor.
Identifiers: Canadiana 20240451198 | ISBN 9781998141074 (softcover) |
ISBN 9781998141081 (hardcover)
Subjects: LCSH: Hutterian Brethren—History—Sources.
Classification: LCC BX8129.H8 F67 2024 | DDC 289.7/3—dc23

Acknowledgments and Permissions: Every effort has been made to locate
the copyright holders for all materials included in this compendium.
Where the copyright holder could not be found or did not respond, the
publisher is willing to rectify any errors or omissions in subsequent edi-
tions if notified. Please contact the publisher with any concerns.

Cover image: A 16th-century large-format drawing, spread over two folios,
that combines two scenes into one: on the front cover (right side) the authorities discovery a nocturnal assembly of Anabaptists, and the back cover
(left side) shows the two missioners being lead away into captivity. Pen and
watercolour, Zentralbibliothek Zürich, Ms. F 23, fol. 394.

Box 40 • MacGregor, MB • R0H 0R0
p. 204–272–5132 • f. 204–252–2381 • e. orders@hbbookcentre.com

Table of Contents

THE PRE-HUTTERITE PERIOD

Medieval Spirituality and Reform Voices

Reformation Literature

Early Anabaptist Writings

Late 20th-Century Concerns

THE 21ST CENTURY

Index of Illustrations

v

Introduction

The body they may kill; *God's truth* will triumph still.

– Martin Luther

Behold, woe and double woe to all who would persecute, exile, and hate us without cause, simply because we stand *for God's truth*!"

– Jakob Hutter

Envy, stemming from the old serpent, is behind their hatred *of God's truth.*

– Hans Kräl

This, however, was always at the price of great suffering and the shedding of much blood in many lands, towns, and marketplaces for the sake of Jesus Christ and *his divine truth.*

– Kasper Braitmichel

The Hutterites of the 16th century produced and transmitted a substantial literary corpus despite being a persecuted minority in a very intolerant early modern context. Besides the *Great Chronicle* and the smaller versions it is based on, they authored countless letters, confessions, martyr ballads, prayers, homilies, and biblical commentaries. Unfortunately, much of this material remains inaccessible to non-specialists. *For God's Truth: A Hutterite History Reader* seeks to address this gap.

Beginning in 1930, the *Verein für Reformationsgeschichte* [Society for Reformation History] published the more notable 16th century Anabaptist-Hutterite sources in the *Quellen zur Geschichte der Täufer* [Anabaptist History Sources] series. The two-volume *Glaubenszeugnisse oberdeutscher Taufgesinnter* [Confessions of Faith of South German Anabaptists] edited by Lydia Müller and the two volumes edited by Grete Mecenseffy focusing on Austrian sources are particularly relevant for Hutterite history. These volumes, however, are rare, expensive, and almost exclusively in 16th century German.

In Hutterite circles, the four-volume *Hutterischen Episteln 1525–1767* [Hutterite epistles] published by James Valley Book Centre between 1986–1991 is more familiar. It features a significant part of the Hutterite literary heritage (with an emphasis on the epistles), but it too is inaccessible to many readers for a variety of reasons: most of the documents are only available in German and the texts are printed in the foreboding Fraktur typeface. Additionally, the series offers no introductions to contextualize the texts. While this *Reader* cannot reproduce this series, its goal is to make some of the key texts available in English for a wider readership.

Organization of Material

The *Reader* is organized chronologically by era. In the eras with more literary activity, such as the 16th and 20th centuries, subheadings were added to better categorize the selected sources.

Selection Criteria

In selecting the texts for this *Reader*, we attempted to draw a full picture of Hutterite influences, history, theology, spirituality, and contemporary concerns.

One strand of texts focuses on watershed moments in the narrative, such as the first adult baptism at Zürich, the beginning of community-of-goods outside Nikolsburg, the early schisms in Moravia, and so on. In most cases, the *Chronicle* was the go-to source for these entries. Wherever possible we drew on sources beyond the Hutterite tradition to fill out the picture: Wilhelm Reublin's letter to Pilgram Marpeck, for example, appears alongside the *Chronicle*'s account of the Austerlitz Schism of 1531.

A second strand highlights the fact that Hutterites did not appear in a vacuum and, despite their attempt to separate from the world, could never be an island unto themselves. For example, scholars have traced influences on the Hutterite tradition from the monastic tradition (Benedict's *Rule*), the *devotio moderna* (Kempis, *Imitation of Christ*) and humanism (Erasmus). Thus, the texts in the pre-Hutterite section are intended to help readers understand the ideas, influences, and individuals which contributed to the emergence of the Hutterite movement. A number of pieces from Martin Luther and Huldrych Zwingli, as well as a selection of Anabaptist voices, emphasize that Hutterites were part of a larger conversation during the Reformation period. Further, we've included several legal documents and contracts to emphasize the fact that Hutterite existence was always dependent on relationships with hospitable landlords, rulers, and governments.

In some cases, excerpts from secondary sources are used (for example, the Forest River conflict, and the 1974 reuniting with the Bruderhof) to establish the context of a complex event where official documents are either not available or where the story is not easily represented through primary sources.

A third strand of texts highlights sources of theological interest, including a variety of early confessions, letters dealing with burning questions of the day, representative *Ordnungen*, and texts relating to inter-confessional conversations. These sources give voice to the community's theological commitments, the process of translating these into a shared life, and their development over time. We also added a number of songs and prayers in order to reflect elements of the contemporary spirituality. The inclusion of historically significant images reflects the importance of visual culture in history.

Finally, we included a number of more recent documents to prompt critical reflection about how we remember our history: two pieces relating to Hutterite-Indigenous relations in Manitoba in the 20th and 21st centuries; and two texts reflecting recent efforts towards reconciliation and right remembering, spearheaded by the *Hutterer Arbeitskreis von Tirol und Südtirol*.

We intentionally decided against including any documents directly relating to the 1992 Schmiedeleut schism. The challenge of telling the complex story of the schism through primary sources is a daunting one, and we do not feel that we are in a position to do justice to this work at this time.

Intended Audience

The *Reader* was originally conceived and tested as a companion text for an introductory high school Hutterite history course taught via the HBNIITV (Hutterian Brethren Network Interactive Instructional Television) network. We hope that it will be useful as further reading for those familiar with the general Hutterite story but desiring a deeper dive into the primary sources in order to encounter, weigh, and interpret the historical evidence for themselves.

The difference between encountering primary texts and simply relying on secondary sources for understanding historical events is similar to a detective visiting a crime scene to gather and analyze clues as opposed to simply relying on reports or newspaper accounts of what happened. This *Reader* allows students of Hutterite History to put on their detective hats and begin sleuthing for themselves. Generous outer margins have been added to encourage annotation and visual reflections. Those wanting to dig deeper on a particular period or theme in Hutterite history are encouraged to consult the selected bibliography at the end of this volume.

Introductions

The introductions were written to provide important background information and draw attention to important issues in the texts without doing the work of analysis and interpretation for readers. We have taken the first occurrence of a genre that appears numerous times (e.g., *Ordnungen* and confessions of faith) as an opportunity to provide a longer overview of the place of this genre in the *Reader* and a consideration of its significance within Hutterite history.

Translations

Over time, translations can lose their luster, as language evolves and as we learn more about the world of a given text. Thus, about half of the Hutterite texts have been newly translated for the *Reader* and a few appear in English for the first time: Handbüchlein excerpts, *Allgemeine Dienstordnung*, Anabaptist legends, court testimonies of the crypto-Protestants, and *Decline of the Community in Russia*.

About the Title: *For God's Truth*

The tone of many 16th century texts commonly strikes 21st century ears as severe, uncompromising, and judgemental. Of course, this says as much about our world and our values today as it does about what we find in the past. One way to make sense of this phenomena is to recognize that something very significant was at stake for these writers: they believed themselves to be engaged in a struggle for God's truth, a phrase that appears frequently in these texts. They regularly dispensed with common courtesy in order to get to the heart of the matter. Christendom and the social order as they knew it were unravelling, and there was great concern for what would emerge in their place. As the foundations of society were quaking, they were convinced that a more hopeful future was to be found in striving to better understand and live according to the truthful vision of human flourishing otherwise known as "God's will."

As empathetic and truth-seeking readers of these texts, we too can participate in a larger conversation about what living God's truth means for us today.

The cover image depicts Anabaptist believers gathering secretly in the woods to hear and discuss Scripture and to consider how God's truth should transform their lives, even while the authorities are closing in. Many experienced first-hand what is partly illustrated in the second half of the image: arrest, imprisonment, torture, and even execution. But God's truth, as Balthasar Hubmaier pointed out, is indestructible. And so the Hutterite fire of devotion kept burning despite the draconian measures introduced to snuff it out.

Acknowledgements

We are grateful to the various individuals, organizations, and publishers who have graciously granted permission to reprint various texts and images especially the Mennonite Quarterly Review and Plough Publishing.

We also wish to acknowledge the influence of the Riedemann Arbeitskreis (2014–2017) and the guidance of our mentor, Lothar Korff. The time spent carefully reading texts with this group has been formative for how we value primary sources, and for how we think about and appreciate our heritage. At various times, we were enriched by the participation of the following members: Lothar Korff from Neepawa, Manitoba, Conrad Hofer from Acadia, Ian Kleinsasser, Anita Kleinsasser, and Edward Kleinsasser from Crystal Spring, Kathy Waldner and Mark Waldner from Decker, Linda Maendel from Elm River, Dora Maendel from Fairholme, Wanda Waldner and Paul Waldner from Green Acres, Markus Hofer from Netley, Doris Wurtz from Oak River, Cynthia and Harry Stahl from Odanah, Zacharias Hofer from Silverwinds, Paul Hofer from Springhill, and Stanley Kleinsasser from Wingham.

Thank you also to the following individuals for their suggestions and editorial assistance: Emmy Barth Maendel, Paul Doerksen, Jonathan Seiling, Astrid von Schlachta, Jason Stahl, Julian Waldner, and Mark Waldner.

We are particularly excited to publish this volume on the cusp of the 500th anniversary of the Anabaptist movement. May it inspire deeper reflection about the roots of the movement, with a view to cultivating more thoughtful engagement with the past, and more faithful discipleship today.

August 2024

Hutterite History in a Nutshell

The date of January 21, 1525 is commonly considered the beginning of the Anabaptist movement. On this day Conrad Grebel, Felix Manz, Georg Blaurock, and others met for prayer in a home in Zürich and began the practice of adult baptism based on their reading of Scripture. We should question this date as the 'beginning' of 'Anabaptism' for two reasons that Grebel, Manz, and Blaurock would also have insisted on: They saw themselves not as beginning a new movement, but as restoring the Church begun by the Holy Spirit at Pentecost; further, they saw their baptisms not as a 'rebaptism' (as the moniker *Wiedertäufer* or Anabaptist suggests) but as the only true and valid baptism made voluntarily and upon confession of faith.

Connected with this commitment to believer's baptism was the Anabaptist's understanding of the church as a voluntary community of believers. Alongside this, they were committed to non-violence, mutual aid, and economic sharing. Some even practiced a form of commun-

ity-of-goods. However, putting it into a concrete, visible form was not possible due to severe repression under Ferdinand I. This was true especially in the Tyrol where Georg Blaurock spread the Anabaptist message after fleeing persecution in Zürich. The Tyrol was the homeland of many early Hutterites.

This persecution, however, soon pushed many Anabaptist believers to move northeast to Moravia, where a measure of tolerance could be found, thanks to a combination of geography, sympathetic lords, and a unique history of reform and dissent.

It is not a coincidence that the Anabaptist movement emerged almost at the same time as the German Peasants' War of 1524–25. The peasants yearned for social and economic justice and were encouraged by Luther's bold writings on "Christian freedom" and a "priesthood of all believers." When Luther made it clear that his reforms were aimed primarily at the spiritual level, many of the peasants embraced the more radical vision of the Anabaptists which sought to create an alternative society where all aspects of life—social, political, economic, and yes, spiritual—were reformed and impacted by the good news of the gospel. Discipleship and a voluntary faith were central, which translated to a high degree of commitment and accountability to the church community.

By 1528, the first commune was established outside the Anabaptist city of Nikolsburg by a splinter group that emerged from a conflict between Balthasar Hubmaier and Hans Hut over the use of the sword and other issues. Following a series of divisions over leadership, Jakob Hutter emerged as a unifying, charismatic figure who set a direction for the beleaguered company in part through an unwavering commitment to his people and the principle of radical economic sharing. Martyred in 1536 in the wake of intensified imperial attention following the Münster debacle (1534–35), Hutter's organizational genius set the tone for the movement.

The founding years were characterized by intermittent raids, countless martyred missioners, the formidable challenge of integrating newcomers, and a growing literary corpus, including countless epistles, Peter Riedemann's notable *Confession of Faith* (1542), and the *Great Chronicle* (1560s), a running record of the movement's history.

During the Golden Years (1565–1590), Hutterites were able to grow to an estimated population of 20,000–30,000. Persecution of the movement lessened significantly, missioners were routinely sent out to gather more converts, and their economic enterprises, focused primarily on manufacturing luxury items such as pottery and cutlery, flourished. They established boarding schools where boys and girls learned to read, a standard that was exceptional for the 16th century.

The downturn in their fortunes in Moravia began in the 1590s, with the Turkish War (1593–1606), followed by the Thirty Years' War (1618–1648) and their expulsion to neighbouring Slovakia in Northern Hungary in 1622. A year earlier, several hundred members were taken to Transylvania to establish communes on Prince Gabor Bethlen's properties near Sibiu (Hermannstadt, Romania).

Over the next 130 years, the communities in Hungary and Transylvania struggled to maintain their faith in the face of determined Jesuit strategies to reclaim them for the Catholic Church. Besides this threat, they were frequently overrun by soldiers taking part in various conflicts, and struggled under a growing tax burden. In an attempt to spark renewal, Elder Andreas Ehrenpreis (1589–1662) introduced new *Gemeindeordnungen*, sent out missionaries, and oversaw the writing of a collection of homilies (*Lehren und Vorreden*) still widely used today. Community-of-goods, however, was eventually abandoned by both groups, and they became known as 'Habaner.'

In 1755, renewal came from an unexpected, unlikely source. A group of crypto-Protestants were deported from their home province of Carinthia by Empress Maria Theresa, a staunch Catholic. They initially settled close to the Hutterites who lived at Alwinz in Transylvania and soon encountered them while looking for work. They learned about the community's history and beliefs and were so impressed and attracted by what they heard, they enthusiastically revived community-of-goods and established a few communities, despite the authorities' ongoing efforts to prevent them.

By 1767, the Jesuits had designs to place Hutterite children in Catholic-run boarding schools in a last-ditch attempt to convert them. Learning of this ploy, a small group of 67 Hutterites arranged for an escape across the Carpathian Mountains into Wallachia, where they stayed for a short three years before once again being forced to move northeast of Kiev to settle at Vishenka (Ukraine) due to armed conflict in the area.

After about 30 years at Vishenka they moved to nearby crown lands at Radicheva because they were not able to renew their contract with their landlord's sons. The community at Radicheva failed to flourish for a number of reasons and eventually gave up communalism and divided

in 1819. By 1842, with the help of Mennonite leader and entrepreneur, Johann Cornies, they were able to relocate to the Molotschna Colony near what is Melitopol, Ukraine today. They established a number of villages, learned modern farming techniques and received schooling. But integration in the Molotschna was always fraught with tensions, and these tensions revived a yearning for the old ways. In 1859, following a vision in which an angel instructed him to restore the ark of the commune, Michael Waldner led efforts to re-establish *Gütergemeinschaft*, community-of-goods.

In 1874, responding to nationalization efforts by the Russian government which would have meant a loss of their military exemption, the Hutterites migrated to the Dakota territories in North America, despite the fact that they could not get assurance from the government that they would receive an exemption from military service. With the help of two German-speaking communal societies, Amana (Iowa) and Harmony (Pennsylvania), they were able to overcome a multitude of pioneering hardships and establish thriving agricultural operations.

During World War I (1914–18), the communal, German-speaking, pacifist Hutterites began attracting public attention. Their communities were targeted with anti-German sentiment. A number of their young men were conscripted into the American army and two of them—

Michael and Joseph Hofer—died in military custody following mistreatment during their imprisonment at Alcatraz. Feeling betrayed and besieged, the Hutterites packed their bags once more and headed north to Canada, where they were able to secure similar religious freedoms as the Mennonites had some forty years earlier.

During the first decades in Canada, the handful of communities were burdened by the significant debt incurred from the initial land purchases, and by the challenges posed by the Great Depression (1929–39). During World War II (1939–45), many young Hutterite men performed alternative service as conscientious objectors to the war, mostly in national parks. Resentment expressed by returning veterans led to legislation in Alberta that restricted the amount of land Hutterites could buy (Land Sales Prohibition Act, 1942–47), and limited how close a daughter community could be built to other Hutterite communities (Communal Property Act, 1947–73).

Beginning in 1931, the Hutterites entered into a relationship with the Bruderhof. The Bruderhof is a German communal society founded by Eberhard and Emmy Arnold following the social, economic and spiritual turmoil unleashed by World War I. The partnership was mutually beneficial in many ways, but also created ongoing conflicts around education, mission, compliance with the *Ordnungen*, cultural expressions, and the larger vision and direction of the church. The union ended formally in 1955, was restored in 1974, but another parting of ways occurred in the 1990s. Today, the two groups are formally separate entities, with some ongoing influences and exchanges.

Today, there are about 500 Hutterite communities which are home to some 50,000 Hutterites, mostly in the prairie states and provinces of North America. Settled far from their origins in Moravia, speaking a dialect that reflects the pilgrimage they have collectively embarked on, Hutterites are a familiar part of the Canadian and American landscapes.

Hutterites have not faced any significant external threats since World War I. For over 100 years they have been mostly left to their own to build their communities and practice their faith in peace. Part of their challenge is to keep alive and vibrant their identity as a people of faith in these relaxed circumstances, to wrestle with what it means to be radical, communal Christians in a highly individualized Western society. What does it mean to live with increasing prosperity within a technological, pluralistic, and secular society? What should engagement with larger society look like? How should we prepare our children to meet the challenges of the future? These urgent questions will require a courageous biblically and historically informed vision to point Hutterites to revitalizing answers.

Reading Primary Sources Empathetically and Critically: A Gift and a Challenge

Historians commonly distinguish between two types of texts: Primary sources and secondary sources. Primary sources are texts produced in the time period that the historian is interested in. Secondary sources are texts written about a particular time period. For example, John Hofer's book *The History of the Hutterites* is a secondary source about Hutterite history that draws on a number of primary sources including the Hutterite Chronicles. This Hutterite history reader collects primary sources from over 500 years of Hutterite history.

Reading primary sources can be exciting and intimidating. Exciting because these texts offer the opportunity to step outside of our time and culture and into the very different world of a different historical period. Reading primary sources has some of the excitement of being a tourist visiting a different country or culture. As L.P. Hartney put it, "The past is a foreign country; they do things differently there." If you read the texts in this reader carefully, you will have the opportunity to experience some of this excitement for yourself. You might be surprised at what Hutterites in the past thought or did that is different from what we think and do today. For example, while we think of the family as central to Hutterite life, Hutterites in the past raised children communally and discouraged strong familial ties. This should raise questions. Do our contemporary assumptions need to be unsettled by the past? Are contemporary ideas and practices in Hutterite life 'true for all time' or are they temporary and worth questioning?

Reading primary sources is intimidating for the same reason it is exciting: to our contemporary eyes, texts from the past can be challenging, shocking, disturbing, or unsettling. On the most basic level, reading texts from the past can be challenging because writers use words and language differently, and it can sometimes take some work to understand what is being said. Sometimes, this difference can be shocking. For example, many readers are taken aback by the angry and militant tone of Reformation era polemics (see "Sixteenth Century Visual Polemics," 55). We can find it hard to look past the language to see the issues at stake underneath. Further, we might find ourselves disturbed by the beliefs held by our ancestors. Some readers might feel this way when reading Peter Riedemann's defence of the practice of "double honour" by which ministers in the community were afforded special food and other privileges (see Riedemann, "Double Honour" Letter, 191). Finally, reading primary sources can challenge our dearly held modern assumptions in ways that can be unsettling in a potentially fruitful way. For example, how do modern ideas about individualism and the pursuit of prosperity and the American Dream line up with the vision of Andreas Ehrenpreis (see Ehrenpreis: An Open Letter, 279)? Along this same vein, C.S. Lewis has some wise words about the value of reading 'old books' to help break us free from present assumptions:

> Every age has its own outlook. It is specially good at seeing certain truths and specially liable to make certain mistakes. We all, therefore, need the books that will correct the characteristic

mistakes of our own period. And that means the old books.[1]

Because the gift and challenge of reading primary texts comes from stepping outside of our time into a different world, doing this well requires attentive reading. Such reading begins with empathy and imagination as we try to understand a world quite different from our own. Readers should avoid the 'sin' of presentism, that is, judging the past by present day standards and refusing to give writers of the past a fair hearing. At the same time, because many of these texts continue to shape Hutterite life and theology, there is room for discerning judgement.

Doing good historical reading requires asking certain critical questions of the text. Included below are suggestions for questions to ask when reading primary texts. These can help us enter into the world of the author and develop a reasonable interpretation. The short introductions before each primary text in this collection are designed to aid the reader in answering these questions:

Context

What is the historical or cultural context of the text? When was this text written; how does it fit into the broader history? What are important historical events that are significant for understanding this text? For

---

[1]   C.S. Lewis, preface to *On the Incarnation*, by Athanasius, translated by John Behr (New York: St. Vladimir's Seminary Press, 2011), 10.

example, the historical context of Martin Luther's 1525 text is the ongoing violence of the German Peasants' War (see 35).

Authorship

Who is the author? What about the writer's life experiences, beliefs, or biases might be shaping this text? For example, Tony Waldner is a member of Forest River Community. How might that shape how he writes his history of Forest River?

Genre

What kind of text is it: a letter, hymn, diary, narrative, contract, or something else? How does the genre shape the content? For example, several hymns are included in this collection. How does this genre differ from a Chronicle excerpt?

Purpose and Audience

Why is the author writing this text? Who is the author writing to? What are they intending to accomplish by writing this text? For example, Johannes Waldner, writer of *Chronicle*, vol 2, provides his own rationale for the writing of the *Chronicle* (see Waldner, Rationale for Writing Church History, 313).

Themes and/or Arguments

What are the main themes and arguments in the text? This can help you understand the overarching argument and therefore the purpose of the text. For example, what are the key arguments Martin Luther makes against adult baptism, and how do they fit together?

Key terms

What are some of the key terms the author uses to make their argument? Does the author mean something specific by these terms? These can provide clues to the central concerns and aims of the author. For example, the term *Gelassenheit* used by Andreas Ehrenpreis is central to his argument and to Hutterite spirituality.

Tone

What tone is the author using, and how might this help you understand the purpose of the text? Is the tone passionate, polemical, reverent, or neutral? For example, compare the tone of the *Chronicle* excerpts on the first baptism (see "Account of First Rebaptism in 1525," 71) and the origin of community-of-goods (see "Beginning of Community-of-Goods in 1528," 109). Are there similarities?

Reliability

How reliable is the text? Consider the author's expertise, biases, and the evidence that is being presented. Compare the text with other primary sources dealing with the same events. What are some differences or areas of agreement you can identify? For example, compare Jakob Hutter's letter (see Hutter: Letter to Moravian Governor, 155), with Gabriel Ascherham's critical take on Hutter and his leadership (see "Lost Chronicle Fragment," 163).

Historical Significance

What impact has this text had on historical events, movements, or ideas? How does it shape our understanding of the past? How does it continue to shape the present? For example, consider the Community Ordinances and the role they have had in Hutterite communal life past and present.

Critical Reading

Do you agree or disagree with the argument or parts of the argument? Reflect critically on the views and arguments of the text and bring yourself into the conversation. For example, consider Martin Luther's arguments against adult baptism; do you find his argument or parts of his argument convincing or compelling?

By carefully engaging with these and other questions, the process of reading primary sources becomes lively and invigorating.

written by Julian Waldner

THE PRE-HUTTERITE PERIOD
Medieval Spirituality and Reform Voices

Illustration of Benedict delivering his Rule to Maurus and other monks of his order. Monastery of St. Gilles, France, painting, 1129. [*Wikicommons*]

Benedict of Nursia (ca. 480–550)
Regula Benedicti / The Rule of St. Benedict, 530

Benedict of Nursia is regarded as the father of Western cenobitic or communal monasticism. He founded a number of monasteries in Italy, the most famous of which is located at Monte Cassino. Benedict's *Rule* was widely admired for its sensible and moderate approach, and was therefore adopted by many other monastic orders.

With its emphasis on community, asceticism, and discipline, the character of early Anabaptism owes something to the influence of the monastic tradition. Michael Sattler, one of the earliest Swiss Anabaptist leaders and likely author of the influential *Schleitheim Confession*, was a Benedictine prior (See *Schleitheim*, 89). Their opponents criticized Anabaptists for adopting another form of monkery.

Prologue

[…]

We are going to establish a school for the service of the Lord. In founding it we hope to introduce nothing harsh or burdensome. But if a certain strictness results from the dictates of equity for the amendment of vices or the preservation of charity, do not be at once dismayed and fly from the way of salvation, whose entrance cannot but be narrow (Matt. 7:14). For as we advance in the religious life and in faith, our hearts expand and we run the way of God's command-

ments with unspeakable sweetness of love. Thus, never departing from His school, but persevering in the monastery according to His teaching until death, we may by patience share in the sufferings of Christ (1 Peter 4:13) and deserve to have a share also in His kingdom.

I. On the Kinds of Monks

It is well known that there are four kinds of monks. The first kind are the Cenobites: those who live in monasteries and serve under a rule and an Abbot.

The second kind are the Anchorites or Hermits: those who, no longer in the first fervour of their reformation, but after long probation in a monastery, having learned by the help of many brethren how to fight against the devil, go out well armed from the ranks of the community to the solitary combat of the desert. They are able now, with no help save from God, to fight single-handed against the vices of the flesh and their own evil thoughts.

The third kind of monks, a detestable kind, are the Sarabaites. These, not having been tested, as gold in the furnace (Wis. 3:6), by any rule or by the lessons of experience, are as soft as lead. [...] They live in twos or threes, or even singly, without a shepherd, in their own sheepfolds and not in the Lord's. Their law is the desire for self-gratification: whatever enters their mind or appeals to them, that they call holy; what they dislike, they regard as unlawful.

The fourth kind of monks are those called Gyrovagues. These spend their whole lives tramping from province to province, staying as guests in different monasteries for three or four days at a time. Always on the move, with no stability, they indulge their own wills and succumb to the allurements of gluttony, and are in every way worse than the Sarabaites. [...]

Passing these over, therefore, let us proceed, with God's help, to lay down a rule for the strongest kind of monks, the Cenobites.

2. What Kind of Person the Abbess Ought to Be

An Abbess who is worthy to be over a monastery should always remember what she is called, and live up to the name of Superior. [...]

The Abbess ought not to teach or ordain or command anything which is against the Lord's precepts; on the contrary, her commands and her teaching should be a leaven of divine justice kneaded into the minds of her disciples.

Let the Abbess always bear in mind that at the dread Judgment of God there will be an examination of these two matters: her teaching and the obedience of her disciples. And let the Abbess be sure that any lack of profit the master of the house may find in the sheep will be laid to the blame of the shepherd. On the other hand, if the shepherd has bestowed all her pastoral diligence on a restless, unruly flock and tried every remedy for their unhealthy behaviour, then she will be acquitted at the Lord's Judgment. [...]

3. On Calling the Brethren for Counsel

Whenever any important business has to be done in the monastery, let the Abbot call together the whole community and state the matter to be acted upon. Then, having heard the brethren's advice, let him turn the matter over in his own mind and do what he shall judge to be most expedient. [...]

This architectural model of Fontevraud Abbey, founded in 1101 in France, shows how extensive and self-contained monasteries were. [*Creative Commons*]

7. On Humility

Holy Scripture, brethren, cries out to us, saying, "Everyone who exalts himself shall be humbled, and he who humbles himself shall be exalted" (Lk 14:11). [...]

Hence, brethren, if we wish to reach the very highest point of humility and to arrive speedily at that heavenly exaltation to which ascent is made through the humility of this present life, we must by our ascending actions erect the ladder Jacob saw in his dream, on which Angels appeared to him descending and ascending. By that descent and ascent we must surely understand nothing else than this, that we descend by self-exaltation and ascend by humility. [...]

The first degree of humility, then, is that a person keep the fear of God before his eyes and beware of ever forgetting it. Let him be ever mindful of all that God has commanded; let his thoughts constantly recur to the hell-fire which will burn for their sins those who despise God, and to the life everlasting which is prepared for those who fear Him. Let him keep himself at every moment from sins and vices, whether of the mind, the tongue, the hands, the feet, or the self-will, and check also the desires of the flesh. [...]

As for self-will, we are forbidden to do our own will by the Scripture, which says to us, "Turn away from your own will" (Ecc 18:30), and likewise by the prayer in which we ask God that his will be done in us. And rightly are we taught not to do our own will when we take heed to the warning of Scripture: "There are ways which seem right, but the ends of them plunge into the depths of hell" (Pro 16:25). [...]

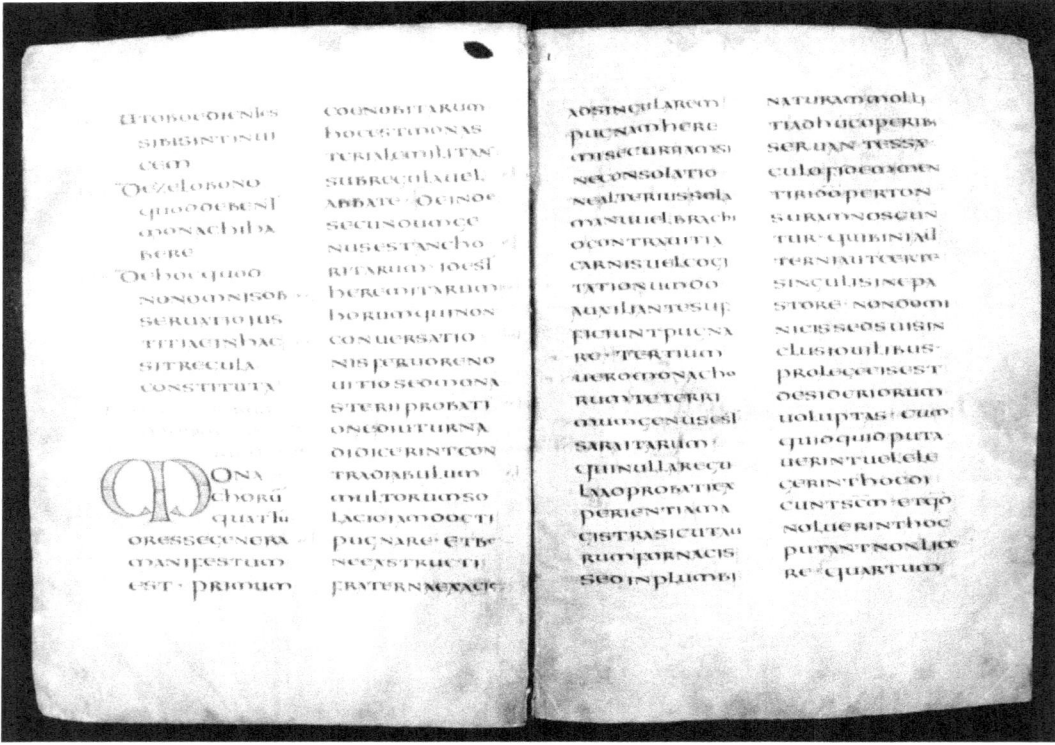

The oldest copy of Benedict's Rule, eighth century, Bodleian Library, Oxford. [*WikiCommons*]

And as for the desires of the flesh, let us believe with the Prophet that God is ever present to us, when he says to the Lord, "Every desire of mine is before You" (Ps [38]:10). We must be on our guard, therefore, against evil desires, for death lies close by the gate of pleasure. Hence the Scripture gives this command: "Go not after your concupiscences" (Ecc 18:30). [...]

The second degree of humility is that a person love not his own will nor take pleasure in satisfying his desires, but model his actions on the saying of the Lord, "I have come not to do My own will, but the will of Him who sent Me" (Jn 6:38). It is written

also, "Self-will has its punishment, but constraint wins a crown."

The third degree of humility is that a person for love of God submit himself to his Superior in all obedience, imitating the Lord, of whom the Apostle says, "He became obedient even unto death."

22. How the Monks Are to Sleep

Let each one sleep in a separate bed. Let them receive bedding suitable to their manner of life, according to the Abbey's directions. If possible let all sleep in one place; but if the number does not allow this, let them take their rest by tens or twenties with the seniors who have charge of them.

A candle shall be kept burning in the room until morning.

Let them sleep clothed and girded with belts or cords—but not with their knives at their sides, lest they cut themselves in their sleep—and thus be always ready to rise without delay when the signal is given and hasten to be before one another at the work of God, yet with all gravity and decorum. The younger shall not have beds next to one another, but among those of the older ones. [...]

31. What Kind of Man the Cellarer of the Monastery Should Be

As cellarer of the monastery let there be chosen from the community one who is wise, of mature character, sober, not a great eater, not haughty, not excitable, not offensive, not slow, not wasteful, but a God-fearing man who may be like a father to the whole community.

Let him have charge of everything. He shall do nothing without the Abbot's orders, but keep to his instructions. Let him not vex the brethren. If any brother happens to make some unreasonable demand of him, instead of vexing the brother with a contemptuous refusal he should humbly give the reason for denying the improper request.

33. Whether Monks Ought to Have Anything of Their Own

This vice especially is to be cut out of the monastery by the roots. Let no one presume to give or receive anything without the Abbot's leave, or to have anything as his own—anything whatever, whether book or tablets or pen or whatever it may be—since they are not permitted to have even their bodies or wills at their own disposal; but for all their necessities let them look to the Father of the monastery. [...] Let all things be common to all, as it is written (Acts 4:32), and let no one say or assume that anything is his own.

But if anyone is caught indulging in this most wicked vice, let him be admonished once and a second time. If he fails to amend, let him undergo punishment.

45. On Those Who Make Mistakes in the Oratory

When anyone has made a mistake while reciting a Psalm, a responsory, an antiphon or a lesson, if he does not humble himself there before all by making a satisfaction, let him undergo a greater punishment because he would not correct by humility what he did wrong through carelessness.

But boys shall be whipped for such faults.

53. On the Reception of Guests

Let all guests who arrive be received like Christ, for he is going to say: "I came as a guest, and you received Me."[1] And to all let due honour be shown, especially to the domestics

---

1   Mt 25:35.

of the faith and to pilgrims. As soon as a guest is announced, therefore, let the superior or the brethren meet him with all charitable service. [...]

In the salutation of all guests, whether arriving or departing, let all humility be shown. Let the head be bowed or the whole body prostrated on the ground in adoration of Christ, who indeed is received in their persons. [...]

In the reception of the poor and of pilgrims the greatest care and solicitude should be shown, because it is especially in them that Christ is received; for as far as the rich are concerned, the very fear which they inspire wins respect for them.

Let there be a separate kitchen for the Abbot and guests, that the brethren may not be disturbed when guests, who are never lacking in a monastery, arrive at irregular hours. [...]

On no account shall anyone who is not so ordered associate or converse with guests. But if he should meet them or see them, let him greet them humbly, as we have said, ask their blessing and pass on, saying that he is not allowed to converse with a guest. [...]

[**SOURCE:** *Saint Benedict's Rule for Monasteries*, translated from the Latin by Leonard J. Doyle. Copyright 1948, 2001 by Order of Saint Benedict, published by Liturgical Press, Collegeville, Minnesota. Used by permission.]

Thomas à Kempis (ca. 1380–1471)
De Imitatione Christi / The Imitation of Christ, ca. 1418–1427

Thomas à Kempis was a member of the Brethren of the Common Life, a network of semi-monastic communities whose members practiced poverty, chastity, and obedience, but did not take formal vows. Members were free to leave the brotherhood. The Brethren were part of a renewal movement known as the *devotia moderna* (the modern way of serving God), which flowered in northern Europe in the late fourteenth century.

It has been estimated that, apart from the Bible, no other book has been as widely read as *The Imitation of Christ*.

Excerpts of the *Imitation* can be found in 16th century Hutterite manuscripts and its spirituality of withdrawal from the world and imitating Christ in simplicity has parallels in the Hutterite tradition.

Imitating Christ and Despising All Vanities on Earth

"He who follows me, walks not in darkness," says the Lord.[1] By these words of Christ, we are advised to imitate his life and habits, if we wish to be truly enlightened and free from all blindness of heart. Let our chief effort, therefore, be to study the life of Jesus Christ.

The teaching of Christ is more excellent than all the advice of the saints, and he who has his spirit will find in it a hidden manna. Now, there are many who hear the Gospel often but care little for it because they have not the spirit of Christ. Yet whoever wishes to understand fully the words of Christ must try to pattern his whole life on that of Christ.

What good does it do to speak learnedly about the Trinity if, lacking humility, you displease the Trinity? Indeed it is not learning that makes a man holy and just, but a virtuous life makes him pleasing to God. […] This is the greatest wisdom—to seek

---

1   Jn 8:12.

9

the kingdom of heaven through contempt of the world. [...]

The Love of Solitude and Silence

Seek a suitable time for leisure and meditate often on the favours of God. Leave curiosities alone. Read such matters as bring sorrow to the heart rather than occupation to the mind. If you withdraw yourself from unnecessary talking and idle running about, from listening to gossip and rumours, you will find enough time that is suitable for holy meditation.

Very many great saints avoided the company of men wherever possible and chose to serve God in re-

Thomas von Kempen, unknown artist, painting, 1460. [*WikiCommons*]

tirement. "As often as I have been among men," said one writer, "I have returned less a man." [...] To stay at home is easier than to be sufficiently on guard while away. Anyone, then, who aims to live the inner and spiritual life must go apart, with Jesus, from the crowd. [...]

A Meditation on Death

Very soon your life here will end; consider, then, what may be in store for you elsewhere. Today we live; tomorrow we die and are quickly forgotten. [...] Therefore, in every deed and every thought, act as though you were to die this very day. If you had a good conscience you would not fear death very much. [...]

What good is it to live a long life when we amend that life so little? Indeed, a long life does not always benefit us, but on the contrary, frequently adds to our guilt. [...]

If you have ever seen a man die, remember that you, too, must go the same way. In the morning consider that you may not live till evening, and when evening comes do not dare to promise yourself the dawn. Be always ready, therefore, and so live that death will never take you unprepared. Many die suddenly and unexpectedly, for in the unexpected hour the Son of God will come. When that last moment arrives you will begin to have a quite different opinion of the life that is now entirely past and you will regret very much that you were so careless and remiss. [...]

Ah, foolish man, why do you plan to live long when you are not sure of living even a day? How many have been deceived and suddenly snatched away! How often have you heard of persons being killed by drownings, by fatal falls from high places, of persons dying at meals, at play, in fires, by the sword, in pestilence, or at the hands of robbers! Death is the end of everyone and the life of man quickly passes away like a shadow. [...]

Keep yourself as a stranger here on earth, a pilgrim whom its affairs do not concern at all. Keep your heart free and raise it up to God, for you have not here a lasting home. To Him direct your daily prayers, your sighs and tears, that your soul may merit after death to pass in happiness to the Lord.

On Judgment and the Punishment of Sinners

In all things consider the end; how you shall stand before the strict Judge from whom nothing is hidden and who will pronounce judgment in all justice, accepting neither bribes nor excuses. [...]

It is better to atone for sin now and to cut away vices than to keep them for purgation in the hereafter. In truth, we deceive ourselves by our ill-advised love of the flesh. What will that fire feed upon but our sins? The more we spare ourselves now and the more we satisfy the flesh, the harder will the reckoning be and the more we keep for the burning. [...]

You must, therefore, take care and repent of your sins now so that on the day of judgment you may rest secure with the blessed. [...]

He who loves God with all his heart does not fear death or punishment or judgment or hell, because perfect love assures access to God. It is no wonder that he who still delights in sin fears death and judgment.

It is good, however, that even if love does not as yet restrain you from evil, at least the fear of hell does. The man who casts aside the fear of God cannot continue long in goodness but will quickly fall into the snares of the devil.

Zeal in Amending our Lives

Be watchful and diligent in God's service and often think of why you left the world and came here. Was it not that you might live for God and become a spiritual man? Strive earnestly for perfection, then, because in a short time you will receive the reward of your labour, and neither fear nor sorrow shall come upon you at the hour of death. [...] Continue to have reasonable hope of gaining salvation, but do not act as though you were certain of it lest you grow indolent and proud. [...]

Study also to guard against and to overcome the faults which in others very frequently displease you. Make the best of every opportunity, so that if you see or hear good example you may be moved to imitate it. On the other hand, take care lest you be guilty of those things which you consider reprehensible, or if you have ever been guilty of them, try to correct yourself as soon as possible. As you see others, so they see you. […]

A fervent and diligent man is ready for all things. It is greater work to resist vices and passions than to sweat in physical toil. He who does not overcome small faults, shall fall little by little into greater ones.

If you have spent the day profitably, you will always be happy at eventide. Watch over yourself, arouse yourself, warn yourself, and regardless of what becomes of others, do not neglect yourself. The more violence you do to yourself, the more progress you will make.

[**Source:** Thomas à Kempis, *Of the Imitation of Christ: With Photogravures After Celebrated Paintings.* Translated by William Benham. London: George Routledge and Sons, 1905.]

Desiderius Erasmus (1466–1536)
Stultitiæ Laus / In Praise of Folly, 1509

Known as "the prince of humanists," Desiderius Erasmus traveled widely and was very active in humanist circles. He had a decisive influence on the early Swiss Anabaptists, especially with respect to ideas about discipleship, baptism, peace and nonviolence, the apostolic church, and the centrality of the Sermon on the Mount.

Erasmus was a prolific writer, and especially well-known for his critical edition of the Greek New Testament. *In Praise of Folly* shows Erasmus at his satirical best, poking fun at the scholastic theologians and self-righteous monks of his day. Many people shared Erasmus' anti-clerical views, and this resentment is one of the main factors that inspired the spirited debates and life-altering decisions during the Reformation period.

As for the theologians, perhaps it would be better to pass them over in silence, "not stirring up the hornets' nest" and "not laying a finger on the stinkweed," since this race of men is incredibly arrogant and touchy. For they might rise up *en masse* and march in ranks against me with six hundred conclusions and force me to recant. And if I should refuse, they would immediately shout "heretic." For this is the thunderbolt they always keep ready at a moment's notice to terrify anyone to whom they are not very favourably inclined.

Certainly, though no one is less willing than they are to recognize my good will toward them, still these men are also obliged to me for benefits of no little importance. They are so blessed by their self-love as to be fully persuaded that they themselves dwell in the third heaven, looking down from high above on all other mortals as if they were earth-creeping vermin almost worthy of their pity. They are so closely hedged in by rows of magistral definitions, conclusions, corollaries, explicit and implicit propositions, they have so many "holes they can run to," that Vulcan himself couldn't net

Desiderius Erasmus
of Rotterdam with
Renaissance Pilaster,
Hans Holbein, oil
on panel, 1523.
[*WikiCommons*]

proportion, in how short a period of time Christ was fully formed in the virgin's womb, how accidents subsist in the Eucharist without any domicile. But such questions are run-of-the-mill. There are others which they think worthy of great and "illuminated" theologians, as they say. If they ever encounter these, then they really perk up. Whether there is any instant in the generation of the divine persons? Whether there is more than one filial relationship in Christ? Whether the following proposition is possible: God the Father hates the Son. Whether God could have taken on the nature of a woman, of the devil, of an ass, of a cucumber, of a piece of flint? And then how the cucumber would have preached, performed miracles, and been nailed to the cross? And what Peter would have consecrated (if he had consecrated) during the time Christ was hanging on the cross? And whether during that same time Christ could be called a man? And whether it will be permissible to eat and drink after the resurrection?—taking precautions even now against hunger and thirst.

them tightly enough to keep them from escaping by means of distinctions, with which they cut all knots as cleanly as the fine-honed edge of "the headsman's axe"—so many new terms have they thought up and such monstrous jargon have they coined. Moreover, they explicate sacred mysteries just as arbitrarily as they please, explaining by what method the world was established and arranged, by what channels original sin is transmitted to Adam's posterity, by what means, by what

There are numberless petty quibbles even more fine-spun than these, concerning notions, relations, instants, formalities, quiddities, ecceities—things to which no eyesight could ever penetrate, unless it were an "x-ray vision" so powerful it could perceive through the deepest darkness things that are nowhere. Also throw in those *sententiae* of theirs, so paradoxical that those oracular sayings which the Stoics called paradoxes seem downright crude and commonplace by comparison—such as this, for example: it is a less serious crime to murder a thousand men than to fix just one shoe for a poor man on the Lord's day; or it would be better to let the whole world be destroyed—"lock, stock, and barrel," as they say—than to tell just one, tiny, little white lie. And then these most subtle subtleties are rendered even more subtle by the various "ways" or types of scholastic theology, so that you could work your way out of a labyrinth sooner than out of the intricacies of the Realists, Nominalists, Thomists, Albertists, Occamists, Scotists—and I still haven't mentioned all the sects, but only the main ones.

In all of these there is so much erudition, so much difficulty, that I think the apostles themselves would need to be inspired by a different spirit if they were forced to match wits on such points with this new breed of theologians. Paul could provide a living example of faith, but when he said "Faith is the substance of things to be hoped for and the evidence of things not seen," his definition was not sufficiently magisterial. So too, he lived a life of perfect charity, but he neither distinguished it nor defined it with sufficient dialectical precision in the first epistle to the Corinthians, chapter 13.

Certainly the apostles consecrated the Eucharist very piously, but still

if they had been asked about the "*terminus a quo*" and the "*terminus ad quern*," about transubstantiation, about how the same body can be in different places, about the difference between the body of Christ as it is in heaven, as it was on the cross, and as it is in the Eucharist, about the exact point at which transubstantiation takes place (since the speech through which it is accomplished is a divisible quantity which takes place in a flowing period of time), I don't think they would have responded with a subtlety equal to that of the Scotists when they dis-

"The Fool and his Sceptre," Hans Holbein the Younger, marginal drawing in the first edition of *In Praise of Folly*, ink on paper, 1515. [*WikiArt*]

cuss and define these points. They knew Jesus' mother, but which of them has shown how she was preserved from the stain of Adam's sin as philosophically as our theologians have done it? Peter received the keys, and received them from one who would not have committed them to someone unworthy of them, but still I don't know whether he understood—certainly he never attained sufficient subtlety to understand—how even a person who does not have knowledge can still have the keys of knowledge. They baptized everywhere, but nowhere did they teach what are the formal, material, efficient, and final causes of baptism, nor do they even so much as mention the delible and indelible marks of the sacraments. Certainly they worshipped God, but they did so in the spirit, following no other directive than the one given in the gospel: "God is a spirit and those who worship him should worship him in the spirit and in truth."[1] But it is hardly clear that it was also revealed to them that a charcoal sketch drawn on a wall should be worshipped with the same worship as Christ himself, provided that the picture has two fingers extended, long hair, and three rays in the halo stuck on the back of the skull. For who could perceive these things unless he had spent 36 whole years in studying the physics and metaphysics of Aristotle and the Scotists? So too, the apostles preach grace very forcefully, but nowhere do they distinguish between grace "*gratis data*" and grace "*gratificans*." They exhort us to good works, without distinguishing "*opus operans*" from "*opus operatum*." Everywhere they inculcate charity, without separating infused from acquired charity or explaining whether charity is an accident or a substance, a created or an uncreated thing. They detest sin, but I would stake my life they couldn't define scientifically what it is that we call sin, unless perchance they had been instructed by the spirit of the Scotists. Nor can I bring myself to believe that Paul, from whose learning we may judge that of the others, would so often have condemned questions, disputes, genealogies, and (as he calls them) quarrels about words, if he had been so expert in subtle argumentation, especially since all the quarrels and disputes of that time were coarse and crude by comparison with the supersubtleties of our doctors of theology.

[**Source:** Desiderius Erasmus, *The Praise of Folly*, translated by Clarence H. Miller (New Haven: Yale University Press, 1979), 87–106, 110–15.]

---

1   Jn 4:24.

Der Buchdrücker.

This llustration shows the interior of a printing press. Two men are working at the press—the right man applying ink onto the letterpress matrix and the left man taking off a freshly printed sheet. In the background, two men are seated in front of type drawers, holding a composition stick; in the foreground are two piles of printed and blank sheets of paper. "*Der Buchdrucker* / The Bookbinder," Jost Amman, woodcut, 1568. [*WikiCommons*]

Ich bin geschicket mit der preß/
So ich aufftrag den Firniß reß/
So bald mein dienr den bengel zuckt/
So ist ein bogn papyrs gedruckt.
Da durch kombt manche Kunst an tag/
Die man leichtlich bekommen mag.
Vor zeiten hat man die bücher gschribn/
Zu Meintz die Kunst ward erstlich triebn.

The English states-
man and humanist
Thomas More
published *Utopia*
in 1516 to critique
contemporary social
and political struc-
tures, which had
contributed to wide-
spread poverty and
inequality, incessant
warfare, and crime.
More proposed an
alternative society
characterized by uni-
versal employment,
sharing of material
wealth, just govern-
ance, and religious
tolerance.
While life on the
island of Utopia is
based on secular,
rational principles
of governance, only
12 years later the
Hutterites estab-
lished communes in
Moravia committed
to similar ideals of
peace, equality, and
community-of-goods
based on Christian
principles. No direct
connection has been
established between
More's book and the
early Anabaptists and
Hutterites. *Vtopiae
Insulae Figura*, Thom-
as More, *Utopia*, 1516.
[*Wikicommons*]

THE PRE-HUTTERITE PERIOD
Reformation Literature

Martin Luther's *Disputatio pro declaratione virtutis indulgentiarum* of 1517. Its complete title reads: "Out of love and zeal for clarifying the truth, these items written below will be debated at Wittenberg. Reverend Father Martin Luther, Master of Arts and of Sacred Theology and an official professor at Wittenberg, will speak in their defense. He asks this in the matter: That those who are unable to be present to debate with us in speech should, though absent from the scene, treat the matter by correspondence. In the Name of Our Lord Jesus Christ. Amen." [*WikiCommons*]

Amore et studio elucidande veritatis:hec subscripta disputabūtur Wittenberge. Presidente R. P. Martino Luther:Artiū et S. Theologie Magistro:eiusdemq̃ ibidem lectore Ordinario. Quare petit:vt qui nō possunt verbis presentes nobiscū disceptare:agant id literis absentes. In noie dṅi nostri Iesu chri. Amē.

Martin Luther (1483–1546)

Disputatio pro declaratione virtutis indulgentiarum / Propositiones wider das Ablas / [Ninety-five Theses:] Disputation on the Power and Efficacy of Indulgences, 1517

Without question, Martin Luther is one of the central characters in the tumultuous drama of the 16th century Reformation. Yet, when he posted the 95 theses against the sale of indulgences in Wittenberg in 1517, Luther had no idea he would become the founder and leader of the "Protestant" movement. He would go on to produce a wide variety of writings—books, a translation of the Bible, bible commentaries, articles, letters, sermons, hymns, catechisms, etc.—that fill 100 volumes in the modern critical edition.

Luther's theology was forged in the crucible of his deep personal anxiety over his sinfulness and alienation from God and his eventual discovery of the gospel of justification by faith. There is a unique urgency and forcefulness to his writing as he seeks to respond to his critics and also develop resources for the emerging Protestant tradition.

The publication of the "Ninety-five Theses" in 1517 is customarily designated as the beginning of the Reformation. The Theses were originally written in Latin to initiate an academic debate about the validity of indulgences, purgatory, and the sacrament of penance in a university context. In hindsight, this document proved to be the spark for the Protestant Reformation. Although he was critical of the practices surrounding the selling of indulgences, Luther is seeking reform rather than a break from the Catholic Church at this point in time.

[…] 1. When our Lord and Master Jesus Christ said, "Repent,"[1] he willed the entire life of believers to be one of repentance.

2. This word cannot be understood as referring to the sacrament of penance, that is, confession and satisfaction, as administered by the clergy.

---

1 Mt 4:17.

"*On Aplas von Rom kan man wol selig werden* [One can indeed be saved without an indulgence from Rome]," unknown, Augsburg, woodcut, 1521. [*WikiCommons*]

mean "all penalties," but only those imposed by himself.

27. They preach only human doctrines who say that as soon as the money clinks into the money chest, the soul flies out of purgatory.

37. Any true Christian, whether living or dead, participates in all the blessings of Christ and the church; and this is granted him by God, even without indulgence letters.

43. Christians are to be taught that he who gives to the poor or lends to the needy does a better deed than he who buys indulgences.

45. Christians are to be taught that he who sees a needy man and passes him by, yet gives his money for indulgences, does not buy papal indulgences but God's wrath.

50. Christians are to be taught that if the pope knew the exactions of the indulgence-preachers, he would rather that the basilica of St. Peter were burned to ashes than built up with the skin, flesh, and bones of his sheep.

52. It is vain to trust in salvation by indulgence letters, even though the indulgence commissary, or even the pope, were to offer his soul as security.

54. Injury is done the Word of God when, in the same sermon, an equal or larger amount of time is devoted to indulgences than to the Word.

62. The true treasure of the church is the most holy gospel of the glory and grace of God.

5. The pope neither desires nor is able to remit any penalties except those imposed by his own authority or that of the canons.

6. The pope cannot remit any guilt, except by declaring and showing that it has been remitted by God; or, to be sure, by remitting guilt in cases reserved to his judgment. [...]

13. The dying are freed by death from all penalties, are already dead as far as the canon laws are concerned, and have a right to be released from them.

20. Therefore the pope, when he uses the words "plenary remission of all penalties," does not actually

63. But this treasure is naturally most odious, for it makes the first to be last.[2]

64. On the other hand, the treasure of indulgences is naturally most acceptable, for it makes the last to be first.

65. Therefore the treasures of the gospel are nets with which one formerly fished for men of wealth.

66. The treasures of indulgences are nets with which one now fishes for the wealth of men.

75. To consider papal indulgences so great that they could absolve a man even if he had done the impossible and had violated the mother of God is madness.

81. This unbridled preaching of indulgences makes it difficult even for learned men to rescue the reverence which is due the pope from slander or from the shrewd questions of the laity,

82. Such as: "Why does not the pope empty purgatory for the sake of holy love and the dire need of the souls that are there if he redeems an infinite number of souls for the sake of miserable money with which to build a church? The former reasons would be most just; the latter is most trivial."

86. Again, "Why does not the pope, whose wealth is today greater than the wealth of the richest Crassus, build this one basilica of St. Peter with his own money rather than with the money of poor believers?"

94. Christians should be exhorted to be diligent in following Christ, their head, through penalties, death, and hell;

95. And thus be confident of entering into heaven through many tribulations rather than through the false security of peace.[3]

[**Source:** *Luther's Works,* Volume 31 (Minneapolis: Fortress Press, 1957), 25–33. Used by permission.]

---

2   Mt 20:16.
3   Acts 14:22.

"Martin Luther."
The text reads, "In quietness and hope is your strength." Lucas Cranach the Elder, painting, 1529. [*WikiCommons*]

POPE LEO X (1475–1521)
Exsurge Domine: Condemning the Errors of Martin Luther, June 1520

A papal bull is an important official document released by the pope; "bull" comes from the Latin *bulla*, which refers to the seal affixed to an official letter. On June 15, 1520, Pope Leo X issued the papal bull titled, "*Exsurge Domine* / Arise, O Lord"). This bull begins with the opening phrase from Psalm 7:6 (Psalm 7:7 in the Latin Vulgate), and is also the source of the bull's name.

"Portrait of Leo X." Raphael, oil on wood, ca. 1518–1520. [*WikiCommons*]

Exsurge Domine officially condemned forty-one statements found in Martin Luther's writings as heretical. The text goes on to "condemn, reprobate, and reject completely the books and all the writings and sermons of the said Martin...." Luther responded with a pamphlet, "Against the Execrable Bull of the Antichrist," and by burning a copy of the bull. In another bull issued on January 3, 1521, the pope officially declared Luther a heretic and excommunicated him from the Catholic Church.

Although Luther's tone had become increasingly militant and belligerent, these events would mark the end of Luther's reform movement as taking place within the Catholic Church. From this point onward, Luther would be forming a breakaway "Protestant" movement.

"Bull against the errors of Martin Luther and his followers," 1520. [*WikiCommons*]

administration of this vineyard to Peter as head and to thy representatives, his successors, as the Church triumphant. A roaring sow of the woods has undertaken to destroy this vineyard, a wild beast wants to devour it.[6]

Arise, O Peter, according to thy responsibility and care, bestowed upon thee by God. Be eagerly mindful of the cause of the holy Roman Church. [...]

Arise, O Paul, we pray, for thou hast enlightened the Church with thy teaching and the same martyrdom. A new Porphyry has arisen who, like the one of old, attacks the holy twelve apostles, strives against the holy popes, our predecessors, and against thy teaching. [...]

We have unfortunately seen and read with our own eyes many and various errors, some of which have already been condemned by the councils and definitions of our predecessors, since they incorporate the heresies of the Greeks and the Bohemians. [...]

This we find all the more painful because [...] The German people have truly been the friends of Christian truth and always the most serious opponents of heresy. This is shown by the commendable laws of the German emperors for the

Leo, Bishop, servant of the servants of God, to eternal memory.

Arise, O Lord,[1] and judge thy cause. Be mindful of the daily slander against thee by the foolish,[2] incline thine ear to our supplication.[3] Foxes have arisen which want to devastate thy vineyard,[4] where thou hast worked the wine-press.[5] At thy ascension into heaven thou hast commanded the care, rule and

1	Ps 7:6.
2	Ps 74:22.
3	Ps 88:2.
4	Song of Sol 2:15.
5	Isa 63:3.
6	Ps 80:12–13.

freedom of the Church and their laws always to suppress heretics from German territory. If these laws were kept today we would not find ourselves in this difficult situation. This is furthermore shown by the condemned and punished faithlessness of the Hussites, of Wycliffe and Jerome of Prague at the Council of Constance. This is indeed shown by the German blood shed so often against the Bohemians. [...]

Since these errors, as well as many others, are found in the writings or pamphlets of a certain Martin Luther, we condemn, reject and denounce these pamphlets and all writings and sermons of this Martin, be they in Latin or in other languages, in which one or more of these errors are found. [...]

We order in the name of the holy obedience and the danger of all punishment each and every Christian believer of either sex, under no circumstances to read, speak, preach, laud, consider, publish or defend such writings, sermons, or broadsides or anything contained therein. [...]

Indeed, they are, upon learning of this bull, wherever they may be, to burn his writings, publicly and in the presence of clerics and laity in order to avoid the punishment stated above.

As regards Martin: dear God, what have we failed to do, what have we avoided, what paternal love did we not exercise, to call him back from his errors? [...] We reminded him through our writings that he should desist from his error or else, with safe conduct and the necessary provisions, without fear or trembling (which perfect love casts out), to come to us and talk with us, not secretly, but publicly as our Saviour and the holy Apostle Paul did. Had he done so... We would have clearly instructed and taught him that the holy popes, our predecessors, whom he chides without all reason, never erred in their statutes and regulations which he boldly destroys.

We prohibit this Martin from now on and henceforth to contrive any preaching or the office of preaching. And even though the love of righteousness and virtue did not take him away from sin and the hope of forgiveness did not lead him to penance, perhaps the terror of the pain of punishment may move him. [...]

We ask him earnestly that he and his supporters, adherents and accomplices desist within sixty days (which we wish to have divided into three times twenty days, counting from the publication of this bull at the places mentioned below) from preaching, both expounding their views and denouncing others, from publishing books and pamphlets concerning some or all of their errors. Furthermore, all writings which contain some or all of his errors are to be burned. Furthermore, this Martin is to recant perpetually such errors and views. He is to inform us of such recantation through an open document, sealed by two prelates, which we should receive within another sixty days. Or he should personally, with safe conduct, inform us of his recantation by coming to Rome. […]

If, however, this Martin, his supporters, adherents and accomplices, much to our regret, should stubbornly not comply with the mentioned stipulations within the mentioned period, we shall, following the teaching of the holy Apostle Paul, who teaches us to avoid a heretic after having admonished him for a first and a second time, condemn this Martin, his supporters, adherents and accomplices as barren vines which are not in Christ, preaching an offensive doctrine contrary to the Christian faith and offend the divine majesty, to the damage and shame of the entire Christian Church, and diminish the keys of the Church as stubborn and public heretics. […]

[**Source:** Hans J. Hilderbrand, *The Reformation in its own Words* (London: SCM Press, 1964), 80–84. Public Domain.]

An indulgence note bearing the papal seal and Johann Tetzel's signature. In English the text reads, "By the authority of all saints and in compassion toward you, I absolve you from all sins and misdeeds, and pardon you from all punishments for ten days." [WikiCommons]

Martin Luther (1483–1546)
Von der Freyheyt eyniß Christen menschen /
The Freedom of a Christian, 1520

This text was written in November 1520, and Luther sent it to Pope Leo X along with a lengthy cover letter. With it, Luther gave a succinct account of his fundamental theological idea of justification by faith alone—*sola fide.*

[…]

To make the way smoother for the unlearned—for only them do I serve—I shall set down the following two propositions concerning the freedom and the bondage of the spirit:

A Christian is a perfectly free lord of all, subject to none.

A Christian is a perfectly dutiful servant of all, subject to all.

These two theses seem to contradict each other. If, however, they should be found to fit together they would serve our purpose beautifully. [...]

First of all, remember what has been said, namely, that faith alone, without works, justifies, frees, and saves. [...] Here we must point out that the entire Scripture of God is divided into two parts: commandments and promises. [...] [T]he commandments show us what we ought to do but do not give us the power to do it. They are intended to teach man to know himself, that through them he may recognize his inability to do good and may despair of his own ability. [...]

[T]hen, being truly humbled and reduced to nothing in his own eyes, he finds in himself nothing whereby he may be justified and saved. Here the second part of Scripture comes to our aid, namely the promises of God. [...] Thus the promises of God give what the commandments of God demand and fulfill what the law prescribes. [...]

From this anyone can clearly see how a Christian is free from all things and over all things so that he needs no works to make him right-

29

eous and save him, since faith alone abundantly confers all these things. [...]

Now let us turn to the second part, the outer man. Here we shall answer all those who, offended by the word "faith" and by all that has been said, now ask, "If faith does all things and is alone sufficient unto righteousness, why then are good works commanded? [...] This is the place to assert that which was said above, namely, that a Christian is the servant of all and made subject to all. Insofar as he is free he does no works, but insofar as he is a servant he does all kinds of works. [...]

The following statements are therefore true: "Good works do not make a man good, but a good man does good works; evil works do not make a man wicked, but a wicked man does evil works." [...]

Illustrations [...] can be seen in all trades. A good or a bad house does not make a good or bad builder, but a good or bad builder makes a good or a bad house. [...]

Our faith in Christ does not free us from works but from false opinions concerning works, that is, from the foolish presumption that justification is acquired by works. Faith redeems, corrects, and preserves our consciences so that we know that righteousness does not consist in works, although works neither can nor ought to be wanting; just as we cannot be without food and drink and all the works of this mortal body, yet our righteousness is not in them, but in faith; and yet those works of the body are not to be despised or neglected on that account. [...]

[**Source:** *Luther's Works*, Volume 31 (Minneapolis: Fortress Press, 1957): 334–59. Used by permission.]

[Sebastian Lotzer (ca. 1490–after 1525) and Christoph Schappeler (1472–1551)]

Dye Grundtlichen Vnd rechten Haupt Artickel aller Baurschafft vnnd Hyndersessen der Gaistlichen vn Weltlichen oberkayten, von wolchen sy sich beschwert vermainen / [The Twelve Articles of the Upper Swabian Peasants:] The Fundamental and Truly Essential Articles of all Peasantry and Subjects against the Spiritual and Secular Authorities by whom they consider themselves to be Burdened, 1525

In the century before the Reformation, German peasants had experienced a significant deterioration in their living conditions. A large portion of their harvest went toward church tithes and taxes, and access to the common land for hunting, fishing, and gathering firewood had been restricted by their landlords. Their legal rights had also undergone significant change.

Thus, when the peasants heard Martin Luther speak about "Christian freedom" and "the priesthood of all believers" they applied his message to their situation: they expected the new teaching to improve their social and economic situation. When it became clear that this was not Luther's intention, and that most of the landlords would not agree to make changes in how they treated the peasants, the peasants organized in assemblies and put their demands in writing. They eventually resorted to violence in an attempt to realize their demands.

Of the various lists of peasant grievances that circulated in 1524–25, "The Twelve Articles of the Upper Swabian Peasants," written by craftsman Sebastian Lotzer and pastor Christian Schappeler in Memmingen on behalf of the local peasants, became the most well-known manifesto of the peasant movement.

Couched in the language of *sola scriptura*, the *Twelve Articles* give voice to a vision of reform that would find sympathy in the emerging Anabaptist movement. Many early Anabaptists had links to the peasant movement.

To the Christian reader peace and the grace of God through Christ.

There are many Antichrists who on account of the assembling of the peasants, cast scorn upon the gospel, and say: Is this the fruit of the new teaching, that no one obeys but all everywhere rise in revolt, and band together to reform, extinguish, indeed kill the temporal and spiritual authorities?

The following articles will answer these godless and blaspheming faultfinders. They will first of all remove the reproach from the Word of God and secondly give a Christian excuse for the disobedience or even the revolt of the entire peasantry.[…] Therefore, Christian reader, read the following articles with care, and then judge. Here follow the articles:

The First Article. First, it is our humble petition and desire, indeed our will and resolution, that in the future we shall have power and authority so that the entire community should choose and appoint a minister, and that we should have the right to depose him should he conduct himself improperly. The minister thus chosen should teach us the holy gospel pure and simple, without any human addition, doctrine or ordinance. For to teach us continually the true faith will lead us to pray God that through his grace his faith may increase within us and be confirmed in us. For if his grace is not within us, we always remain flesh and blood, which avails nothing; since the Scripture clearly teaches that only through true faith can we come to God. Only through his mercy can we become holy. […]

The Second Article. Since the right tithe is established in the Old Testament and fulfilled in the New, we are ready and willing to pay the fair tithe of grain. Nonetheless it should be done properly. The Word of God plainly provides that it should be given to God and passed on to his own. If it is to be given to a minister, we will in the future collect the tithe through our church elders, appointed by the congregation, according to the judgment of the whole congregation. The remainder shall be given to the poor of the place, as the circumstances and the general opinion demand. […]

The Third Article. It has been the custom hitherto for men to hold us as their own property, which is pitiable enough considering that Christ has redeemed and purchased us without exception, by the shedding of his precious blood, the lowly as well as the great. Accordingly, it is consistent with Scripture that we should be free and we wish to be so. Not that we want to be absolutely free and under no authority. God does not teach us that we should lead a disorderly life according to the lusts of the flesh, but that we should live by the commandments, love the lord our God and our neighbour. […]

The Fourth Article. In the fourth place it has been the custom heretofore that no poor man was allowed to catch venison or wild fowl, or fish in flowing water, which seems to us quite unseemly and unbrotherly, as well as selfish and not according to the Word of God.... Accordingly, it is our desire if a man holds possession of waters that he should prove from satisfactory documents that his right has been wittingly acquired by purchase. We do not wish to take it from him by force, but his rights should be exercised in a Christian and brotherly fashion. [...]

The Fifth Article. In the fifth place we are aggrieved in the matter of woodcutting, for our noble folk have appropriated all the woods to themselves alone. [...] It should be free to every member of the community to help himself to such firewood as he needs in his home. Also, if a man requires wood for carpenter's purposes he should have it free, but with the approval of a person appointed by the community for that purpose. [...]

The Sixth Article. Our sixth complaint is in regard to the excessive services demanded of us, which increase from day to day. We ask that this matter be properly looked into, so that we shall not continue to be oppressed in this way, and that some gracious consideration be given to us, since our forefathers served only according to the Word of God.

Handlung / Artickel / vnnd Instruction / so furgenommen worden sein vonn allen Rottenn vnnd hauffen der Pauren / so sich desamen verpflicht haben: M: D: xxv:

The Seventh Article. Seventh, we will not hereafter allow ourselves to be further oppressed by our lords. What the lords possess is to be held according to the agreement between the lord and the peasant. [...]

Pamphlet cover of the *Twelve Articles*, 1525, woodcut. [*WikiCommons*]

The Eighth Article. In the eighth place, we are greatly burdened by holdings which cannot support the rent exacted from them. The peasants suffer loss in this way and are ruined. We ask that the lords may appoint persons of honour to inspect these holdings and fix a rent in accordance with justice, so that the peasant shall not work for nothing, since the labourer is worthy of his hire.

The Ninth Article. In the ninth place, we are burdened with the great evil in the constant making of new laws. We are not judged according to the offense but sometimes with great ill will, and sometimes much too leniently. In our opinion we should be judged according to the old written law, so that the case shall be decided according to its merits, and not with favours.

The Tenth Article. In the tenth place we are aggrieved that certain individuals have appropriated meadows and fields which at one time belonged to the community. These we will take again into our own hands unless they were rightfully purchased.

The Eleventh Article. In the eleventh place we will entirely abolish the custom called *Todfall*,[1] and will no longer endure it, nor allow widows and orphans to be thus shamefully robbed against God's will. […]

Conclusion. In the twelfth place it is our conclusion and final resolution, that if any one or more of these articles should not be in agreement with the Word of God, which we do not think, we will willingly recede from such article when it is proved to be against the Word of God by a clear explanation of the Scripture. For this we shall pray God, since he can grant all this and he alone. The peace of Christ abide with us all.

[**Source:** Hans J. Hillerbrand, ed. *The Protestant Reformation* (New York: Harper Torchbooks, 1968), 63–66. Public domain.]

---

1   The practice of heriot was the right of a lord in feudal Europe to seize a serf's best horse, clothing, or both, upon his death. This emerged from the tradition of the lord lending a serf a horse or armour or weapons to fight; upon the death of the serf the lord would reclaim his property. This developed into a tribute coming from the belongings of a deceased tenant, often a live animal.

MARTIN LUTHER (1483–1546)
Wider die Mordischen und Reubischen Rotten der Bawren / Against the Murdering and Robbing Hordes of Peasants, 1525

With the outbreak of the Peasants' War in 1524, Martin Luther faced the radical consequences of the movement he had unleashed. Initially, he had been somewhat sympathetic to the peasants' plight and urged the lords to respond to their grievances, while calling the peasants to take a peaceful route. (*Admonition to Peace*, April 1525). When the peasants' calls for justice went unheeded, the movement first threatened violence and then turned into a full-scale uprising.

For Luther, governing authorities were put in place by God and ought to be respected as such. Nothing was worse than a rebel because they were a threat to society and divine order. After the violent turn of the movement, Luther's tone switched to total support of the authorities. In his May 1525 text, *Against the Murdering and Robbing Hordes of Peasants*, Luther advised the princes to crush the peasants, infamously urging them to "smite, slay, and stab," just as "one must kill a mad dog." When the peasants were subsequently slaughtered by the princes to bring the Peasants' War to a close, Luther was critiqued for inciting such a brutal response. In response to his critics, Luther later defended his harsh language against the peasants (*An Open Letter on the Harsh Book Against the Peasants*, June–July 1525).

In the former book I did not venture to judge the peasants, since they had offered to be set right and to be instructed, [...] but before I look around they go on, and, forgetting their offer, they betake themselves to violence, and rob and rage and act like mad dogs. [...]

[T]hey are starting a rebellion, and violently robbing and plundering monasteries and castles which are not theirs, by which they have a doubly deserved death in body and soul, if only as highwaymen and murderers. [...] For if a man is an open rebel every man is his judge and executioner, just as when a fire starts, the first to put it out is the best man. For rebellion is not simple murder, but is like a great fire, which attacks and lays waste a whole land. Thus rebellion brings with it a land full of murder and bloodshed, makes widows and orphans, and turns everything upside down, like the greatest disaster. Therefore let everyone who can, smite, slay and stab, secretly or openly, remembering that nothing can be more poisonous, hurtful or devilish than a rebel. It is just as when one must kill a mad dog; if you do not strike him, he will strike you, and a whole land with you. […]

I will not oppose a ruler who, even though he does not tolerate the Gospel, will smite and punish these peasants without offering to submit the case to judgement. For he is within his rights, since the peasants are not contending any longer for the Gospel, but have become faithless, perjured, disobedient, rebellious murderers, robbers and blasphemers, whom even heathen rulers have the right and power to punish. […]

[**Source:** *Works Of Martin Luther*, Volume 4 (Philadelphia: Muhlenberg Press, 1931), 248–254. Used by Permission.]

Martin Luther (1483–1546)
Wider die himelischen Propheten: Von den bildern vnd Sacrament / Against the Heavenly Prophets: Concerning Images and the Sacraments, 1525

In his 1525 text, *Against the Heavenly Prophets* Luther vehemently attacks the views of his former associate, Andreas Karlstadt, and those he dismissively calls "the heavenly prophets." Karlstadt, like the radicals at Zürich, drew Luther's ire when he became impatient with Luther's slow pace of reform, and instituted radical reforms and performed iconoclastic acts in 1521 at Wittenberg.

In this text, Luther makes a spirited critique of the "heavenly prophets," a broad term for radical reformers, Anabaptists, and spiritualists of various stripes. In Luther's reading, by prioritizing the spiritual over the external, these 'heavenly prophets' are led to rebellion, legalism, sectarianism, and subjective and arbitrary interpretations of Scripture. They have, in Luther's words "devoured the Holy Spirit, feathers and all." Further, by emphasizing good works over sound doctrine, they can give no comfort to the tormented conscience that was so close to Luther's own experience. The vehement tone of this document shows Luther's increasing concern about the radical extremes of the movement he spawned.

[…]

These honour-seeking prophets who do nothing but break images, destroy churches, manhandle the sacrament, and seek a new kind of mortification, that is, a self-chosen putting to death of the flesh […].

And if they had now altogether succeeded so that there were no more images, no churches remained, no one in the whole world held that the flesh and blood of Christ were in the sacrament and all went about in grey peasant garb, what would be accomplished thereby? […]

Fame, vainglory, and a new monkery would well thereby be achieved, as happens in all works, but the con-

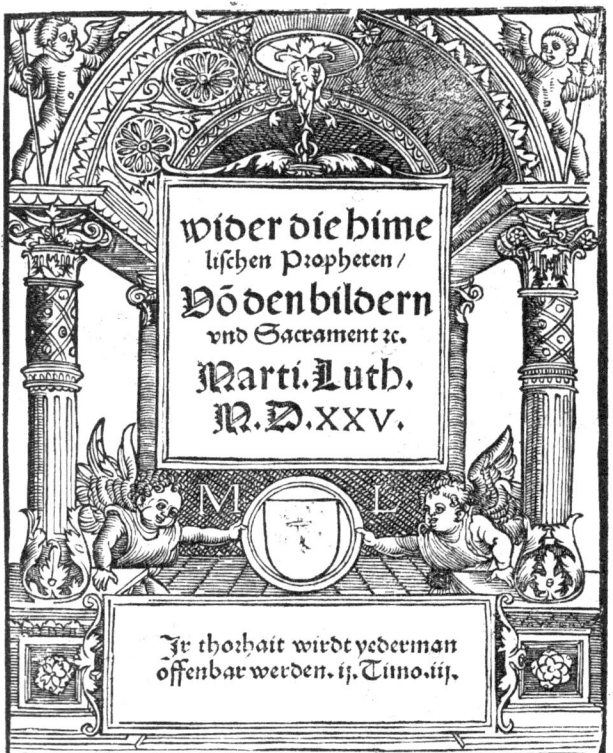

wider die hime
lischen Propheten/
Vö den bildern
vnd Sacrament ıc.
Marti.Luth.
N.D.xxv.

Ir thorhait wirdt yederman
offenbar werden. ıj. Timo.iij.

Title page of "Wider
die himelischen
Propheten," 1525.
[WikiCommons]

dash, stab, strike, run, throw, hit the idols in the mouth! If you see a crucifix, spit in its face, etc. This is to do away with images in a Karlstadtian manner, to make the masses mad and foolish, and secretly to accustom them to revolution. Those who rush into this thing think they are now great saints, and become proud and impudent beyond all measure. [...]

Dr. Karlstadt's spiritual interpretation seems to him and his followers to be a remarkably precious one. But when one examines it under the light and according to the text, it is revealed as pure jugglery. Devoid of foundation or truth, it is the product of his own fancy, and forced upon the text. [...]

There you have their theology: Others are to learn outwardly by their word, which they call an external witness. But they themselves are better and superior to the apostles, and pretend to learn inwardly in their spirit without an external Word and without means, though this possibility was not given to the apostles, but alone to the only Son, Jesus Christ. [...]

He despoils the sacrament by making it merely bread and wine. [...]

Further, the mad spirit is so ignorant of Scripture that he interprets the word, "remembrance," where Christ says, "This do in remembrance of me," only [...] to mean, the inner thoughts of the heart, as one would think of any one. For this spirit must

science would in no way be helped. [...]

From which you now see that Dr. Karlstadt and his spirits replace the highest with the lowest, the best with the least, the first with the last. Yet he would be considered the greatest spirit of all, he who has devoured the Holy Spirit feathers and all. [...]

This breaking of images has also another weakness in that they themselves do it in a disorderly way, and do not proceed with proper authority. As when their prophets stand, crying and arousing the masses, saying: heigh, hew, rip, rend, smash, be inward, and make inward and spiritual what God wants to be outward, so that nothing will be external. [...]

The entire teaching of Dr. Karlstadt is a fantasy of this kind. For by his high-sounding words, "passionate remembrance, ardent knowledge, experiential taste of the suffering of Christ," he mocks us and does not bring us any farther than showing the health-giving treasure in a glass or vessel. [...]

Whoever has a bad conscience from his sins should go to the sacrament and obtain comfort, not because of the bread and wine, not because of the body and blood of Christ, but because of the word which in the sacrament offers, presents, and gives the body and blood of Christ, given and shed for me. [...]

Even if only bread and wine were there present, as they claim, as long as the word, "Take, eat, this is my body given for you," etc., is there, the forgiveness of sins, on account of this word, would be in the sacrament.

In closing, I want to warn everyone truly and fraternally to beware of Dr. Karlstadt and his prophets, for two reasons. First, because they run about and teach, without a call. This God condemns through Jeremiah [23:21], who says, I did not send them, yet they ran. I did not speak to them, yet they prophesied." [...] They boast of possessing the Spirit, more than the apostles, and yet for more than three years now have secretly prowled about and flung around their dung. [...]

The second reason is that these prophets avoid, run away from, and are silent about the main points of Christian doctrine. For in no place do they teach how we are to become free from our sins, obtain a good conscience, and win a peaceful and joyful heart before God. This is what really counts. This is a true sign that their spirit is of the devil, who can use unusual new words to excite, terrify, and mislead consciences. But their spirit cannot give quietness or peace, but goes on and teaches special works in which they are to exercise and discipline themselves. They have no idea how a good conscience can be gained or ought to be constituted. For they have not felt or ever recognized it. How can they know or feel it, when they come and teach of themselves, without a call. No good can come in this way.

[**Source:** *Luther's Works: Church and Ministry II*, Vol. 40. Conrad Bergendoff and Helmut T. Lehmann, editors. (Philadelphia: Fortress Press, 1958), 80–222. Used by permission.]

An extremely rare early second edition printing of Luther's hymn, *Ein feste Burg ist unser Gott*. There are no first edition printings extant. [*WikiCommons*]

Martin Luther (1483–1546)
Ein feste Burg ist unser Gott / A mighty fortress is our God, ca. 1527–1529

In addition to his voluminous collected writings, Luther also penned about 36 hymns, including his most famous, *Ein feste Burg ist unser Gott.* Within Protestantism, hymns were instrumental for teaching and inspiring faith.

1.

Ein feste Burg ist unser Gott,
ein gute Wehr und Waffen.
Er hilft uns frei aus aller Not,
die uns jetzt hat betroffen.
Der alt böse Feind
mit Ernst er's jetzt meint,
groß Macht und viel List
sein grausam Rüstung ist,
auf Erd ist nicht seins gleichen.

2.

Mit unsrer Macht ist nichts getan,
wir sind gar bald verloren;
es streit' für uns der rechte Mann,
den Gott hat selbst erkoren.
Fragst du, wer der ist?
Er heißt Jesus Christ,
der Herr Zebaoth,
und ist kein andrer Gott,
das Feld muss er behalten.

3.

Und wenn die Welt voll Teufel wär
und wollt uns gar verschlingen,
so fürchten wir uns nicht so sehr,

1.

A mighty fortress is our God,
a bulwark never failing;
Our helper he, amid the flood
of mortal ill prevailing.
The old deadly foe
means us deadly woe
deep guile and great might,
are his dread arms in fight;
on earth there is no equal.

2.

If we in our own strength confide,
our striving would be losing;
but there is one who takes our side,
the one of God's own choosing.
You ask, "Who is this?"
Jesus Christ it is,
the Lord Sabaoth,
and there's no other God;
he holds the field forever.

3.

And though this world, with devils filled,
should threaten to undo us,
we will not fear, for God has willed

es soll uns doch gelingen.   that truth will triumph through us.
Der Fürst dieser Welt,   This world's prince may still
wie sau'r er sich stellt,   scowl fierce as he will,
tut er uns doch nicht;   he can harm us none.
das macht, er ist gericht':   He's judged; the deed is done;
ein Wörtlein kann ihn fällen.   one little word can fell him.

4.   4.

Das Wort sie sollen lassen stahn   That Word beyond all earthly pow'rs,
und kein' Dank dazu haben;   no thanks to them, is sounding.
er ist bei uns wohl auf dem Plan   The Spirit and the gifts are ours,
mit seinem Geist und Gaben.   by God's good grace abounding.
Nehmen sie den Leib,   And take they our life,
Gut, Ehr, Kind und Weib: goods, fame, child, and wife,
lass fahren dahin,   though all may be gone,
sie haben's kein' Gewinn,   our victory is won;
das Reich muss uns doch bleiben.   God's reign endures forever.

[**SOURCE:** Translation composite, 1866.]

Ein feste Burg ist unser Gott

M.L., 1529   Martin Luther, 1529

Martin Luther (1483–1546)
Von der Widertauffe / Concerning Anabaptism, 1528

In late 1527, Martin Luther was approached by two Roman Catholic priests who sought advice about how to respond to Anabaptist arguments. This text from 1528 is Luther's response. Luther vehemently critiques Anabaptist views, taking particular offence at their assertion that the first (infant) baptism is null and void because infants are incapable of saving faith, and that therefore a second baptism upon genuine confession of faith needs to be performed. Alongside his critique, Luther articulates his own theology of baptism and defends infant baptism. Luther claims that he is eager to distance his own views from the Anabaptists because he is aware of some, such as Balthasar Hubmaier, who falsely claimed Luther was opposed to infant baptism. In the course of his argument Luther compares the Anabaptist view to the ancient heresy of Donatism and makes reference to the practice of some Anabaptist groups (notably the Hutterites) to encourage spouses to separate from their unbelieving partners. A Hutterite response of sorts might be found in the 1560 *Ein Handbüchlein wider den Prozess zu Worms am Rhein gegen die Brüder so man die Hutterischen nennt*, where Hutterite theologians responded to similar critiques from Lutheran theologians (see *Handbook*, 215).

Martin Luther, to the worthy and beloved pastors N. and N., my dear friends in Christ:

Grace and peace be with you in Christ our Lord.

Unfortunately, I know full well, dear sirs, that Balthasar Hubmaier has included my name among others in his blasphemous booklet on re-baptism, as if I shared his perverted views. [...]

These Anabaptists and enthusiasts say, "Whatever is of the pope is wrong," or, "Whatever is in the papacy we must have and do differently," thinking thereby to prove themselves the foremost enemy of Antichrist. Not realizing that they thus give him most help, they hurt Christendom most and deceive themselves. [...]

In fact they remind us of what one brother in the forest of Thuringia did to the other. They were going through the woods with each other when they were set upon by a bear who threw one of them beneath him. The other brother sought to help and struck at the bear, but missed him and grievously wounded the brother under the bear... They take a severe stand against the pope, but they miss their mark and murder the more terribly the Christendom under the pope. […]

Those who depend on such arguments say that they know nothing of their baptism, and exclaim, "How do you know you have been baptized? You believe people who say you have been baptized. But you should believe God himself and not people, and you must be sure of your baptism." […] I might reply, "My friend, how do you know that this man is your father, this woman is your mother? You cannot trust people; you must be sure of your own birth." […]

Indeed I might then claim that holy Scripture meant nothing, Christ meant nothing. The apostles, too, never preached. For I have not seen nor felt these things. I've only heard them from people. So I won't believe them unless they are re-enacted anew and happen and are done again before my eyes. […]

God's work progresses in public so that neither devil nor man can controvert it, but every man can so know and declare it as he declares that you are living. When anyone

bears witness to the work of God it does not mean believing others, but God. […]

I also have read, that they base their faith on this verse, "He who believes and is baptized will be saved" [Mark 16:16]. This they interpret to mean that no man should be baptized before he believes. I must say that they are guilty of a great presumption. For if they follow this principle, they cannot venture to baptize before they are certain that the one to be baptized believes. How and when can they ever know that for certain? Have they now become gods so that they can discern the hearts of men and know whether or not they believe? […]

When they say, "Children cannot believe," how can they be sure of that?... There are Scripture passages that tell us that children may and can believe, though they do not speak or understand. […]

But, you say, he has not commanded the baptism of children... But he has commanded us to baptize all Gentiles, none excepted, when he said, "Go and baptize all heathen in my name," etc. (Matt. 28[:19]). Now children constitute a great part of the heathen. […]

Yet even if they could establish that children are without faith when they are baptized, it would make no difference to me. I would want to know their reason for re-baptizing when later on faith or the confession of faith is supposed to be present. […]

It is as if a girl married a man reluctantly and altogether without a wife's affection for the man. She is before God hardly to be considered his true wife. But after two years she gains affection for him. Would then a second engagement be required, a second wedding be celebrated, as if she had not previously been a wife, so that the earlier betrothal and wedding were in vain? [...]

Likewise God provides for the preaching of the Ten Commandments. But since some people only grasp them with their ears, albeit improperly, they are not Ten Commandments, are no good, and God ought hence to issue ten new commandments in place of the former. It can't be enough that people let themselves be rightly converted and give heed to the original Ten Commandments. [...]

We see among them the natural fruit of the devil, namely, that some of them on account of rebaptism desert wife and child, house and land, and will recognize no authority. Yet St. Paul teaches that whoever does not provide for his own has disowned his faith and is worse than an unbeliever (1 Tim. 6[5:8]). And in 1 Corinthians 7[:13] he expresses as his desire that a wife who believes should not divorce an unbelieving husband. Nor does Christ want a marriage broken, except where adultery becomes a reason for it. [...]

Even if St. Peter baptized, no one would know for certain if in that moment he stood in faith or in doubt. For no one can discern his heart. In brief, such arguments once led the Donatists to separate themselves and to re-baptize, when they saw how unholy some were who preached and baptized. They began to base baptism on the holiness of men, though Christ had based it on his Word and commandment. That is also the attempt of our rebellious spirits, the foes of the sacrament. They maintain, of course, that the truth and Scripture compel them, but they lie nevertheless. They are offended (as they sometimes experience) that any rogue may bring Christ into the bread of the sacrament, as if the entire world were sure that they themselves have faith and are completely holy. They act as though they were not great rogues in the eyes of God, just as much as they who sharply condemn wickedness and call others rascals, forgetting the beam in their own eye...And Christ bids us hear the godless Pharisees in the seat of Moses, though they are godless teachers. [...]

There is quite a difference between having faith, on the one hand, and depending on one's faith and making baptism depend on faith, on the other. Whoever allows himself to be baptized on the strength of his faith is not only uncertain. He is also an idolater. He denies Christ, because he trusts in and builds on something of his own, namely, on a gift which he has from God, and not on God's Word alone. So another may build on and trust in his strength, wealth, power, wisdom, holiness, which also are gifts given him by God. But a baptism on the Word and command of God even when faith is not present is still a correct and certain baptism if it takes place as God commanded. Granted, it is not of benefit to the baptized one who is without faith, because of his lack of faith, but the baptism is not thereby incorrect, uncertain, or of no meaning. [...]

I want to be baptized because it is God's command that I should be, and on the strength of this command I dare to be baptized. In time my faith may become what it may. If I am baptized on his bidding I know for certain that I am baptized. If I were to be baptized on my own faith, then I might tomorrow find myself unbaptized—if faith failed me or if I became worried that I might not yesterday have had the faith rightly. [...]

Of his baptism as a child he would say, I thank God and am happy that I was baptized as a child, for thus I have done what God commanded.

In sum, the Anabaptists are too frivolous and insolent. For they consider baptism, not as a God-given ordinance or command, but as a human trifle, like many other customs under the papacy relating to the consecration of salt, water, or herbs... So they carry on and call it a dog's bath, or a handful of water, and other such vile things.

Very much in the same manner the devil also deceives those who blaspheme the sacrament. When he realizes that his lies do not produce much effect, he fares forth and fills the ears of the mad mob with high-sounding sacrilege, such as our sacrament is an eating of flesh and guzzling of blood and the like. [...]

[**Source:** Timothy F. Lull and William R. Russel, editors, *Martin Luther's Basic Theological Writings*, 3rd edition (Philadelphia: Fortress Press), 240–261. Used by permission.]

HULDRYCH ZWINGLI (1484–1531)
"On Baptism," 1525

Huldrych Zwingli, one of the principal leaders of the Swiss Reformation, was a mentor to the young radicals, Conrad Grebel, Felix Manz, and others in their circle.

Alongside Zwingli—who arrived at his conclusions independently from Luther—they refined their thinking about justification by faith, *sola scriptura*, a memorial view of the Lord's Supper, and the rejection of singing.

On January 1, 1519, Zwingli came to Zürich to fill the position of *Leutprediger* at the Grossmünster. During Lent 1522, the group associated with him publicly expressed their protest in the famous "Sausage Affair" as a way to highlight the importance of Scripture over and against tradition and church rules. Beginning in the fall of 1523, the Radicals diverged from Zwingli primarily over questions about the authority of the city council, the pace of reform, and the issue of infant baptism. Public disputations were introduced to resolve the religious questions in Zürich, but they did not satisfy the radicals who were on the losing end of the contests.

The following texts give us a sense of the nature of the disagreements and tensions between Zwingli and his former students.

May 27, 1525

The Anabaptists claim that only those who know that they can live without sin ought to receive the sign of baptism. In so doing they make God a liar and bring back the hypocrisy of legal righteousness. [...] [I]s not that the height of presumption? As long as we are in the flesh, we are never without sin. [...]

But the Anabaptists do hold that they live without sin. This is proved by what they and some others write and teach concerning the [...] perseverance of saints. In this they are committed absolutely to the view that they can and do live without sin. How far that claim is borne out by their envy, lying, clamour, evil-speaking, and blasphemy I leave on one side. [...]

Clearly, then, baptism cannot bind us in such a way that we must not accept it unless we know that we can live without sin: for if that be the case, baptism was instituted in vain, for not one of us can claim to do that before God. Therefore we will turn to the Word of God and learn there both what baptism is and when it was instituted. As regards the first question, baptism is a covenant sign which indicates that all those who receive it are willing to amend their lives and to follow Christ. In short, it is an initiation to new life. Baptism is therefore an initiatory sign. [...]

[I]t is not the pouring of water which washes away sin. And that was what we once believed, although without any authority in the Word of God. We also believed that the water of baptism cleanses children from a sin which they never had, and that without it they would be damned. All these beliefs were erroneous, [...] Water-baptism cannot contribute in any way to the washing away of sin. [...] [A]lthough baptism may wash the body—and that is all that water-baptism can do—it cannot take away sin. Sin is taken away only when we have a good conscience before God. But no material thing can purge the conscience, [...] The sacrament can never cleanse the soul for it is only an external thing. The Word which saves the soul is not the word outwardly spoken, but the word inwardly understood and believed. And it is to that water that Christ is here referring, [...] But that water can be none other than Christ himself. [...]

Hence water-baptism is nothing but an external ceremony, that is, an outward sign that we are incorporated and engrafted into the Lord Jesus Christ and pledged to live to him and to follow him. And as in Jesus Christ neither circumcision nor uncircumcision avails anything, but a new creature, the living of a new life,[1] so it is not baptism which saves us, but a new life. [...] The root of the trouble is that the Anabaptists will not recognize any Christians except themselves or any Church except their own. And that is always the way with sectarians who separate themselves on their own authority. [...] For if every blockhead who had a novel or strange opinion were allowed to gather a sect around him, divisions and sects would become so numerous that the Christian body which we now build up with such difficulty would be broken to pieces in every individual congregation. Therefore no innovations ought to be made except with the common consent of the churches, and not merely of a single church. For the judgment of Scripture is not mine or yours, but the churches. [...]

[**Source:** G.W. Bromiley, *Zwingli and Bullinger* (Louisville: Westminster John Knox Press, 1979), 139–141, 153–154, 156–158. Used by permission.]

---

1   Gal 6.

Mandate of the Zürich council against the Anabaptists, 1526

The Zürich city council sought to bridge the theological differences between Zwingli and the Anabaptists by means of disputations or formal debates. In early January of 1525, the council sided with Zwingli on the issue of infant baptism and issued a mandate stating that anyone who refused to have their babies baptized must leave the city. When the Anabaptists refused to heed these rulings, the council produced a sharper mandate threatening death by drowning for anyone who baptized adults.

March 7, 1526

Although our lords, the mayors, the Council and the Great Council, which is called the Two Hundred, of the town of Zürich, have striven for a long time with special concern to bring the mistaken, wayward Anabaptists back from their errors, etc. some of them have remained quite stubborn in their opinions, contrary to their oaths, vows and promises, and have exhibited a disobedience against the rule of the government with disadvantageous and destructive consequences for the common weal and Christian life, and some of them, men, women and girls, have been severely punished by our lords and put in prison. Thereupon, our said lords now publish the grave command, order and warning, that henceforth, whether in the town, on the land or in the [subordinate] districts, no one, be they man, woman or maid, may re-baptize another. In future, if anyone baptizes another in this way, our lords will seize him and have him drowned without mercy according to the ruling they have just made. Accordingly, let everyone take care and pay attention, so that no one occasions their own death.

[**Source:** Hans Jürgen-Goertz, *The Anabaptists* (Oxon/New York: Routledge, 1996), 158. Reproduced by permission of Taylor and Francis Group, LLC, a division of Informa plc.]

HULDRYCH ZWINGLI (1484–1531)
Refutation of the Tricks of the Catabaptists, 1527

This text reveals the growing gap between the reforms of Zwingli and his Anabaptist offspring. Zwingli here paints his former friends as dangerous and radical opponents of public order. In the process he helps spread what would become a common malicious rumour about the Anabaptists: that their sharing of goods extended to their wives. Zwingli's rhetoric would bear its fruit on January 5, 1527, when Felix Manz, the first Anabaptist martyr, was drowned in the River Limmat.

July 31, 1527

[…]

This work is called a "Refutation of the Tricks, etc.," because this class of men [Anabaptists] so abounds and works in tricks that I have never seen anything equally oily or changeable. […] [T]hey deceive not only the simple, but even the elect. […] For you must know, most pious reader, that their sect arose thus. When their leaders, clearly fanatics, had already determined to drag into carnal liberty the liberty we have in the gospel, they addressed us who administer the Word at Zürich first, kindly, indeed, but firmly. […] They denounced infant baptism tremendously as the chief abomination, proceeding from an evil demon and the Roman pontiff. We met this attack at once, promised an amicable conference. It was appointed for Tuesday of each week. At the first meeting the battle was sharp but without abuse, as we especially took in good part their insults. Let God be the witness and those who were present, as well from their side as from ours. The second was sharper. […] Within three, or at most four, days it was announced that the leaders of the sect had baptized fifteen brethren. Then we began to perceive why they had determined to collect a new church and had opposed infant baptism so seriously. We warned the church that it could not be maintained, […] They had attempted a division and partition of the church, and this was

Depiction of the first Zurich Disputation of 1523 in a copy of Bullinger's History of the Reformation, pen and water colour, ca.1600. [*WikiCommons*]

just as hypocritical as the superstition of the monks. […] Then […] in great swarms they came into the city, unbelted and girded with rope or osiers, and prophesied, as they called it, in the market place and squares. They filled the air with their cries about the old dragon, as they called me, and his heads, as they called the other ministers of the Word. They also commended their justice and innocence to all, for they were about to depart. They boasted that already they hold all things in common, and threatened with extremes others unless they do the same. They went through the streets with portentous uproar, crying "Woe, woe, woe to Zürich!" Some imitated Jonah, and gave a truce of forty days to the city. What need of more? I should be more foolish than they were I even to name all their audacity. […] When the evil had somewhat subsided, so that the majority seemed likely to judge the matter impassively, joint meetings were appointed […] In the presence of the church the contest raged for three whole days more, with so great damage to them that there were few who did not see that the wretched people were struggling for the sake of fighting, and not to find the truth.

HIER WURDEN MITTEN IN DER LIMMAT
VON EINER FISCHERPLATTFORM AUS
FELIX MANZ UND FÜNF WEITERE TÄUFER
IN DER REFORMATIONSZEIT
ZWISCHEN 1527 UND 1532 ERTRÄNKT
ALS LETZTER TÄUFER WURDE IN ZÜRICH
HANS LANDIS 1614 HINGERICHTET

[...] After that conference [...] the senate decreed that he should be drowned who rebaptized another. [...]

So much about their division and betrayal of the church. They have gone out from us, for they were not of us. [...]

In describing their deeds I shall be free and brief. They have their wives common in such a manner as to desert their own marriage partner, and take others; so with the children, as to desert them and leave them for others to support. These fine fellows, when lust persuades, make common a brother's wife, even his virgin daughter. Though the very force of nature requires that they cherish their children by the sweat of the body, they make them common to others. [...]

At St. Gall public charges were made against two girls who had been of unblamed modesty until they had gone over to the Catabaptists, but whose modesty had suffered shipwreck when their bodies were immersed in catabaptism, They affirmed that they were betrothed in spiritual marriage, the rings be-

ing accepted, and in one night on one couch two Catabaptists had so loosed their virgin belts that the couch, groaning for a long time, at length, impatient of the burden, threw on the floor with one crash the two marriages. Those who heard the downfall swore solemnly that those spirits made such a sound that it appeared as if four bodies had fallen from on high. [...] But who can fittingly tell of the awful murder which a brother perpetrated upon his own brother [Thomas Schinker upon his brother Leonhard] in St. Gall? What ability in words can worthily set forth so great atrocity? Or who is so dull as not to see that God has set forth this example for the good of all, so as the more to deter from this pernicious sect? A brother calls in a brother who is thinking of no such thing into the presence of his father, mother, listers and the whole family, and orders him to kneel in the midst. The fanatical fellow obeys, thinking his brother is going to show some wonder. Doubtless the parents had the same expectation. [...] But when this one had knelt, the other seized a sword which he had brought for this purpose, drove it through his neck

A memorial plaque on the Limmat River commemorating the Anabaptists killed in early 16th century by the Zürich city government. In English it reads, "Here, from a fishing platform in the middle of the Limmat, Felix Manz and five other Anabaptists were drowned during the Reformation of 1527 to 1532. Hans Landis was the last Anabaptist executed in Zurich in 1614." [WikiCommons]

and cut off his head, which rolled to the feet of his parents, and left him lifeless. From his trunk poured a great quantity of blood. All there fell and became [as] lifeless in madness. The murderer himself shouted: The will of God is fulfilled. Like a madman he came into the city and cried out to the Burgomaster: I announce to you the day of the Lord. For at that time they were appointing as the day of the low that Ascension Sunday that passed two years ago. I cannot jest here at that murderous sect, for the deed was too atrocious to admit any mirth. […]

[**Source:** Samuel Macauley Jackson, *Selected Works of Huldreich Zwingli, (1484–1531):The Reformer of German Switzerland*. (Philadelphia: University of Pennsylvania, 1901), 131–137, 170–171.]

Sixteenth Century Visual Polemics

Life in the sixteenth century was marked by instability. Numerous factors, including the religious upheaval of the Protestant Reformation, political power struggles among emerging nation-states, economic turbulence from the discovery of the "New World," and widespread social unrest due to poor harvests and food shortages all contributed. The result was an intense political and social climate.

During this period, the battle of ideas was in part fought through the distribution of polemical pamphlets known as *Flugschriften*. These pamphlets were booklets that made a social or theological argument targeting an uneducated audience. Like the internet makes it possible for a message to go "viral" today, the invention of the printing press made it possible to mass produce them. They were often illustrated with woodcuts that vividly illustrated the issue at stake. These were precursors to modern political cartoons and very effectively lampooned opponents, bringing ideas to a large audience like never before. Most ordinary people would not have been able to understand the intricate debates about justification or the true nature of the eucharist, but a degree in theology was not needed to comprehend the point of a woodcut showing Martin Luther with seven heads, or a seven-headed papal monster sitting on an indulgence chest. Woodcuts like these would have functioned like modern day memes that allow political movements to mobilize the energy of the masses.

Polemical pamphlets and woodcuts were used by both Catholics and Protestants.

Christ places the Gospel writers and apostles into the divine mill along with the Holy Spirit. Erasmus and Luther distribute the resulting bibles to the clergy. "*Göttliche Mühle* / Divine Mill," woodcut, 1521. [Deutsche Digitale Bibliothek]

This woodcut depicts Luther as a nightingale singing the tones of the Gospel surrounded by his opponents, depicted as ravenous wolves. "*Die Wittenbergisch Nachtigall* / The Wittenberg Nightingale," woodcut, unknown artist, 1523. [*WikiCommons*]

The title page of Johannes Cochelus's "*Sieben köpfe Martini Luthers: Vom Hochwirdigen Sacrament des Altars / The Seven Heads of Martin Luther: Concerning the Holy Sacrament of the Alter*" shows Luther as the seven-headed beast of the apocalypse, with each head bearing a different title: Doctor, Martinus (wearing clerical clothing), Luther (wearing a Turkish hat), Clergyman, Fanatic, Visitor in the Church, and a wild Barrabas. Hans Brosamer, woodcut, 1529. [British Library]

Das sibénhabtig Pabſtier Offenbarung Johannis Teſſaloni. 2. Cap.

Umb gelt ein ſack vol ablas.

Regnum.

Diaboli.

This image depicts the papacy as a diabolical institution and was a response to the "The Seven Heads of Luther." A cross with the instruments of Christ's Passion and Crucifixion can be seen, to which is attached a letter of indulgence with the ironic inscription "*Umb Gelt ein Sack vol Ablas* / For money, a sack full of indulgences" in place of the typical INRI. Below it, framed by flags with the papal coat of arms, the seven-headed papacy is depicted as a devilish monster. The heads of the monster are those of the Pope, his cardinals, bishops, and monks. The monster sits on an indulgence chest, intended to represent an alter, leading to the devil's kingdom below. Unknown artist, "*Das sibnha[u]ptige Papsttier*," woodcut, ca. 1530. [Deutsche Digitale Bibliothek]

A caricature depicting a rotund monk being "played like a bagpipe" by the devil. The monk/bagpipe is not Martin Luther, as commonly suggested, but representative of monasticism in general. Eduard Schön, woodcut, ca. 1530. [*WikiCommons*]

A woodcut showing Luther wearing his friar's robes in the centre as he out-bowls the pope and his cardinals with a ball representing the holy Scriptures (*hailig gschrifft*). [Otto Clemen, *Flugschriften aus den ersten Jahren der Reformation*, vol. 3, Leipzig: R. Haupt, 1907–11.]

Johannes Tezelius Dominicaner Münch/mit sei
nen Römischen Ablaßkram/welchen er im Jahr Christi 1517. in Deutschen-
landen zu marckt gebracht/wie er in der Kirchen zu Pirn in seinem
Vaterland abgemahlet ist.

O ihr deutschen mercket mich recht/
   Des heiligen Vaters Papstes Knecht/
Bin ich/vnd br ing euch jst allein/
   Zehn tausent vnd neun hundert carein/
Gnad vnd Ablaß von einer Sünd/
   Vor euch/ewer Eltern/Weib vnd Kind/
Sol ein jeder gewehret sein
   So viel jhr leg eins Kästelein/
So bald der Gülden im Becken klingt/
   Im hup die Seel in Himel springt/

A caricature showing Johann Tetzel selling indulgences. The German verse concludes with the famous sales jingle attribut-
ed to him: "As soon as the coin in the coffer rings, the soul into heaven springs."

Pre-Hutterite Period
Early Anabaptist Writings

TOMAS MVNCER PREDIGER ZV HLSTET IN DVRINGEN.

CONRAD GREBEL AND CIRCLE
Letter to Thomas Müntzer, 1524

Written in the vernacular German instead of the scholarly Latin, Grebel's letter to Müntzer is one of the most important documents for understanding the convictions and development of Swiss Anabaptism. Grebel is writing on behalf of a larger circle of Radicals in an attempt to gain support and guidance for the beleaguered movement. The letter portrays a self-confident movement that is seeking to network with like-minded individuals in imagining an alternative understanding of the church. It is not known whether Müntzer received the letter.

Thomas Müntzer was a revolutionary reformer who initially supported Luther but later led a movement that sought to overthrow the social-political order. He actively participated in the Peasants' War and was killed in the battle at Frankenhausen along with 6,000 peasants. Müntzer significantly influenced Hans Hut, Hans Denck, and other early Anabaptist leaders.

The Radicals were impressed by Müntzer's writings on baptism, his emphasis on the "priesthood of all believers," and his boldness in calling out Luther's cautious approach to reform and its failure to produce a change in people's lives.

ZÜRICH, September 5, 1524

May peace, grace, and mercy from God our Father and Jesus Christ our Lord be with us all, Amen.

Dear Brother Thomas, for God's sake do not marvel that we address you without title and as a brother request you to correspond with us, and that we have ventured without your asking, and unknown to you, to initiate dialogue. God's Son, Jesus Christ, who presents himself as the one master and head of all those who are to be saved, and who calls us brethren through the one common word to all brethren and believers, has moved and constrained us to establish friendship and brotherhood [with you] and to call your attention on the following articles. Your writing of two booklets on spurious faith also moved us to write to you.[1] Therefore may you receive it favourably for the sake of Christ our Saviour, and if God wills, it shall also serve and work for our good. Amen.

Just as our ancient forefathers fell away from the true God and from the knowledge of Jesus Christ, and from true faith in him, and from the one true, common, divine Word, and from the divine rites of Christian love and being, and lived without God's law and gospel in human, unprofitable, and unchristian rites and ceremonies, and thought that thereby they would obtain salvation, and yet fell far short of it, as the evangelical preachers have pointed out, and are still in part pointing out, so also today everybody wants to be saved by a make-believe faith, without faith's fruits, without the baptism of trial and testing, without love and hope, without proper Christian rites, and while continuing in the old blasphemous way of life, and in the common ceremonial, anti-Christian rites of baptism and Christ's Supper: thus despising the divine Word and following the papal word as well as the word of the antipapal preachers which is not identical with nor agreement with the divine Word. [...]

While we were taking note of and lamenting these things your writing

against spurious faith and baptism[2] was brought to us, and we were more fully informed and confirmed. It made us wonderfully happy to have found one who was one with us in a common Christian understanding, and who ventured to point out to the evangelical preachers their deficiency. [...]

[On the Mass and Singing]

We understand and have noted that you have translated the mass into German, and have begun to use German hymnody.[3] That cannot be right, when we find no teaching in the New Testament about singing, and no example of singing, Paul scolds the learned at Corinth more than he praises them because they chanted in the church service, just as if singing,[4] as the Jews and Italians pronounce their words in a singsong manner.

Since singing in the Latin tongue arose without divine teaching and apostolic precedent and practice, and neither resulted in good nor brought edification, it will much less edify in German, but will result in an outward make-believe faith.

Paul quite explicitly forbids singing in Ephesians 5 and Colossians 3, when he teaches that they shall teach and admonish one another with psalms and spiritual songs, and

---

1   *Von den getichten glauben* (1524) and *Protestation odder Empietung und zum Anfang von dem rechten Christenglawben und der taufe* (1524).
2   *Protestation*, 1525.
3   Grebel may have seen Müntzer's three liturgical works.
4   cf. I Cor 14:9, 16.

if anyone wishes to sing, he shall sing and give thanks in his heart.

That which is not taught by clear instruction and example we shall regard as forbidden to us—just as if it stood written: Do not do this; do not sing.

The only command Christ gave his ambassadors [*boten*] in the Old [Testament] was to preach the Word; the same in the New. Paul likewise commands that the Word of Christ shall dwell in us, not singing. He who sings poorly is vexed; he who is able to sing well becomes conceited. [...]

If you wish to abolish the mass, do not introduce German singing. That is perhaps your idea, or it originated with Luther. [...] [Singing in the meeting] was not established by God.

[On the Lord's Supper]

The Supper of unity was set up by Christ and established by Him.

Only the words of Matthew 26, Mark 14, Luke 22, and 1 Corinthians 11 shall be used: no more and no less.

The minister of the congregation shall pronounce them, reading from one of the Gospels or Paul.

They are the words of institution of the Supper of unity, not of consecration.

Common bread shall be used, with no idolatry and with no additions: for these [human additions] introduce a make-believe reverence and adoration of the bread, as well as a turning away from the inward. Also a common drinking vessel shall be used.

This will eliminate the adoration, and guarantee a true knowledge and understanding of the Supper. For the bread is simply bread, yet by faith the body of Christ, and an incorporation into the body of Christ and with the brethren. One must eat and drink in the Spirit and in love, as John 5 and elsewhere indicate, as Paul points out in 1 Corinthians 10 and 11, and as Acts 2 clearly teaches.

Although it is simply bread, where faith and brotherly love prevail it shall be partaken of with joy. When observed in that way in the congregation it shall signify to us that we are truly one loaf and one body, and that we are and intend to be true brothers one with another. [...]

It shall be observed often and much. [...]

As to the time, we know that Christ gave it to the apostles at supper time, and that the Corinthians so observed it. Yet we do not designate any specific time, etc.

We know that you are far better instructed about the Supper of the Lord than we are; we only indicate our understanding. If we are not right about this, instruct us better. But do drop the singing and the mass and operate only according to the Word [...]. If that cannot be done it were better just to leave everything in Latin, unchanged and unmodified. [...]

We give this admonition the more freely because you listened to our brother[5] in such a friendly manner, also acknowledging to him that you too have given way a bit too much, also because we regard you and Carlstadt[6] as the purest proclaimers and preachers of the purest Word of God. And if you both justly rebuke those who mix human words and rites with the divine, you really ought also to dissociate yourselves from the priesthood, benefices, and all sorts of new and old usages, and from all other notions, both your own and those which are ancient, and thereby become entirely sound. [...]

Press forward with the Word and create a Christian church with the help of Christ and his rule as we find it instituted in Matthew 18 and practiced in the epistles. [...] There is more than enough wisdom and counsel in the Scripture, how all classes and all men shall be taught, governed, instructed, and made God-fearing. Whoever will not repent and believe, but resists the Word and the moving of God, and so persists [in sin] [...], such a man, we declare, on the basis of God's Word, shall not be killed, but

regarded as a heathen and publican, and left alone. One should also not protect the gospel and its adherents with the sword, nor themselves. [...]

[On Baptism]

On the subject of baptism we are really pleased with your book, and we desire further instruction from you. We understand that even an adult is not to be baptized apart from Christ's rule of binding and loosing. Scripture describes baptism for us as signifying that through faith and the blood of Christ our sins are washed away: to the one baptized that this inner self has been changed, and that he believes, both before and afterward. It signifies that one should be and is dead to sin, and walking in newness of life and spirit; also that he shall certainly be saved by the inward baptism if he lives his faith according to this significance. But the water does not strengthen nor increase—as the learned ones at Wittenberg say—and that it gives very great comfort, and is even one's final refuge on one's deathbed! Furthermore, it does not save, as Augustine, Tertullian, Theophylact, and Cyprian taught; and by such teaching they brought faith and the suffering of Christ to shame, in relation to adults; and also in relation to the unbaptized infants they brought shame upon the suffering of Christ. [...]

5   This is undoubtedly Hans Hujuff.
6   Andreas Bodenstein von Carlstadt, originally an ally of Luther in Wittenberg, subsequently an opponent on the issues of the Supper and Scripture. He died, a professor in Basel, in 1541.

If you or Carlstadt do not write sufficiently against infant baptism, and all that is associated with it, how and why one is to baptize, etc., I [Conrad Grebel] will try my hand at it, and will complete what I have begun, to write against all those (except yourself) who hitherto have written misleadingly and wilfully on baptism, and who have translated into German the senseless and blasphemous liturgy for infant baptism—such as Luther, Loew, Osiander, and those of Strassburg; and some have been even more shameful. Unless God avert it, I and my colleagues are more certain to suffer persecution from the learned ones than from other people. We entreat you not to use nor adopt the old antichristian rites, such as sacrament, mass, signs, etc. Hold to the Word alone, and rebuke as ambassadors should, especially you and Carlstadt, for you are doing more than all the preachers of all nations.

Count us as your brethren, and take this our letter as our confident expression of great joy and hope toward you through God. […]

One thing more. We are eager for a reply from you. And if you publish anything, send it to us with this messenger or others. We are also eager to learn whether you and Carlstadt are of one mind. We hope and believe that you are. […]

God be with us! Whatever we have not rightly understood, inform and instruct us.

[SIGNED:] Conrad Grebel, Andrew Castelberg, Felix Manz, John Ockenfuss, Bartholomew Pur, Henry Aberly, and others of your brethren in Christ, if God will, who joined in writing this to you, wish for you and all of us, until we write again, the true Word of God, and true faith, love, and hope, with all peace and grace from God through Christ Jesus, Amen.

[**Source:** William R. Estep Jr., ed., *Anabaptist Beginnings: A Source Book* (Nieuwkoop: B. De Graaf, 1976), 31–37. Used by permission.]

A detail from a 16th century schematic of Zurich showing the Grossmünster and the fishing huts on the Limmat River. Josua Murer (artist), Christoffel Froschauer (printer), woodcut, 1576. [*WikiCommons*]

Kaspar Braitmichel (d. 1573)
"Account of the First Re-baptism in 1525," written ca. 1570

The following account of the first re-baptisms in Zurich in 1525 is the only written evidence historians have of this watershed moment for the Anabaptist movement. Writing over forty years after the events he is describing, Hutterite chronicler Kaspar Braitmichel likely relied on oral accounts of this event in his retelling.

Because God wanted one united people, separated from all other peoples, he brought forth the Morning Star, the light of his truth, to shine with all its radiance in the present age of this world. He wanted in particular to visit the German lands with his Word and to reveal the foundation of divine truth, so that his holy work could be recognized by everyone. It began in Switzerland, where God brought about an awakening. First of all a meeting took place between Ulrich Zwingli, Conrad Grebel (a member of the nobility), and Felix Manz. All three were men of learning with a thorough knowledge of German, Latin, Greek, and Hebrew. They started to discuss matters of faith and realized that infant baptism is unnecessary and, moreover, is not baptism at all.

Two of them, Conrad and Felix, believed that people should be truly baptized in the Christian order appointed by the Lord, because Christ himself says, "Whoever believes and is baptized will be saved."[1] Ulrich Zwingli (who shrank from the cross, race, and persecution that Christ suffered) refused to agree—he said it would cause an uproar. But Conrad and Felix said that was no reason to disobey the clear command of God.

At this point a man came from Chur, a priest named Georg from the House of Jakob, later known as Georg Blaurock. Once, when they were discussing questions of faith, Georg shared his own views. Some-

---

1   Mk 16:16.

71

one asked who had just spoken. "It was the man in the blue coat [*blauer Rock*]." So he was given this name because he had worn a blue coat. This same Georg had come because of his extraordinary zeal. Everyone thought of him as a plain, simple priest; but he was moved by God's grace to holy zeal in matters of faith and worked courageously for the truth.

He, too, had first approached Zwingli and discussed questions of faith with him at length, but he had got nowhere. Then he was told that there were other men more on fire than Zwingli. He enquired eagerly about them and met with them, that is, with Conrad Grebel and Felix Manz, to talk about questions

of faith. They came to unity about these questions. In the fear of God they agreed that from God's Word one must first learn true faith, expressed in deeds of love, and on confession of this faith receive true Christian baptism as a covenant of a good conscience with God, serving him from then on with a holy Christian life and remaining steadfast to the end, even in times of tribulation.

One day when they were meeting, fear came over them and struck their hearts. They fell on their knees before the almighty God in heaven and called upon him who knows all hearts. They prayed that God grant it to them to do his divine will and that he might have mercy on them. Neither flesh and blood nor human

Felix Manz was drowned in the Limmat on January 5, 1527. The executioner tied him up, put him on the platform of the fisherman's hut and pulled him into the water with a rope. Heinrich Thomann, *Kopienband zur zürcherischen Kirchen- und Reformations- geschichte*, ca. 1605. [*WikiCommons*]

wisdom compelled them. They were well aware of what they would have to suffer for this.

After the prayer, Georg Blaurock stood up and asked Conrad Grebel in the name of God to baptize him with true Christian baptism on his faith and recognition of the truth. With this request he knelt down, and Conrad baptized him, since at that time there was no appointed servant of the Word. Then the others turned to Georg in their turn, asking him to baptize them, which he did. And so, in great fear of God, together they surrendered themselves to the Lord. They confirmed one another for the service of the Gospel and began to teach the faith and to keep it. This was the beginning of separation from the world and its evil ways.

Soon after this, more people joined them, like Balthasar Hubmaier of Friedberg and Ludwig Haetzer, and other scholars of German, Latin, Greek, and Hebrew, well acquainted with the Scriptures, as well as priests and preachers and other people. Soon they all gave witness with their blood.

Felix Manz was drowned at Zürich for the sake of the true faith and baptism, thus giving his life in steadfast witness to the truth.

Later, Wolfgang Uliman was condemned to death and burned at Waldsee, also in Switzerland his ten companions, including his own brothers, were executed with him. Valiantly and resolutely they gave their lives as a witness that their faith and baptism were founded on divine truth.

Melchior Vet, Georg Blaurock's traveling companion, was burned at Ettach for the sake of his faith.

So the movement spread through persecution and great tribulation. The church increased daily, and the number of the Lord's people grew quickly.

[**Source:** *The Chronicle of the Hutterian Brethren*, Volume 1. Translated and edited by the Hutterian Brethren. (Ulster Park: Plough Publishing House, 1987), 43–46. Used by permission.]

Portrait of Balthasar
Hubmaier, Chris-
toffel van Sichem,
engraving, 1650.
[*WikiCommons*]

Balthasar Hubmaier (ca.1480–1528)
Ein Christennliche Leertafel, die ein yedlicher mensch, ee vnd er im Wasser getaufft wirdt, vor wissenn solle / A Christian Catechism, which every Person should know before they are Baptized in Water, 1526–1527

Balthasar Hubmaier was the only university trained theologian among the first generation of Anabaptists. He began his career as a priest in Regensburg, then moved on to Waldshut, where he introduced a civic or town-wide form of Anabaptism. The town of Waldshut sided with the peasants, but when it was defeated, Hubmaier fled to Nikolsburg in Moravia and again introduced civic Anabaptism with the support of the local lord, Leonard von Liechtenstein.

Hubmaier clashed with Hut at Nikolsburg over Hut's apocalyptic ideas and his refusal to pay war taxes and accept governing authorities as Christians. Hubmaier defended the use of the sword by the authorities and saw Hut's ideas as destabilizing what he was trying to accomplish at Nikolsburg.

Scholars believe that Hubmaier's writings significantly influenced Peter Riedemann's *Rechenschaft*, particularly the arguments concerning infant baptism, and his discussion of the Lord's Supper. The Hutterite *Chronicle* acknowledges Hubmaier's contributions in this way: "Two hymns are still in our brotherhood which this Balthasar Hubmaier composed. There are also other writings by him from which one learns how he had so forcefully argued the right baptism, and how infant baptism is altogether wrong—all this proved from the Holy Scriptures. Likewise he brought to light the truth of the Lord's Supper, and refuted the idolatrous sacrament and the great error and seduction by it."[1]

Hubmaier wrote numerous books and pamphlets to defend religious tolerance, believers' baptism, a memorial understanding of the Lord's Supper, church discipline, and the freedom of the will. He also penned a devotional on the

---

1   A.F.J. Zieglschmied, *Die Älteste Chronik der Hutterischen Brüder*, (Philadelphia: Carl Schurz Memorial Foundation, 1943), 52.

Lord's Prayer and a catechism, part of which is included here. The two speakers in the catechism, Leonhart and his presumably unbaptized nephew Hans, represent the Lords von Liechtenstein, Hubmaier's patrons at Nikolsburg.

On three-fold baptism

Leon: What do you desire subsequent to faith?

Hans: Baptism in water.

Leon: How many kinds of baptism are there?

Hans: Three.

Leon: Which?

Hans: The baptism of the spirit; the baptism in water; a baptism in blood.

Leon: What is the baptism of the spirit?

Hans: It is an inward enlightenment of our hearts, caused by the Holy Spirit through the living Word of God.

Leon: What is water baptism?

Hans: It is an outward and public testimony to the inward baptism of the spirit. A man makes it by receiving the water, when in the sight of all he acknowledges his sins. He also testifies hereby that he believes in the pardon of those sins through the death and resurrection of our Lord Jesus Christ. He then allows himself to be outwardly marked, enrolled, and incorporated into the community of the church by baptism. This is in accordance with the behests of Christ. Thus man publicly and orally makes his pledge to God before the church in the strength of God the Father and the Son and the Holy Spirit, that henceforth he will believe and live according to the divine Word.

And if he should err therein he will submit to fraternal punishment according to the order of Christ.[2] That is the proper baptismal vow which was lost for the space of a thousand years. In the meantime Satan with his monastic vows and priests' oaths has pressed in and taken his seat in the holy place.

Leon: What is the baptism of blood?
Hans: It is the daily mortification of the flesh even unto death.

[**Source:** *Anabaptism in Outline: Selected Primary Sources*. Edited by Walter Klaassen. Scottdale: Herald Press, 1981; Walden: Plough Publishing House, 2019), 167–168. Used by permission.]

---

2   Mt 18.

On the Lord's Supper

Leon: What is the Lord's Supper?

Hans: It is a public token and testimony of love, in which one brother pledges himself to another before the church. Just as they are now breaking bread and eating with one another, and sharing the cup, so each will offer up body and blood for the other, relying on the power of our Lord Jesus Christ. They are mindful of his sufferings, when they break the bread and share the cup and the Supper, and show forth his death till he comes. That is the loving duty of the Supper of Christ which one Christian fulfils toward another so that every brother may know what good he can expect from the other.

Leon: Is not the bread the body of Christ and the wine his rose-coloured blood as the sayers of the Mass have told us hitherto?

Hans: By no means. Bread and wine are only memorial signs of the suffering and death of Christ for the pardon of our sins through the institution of Christ on Maundy Thursday. On that day he had determined to go forth and show the greatest of all the signs of love, the sacrifice of his flesh and blood for our sakes, even unto death on the next day. This was by our forefathers called Good Friday *a caritate*, that is, from love. Let me say at once: the Supper is a sign of brotherly love to which we are obliged, just as baptism is a vow and token of faith. The water concerns God; the Supper concerns our neighbour. Thereon hang all the law and the prophets. No other rites has Christ enjoined upon us and left behind him on earth. He who teaches these two signs aright, teaches faith and love aright.

[**SOURCE:** *Anabaptism in Outline: Selected Primary Sources.* Edited by Walter Klaassen. Scottdale: Herald Press, 1981; Walden: Plough Publishing House, 2019), 194.]

Portrait of Hans
Hut, Christoffel van
Sichem, engraving,
17th century.
[*WikiCommons*]

JOANNES HVT   IN MERHERN.

HANS HUT (ca. 1490–1527)
Von dem geheimnis der tauf, baide des zaichens und des Wesens, ein anfang eines rechten wahrhaftigen christlichen Lebens / On the Mystery of Baptism, both the Sign and the Essence of the Beginning of a True Christian Life, 1527

Hans Hut was a bookbinder and traveling book salesman who hailed from the village of Bibra near Meiningen in Thuringia. According to Werner Packull "Hut was without question the most influential missionary of early Anabaptism in Central and Southern Germany."[1] Hut's interest in the transformation of society as a whole attracted him to Thomas Müntzer's revolutionary vision of social and political reform. He was present at the Battle of Frankenhausen until the "shooting became too thick" and he fled.

Hut was intensely interested in the end times and identified Pentecost 1528 as the time when God's judgement would be unleashed on the ungodly via the invading Turks and God's elect, the Anabaptists (his hope in the peasants had not panned out). His frenetic pace of baptizing converts appears to be associated with an understanding of baptism as "an apocalyptic sealing of the faithful remnant."[2] Following Müntzer, he taught "the bitter Christ" of suffering and added his unique emphasis, the "Gospel of all creatures," which likewise promoted cleansing through suffering and freed humanity from servitude to this world.[3]

Hut died by suffocation when a candle left in his cell ignited some straw. Although he died before the first communes were established in Moravia, the Hutterite chroniclers speak favourably about Hut, probably because he advocated for a form of communal sharing, and associated with the non-resistant group at Nikolsburg, even though his own pacifism was more provisional and complex.

---

1   Werner O. Packull, *Hutterite Beginnings: Communitarian Experiments during the Reformation* (Baltimore/London: Johns Hopkins University Press, 1995), 56.
2   Werner Packull, *Hutterite Beginnings*, 57.
3   Hans Jürgen Goertz, *Profiles of Radical Reformers* (Scottdale: Herald Press, 1982), 57.

First then, Christ says, "Go into all the world and preach the gospel of all creatures [*aller creaturen*]." Here the Lord shows how humanity shall come to the knowledge of God and himself, namely through the "gospel of all creatures." But we must first of all learn and know what is this "gospel of all creatures." For, God have mercy, the whole world is utterly ignorant of it, and it is also never preached in our age. And though it be preached and spoken by the poor in spirit, despised of the world, as it should be, to those to whom it is revealed, yet to the soft and carnal men, especially the hireling preachers, who nonetheless boast that they preach the gospel, it is the very greatest folly and fanaticism, and those who so preach are railed at as the most scandalous false prophets and lying spirits. Ah well, they have their little day, and, as Paul has so well said, the Word of the cross is foolishness to them that are perishing; but to those who shall be saved (that is, us) it is the power of God.

In the "gospel of all creatures" is nothing else signified and preached than simply Christ crucified, but not Christ alone as Head, but the whole Christ with all members; this is the Christ which all creatures preach and teach. The whole Christ has to suffer in all members, and not as our scribes preach Christ (who nevertheless want to be the best, as we hear daily from them), that Christ as the Head has borne and accomplished everything. But then what happens to the members and the whole body in which the suffering of Christ must be fulfilled? Of this Paul bears witness, when he says, "I rejoice in my suffering, for I fulfill what is lacking in the suffering of Christ in my body." And therefore, in a short time, which has already begun, they must with their wisdom be turned into fools, for it is God's good pleasure through foolish, silly, and fanatical preaching, as the clever ones call it, to save those who believe it, though these rage against it never so much. So they must in a short time, for all their wisdom and pride, give way to the poor in spirit who, as Paul says, are simply fanatics to them. Now this you are to understand with diligence, my dearly beloved brethren, and mark the Word which Christ calls "the gospel of all creatures" [*das evangelium aller creaturen*]. For it is not here to be understood as though the gospel is to be preached to the creatures, cats and dogs, cows and calves, leaves and grass, but as Paul says, the "gospel which is preached to you, in all creatures." This he also shows when he says that the eternal power and divinity will be perceived when a man truly recognizes it in the creatures or works from the creation of the world. [...]

Thus it is nothing else, as he expounds it in another place, than a power of God which saves all who believe in it. But if a man will understand and confess God's eternal power and divinity, or his invisible being, by the works or creatures from the creation of the world, he must then mark and consider how Christ always showed the kingdom of heaven and the power of the Father to the common man in a creature, through a parable, through handicrafts, in all manner of works with which men are occupied. He did not direct the poor man to books, as now our senseless scribes do, but he taught them and showed them the gospel by means of their work, the peasants by their field, seed, thistle, thorn and rock. In the prophets God says men are not to sow amongst thorns, but are first to clear the ground, plough it or turn it up, and then plant afterwards. The power of God, as it is shown us here, is God's work towards us, that God's power must be exercised towards us, as the work of the peasants towards the field. This Christ shows with the field, and Paul says, "you are God's husbandry." As the peasant does with his field, before he sows seed in it, so does God also with us, before he plants his Word in us, that it may grow and bear fruit. He teaches the gardener the gospel from his trees, the fisherman from his catch, the builder from his house, the goldsmith by the testing of his gold, the housewives from their dough, the vine dresser by his vineyard, vine and shoots, the tailor by the patching on an old garment, the merchant by the pearls, the reaper by the harvest, the woodcutter by the axe laid to the tree, the shepherd by his sheep, the potter by his pottery, the steward and the bailiff by their accounts, the pregnant woman by her childbearing, the thresher by his winnowing fan, the butcher by his slaughtering. Paul illustrates the body of Christ in and through a human body, and so Christ always preached the gospel of the kingdom of God by the creatures and in parables and without a parable he did not preach to them. And so David says "I will open my mouth and speak in parables."

From such parables men are diligently to mark how all the creatures have to suffer the work of men, and come through the suffering to their end, for which they were created, and also how no man can come to salvation, save through suffering and tribulation which God works in him, as also the whole Scripture and all the creatures show nothing else but the suffering Christ in all his members.

[**Source:** *Anabaptism in Outline: Selected Primary Sources*. Edited by Walter Klaassen. Scottdale: Herald Press, 1981; Walden: Plough Publishing House, 2019), 48–51. Used by permission.]

"The Flammarion" first appeared in Camille Flammarion's *L'Atmosphère: Météorologie populaire* in 1888. It shows a man crawling under the edge of the sky, depicted as if it were a solid hemisphere, to look at the mysterious celestial realm beyond. The caption underneath the engraving translates to, "A medieval missionary says he has found the point where heaven and earth meet." Wood engraving, unknown artist, ca. 1888. [*WikiCommons*]

Anabaptist Apocalypticism, 1527–1528

The 15th and 16th centuries were a tumultuous time of transition with the discovery of the "New World," the Copernican Revolution, the invention of the printing press, the Peasants' War, and the Protestant Reformation. The medieval world was being radically shaken, expanded, and transformed imaginatively, culturally, politically, and even cosmologically. Is it any wonder then, that many Europeans at the time had a sense that the world was coming to an end? In fact, a world was coming to an end: the medieval world was giving way to the modern.

Reading their times through the lens of biblical apocalyptic writings, many saw the events of their day reflected in the symbols found in Daniel and Revelation. It was a common view held by most Reformers—from magisterial to radical—that they were living in the "last days." In the case of the Anabaptists, this expectation fostered a sense of urgency that led them to imitate the radicalism of the early church as they sought to detach from worldly affairs.

On the more extreme ends of the Reformation, apocalyptic expectation fuelled revolution. Two prominent Anabaptists, Hans Hut and Melchior Hoffman saw the time of the end as the time when the righteous should take up the sword against the unjust to usher in God's reign.

The consequences of this violent apocalypticism bore their horrible fruit at the Münster Rebellion. In 1534, led by charismatic leaders Jan Matthys and later Jan van Leiden, Anabaptists seized control of the city of Münster in present-day Germany and attempted to establish a theocracy. Under Jan van Leiden, Münster was declared the "New Jerusalem;" they forcibly baptized people, implemented polygamy, and practiced a form of community-of-goods. Bernard Rothmann, a preacher, provided the theology to defend many of the bizarre practices introduced in Münster.

In 1535, the Catholic and Lutheran armies broke through the city's defences and executed the leaders, placing their corpses in cages that were hung in the church tower. The shadow of Münster hung over the Anabaptists and especially the communal Hutterites for almost a century.

Hans Hut on the end times, 1527

It had been his view that God the Lord had given three and one-half years for repentance according to Revelation 13. Whoever repented would be persecuted and would have to suffer, as we read in [2] Timothy 3. All who would lead a godly life would have to suffer persecution. Daniel 12 says that they will all be scattered. He also talked about the three and one-half years and predicted famine, pestilence, and war. Only after these had happened would the Lord gather his own in all countries, and in each country they would punish the governments and all sinners. He based this on the passage where it says that the Lord would send his angels to the four corners of the earth to gather his elect. Then the new heaven and earth and a habitation for all the pious and elect here on earth would appear. This he called the future world according to Ezekiel 37 and Psalm 37, when the godless would be rooted out and the just would live in the land in perpetual peace.

Those who in these last times repent, remain steadfast to the end, and are not killed but remain, they will not die, but possess the earth and reign after the day and judgment of the Lord, as is stated in 1 Corinthians 15.

[**Source:** *Anabaptism in Outline: Selected Primary Sources*. Edited by Walter Klaassen. Scottdale: Herald Press, 1981; Walden: Plough Publishing House, 2019), 320–321. Used by permission.]

Balthasar Hubmaier Responds to Hut's end-times speculation, 1528

The day of the Lord is nearer to us than we expect. Therefore we should be prepared in daily worship, piety, and the fear of God.

Concerning this I very strongly opposed Hans Hut and his followers when they hoodwinked the simple people by claiming a definite time for the last day, namely next Pentecost. They convinced them to sell their property and leave wife and child, house and field behind, and are now without means of support. Thus the poor people were convinced to follow him by a seductive error which arose out of ignorance of Scripture.

The Scripture speaks of four years which Daniel calls a time, times, and half a time.[1] John in the Revelation calls the time 42 weeks which also make three and one-half years. That will be the time in which antichrist (whom Paul calls the man of sin and son of perdition[2]) will move and reign. At the end of that time God

---

1　　Dan 12.
2　　2 Thes 2.

will destroy him with the breath of his mouth.[3] Out of these three and one-half years which are sun and Daniel years, this ignorant Hut has made common years which is a great mistake. For a sun year is that time in which the sun makes one circuit which happens in one year with a little time remaining. That's where leap year comes from. Thus one common year is one day of the sun year. From this it follows that when Hut teaches about three and one-half years as in Daniel or the forty-two weeks in the Revelation and regards them as common years, he is mistaken. It is in fact according to the true understanding of Scripture three and one-half sun years which makes 1277 common years. By that much his calculations are in error which I seriously and openly flung into his face. I chastised him severely that he misled the simple people with his ungrounded claims.

[**Source:** *Anabaptism in Outline: Selected Primary Sources*. Edited by Walter Klaassen. Scottdale: Herald Press, 1981; Walden: Plough Publishing House, 2019), 324–325. Used by permission.]

Bernhard Rothmann: *Eyne Restitution edder Eine wedderstellinge rechter unnde gesunder Christliker leer* / A Restitution or a Vindication of True and Sound Christian Teaching, 1534

From the history of the people of God we learn that God brings about a restitution after each fall. [...]

God the Almighty rightly began the restitution when he awakened Martin Luther. When Luther, however, would not further God's grace, but remained lying in his own pride and filth, then the Antichrist became evident, and the true gospel began to appear. But the fullness of truth was magnificently introduced in Melchior Hofmann, John Matthys, and here in our brother, John of Leiden. Thus the kingdom of Christ has begun in Münster. What has been restored by God in the New Zion will now be shown, point by point.

1. God has again restored the Scripture through us. He has abundantly made his will known to us. And as we earnestly put into practice what we understand, God teaches us further every day.

2. The Münsterites hold to the true understanding of Scripture. [...] Everything is portrayed previously in the Old Testament before it is dealt with in the New Testament. Much more, everything which we await in the New Testament, has been openly anticipated in the Old Testament. [...]

6. Baptism is here restored. The Antichrist began child-washing, and made an idol out of water, with his magic. True baptism belongs only to

---

3   Isa 1, Dan 8.

those who understand and believe in Christ.

7. Through God's grace, the true church has been restored to Münster. For 1400 years, the truth has been falsified and repressed. [...] The true, holy church cannot be found either among Catholics or Evangelicals [i.e., Lutherans]. The latter would have better remained papists, than to have taught half-truths, for a half-truth is no truth. [...]

10. The living communion of saints has been restored, which provides the basis for community-of-goods among us. [...] And accordingly everything which has served the purposes of self-seeking and private property, such as buying and selling, working for money, taking interest and practicing usury—even at the expense of unbelievers—or eating and drinking the sweat of the poor (that is, making one's own people and fellow-creatures work so that one can grow fat) and indeed everything which offends against love—all such things are abolished amongst us by the power of love and community. [...]

11. We have again been given a sound understanding of the Lord's Supper. [...]

The Antichrist teaches that he can make a God out of bread. [...] Rather, the Lord's Supper is a remembrance of the Lord. [...]

12. God has restored the true practice of holy matrimony amongst us. Marriage is the union of man and wife—"one" has now been removed—for the honour of God and to fulfill his will, so that children might be brought up in the fear of God. [...]

Freedom in marriage for the man consists in the possibility for him to have more than one wife. [...] This was true of the biblical fathers until the time of the Apostles, nor has polygamy been forbidden by God. [...]

But the husband should assume his lordship over the wife with manly feeling and keep his marriage pure. Too often wives are the lords, leading their husbands like bears, and all the world is in adultery, impurity, and whoredom. Nowadays, too many women seem to wear the trousers. The husband is the head of the wife, and as the husband is obedient to Christ, so also should the wife be obedient to her husband, without murmuring and contradiction. [...]

13. Previously, there has been no true understanding of the glory of the kingdom of Christ on earth. [...] We know, however, that this kingdom must be fulfilled during our generation, and that the scriptural reference to the kingdom of Christ must be awaited here on earth. [...]

With his well-armed servants, Christ will defeat the devil and all unrighteousness, and then he will enter into his kingdom, in full justice and peace. [...] In sum, the people of Christ must inherit the earth. The prophets and the psalmist, together with Christ's parables and the Apocalypse, undeniably give proof of this. [...]

[**Source:** "A Restitution of Christian Teaching, Faith, and Life" by Bernhard Rothmann from *Christianity and Revolution: Radical Christian Testimonies 1520-1650*, edited by Lowell H. Zuck, 98–101. Used by permission of Temple University Press. © 1975 by Temple University. All Rights Reserved.]

Brüderlich vereini-
gung etlicher Kinder
Gottes / sieben artickel
betreffend.

Item / ein sendbrieff Michael Sat
lers / an ein gemein Gottes / sampt kur-
zem / doch warhafftigem anzeig /
wie er seine leer zu Rotten
burg am Necker / mit
seinem blut bezeu-
get hat.

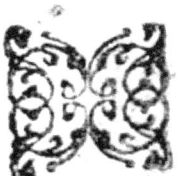

[MICHAEL SATTLER] (ca. 1490–1527)
Brüderliche Vereinigung etlicher Kinder Gottes, sieben artikel betreffend / [The Schleitheim Confession:] A Brotherly Agreement by Several of God's Children Concerning Seven Articles, 1527

Likely written by former Benedictine monk Michael Sattler in February of 1527, the *Brotherly Union* (aka the *Schleitheim Confession*) is the earliest known summary of Swiss Anabaptist beliefs.

The *Brotherly Union* is found in several Hutterite manuscripts, and formed part of the confession produced by the prisoners at Falkenstein (1539). The document influenced Hutterite theology on baptism, the Lord's Supper, the use of violence, separation from the world, and other areas.

By 1527, Swiss Anabaptism was without political protection and faced persecution from all sides. Internally, it also faced the temptation of spiritualism, the tendency to downplay outer forms as well as the material reality of the church. The young Anabaptist movement was in full survival mode.

To discern a way ahead, Anabaptist leaders met at the Swiss border village of Schleitheim. The seven articles that were hammered out at this conference are an attempt to reimagine the nature of the church: What does a church of voluntary believers committed to following Jesus in all areas of life look like in a society that considers everyone to be Christian and where church and state are closely connected? The topics of baptism, the ban, communion, separation from the world, leaders in the community, the sword, and swearing of oaths are addressed. Most scholars believe that the cover letter was a later addition.

[Cover Letter]

Joy, peace, and mercy from our Father, through the reconciling blood[1] of Christ Jesus, along with the gifts of the Spirit (who is sent by the Father to all believers for encouragement, consolation, and endurance in all tribulation until the end, amen) be with all who love God and the children of the light who are scattered about wherever God has deigned [*verordnet*] to place them and wherever they are gathered in unity in the one God and Father of us all. Grace and peace of heart be with you all. Amen.

Beloved in the Lord—brothers and sisters,

Your consolation and assurance of conscience (which has been somewhat confused) is always our first and primary concern so that you do become cut off from us like outsiders[2] [*auslendigen*] and completely, however appropriately, separated, but rather that you may again return to the members of Christ who are fully grafted in, armed with patience and self-knowledge, and become reunited with us

by the power of a divine Christian spirit and passion for God.

It is also clear to us what great deception [*tausent listigkeit*] the devil has brought against us so that he might destroy and demolish the work God has mercifully and graciously begun in us. However, the true shepherd of our souls, Christ, who is the source of this [i.e. God's work] in us, will guide and teach this [*dasselbe*] to the end to his glory and our salvation, amen.

Beloved brothers and sisters, we, who have been assembled in the Lord at Schleitheim on the Randen[3] declare to all who love God in point and article form that we have agreed to stand fast in the Lord as obedient children of God, as sons and daughters who have been and shall be separated from the world in all that we do (the praise and glory be to God alone), without any brothers contradicting, but completely at peace. In this we have felt that the unity of the Father and our mutual [*gemeinen*] Christ were present with us in their Spirit, for the Lord is a Lord of peace and not of quarrelling, as Paul indicates.[4]

---

1   In German: "*vereinigung des blutes.*" John Howard Yoder notes that *vereinigung* is a "most significant concept" for Sattler. John Howard Yoder, trans. and ed., *The Legacy of Michael Sattler* (Walden: Plough Publishing House, 2019), n1. In English, depending on context, it is variably translated as agreement, unification, or reconciliation. In this instance, Yoder chose to use "at-one-ment," a quite literal, yet theologically laden, rendering. This translation uses "reconciling," in an attempt to correspond more closely with the document's overall theme of unification and coming-together.

2   An allusion to Eph 2:12 and 19, indicating those outside the faith or Christ.

3   In German: "*zu Schlaten am Randen.*" There are several towns with the name Schlaten, but the subsequent reference, "on the Randen," refers to the hills overlooking Schleitheim. According to Yoder, there is a *Langer Randen* and a *Hoher Randen*. John Howard Yoder, *The Legacy of Michael Sattler*, n5.

4   1Cor 14:33. Note the membership overtones implicit in this phraseology.

So that you may know and understand why we came to this agreement, we must tell you the following: Some false brothers[5] did much damage among us, causing several to turn from the faith, by teaching that in Christ one may do whatever one feels like. But they have fallen short of the truth and (to their own condemnation) have been given over to the lust and desires [*geylheyt unnd freyheyt*] of the flesh. They thought that faith and love could accomplish and tolerate everything, and nothing would harm nor condemn them because they were also believers.

Take note, members of God in Christ Jesus: faith in the heavenly father through Jesus Christ is not like this; it does not produce such things nor deal as these false brothers and sisters practice and teach. Protect yourself and be warned from such [people], for they do not serve our father, but rather their father, the devil. Do not be like this, for those who belong to Christ have crucified their flesh along with all [misguided] lusts and desires. I am sure you understand me clearly and know which brothers I mean.[6] Separate yourself from them, for they are corrupted. Pray to the Lord that they may acknowledge [their need] for repentance and also for our on-going faithfulness in traveling the path we have chosen for the glory of God and Christ, his son. Amen.

[The Seven Articles]

The articles we have deliberated and reached agreement on are as follows: 1. baptism, 2. the ban, 3. the breaking of bread, 4. separation from abomination, 5. shepherds in the community, 6. the sword, and 7. the oath.

[Baptism]

FIRSTLY, REGARDING BAPTISM PLEASE NOTE: Baptism should be given to all those who have been taught repentance and transformation of life and who truly believe that their sins are removed through Christ, and all those who desire to walk in the resurrection of Jesus Christ so that they may rise with him, and all those who share this understanding and request and demand it of themselves. With this we rule out pedobaptism, the chief and primary abomination of the pope. Of this you have reason and testimony from Scripture and the practices of the apostles: Mt 28[:19], Mk 16[:6], Acts 2[:38], 8[:36], 16[:31–33], 19[:31–33].[7] To this we want to hold firm in simplicity and assurance.

---

5   See H.W. Meihuizen, "Who are the 'False Brethren' in the Schleitheim Articles." *Mennonite Quarterly Review* 41 (1967), 22ff.

6   The use of first person singular suggests that the cover letter was a later addition by an individual. Some manuscripts do not include it and the articles were commonly circulated without it.

7   The article on Baptism is the only one of the seven supported by biblical references. Only chapter numbers are given in the original.

[The Ban]

SECONDLY, WE REACHED AN AGREE-
MENT REGARDING THE BAN IN THE
FOLLOWING WAY: The ban should be
utilized against all those who have
submitted themselves to the Lord,
[committed to] following his commandments, [and] with all those
who have been baptized into the one
body of Christ and let themselves be
called brothers and sisters, but have
slipped [*entschlipffen*] and fallen into
error and sin or have been uninten-
tionally overcome.[8] They should be
admonished twice in private, but
for the third offence, they should be
disciplined or banned[9] publicly before the entire community according to the command of Christ (Mt
18).[10] This should take place under
the guidance of God's Spirit before
the breaking of bread so that we can
break and eat the bread and drink
the cup in unity and love.

[Communion]

THIRD, WE WERE UNITED AND IN
AGREEMENT CONCERNING THE
BREAKING OF BREAD: All those who
want to break bread for the remembrance of Christ's broken body, and
all who want to drink from one cup
for a memorial of the shed blood of
Christ, should first be members in
the singular body of Christ, that is,
in the community of God of which
Christ is the head through baptism.
For as Paul indicates,[11] it is not possible to participate at the table of the
LORD[12] and the table of the devil;
we can also not participate and
drink from the LORD's[13] cup and
the devil's cup simultaneously. That
is, all those who have communion
with the dead works of darkness
have no part in the light; in the same
way, all those who follow the devil
and the world do not participate
with those whom God has called out
of the world; all those who lie in evil
have no part in the good.

---

8   This turn of phrase raises interesting interpretive questions that defy clear answers.
    Yoder suggests two possible readings: 1. "unknowingly overcome" is a parallelism to
    "have slipped," and suggests that all sin is rooted in ignorance, i.e., individuals cannot
    fully comprehend the will of God, or 2. a distinction between 'forgivable' and 'un-
    forgivable' sins. Calvin read it the second way and understood it to mean that Anabap-
    tists were only concerned with forgiving inadvertent sins within their congregations.
    John Howard Yoder, *The Legacy of Michael Sattler*, n18.
9   The print edition inserts "*oder gebant werden.*"
10 This reference to the 'crescendo of care' is the singular biblical reference present in
    the earliest manuscript. Yoder notes that, given the abundant use of "scriptural lan-
    guage," the absence of references could be interpreted as evidence of the Anabaptists
    fluency in biblical vocabulary; he also points out that these texts were not seen as
    "proof texts," but rather plainly understood truths. John Howard Yoder, *The Legacy of
    Michael Sattler*, n20.
11 1Cor 10:21.
12 As in the print edition.
13 As in the print edition.

Consequently, whoever does not share the calling from one God to one faith, to one baptism, to one spirit, to one body[14] with all of God's children can also not be formed into one [loaf of] bread, as it must be if we [*man*] desire to break the bread rightly, according to the command of Christ.

[Separation from the world]

FOURTH, WE HAVE COME TO AN UNDERSTANDING CONCERNING SEPARATION [FROM THE WORLD]: This must occur toward the wicked and evil people that the devil has planted in the world. Thus: simply that we have no fellowship [*gemeinschaft*] with them, refusing to go along with [*laufen*] the masses in their abomination. This is because all those who have not entered into obedience of faith[15] and refused to unite themselves with God, so that they want to do his will, are a great abomination before God. Because of this, nothing but abominable things can and will [*kann und mag*] be manifested by them. Everything in all of creation is either good or evil, believing or unbelieving [*glaubig unnd unglaubig*], darkness or light, worldly or those who are separated from the world, temples of God or idols, Christ or Belial—nothing can have anything to do with the other.

To us, therefore, the command of the Lord in which he calls us to be and become separate from evil is obvious. Thus, he will be our God and we will be his sons and daughters.[16]

Further, and to that end, he admonishes us to leave Babylon and earthly Egypt behind so that we do not also participate in their torment and suffering that the Lord will bring upon them.[17]

From all this we ought to realize that everything unreconciled to our God and Christ is an abomination which we must avoid and flee.[18] This means [*vermeint*] all Catholic and Reformed [*pepstliche und widerbepstliche*][19] works and rituals [*Gottesdienste*[20]], assemblies, church attendance, [going to the] tavern, citizenship, and com-

---

14   Eph 4:5–6.
15   The print edition repeats "*und die gehorsam des glaubens*."
16   2Cor 6:17.
17   Rev 18:4–8.
18   The print edition inserts "*und fliehen*."
19   "*Wider*" can either mean 'against' or act as a 're-' suffix. Yoder points out that in the case of "*widerbepstliche*" both meanings are invoked: the Reformed churches were certainly anti-Catholic, but according to the Anabaptists they had also re-assumed characteristics of the papacy such as using the sword. In other words, the Reformed churches had become like the Catholic Church in significant ways. This polemical double meaning is lost in translation.
20   Although the early manuscripts and printings have "*Gottesdienst*," Zwingli read "*Götzendienst*." For Zwingli, this "idolatry" referred to statues and images used in Catholic worship.

mitments of unbelief,[21] and anything else like this in the world that is unjust by any measure. From all this we should become separate and have no part in it for it is an abomination [*eitel grewel*] that causes us to be despised by Christ Jesus who has delivered us from the servitude of the flesh and prepared us for the service of God through the Spirit which he has given us.

We therefore also repudiate without hesitation[22] the unchristian and[23] diabolical weapons of violence—such as swords, armour, and the like—and any use thereof to protect friends or oppose enemies. According to the teachings of Christ, "you should not resist evil."[24]

[Leaders in the Community]

FIFTH, WE REACHED AGREEMENT REGARDING SHEPHERDS IN THE CONGREGATION [*GEMEIN*] OF GOD AS FOLLOWS: The shepherd in the community of God should be a person in accordance with the rule of

[the apostle] Paul, [namely] have an overall positive [*ganz und gar gut*] reputation with those outside the faith.[25] This office includes reading [the Scriptures],[26] encouraging, and teaching, admonition, discipline, exclusion [*bannen*] within the community, and interceding in prayer for the improvement [*besserung*] of all brothers and sisters, breaking the bread,[27] and carefully heeding [*acht haben*] to all things concerning the body of Christ so that it flourishes [*gebawr unnd gebessert*] and the mouth of the mocker is sealed [*verstopfft*].

[The shepherd] should be supported [materially] wherever needed by the community who has chosen him, so that those who serve the Gospel can also be sustained by it, as the Lord has ordained.[28] If a shepherd does something that is worthy of correction, no action should be taken against him without two or three witnesses. If they [the shepherds] sin, they should be disciplined publicly so that others are warned.[29]

---

21 The Bern manuscript has "*Burgschaft,*" referring to a guarantee or security toward a financial or social commitment. The "commitments of unbelief" in the print edition refers to signing notes, mortgages, and affidavits in bad faith.

22 The print edition inserts "*angezweifelt.*"

23 The print edition inserts "*unchristlichen / auch.*"

24 Mt 5:39.

25 I Tim 3:7.

26 Yoder suggests that "reading" also implied providing an exegesis on the biblical text because "'readings' had been one of the earliest names given to the study meetings held in Zürich and St. Gall prior to the foundation of Anabaptist congregations." John Howard Yoder, *The Legacy of Michael Sattler*, n73.

27 The print edition inserts, "*und allen Brüdern und Schwestern zur besserung vorbeten / das Brot anheben zu brechen.*"

28 I Cor 9:14.

29 Literally, "have fear [*forcht haben*]." I Tim 5:20.

If this shepherd is persecuted or led to the Lord by the cross,[30] in the same hour another should be chosen to take his place so that the little flock and assembly of God is not destroyed.

[The Sword][31]

SIXTH, WE HAVE REACHED UNITY CONCERNING THE SWORD IN THE FOLLOWING WAY: The sword is an ordinance of God, outside the perfection of Christ; it punishes and kills the wicked and guards and protects good [people]. In the [Mosaic] law the sword is put in place [...] for use by secular authorities. Within the perfection of Christ, however, the ban, which doesn't kill the body, is used solely for admonition and exclusion of those who sin. This is done simply with a warning and command to abstain from sin.

Many who do not understand the will of Christ ask if the sword can or should be used against the wicked for the defense and protection of good [people], or for the sake of love.

[Our] unanimous answer is as follows: Christ teaches and commands us that we ought to learn from him because he is meek and humble at heart and thus we will find rest for our souls.[32] Christ said that the gentile [*heidnischen*] woman caught in the act of adultery[33] should not be stoned according to the [Mosaic] law of his father (and yet he says, "I do what the father has commanded me to do.")[34] but rather, be extended mercy and forgiveness; with the admonition to abstain from sin, he said, "Go and sin no more."[35] We should therefore do just that, according to the rule of the ban.

Secondly, we are asked, with regard to the sword, if a Christian should pass judgment in the secular disputes and conflicts that the unbelievers have among themselves.

This is our united response: Christ refused to pass judgment or sentence between two brothers concerning their inheritance;[36] we should follow his lead.

The third question posed regarding the sword is, "Should [a Christian] be a magistrate, if elected to the position?"

We answer as follows: Christ was supposed to be made into a king, but he fled because he did not see it as the will of his father.[37] We ought

---

30 Yoder notes that by this time, the notion of "cross" was already a direct reference to martyrdom within the fledgling Anabaptist movement. John Howard Yoder, *The Legacy of Michael Sattler*, n42.

31 "The sword" is classic Anabaptist nomenclature for the power the state exerts in judicial matters.

32 Mt 11:29.

33 Jn 8:3–11.

34 Jn 8:22.

35 Jn 8:11.

36 Lk 12:13.

37 Jn 6:15.

to do the same and flee with him [*ihm nachlaufen*]. In this way we will not wander in darkness, for [Christ] himself said, "Whoever wants to become my follower, let him deny themselves, take up their cross and follow me."[38] He also directly forbade the violence of the sword by saying, "[…] the rulers of the Gentiles lord it over them, [and their great ones are tyrants over them.] It will not be so among you."[39] Additionally, Paul says, "Those whom God has chosen, they are also ordained that they are glorified to the image of the son…."[40] Peter also says, "[To this you were called, because] Christ suffered (not ruled), leaving us an example, that you should follow in his steps."[41]

Finally, it is noted that it is inappropriate for a Christian to be a magistrate because of the following points:

- In the same way the rule of government is according to the flesh, a Christian [lives] according to the Spirit.

- [In the same way the state's] home and residence is in this world, so is the Christian's in heaven, [i.e. divine].[42]

- [The government's] citizenship is of this world, and the Christian's citizenship is in heaven.

- [The government's] weapons of battle and warfare are carnal, attacking only the flesh, while the Christian's weapons are spiritual and fight against the fortifications of the devil.

- The worldly are armed with steel and iron, but Christians are armed with the armour of God, [namely] truth, justice, peace, faith, salvation, and with the Word of God.

In summa,[43] as Christ our head is minded, so must the members of the body of Christ also be minded through him so that there is no division in the body by which it may be destroyed; "every kingdom divided against itself will be destroyed."[44] Because Christ is just as it is written about him, so must also the members be, so that his body remains whole and unified for its own betterment and edification.[45]

[Swearing Oaths]

Seventh, we were united concerning the oath in the following way: The oath is an agreement between those who are quarrelling or making promises. Under [Mosaic] law it was required to be done in the name of God who is truth alone and without falsehood.

---

38   Mt 16:24.
39   Mt 20:25.
40   Rom 8:30.
41   1Pet 2:21.
42   Phil 3:20.
43   Latinism meaning "in conclusion," or "in summary."
44   Mt 12:25. An addition in the print edition.
45   The Bern manuscript has the Mt 12:25 quotation here.

Christ, who teaches the perfection [*vollkommenheit*] of the law, forbids his followers to swear [an oath]— whether true or false, whether by heaven or by earth, whether by Jerusalem or by their own heads—because, as he said shortly thereafter, "you cannot make one hair white or black."[46] Take heed, all swearing [of oaths] is therefore forbidden because we cannot make good on what is promised in [the act of] swearing in the same way we cannot change even the smallest part of our body.

Now there are several who do not put their faith in the simple command of God, but say and ask, "But God swore by himself to Abraham because he was God (when he promised him that he would bless him and would be his God if he kept his commandments). Why, therefore, should I not swear [oaths] as well when I promise something to someone?"

[…] Hear what the Scriptures say: "Because God wanted to make the unchanging nature of his purpose very clear to the heirs of what was promised, he confirmed it with an oath […] by two unchangeable things (in which it is impossible for God to lie), [so that] we […] may be greatly encouraged."[47] Notice the purpose of this passage: God has the authority to do what he forbids you [to do], for with him everything is possible. God swore an oath to

Abraham, says Scripture, to prove to him that his counsel will not falter [*nicht wancket*]. That means, no one can oppose or hinder his will, and therefore he can keep his promise whereas we cannot. As Christ is quoted above, whatever we do or accomplish, we should still not swear [oaths].

Still others further say that God did not forbid swearing [oaths] in the New Testament if he commanded it in the Old. Rather we are prohibited from swearing by heaven, earth, Jerusalem, and on our head. Response: Listen to Scripture: "Whoever swears by heaven, swears by the throne of God and by the one who is seated upon it."[48] Notice that swearing by heaven, which is merely the seat of God, is forbidden, how much more is it forbidden to swear by God himself? You fools and blind [people]! What is greater—the throne, or the one who sits on it?

Still others say that if it is wrong to use God for the sake of truth, then the apostles Peter and Paul also swore.

Response: Peter and Paul only testified to what God promised Abraham by means of an oath, not about a promise they received themselves as the examples clearly demonstrate. Testifying and swearing, however, are two different things, for when someone swears [an oath] it involves something yet to come, like

---

46   Mt 5:34–37.
47   Heb 6:13–20.
48   Mt 5:34–35.

Christ was promised to Abraham, which came to fulfilment much later. When someone testifies, however, one witnesses to what is present, whether it is good or evil, like Simeon said to Mary about Christ: "This [child] is destined for the falling and the rising of many in Israel, and to be a sign that will be opposed."[49]

Christ taught us to do the same when he said,[50] "Your speech shall be yes, yes and no, no, for what is more than that comes of evil."[51] He says, your speech or your word shall be yes and no, so that no one might understand that he had permitted…. Christ is simply yes or no, and all that seek him in simplicity will understand his Word, amen.

[Conclusion]

Beloved brothers and sisters in the Lord, these are the articles that several brothers have misunderstood and missed their true meaning, thereby confusing many weaker consciences through which the name of God was greatly maligned. It was, therefore, essential that we were reconciled in the Lord. To God be glory and praise that this has happened!

Now, because it is abundantly clear to you what the will of God is, as revealed to us at this time, it is impera-

tive that you persevere in fulfilling it without deviation, for you know what the reward of the servant was who knowingly disobeyed [sündet].

Everything you have unknowingly done, but now recognized as wrong, is forgiven through the prayers of the devout offered among us when we gather for our failures and trespasses through the gracious forgiveness of God and through the blood of Jesus Christ, amen.

Be cautious toward all those who do not walk in the simplicity of divine truth [found] in this letter and discerned by us in the assembly so that all among us, governed by the rule of the ban, can prevent false brothers and sisters from infiltrating us in the future.

Cut off from yourselves what is evil and then the Lord will be your God and you will be his sons and daughters.[52]

Dear brothers, keep in mind how Paul admonished his [disciple], Titus. He said, "The grace of God has appeared, bringing salvation to all, training us to renounce impiety and worldly passions, and to live in this world with self-control, upright, and godly, while we wait for the blessed hope and the appearing of the glory of our great God and

---

49 Lk 2:34.

50 In the original "taught" and "said" are in past and present tenses respectively. This translation changed "says" to "said" for ease of reading. The inconsistent use of tenses, according to Yoder, is due to the fact that Scripture is always quoted in the present tense, i.e., "Scripture/Christ/Paul, etc. says."

51 Mt 5:37.

52 2Cor 6:17. This is the second allusion to this text, see n16.

Saviour, Jesus Christ, who gave himself for us so that he might redeem us from all iniquity and purify for himself a people of his own who are zealous for good works."[53]

Reflect on this and practice it and the Lord of peace will be with you.

The name of God is forever blessed and greatly praised, amen. May the Lord give you his peace, amen.

Completed [*Acta*] at Schleitheim on Randen, on St. Matthew's Day,[54] 1527.

[**Source:** Translated by Kenny Wollmann from the third edition from 1550. Two known copies are extant: one at the Mennonite Historical Library in Goshen, IN and a second at the Ortsmuseum Schleitheim. This translation is based on scans of the copy found at the Ortsmuseum Schleitheim (http://www.museum-schleitheim.ch/taeufer_bekenntnis1.htm).]

---

53   Tit 2:11–14.
54   February 24.

Castle Freundsberg
where Hans Schlaffer
was imprisioned.
Photograph, 2013.
[*WikiCommons*]

Hans Schlaffer (d. 1528)
In Todesnöten / In death's agony, 1528

Hans Schlaffer entered the Catholic priesthood in 1511 but resigned from his post in 1526 after encountering Luther's teachings. He was likely baptized by Hans Hut and was a leader in the Anabaptist congregation of Freistadt in Upper Austria for a time before moving on to spread the gospel in Bavaria and North Tyrol. Schlaffer traveled extensively and was in contact with most of the leading early Anabaptists; he was present at the Nikolsburg disputation between Hans Hut and Balthasar Hubmaier in 1527 and possibly at the Martyr's Synod in Augsburg.

Schlaffer and two travelling companions were arrested at Schwaz near Rattenberg, Tyrol and placed in the nearby Freundsberg dungeon. Here he was interrogated about his views on the sacraments, the names of Anabaptist leaders, and his involvement in planning another uprising similar to the Peasants' War.

All except one of his nine known writings, including the moving prayer he wrote the night before his execution, were produced during his eight-week imprisonment; these spiritualistic writings have been preserved in numerous Hutterite manuscripts. Schlaffer's tone is moderate and irenic and shows influence from the *devotia moderna* movement.

On the eve of his departing at Schwaz, [Tyrol,] on the Monday after Candlemas,[1] 1528.

Almighty God, I accept the cup of salvation[2] and call upon your name. I bring you an offering, freely given, and acknowledge your name. I want to settle my debt to you before all people, so that those who fear you will see how I have placed my hope in your Word. Almighty God, show your power and might in my frail and earthly vessel, within which you have revealed to me the precious treasure you placed and hid. Let me pay for everything you have given me with my fragile body

---

1   February 4.
2   Allusion to Ps 116:13.

and wretched life, for I have nothing more to give.

O my God, what misery I suffer here! Only now that the great conflict between spirit and flesh rages, which no one—unless they have endured it themselves—can comprehend, do I confess the grave defect and fall of Adam within me. O my God, what will happen to me?

But now, Lord, I put all my anxiety, distress, and fear upon you. Thus far you have sustained me.[3] You will not withdraw your support from me until the end, but rather show to me in great peril and weakness your greatest support and strength. In my shame and disgrace you will proclaim your glory and reveal eternal life in my temporal death to all those who have submitted to you through faith in Christ and endure in your will to the end.

Therefore come, o dear father, come! The terrible and fearful affliction is at hand; the time is here. Keep your commitments and promise which you have given to all your chosen and faithful, [namely] that—for the sake of your name and Word—you are always the support of the poor, strength and power for the weak, hope for the despairing, refuge for the suffering, and a comfort [Schutz und Schirm] to the dying.

Stretch your arm over us[4] from on high and save us from the might of wicked people [bösen Kinder] whose power is a power of evil. In the midst of the greatest tribulation and distress, you will redeem, deliver, and bring us to life.

Our soul is sorrowful unto death.[5] O father, rescue us from this hour. We now go to Gethsemane [Ölberg] to pray with the Lord: "O Father, not our will, but your will be done!"[6] Help us through this sorrowful night to your eternal life. Amen.

[SOURCE: Translated by Kenny Wollmann from Die Hutterischen Episteln 1527–1763, Volume 3 (Elie: James Valley Book Centre, 1988), 71. Used by permission.]

---

3   Allusion to 1Sam 7:12.
4   At this point the text transitions from an individual to a group perspective (I/my to us/our).
5   Quoting Christ in Gethsemane, see Mk 14:34, Mt 26:38, and Jn 12:27.
6   See Mk 12:36, Mt 26:39, and Lk 22:42.

CHARLES V (1500–1558)
Mandate from the Diet of Speyer, 1529

Charles V was the Catholic Emperor of the Holy Roman Empire from 1519–1556. For much of this time he was preoccupied with defending his territories against the Ottoman Turks in the east and rivals like Francis I of France. He presided at the Diet of Worms, where Luther was condemned in 1521. This mandate reflects his attempt to eradicate the Anabaptist movement.

We, Charles V, etc. greet all of our and the Holy Empire's electors, spiritual and temporal princes, prelates, counts, barons, lords, knights, captains, officials... mayors, judges, councillors, citizens and communes and all the rest of our and the Empire's loyal subjects, whatever their degree, estate or condition, with our friendship, grace and best wishes.

Highborn and worthy friends, nephews, uncles, electors, princes; well-born, noble, honourable, devout and dear subjects!

Although it is ordained and decreed in common [i.e., canon] law that no one who has been baptized once according to the Christian rite should have himself baptized again or for a second time, nor should he baptize others in this way, and that, most notably under im-perial law, this is forbidden on pain of death, whereupon at the beginning of last year, the 28th, as Roman Emperor, highest lord and protector of our holy Christian faith, we instructed you gravely in our public mandate,[1] through your own decrees and also through the pulpit by means of learned, Christian preachers, truly and seriously to alert and warn all of your subjects and people of this, now recently revived, error and sect of the Anabaptists and their malicious, seductive and seditious following, and to remind them too of the legal penalty in such cases and especially of the great punishment which awaits them from God, and to proceed against anyone found, encountered or discovered in the depravity and error of Anabaptism with the punishment prescribed by law, as is done in the case

---

1   *Kaiserliche Patente.*v.4.1.1528.

Portrait of Charles V,, Holy Roman Emperor," Bernard van Orley, oil on wood, ca. 1491. [*WikiCommons*]

over the question of the punishment for Anabaptism, we hereby renew the previous imperial law, together with our aforementioned mandate which stemmed from it, and we order, instruct, declare and desire, in the perfection and knowledge of imperial power, that each and every rebaptizer and rebaptized person of reasoning age, male or female, be executed and taken from life to death by fire, the sword or the like, according to the person's circumstances, without reference to the spiritual judgement of an inquisition; and the preachers, directors, missionaries and rabble-rousers of the said crime of Anabaptism, those who persist in it and those who fall for a second time should be granted no pardon whatsoever, but should be punished severely, in accordance with this, our constitution and decree. However, those people who, either by themselves or after instruction and warning, confess and recant their error and are willing to accept penitence and punishment for it and ask for mercy may be pardoned by their government depending on their intellect, condition, age and other circumstances.

of any other crime, and not to delay in punishing such evil in order to prevent more filth from growing out of it. However, every day we learn that despite the aforementioned common law and our own mandate, the ancient and forbidden sect of Anabaptism, which was damned many centuries ago, is continuing to increase in extent and strength.

To prevent such evil and whatever might result from it, to preserve peace and unity within the Holy Empire and to remove any disagreement and doubt which might arise

We also wish everyone to have their child baptized in infancy according to Christian ordinance, tradition and custom. However, anyone who disdains this and does not do it, thinking nothing of infant baptism, should, if he dares to be stubborn in this, be considered an Anabaptist and subject to our aforementioned constitution. None of those who are pardoned for the aforementioned reasons should be banished and expelled to a different place, but should be forced and bound to remain under their own government, which should then diligently keep them under supervision so that they do not lapse again. No other subject or kin who has left or moved from their state should accommodate or shelter them, but as soon as the government of the land to which they have gone becomes aware of the fact, it should proceed firmly against the people who have escaped, according to our previous sentence, and should not allow or tolerate them to remain, under pain of the ban.

We hereby command each and every one of you individually, whatever your dignity, estate or condition, by the duties and oaths with which you are bound and attached to us and to the Holy Empire, and to avoid our serious disfavour and punishment, and we desire that each and every one of you keep firmly to all the points of our constitution and sentence concerning Anabaptism, judge and act on it, and diligently execute it, and show such obedience as your obligations and the importance of the matter itself require, and we want there to be no doubt that in that you are carrying out our serious intention. Given in our and the Empire's town of Speyer, on the 23rd day of the month of April, in the 1529th year after the birth of Christ, in the tenth year of our Roman rule and in the 13th year of our rule elsewhere.

[**Source:** Hans Jürgen-Goertz, *The Anabaptists* (Oxon/New York: Routledge, 1996), 158. Reproduced by permission of Taylor and Francis Group, LLC, a division of Informa plc.]

Hutterite Beginnings
(1528–1565)

Kasper Braitmichel (d. 1573)
"The Beginning of Community-of-Goods in 1528," written ca. 1570

The beginning of community-of-goods outside Nikolsburg was a watershed moment in pre-Hutterite history. It put into practice an ideal—community-of-goods —that was widely shared among early Anabaptists. Forced to leave the Anabaptist city of Nikolsburg due to rising tensions with the Hubmaier's group, the refugees (*Stäbler*) responded to their desperate economic situation by pooling their possessions and instituting what would become a defining feature of the later Hutterite movement.

At that time several servants and their congregations settled in Moravia: in Znaim, Eibenschitz, Brünn, and elsewhere. A certain Gabriel Ascherham came to Rossitz. Born in Nuremberg, he had been a furrier in Schärding, Bavaria, then moved to Rossitz where he gathered the people and taught them.

At that time, several servants [i.e., leaders] and their congregations came to Moravia to settle at places such as Znaim, Eibenschitz, Brünn[1] and elsewhere. One of them, by the name of Gabriel Ascherham, born in Nuremberg and a furrier at Schirnding, Bavaria, came to Ross-itz[2] where he gathered the people and taught them.

Shortly thereafter, Philip Blauer-mel from Swabia joined him with several people. Gabriel took them into his household and resigned his ministry and position, giving Philip and his assistants the honour and precedence. Soon, how-ever—when Philip did not act to his liking—Gabriel resumed caring for his people, remaining with them in the same household; Philip and his people, however, moved to another house. Despite this, they considered themselves to be brothers to one another, but with different convictions [*aus uneinigen Herzen*]. And thus,

---

1   Modern Czech equivalents are Znojmo, Eibenschitz, and Brno, respectively.
2   Rosice.

two groups emerged: the Philipites and the Gabrielites [...].

With the population of group at Nikolsburg[3] on the increase for the above-mentioned reason, with a good number of them following Jakob Wiedeman and Philip Jäger, Hans Spittelmair along with his assistants and kinsmen publicly began to instruct his followers in Nikolsburg to have nothing to do with them, but leave them completely alone because they were forming a faction. He called all those who followed Jakob Wiedeman a fringe group [*Kleinhäufler*] and "staff-bearers" [*Stäbler*]. Those at Nikolsburg, however, retained the sword, which is why they were called "sword bearers" [*Schwertler*]; now they are called Sabbatarians and have the spirit of Münster.

As a result of this, Lord Leonhard von Liechtenstein once again summoned Jakob Wiedemann and Philip Jäger, along with other of their brothers and stewards. Because they wanted to establish a separate community, he ordered them to clear out, stop [their activities], and vacate his property. Consequently, they put their goods up for sale—some sold, others were left behind—and

the entire group move away. Whatever they had left behind, however, Lichtenstein's people sent after them. Thus, a group of approximately two hundred (without counting the children) from Nikolsburg, Pergen,[4] and the surrounding area gathered outside the town.

Some from the town joined them and, out of great compassion, wept with them; others quarrelled with them. At this point, they set out toward Tannowitz[5] and Muschau,[6] settling in an abandoned village. They remained there for one day and one night to hold counsel with each other in the Lord regarding their crisis. They appointed servants to attend to their temporal needs, namely Franz Intzinger from Leoben, Styria, and Jakob Männdel, who had been the Lord of Lichtenstain's steward. Thoman Arbeiter and Urban Bader were also appointed to assist them.

At that time, these men spread out a mantle before the people, and everyone laid down their possessions, with a willing spirit and without coercion, for the sustenance of those in need, according to the teachings of the prophets and apostles. Isaiah 23[:18], Acts 2[:44–45], 4[:34–5], and 5[:1–11].

[**Source:** Translated by Kenny Wollmann from Rudolf Wolkan, *Geschichtbuch der Hutterischen Brüder* (Wien, 1923), 62–63.]

---

3   Mikulov.
4   Perná.
5   Dunajovice.
6   Mušov.

Unknown
Community Order, 1527/9[1]

Like the various medieval monastic orders, Hutterites emphasized a community life in close proximity which required a rule or order (*Ordnung*), both as a form of discipline befitting the house of God and for practical, organizational purposes. Both traditions emphasized radical discipleship through obedience and accountability, withdrawal from the world in pursuit of holiness and prayer, and pacifism. Michael Sattler, who is the likely author of the *Schleitheim Confession*, was a Benedictine monk prior to this conversion to Anabaptism and his monastic background is clearly evident in this foundational document. Further, there are parallels between Hutterite ordinances and the regulations that governed late medieval guilds.

Ordinances are sometimes divided into temporal ordinances regulating the various trades in the workplace, and spiritual ordinances addressing faith convictions such as non-resistance.[2] This artificial division obscures the fact that for Hutterites all aspects of life—including work, play, conflict, homemaking, worship, economics—were relevant to faith and had spiritual significance.

The following two quotations by Hans Kräl and Johannes Waldner suggest a certain ambivalence about the tradition of writing *Ordnungen*:

> **HANS KRÄL (d. 1569):** There has to be order in all areas for the matters of life can be properly maintained and furthered only where order reigns—even more so in the house of God whose master builder […] is the Lord himself. Where there is no order there is disorder. There God does not dwell, and the house soon collapses.

---

1   The dating of this order is undergoing scholarly debate. This translation is based on the Hutterite *Chronicle* and maintains the date given there while acknowledging that it is likely from an earlier time. See discussion in Werner O. Packull, *Hutterite Beginnings: Communitarian Experiments during the Reformation* (Baltimore/London: Johns Hopkins University Press, 1995), 33–37.

2   Wes Harrison, *Andreas Ehrenpreis and Hutterite Faith and Practice* (Kitchener: Pandora Press, 1997), 37.

JOHANNES WALDNER (1749–1824): Regulations for daily work were not present in the beginning nor were they necessary since each member in a right, simple, and child-like spirit, served God and the devout with all faithfulness and each gave freely of his entire ability.[3]

On one hand, they are necessary to make a community run smoothly and to guide its day-to-day decision-making (Kräl); on the other hand, if they are applied in a legalistic, inflexible manner they can easily become a burden, stifle the Spirit, and undermine the freedom for individual and communal discernment (Waldner). Even today, this is a tension that Hutterite communities need to learn to navigate wisely.

The *Ordnungen* are significant historical sources because they provide a window into the community's approach to decision-making and the formation of its people, as well as its use of the Bible for ethical discernment. Because *Ordnungen* are usually written to address existing or recurring problems they give us a glimpse into the community's problems and priorities. Thus, the *Ordnungen* help to correct the often-idealistic portrayals of communal life found in the Hutterite *Chronicle*.

This *Reader* includes fresh translations of several of the earliest *Ordnungen* that influenced the Hutterites: the *Community Order* of 1527/9 (111), as well as excerpts from the *Allgemeine Dienstordnung* of 1580 (267), which addresses leaders of various work departments. The *Baderordnung* of 1654 (287) reissued by Andreas Ehrenpreis, sheds light on an occupation that appears to have been particularly prone to pushing the envelope on what was permitted by the Hutterites. Finally, it includes a selection of 20th century *Ordnungen* which address a variety of issues, including technology use, substance abuse, home furnishing, and education (385).

In 1529, the church taught, practiced, and agreed to uphold an order about how a Christian who confesses the Apostolic faith ought to live:

FIRST: When the community gathers, we should wholeheartedly pray to God for grace so that he reveals to us and makes known his divine will. When parting ways, we should thank God and pray for all the brothers and sisters in the entire Christian community.

SECOND: We should encourage one another in a heartfelt and Christian way to remain steadfast in the Lord, gathering often—at least four or five times during the week, if possible, whether with half or the entire [*halb oder gar*] [congregation].[4]

THIRD: If a brother or sister lives outside the order, this should be

---

3   *The Chronicle of the Hutterian Brethren*, Vol 2, translated by the Hutterian Brethren. (Ste. Agathe: Crystal Spring Colony, 1998), 761.
4   The meaning of the original text is unclear.

addressed publicly before the community with gentle admonition. If it is a private [offence], it should be disciplined in private, but according to the command of God.

FOURTH: Let every brother and sister commit themselves fully and wholly to the community, yielded to God with body and their whole life [Leben]. All gifts received from God should be held in common according to the practices of the first apostolic church and community of Christ so that the needy in the community are supported like the Christians in the time of the apostles (Acts 2[:44–45], 4[:32–37], 5[:1–11]).

FIFTH: The chosen servants from the community should diligently care for the needs of the poor and do this according to the command of the Lord, giving alms [Notdurft reichen], assisting them on behalf of the community.

SIXTH: Everybody should behave decently among us and also before all people. No one should conduct themselves with frivolous words and deeds neither in the community of God nor among those outside [the community].

SEVENTH: At community gatherings only one should speak and the rest listen and judge what is spoken, and not two or three standing at once. No one should curse or swear and pursue idle chatter so that the weak are spared.

EIGHTH: When we gather, we should not burden ourselves with excessive eating and drinking [Fressen und Saufen]. Rather, we should use creation, which God created as good and pure for our sustenance, with thankfulness and moderation, serving one or two courses. When people are finished eating, everything should be cleared from the table.

NINTH: Whatever is discussed or discerned among the brothers and sisters in the community should not be disclosed to those outside the church [Welt]. To the good-hearted [Gutherzigen, i.e., a sympathetic seeker] the Gospel should first be presented and proclaimed. If that person accepts it, bearing desire and love in their heart for it and seeking to live according to the Gospel, he should be accepted as a member of Christ by Christ's church.

TENTH: We should anticipate the Work of the Lord[5] and the cross [i.e. persecution] every day, because we have chosen to submit ourselves to his discipline, [and are] willing to accept everything he sends our way with thanksgiving, bearing it with patience and not letting ourselves be easily disturbed by every rumour and wind that blows.

ELEVENTH: All those united into one body and [loaf of] bread in the Lord and are of one mind, should observe the Lord's Supper as a memorial of his death; everyone should

---

5   It is unclear whether this is referring to Christ's second coming, or simply God working among them.

be admonished to conform to the Lord in obedience to the Father.

TWELFTH: As we are taught and admonished in the Lord, we should always watch and wait on the Lord so that, when he comes, we are worthy to enter in [-to the Kingdom] with him and flee the evil that will come upon the world.

[**SOURCE:** Translated by Kenny Wollmann from Rudolf Wolkan, *Geschichtbuch der Hutterischen Brüder* (Wien, 1923), 60–61.]

KASPER BRAITMICHEL (d. 1573)
"Table of Martyrs," 1570

From the founding of the first community in 1528 on, martyrdom was a reality that defined Hutterite existence in important ways. Rejected by Catholics and Protestants alike, Hutterites and other Anabaptists were martyred in larger numbers because they were politically vulnerable and often refused to recognize governing authorities as Christians. Hutterites settled in Moravia because of the relative religious and political toleration they found there. From there, they sent *Sendboten* throughout the German-speaking territories to invite others to join the "Church of God."

A theology of martyrdom developed around the historical experience of suffering and martyrdom: Christians should expect to suffer, because their Lord and Master had suffered rejection and a violent execution on a cross. Through martyrdom, believers could identify with the suffering of Jesus, and realize the ideal of costly discipleship. Their three-fold understanding of baptism—baptism by Spirit, water, and blood—signalled the real possibility that Hutterite believers would need to lay down their lives for their commitment and obedience to Jesus. Similarly, their practice of the Lord's Supper emphasized unity and the willingness to suffer rather than to betray fellow believers.[1] As many as four out of every five Hutterite missionaries were executed by various jurisdictions throughout the Holy Roman Empire. Estimates vary, but as many as 4000 Anabaptists were martyred, and about a third of all martyrs were women.[2]

Much of the literature of this era commemorates those who suffered and were killed for their faith. Martyrs were memorialized in many of the ballads, such as "O Father God from Heaven's Realm" (see Falkenstein Song, 187), found in early codices and eventually published in *Die Lieder der Hutterischen Brüder*. Confessions frequently make a case for religious freedom and highlight

---

1   C. Arnold Snyder, *From Anabaptist Seed* (Kitchener: Pandora Press, 1999), 32.
2   Snyder, *From Anabaptist Seed*, 36. See also C. Arnold Snyder and Linda A. Huebert Hecht, eds., *Profiles of Anabaptist Women: Sixteenth Century Reforming Pioneers* (Waterloo: Wilfrid Laurier University Press, 1996), 33.

the necessity and joy of suffering for the sake of the truth. Countless epistles were written by community elders to encourage prisoners to remain faithful; prisoners also wrote back to the community to assure them that they remained steadfast and occasionally, to report on interrogations. The Hutterite *Chronicle* includes many accounts of suffering and martyrdom, several of which are included in this *Reader* (see 125).

The table of martyrs from the *Great Chronicle* records the number of martyrs from various regions where Hutterites were active. To give the reader a sense of the artistry and format of the original, the first two pages of the manuscript are provided alongside a translation. The overall figures are likely not completely reliable, since many of the manuscripts listed Anabaptist martyrs alongside Hutterite martyrs.[3] The blank spaces following each region indicate the expectation that more martyrs would pay the ultimate price in the years to come. The biblical texts that run vertically down the middle of each page remind the reader why martyrdom was to be expected, validating the witness and sacrifice of those who had the courage to be counted among the cloud of witnesses.

The Lord gave his blessing, the church grew, and the number of believers increased daily.

God's messengers and witnesses gave steadfast testimony in word and deed, speaking powerfully of God's kingdom. They urged people to change their lives, to repent and turn away from this world's sin, blasphemy, and injustice and to dedicate themselves to the living God, their Creator, and Jesus Christ, their redeemer. God blessed them and gave them joy in doing his work.

This, however, was always at the price of great suffering and the shedding of much blood in many lands, towns, and marketplaces for the sake of Jesus Christ and his divine truth. God has especially visited Germany with the truth, but Germany has resisted it, just as blind and stubborn Jerusalem resisted the apostles and prophets sent to her. From the beginning of the church community to this day many hundreds of brothers and sisters in Christ have been condemned and put to death for their faith. Even those who had only just begun to recognize the truth and live by it, leaving behind the horrors of the antichrist, were made to suffer for it. As recorded, this was especially so in Austria wherever the royal provost went. If he encountered anyone in field or road who admitted that he was a brother and refused to recant, he ordered him to kneel down and beheaded him on the spot. In the villages he hanged believers on the gateposts, and some he consigned to prisons. It was the same with Aichelin, the imperial provost, who traveled all over Swabia and Würt-

3   Brad S. Gregory, author of *Salvation at Stake: Christian Martyrdom in Early Modern Christianity*, email correspondence, February 10, 2021.

temberg. Wherever brothers and sisters were found or searched out, he put them to death by fire, sword, or rope.

This bloodshed has not ceased yet but continues to this day. On the following pages an attempt is made to tabulate all that can be recalled for certain, though not all are known. We are not concerned with the exact total, which certainly was higher. Our concern is to show how, through the blood of martyrs, faith and divine truth were revealed by God in every comer of the German lands.

[The table of martyrs follows.]

[**Source:** The images of the Martyr Table in manuscript form is from the so-called *Great Chronicle* found in Bon Homme, South Dakota. The English translation is adapted from *The Chronicle of the Hutterian Brethren*, Volume 1. Translated and edited by the Hutterian Brethren. (Ulster Park: Plough Publishing House, 1987), 217–220. Used by permission.]

In Bohemia

At Prague --------------- 11

In Hungary

At Kirchschlag ------------ 3

Loren --------------------- 3

Nusel --------------------- 2

In Moravia

At Brünn ------------------ 4

Behold, I send you out like sheep among wolves · Match the 10th [16] ·

Znaim [Znojmo] --------- 7

Olmütz [Olomouc] ------ 4

In [Lower] Austria

At Vienna --------------- 23

and many secret executions

Neustadt ------------------ 2

Kreuzenstein ------------- 6

Melk --------------------- 3

Grein --------------------- 1

Lembach --------------- 45

Mödling ------------------ 4

Pöggstall ----------------- 1

Ybbs --------------------- 1

Krems -------------------- 3

Böheimkirchen ---------- 2

Ottenthal ---------------- 4

TABLE OF MARTYRS how God through the blood of the faithful testified to his truth and made it known in every corner of the German lands.

Geschicht Buech.   165

Puttenhofen ——— 4   Linz ——————— 72
Volsperg ——— 1
Falckenstain ——— 5

Sie werden auch überantworttet in trübsal, vnnd werden auch tödten. zc. Matth. 24. Marc. am 13.

Im landt ob der Ennß.

Zu Mathausen —— 1
Gmünden ——— 2
Ennß —————— 1
Kropffzall —— 2
Steyer ———— 30
Welß ———— 10
Sessolzprink —— 4
Braunsteten · 3
Freynstat —— 10
Falckndorff —— 1
Sorkolzprink —— 8
Weissenburg —— 2

In Bairn.

Zu München —— 9
Rosenhaim —— 1
Aibling ———— 3
Wasseröing —— 1
Müldorff —— 5
Ötting ———— 7
Landtshiet —— 5
Lampach —— 22
Burkhausen — 7
Riedt ———— 4
Scharding — 3
Passaw ———— 2
Filzhofen —— 1
Monmeß —— 1

E. r. v

Pottenhofen -------------- 4
Feldsberg ---------------- 1
Falkenstein -------------- 5

Linz -------------------- 72

They will deliver you up to tribulation and kill you · Mt 24 · Mk the 13 ·

In Upper Austria
At Mauthausen------------ 1
  Gmunden ---------------- 2
  Enns -------------------- 1
  Kropfing ---------------- 2
  Steyr ------------------- 30
  Wels-------------------- 10
  Fesselsbruck------------- 4
  Gramastetten------------ 3
  Freistadt --------------- 10
  Falkendorf-------------- 1
  Vöcklabruck------------- 8
  Weissenburg ----------- 2

In Bavaria
At Munich---------------- 9
  Rosenheim -------------- 1
  [Bad] Aibling------------ 3
  Wasserburg------------- 1
  Mühldorf --------------- 5
  Altötting---------------- 7
  Landshut --------------- 5
  Lambach---------------- 22
  Burghausen ------------- 7
  Ried [Upper Austria] ---- 4
  Schärding--------------- 3
  Passau ------------------ 2
  Vilshofen --------------- 1
  Mermos ---------------- 1

Ingolstadt-----------------2

Nüneburg ---------------9

Neuburg ----------------3

Freyburg-----------------2

Julback near Braunau ---- 1

In Styria

at Graz ------------------7

Bruck an der

Mur -------------------- 12

Unzmarkt ---------------1

Griesbach----------------5

In Carinthia

at St. Veit -----------------7

Kematen -----------------3

Göpingen-----------------5

Wolfsberg in the

Lavant Valley------------3

In the Puster Valley

At Sillian -----------------3

Taufers-------------------1

St. Lorenzen ------------11

Kiens---------------------5

Schöneck ----------------4

Michelsburg -----------24

In the Adige Region

At Brixen --------------- 16

Klausen -----------------7

Kaltern ------------------4

Kuntersweg--------------9

Bozen ------------------11

Neumarkt ---------------9

Terlan--------------------3

Sterzing ---------------- 30

Gufidaun --------------- 19

Rodeneck----------------4

Schlander----------------2

Trient -------------------1

In the Salzburg Region

at Salzburg ------------- 38

Tittmoning ---------------4

Berchtesgaden---------- 18

Marklibat ----------------2

Kuchl in the Kuchl

Valley -------------------3

Abtenau ------------------1

In the Inn Valley

At Kufstein -------------- 16

Rattenberg---------------71

Schwaz----------------- 20

Hall [Solbad Hall] -------2

Innsbruck ----------------8

Landeck ------------------1

Steinach ------------------4

Kitzbühel -------------- 68

Stams --------------------3

Petersberg ---------------2

Imst----------------------8

Rotholz -------------------1

In Frankenland

at Ansbach ---------------1

Bamberg------------------3

Kitzingen -------------- 20

[Bad] Frankenhausen----1

Fehelsbruck --------------3

Würzburg --------------- 10

In Swabia

at Augsburg --------------2

Landsberg ------------- 19

Lauingen -----------------2

Dillingen -----------------2

Höchstädt ----------------2

Weissenhorn -------------1

Zusmarshausen ---------8

The time is coming when whoever kills you will think he is doing God a service · John 16[:2]

Nördlingen -------------- 1
Schwäbish Gmünd ------- 7
Günzburg --------------- 6
Mantelhof ------------- 20
Kaufbeuren-------------- 5
Sonthofen --------------- 1
Warthausen ------------- 1
Reutte------------------- 1

In Württemberg

At Urach---------------- 1
Esslingen --------------- 2
Schorndorf -------------- 1
Tübingen --------------- 5
Weil--------------------- 2
Stuttgart --------------- 2
Rottenburg on
    the Neckar----------- 13
Rotherburg on
    the Tauber ---------- 24
Herrenberg------------ 12
Schlüsselfeld ----------- 1
Stätz------------------- 18
Deutschnofen [Tyrol]---- 1
Ulmerfeld -------------- 2
Waldshut --------------- 5
Wilhelmsbruck---------- 1
Weiden ----------------- 3
Königsberg ------------- 3
Kürchen on the Eck------ 1
Illingen ---------------- 10

In Margravate of Baden

at Badeb-Baden--------- 20
Pforzheim -------------- 2
Prethaim---------------- 9
Bühl--------------------- 2
Bruchsal ---------------- 1
[Karlsruher] Durlach -- 12
Gernsbach --------------- 1

Therefore I send you prophets, sages, and scribes, some of whom you will kill[.] · Mt 23[:34] ·

Count Palatine

alone was responsible for
executing-------------- 350

On the Rhine

At Speyer --------------- 1
 Pühelsberg ------------- 1
 Kislach----------------- 1

In the Netherlands

At Aurea---------------- 1
 Andorf----------------- 5
 Lagrentzen ------------- 1
 Brussels---------------- 2
 Aachen ----------------- 5

In Velschland

Fuld -------------------- 18

In Alsace

at Ensisheim ----------- 600
 Mühlhausen ------------17

In Switzerland

at Zurich --------------- 16
 Basel ------------------- 3
 Bern -------------------- 1
 Schwyz ----------------- 3
 Appenzell--------------- 1
 Constance on
    Lake Constance ------- 3
 Waldsee [Swabia] -------11
 Ettach------------------ 1
 Baden------------------- 3

In Italy

at Venice --------------- 3
 Lavarone---------------- 3
 Lechensteg ------------- 4

"Accounts of Imprisonment and Martyrdom," ca. late 1570s

While the climate in Moravia was relatively peaceful compared to other parts of the Holy Roman Empire, Hutterite missionaries faced grave danger when entering Catholic, Lutheran, or Reformed territories. Following is a sampling of *Chronicle* accounts of suffering and martyrdom endured by Anabaptist-Hutterite men and women in various contexts from 1529–1567.

Anabaptist Women Martyrs, 1529

CHRISTINE TÖLLINGER from Penon, a widow, testified that brother Georg Blaurock had baptized her in her home with the true Christian baptism. About the mass, she did not believe at all that the priest could bring our Lord into the host; it is nothing but bread, and what the priests do only leads people astray. As for infants being saved without baptism, the Lord said, "Let the children come to me, for of such is the kingdom of heaven."[1] The priests go to the trouble of needlessly baptizing innocent babies, but as the children grow up in this world of sin and vice, the priests make no efforts to turn them away from sin. She believed that Our Lady [Mary] was the mother of Christ and a virgin. She did not believe in confession heard by a priest, but when a person acknowledges and confesses his sin, rejects it, and sins no longer—that, she thought, is true confession. About feast days and Sundays she said that in six days God the Lord created the world, on the seventh he rested; the other feast days were instituted by popes, cardinals, and archbishops. Since she was living in the world, she observed the feast days like other people, to avoid giving offense, but no one would be damned for working. Besides, the priests practice idolatry in the morning and commit fornication in the afternoon. By God's grace and with his help she would die for her convictions.

Barbara from Tiers, the wife of Hans Portz, testified that she had

---

1   Mt 19:14.

125

been baptized according to true Christian command by a servant of the Word of God named Benedict. Her baptism had taken place around Michaelmas [September 29] on a hill near Tramin on the Moos. She did not believe in the priests' idolatrous sacrament of the mass. The priests practice idolatry in the morning and commit fornication in the afternoon. She set no value on the way confession was made to a priest. About Our Lady she had nothing to say. About Sundays and feast days: God the Lord intended the seventh day for rest, and she left it at that. With the help and grace of God, she would remain faithful unto death, for this was the true faith and the only way in Christ.

Agatha Kampner from Breitenberg testified that she was baptized the year before on the Sunday before Christmas at "the hollow" near St. Gall in Switzerland by brother Tobich, a servant of the Word of God. She was against infant baptism, for if children die without baptism, they die in innocence and belong to the Lord. She was against the mass, for Christ did not tell his disciples, "Go out and hold mass," but "Go out and preach the Gospel."[2] About the mass she said that since the confession of faith states that he sits at the right hand of his heavenly Father and will come from there to judge the living and the dead, she in no way believed that he allows the priests to bring him down into the host, handling and transforming him. About Our

Lady, she believed that Mary bore Christ the Lord who redeemed us all and that through her the Word of God became man, who suffered for us on the cross. Concerning feast days she said that no day was more holy than another. The Sabbath was appointed for people to gather for preaching and discussing the Gospel, but now it is used for gluttony and immorality. With the help and grace of God, she would remain steadfast in her faith.

Elizabeth [Kampner], Agatha's sister, testified that she was baptized that summer at Breitenberg by brother Georg Blaurock in the name of the Father, the Son, and the Holy Spirit, according to Christ's command. She did not believe in the priests' sacrament and mass, since there is no evidence that God appointed them. About Our Lady, she believed that Mary was a virgin and bore Christ our Saviour. Mary and the saints had to suffer just as much as she and many others were suffering now, but she did not believe that Mary was a mediator, because all power in heaven and on earth is given to Christ alone. As for feast days, she did not value one above another; we should watch at all times for the great day of the Lord and abstain from sin. She was determined to remain steadfast. After the hearing, these true lovers of God were executed.

In the same year, 1529, two sisters, **Anna Mahler** and **Ursula Ochsentreiber** were sentenced to death

---

2   Mk 16:15, Lk 14:23, Mt 28:19–20.

for the sake of divine truth and drowned at Hall in the Inn Valley. They armed their womanly hearts with such manly courage in God that everyone was astonished at their steadfastness. Thus they witnessed to the truth in life and in death. This testimony is contained in the songs that were written about them and still exist.

Hieronymous Käls, 1536

In the first days of 1536 the church sent brothers to Tyrol: Hieronymus Käls of Kufstein, schoolmaster of the church community of God, and with him Michael Seifensieder from Wallern in Bohemia and Hans Oberecker from the Adige Valley. They reached Vienna in Austria, but already on January 8 they were taken prisoner while sheltering at an inn, a stopping place for the Neustadt wagons. During the evening meal the people there made efforts to get them to drink toasts, as is the devilish custom. The brothers told them plainly that they would not take part in that or in any other horrible practice. When the others noticed this and recognized who the brothers were, they began to slander and tell lies about the community, which the brothers refuted. After the meal one of the men at the table called for paper and ink and wrote a letter in Latin that said, among other things, "There are three persons here who I think are Anabaptists." He did not know that Hieronymus Käls understood Latin.

Hieronymus told the other brothers. They talked it over and agreed to wait and see what would happen. After two hours the judge's servants arrived, bound them, and took them to the judge. When he found out that they were from Jakob Hutter's church, he said they were undoubtedly the right men. They said, "Praise to God, we are indeed the right men!" He had them taken to his house and put in a common prison.

A week later the judge summoned them to appear before his court and urged each of them individually to recant. They replied that with God's grace they would hold to the truth to the end of their lives. In turn they urged their hearers to change from their unbelief and no longer misuse the precious name of Christ. This made the judge furious with Hieronymus. Every time he told them they were not Christians, the judge called him a wicked scoundrel. When he questioned Hieronymus for the tenth time and received the same testimony, the members of the court said, "This evil man is not worthy of your honour's anger."

After another week in prison, all three brothers were summoned by the judge. He had called three especially evil priests, who tried to talk with them, pouring contempt on our calling and slandering our faith. They claimed they were sent to show them their error. Hieronymus answered cheerfully, "We are on the right path, and our mission is from God, as Christ has taught us. We must not listen to an alien voice." He added, "We are ready to give all men an account of our faith and the foundation of our hope, but we have no desire to speak with monks and priests or anyone sent by the pope (who is the antichrist), for there are no greater scoundrels, fornicators, adulterers, deceivers, and corrupters than they."

At that the judge said, "No, no, my Hieronymus. You do not know these good lords."

Hieronymus said, "God is Lord, not they."

Next he was questioned under torture for two and a quarter hours on original sin, on infant baptism, on mission, and on the idolatrous mass. His interrogators implored him to think of his wife and children, to consider his own life, and to take their appeals to heart and pray to God. They would pray too. But he told them the truth and said he would stand by it, regardless of their attitude. After they had also failed to overcome the other two with their poison, the judge ordered them all back to prison. Here they composed songs (which we still have) and often sang them to each other, even at night. They were joyful in the Lord, and when they found

they were able to hear one another, they shouted from their prison cells, greeting, comforting, and strengthening one another. The church still has in its possession letters they wrote to one another, full of love and burning zeal. They also wrote down their confession of faith and defense, fully supported by passages from Holy Scripture, and gave them to the judge and lords at Vienna.

Three times, Hans Oberecker (mentioned above) had a vision of the day of the Lord that is to come over the whole world. We still have the letter he wrote from the prison where he saw with the inner eyes of his heart—as clearly as if he were seeing with the eyes of his head—certain things which words could not express. He saw how it is with the children of God, who have received God's abundant grace, and in contrast, with what overwhelming power and terror this day breaks in upon the ungodly. This made him pray, "O my God, let us never fall under your wrath, which is so great and terrifying for all the children of wickedness."

After all kinds of torture had been used against these brothers, during which they remained steadfast as valiant knights and lovers of God, they were condemned to death by these sons of Pilate and burned to ashes in Vienna on the Friday before Passion Sunday [2 weeks before Easter], Lent 1536. It was this same Hieronymus Käls who wrote [...] prayers for the schoolchildren.

Hans Blüetel, 1545

In 1545 a brother named Hans Blüetel was also captured at Ried, Bavaria, where he had been sent by the church community. The magistrates of Riel had promised a reward to anyone who caught him, and so a man called Gugelwein betrayed him. He spoke to Hans in a friendly way, as if he had been eager to meet him, and invited him into his house. The brother, thinking Gugelwein was concerned for his own soul's salvation, went with him. Once inside, the traitor locked the house and said, "Hans, you are a prisoner."

Hans replied, "God forbid, for I came to you in good will!" Then this traitor demanded money for his release. When Hans refused, Gugelwein went to the magistrates and betrayed him. While the traitor was on his way, his wife, too, demanded money, saying the magistrates would take it from him anyway. If he gave her fifteen gulden, she would set him free. But brother Hans Blüetel refused to give a penny and said that with God's help he was ready for any tribulation.

Meanwhile the magistrates arrived with a crowd of armed men, arrested the brother together with the traitor and his wife, bound them securely with ropes, and set guards over them. When they arrived at the marketplace in Ried, they were racked terribly, the traitor as well as the brother; the magistrates thought Gugelwein had stolen Hans's money because so little was found on him.

To make his wife talk, they squeezed her hands in a vise until they bled, although she and her husband had nothing. So their treachery brought them nothing but disaster. In the end this traitor hanged himself in his despair.

Around St. John's Day [Dec. 27], when brother Hans had been in prison four or five weeks, he received the death sentence: to be burned alive. He was led to the place of execution, and the priests came to him, urging him to abandon his faith. But he told them, "You would do well to turn from your monstrous deception. I will neither agree with it nor listen to your false teaching. Today I have more important things to do than to listen to your false prophecies. I must follow the Lord my God, in Christ, and fulfill my promise to him." And he spoke to them in such a way that the priests drew back and left him in peace.

On the way to his execution, he met a man named Michael Dirk, or *Kramer* [a peddler], whom he knew very well. Hans Blüetel looked at him with a smile on his lips that was a witness of heaven to this Michael. He was amazed that Hans could smile on his way to death by fire. This struck Michael's heart deeply and his wife's too. She went three days without food and mourned and wept over brother Hans's innocent death. Later, both of them joined the church community and became believers, as did others too.

When this dear brother came to the place of execution, he thought of the church community of God and called out in a loud voice that could be heard by the whole crowd, "Oh, if there were someone here who could be trusted to send word to the church in Moravia that I, Hans Blüetel, have been burned to death at Ried in Bavaria for the sake of the Gospel." A man came forward who had encouraged many to embrace the faith, though he himself was unable to do it. He promised to inform the church in Moravia that Hans Blüetel had been burned to death at Ried for the sake of divine truth. This encouraged brother Hans to continue speaking to the people: "This faith of mine is the divine truth, and I want to make this clear to you. I tell you, unless you repent, change your lives, and leave your corrupt ways, God will visit your sins upon you and punish you with the everlasting torment that is prepared for all sinners. He will avenge the innocent blood you have shed and require it at your hands to the last drop."

When the fire was ready, they bound him to a ladder. All this time he went on telling them that this was the truth, the way of eternal life, and the true church of God; heaven and earth should bear witness. "This very day," he said, "God will give a sign in heaven that this is the way to eternal life. "And so it happened. The sun in heaven grew pale and dim, as if it could no longer shed its light. Although the sky was clear and cloudless, the sun cast a shadow on the earth and was nothing but a pale yellow shape. Thus God affirmed this witness.

This lover of God, Hans Blüetel was alive and singing in the fire for quite a long time. He praised Christ and prayed that all who were worthy might be enlightened by God. And so, like pure gold, he endured the fiery test and proved steadfast in faith.

He had foretold as a further sign that the smoke would rise straight upward and his spirit would rise up to heaven with it. It happened just as he said. The smoke from the execution went straight up to the sky. Several people told us that a snow-white dove circled in the fire and soared up into the sky. Praise be to God who stands so faithfully and powerfully with his own and himself bears witness to his divine truth by the miracles he performs for his saints.

Hans Pürchner, 1555

In 1555 brother Hans Pürchner from Saalen was captured at Kortsch in the Adige region and taken to Schlanders by the constables. There he was brought before the governor, a cruel tyrant who was ready to stab Hans to death out of sheer fury. He had him interrogated under torture and put on the rack to make him tell who had given him lodging, and because he refused, they racked him again the same day. But to their great vexation their torture was useless. There was a clerk in attendance named Grimm, who pulled on the rope himself to rack and stretch this brother, though such work belongs only to executioners. They racked Hans again and again. They left him hanging on the rope several hours until he was so torn that he could neither stand on his feet nor walk one step nor bring his hands to his mouth to feed himself. Nevertheless he refused to give in and remained steadfast in the Lord.

Then they put him in stocks, hands and feet, in a dark, stifling dungeon and kept him there over six months.

Many educated people, priests, monks, nobles, and others, attacked his faith for two days and a night, trying to lead him astray. But he put them to shame by pointing out their errors. He was joyful and courageous and would not be intimidated.

Then they condemned him to death and led him to the place of execution. There he called the crowds to repentance. He could not kneel, because they had racked and tortured him so cruelly, so they supported him with a block of wood against his back and then beheaded him. A song written about him gives witness to his suffering.

The constable who arrested him had told Pürchner that he would not let him go at any price. Later, however, he was overcome by remorse and would have been glad to pay any amount to undo what had been done.

One of the priests who had tormented Hans Pürchner in his eagerness to make him recant later became a brother and even a servant of the Word. His name was Leonhard Dax. It was not unlike the prophecy: "Those who destroyed you will hasten to build you again; those who laid you waste will dwell in you." Leonhard Dax remained sincere and steadfast in his new life until the end, as will be recorded in its place.

Leonhard Dax, 1567

On Sunday before St. Martin's Day [Nov.11], brother Leonhard Dax and six others were arrested because of their witness to Christ. Leonhard Dax (as was told earlier) was a former priest who had loathed and persecuted us because of our way of life. After thinking things over, he was converted and abandoned the priesthood. He joined the church community and proved himself as a brother. Later, he was chosen and confirmed as a servant of God's Word and sent out on mission to the lands along the Rhine, where he was captured. The prisoners were taken to the town of Alzey in the Palatinate.

When they had been there two weeks, the superintendent of Alzey (a Zwinglian preacher) and several others came to question him. "Weren't you formerly a priest?" they asked Dax. He admitted that in his blindness and ignorance he had served the idolatrous church of the pope in Bavaria and in Tyrol. Leonhard Dax gave a powerful answer based on Scripture when asked about his mission, the basis of his faith, the reason for our separating from people like themselves, community-of-goods, and infant baptism. Then he was taken back to the dungeon and advised to think it over; they would take serious measures.

On January 12, 1568, he was again brought out for a hearing. The Zwinglian preacher spoke with him about the church, saying there had never been a church without blemish. Magistrates, he said, are Christians and as such may use the sword. He also spoke about separation of

believing and unbelieving marriage partners, but brother Leonhard confuted all he said, and the superintendent was unable to uphold any point. He urged Leonhard to accept his advice and follow the Zwinglian religion. Then the noble lord and sovereign of this country, the count palatine, would provide him with a splendid position and he could live wherever he liked in his country.

But Leonhard told him that he could not show him Christ's truth if he did not live it. Besides, he said, his beliefs were no error but were founded on the true grace of God, and with God's help he would be faithful. Nobody should expect anything else of him.

He was taken back to prison with the threat that he would soon see how serious his situation was. But Leonhard replied that God's will should be done. He was ready to defend his faith and the people of God, not only with words but with his life, if it was God's will. And with God's help no one was going to stop him.

He and his fellow prisoners were held in prison through the winter but then released on February 25, 1568. A written record of Dax's defense and some of his songs are still preserved.

[**Source:** *The Chronicle of the Hutterian Brethren*, Volume 1. Translated and edited by the Hutterian Brethren. (Ulster Park: Plough Publishing House, 1987), 71–73, 147–150, 241–243, 321–22, and 395–96. Used by permission.]

Wilhelm Reublin (ca. 1480–post-1559)
Letter to Pilgram Marpeck, 1531

Proto-Hutterite communities in Moravia faced a number of significant challenges. The *Stäbler* had been forced to leave Nikolsburg in 1528, when they began complete community-of-goods and established a community at Austerlitz. Hundreds of newcomers from diverse backgrounds and bearing significant traumas had to be integrated in a rapidly growing community. Communal norms and leadership roles had not yet been clearly defined. The distribution of food, the organization of schooling, and other practical aspects had to be sorted out.

In this tumultuous context, a crisis erupted at Austerlitz in 1531 which resulted in the community's first schism. The conflicts that emerged seem to centre on the leadership of Jakob Wiedemann, and involved disagreements about who was authorized to preach and whether leaders should be treated differently than the rest of the members.

Wilhelm Reublin, a pastor who was active in the Zürich area in the earliest days of the Anabaptist movement, was among those who was denied the opportunity to preach. When Wiedemann refused to publicly hear complaints raised by another brother, Reublin and Georg Zaunring challenged his decision. Wiedemann refused to back down, which resulted in about 150 members leaving and the founding of a second community at Auspitz.

The following two texts shed light on the factors contributing to the schism. After he was expelled from Auspitz for holding back possessions,[1] Wilhelm Reublin wrote a letter to the Tyrolean native and prominent South German leader, Pilgram Marpeck, in which he lists ten complaints against Jakob Wiedemann. The schism is also recorded from an insider perspective in *Das große Geschichtsbuch*. Reading these accounts side by side gives a fuller picture of the tensions and struggles involved in first-generation community building in Moravia.

---

1 *The Chronicle of the Hutterian Brethren*, vol. 1, translated and edited by the Hutterian Brethren (Ulster Park: Plough Publishing House), 91.

[...]

Dearly beloved brother in the Lord, I am constrained by hearty and divine love, with which I have ever loved you,[2] to inform you about our matters and our life, and what has transpired in the meantime between us and those of Austerlitz. [...]

As soon as my brother Kaspar departed from Austerlitz the elders themselves discussed many points from the Scripture for three days that week, in which points I always found them unsound and untrue in doctrine, and I overcame them always with the truth so that they had to give way and after many disputes they often gave me the kiss of peace, but in their hearts they were not true, as time later demonstrated. It so happened that I took the place of Kilian[3] in preaching during his absence. As I in the course of the sermons prayed the Lord's Prayer several times with the members of Christ, there arose discontent, strife and great rumours so that I was obliged to hold another disputation with the elders. [...]

After this it happened that following an evening meal I wished in God's freedom to proclaim the Word of God with which I have been commissioned, so that I might give to others and to myself joy, comfort and edification according to the gift of the Holy Spirit. So I began with a clear voice[4] to speak that which the Spirit showed me from the open book of the Holy Scripture of 1 Peter 1. The following evening the hearers entreated me to continue further, which I did. But when the elders saw the earnestness of the people, a larger group having assembled on the benches because of their thirst to hear the Word of God, on the third night they sent the people out of the room. They went into another room which was called the School. Thither I followed and taught them with a full voice; and the size of the group increased. At the first only eight or nine persons had been present.

At that time Old Jakob,[5] one of the elders, wished to leave the congregation and having called the people together made a very long address on the marvellous achievements of himself and his brethren at Austerlitz. Finally he called out the names of those brethren who only were permitted to preach, and no one else, neither was anyone to listen to the preaching of anyone else. This speech grieved and saddened me, for I knew well what the outcome would be. I comforted myself much with the Lord's grace and Spirit, and regarded the Lord's command more

---

2   Reublin here indicates a fairly long and intimate friendship with Marpeck.

3   A preacher at Austerlitz. *Chronicle*, vol. 1, 90.

4   The *Chronicle* reports that, "Reublin began reading rather loudly one evening in one of the rooms." *Chronicle*, vol. 1, 87.

5   According to the *Chronicle*, Jakob Widemann was the leader of the struggle with Reublin (*Chronicle*, vol. 1, 94–95), but Jakob Hutter expelled Reublin for not turning over all his money to the Brotherhood (*Chronicle*, vol. 1, 97–98).

highly than that of men. He would certainly speak to me, and I to him, in his own time. But for the sake of greater lenity and peace with the crafty I said to George Zaunriden[6] and to George Prentl, the appointed elders of the Congregation, taking along Thomas Lindner[7] of Schwatz: "May I now no longer preach, and comfort neither myself nor others with God's words, and is the Spirit bound as far as I am concerned?" They replied that I might preach— who could oppose it?—but that I should not extend the hand of reclamation with the grace and gifts of God. Thereupon I launched out with more sermons. When Kilian, Frantz and the other elders heard of this they hurriedly sent messengers to Old Jakob[8] with written messages. He came, summoned me before the elders, and enquired why I was preaching without their command and authorization. I asked them again whether I was teaching the truth. They replied that it was indeed the truth but they wanted to know why I was teaching. I answered: "Ask the people—they are the reason—or go with me before the people who are being taught and I will indicate to you how and why I teach. For I have taught openly, and openly I wish to show the reason, and in corners I will not any more settle this with you." Then they were angry and full of wrath against me,

and counselled day and night how they might expel me. [...]

On the Monday following the New Year the elders took counsel with some of their men, and on Tuesday they demanded of me, George, and Burckhardt, that since we had labelled their elders as false teachers and prophets we should now prove this before them. ... On Wednesday I stood with my brethren George, David and Burckhart before the congregation in the yard and stated that Jakob, Kilian and Franz together with their elders were false teachers and prophets, unfaithful to God and his children, that I would prove this by the truth of Scripture and from living men.

First, I said that they were not a Christian Congregation believing in one God and having one baptism, boasting as they did against me and all the world, which in turn was why they did not possess in truth the fruit of the Holy Church of God, but even hindered others in this attempt, delaying them and falsely accusing me—which they could not deny.

In the second place, the Christian Church which has its being, work and power in the Holy Ghost, they have troubled, and the springs of divine grace and mercy which should flow in the Spirit to the children of God they have rejected, diverted and ruined. They have

---

6   Zaunring in the *Chronicle*.
7   Thomas Lindi in the *Chronicle*.
8   The *Chronicle* also reports the dispatching of messengers to fetch Jakob Widemann the founder of Moravian communistic Anabaptism. *Chronicle*, vol. 1, 93.

robbed, extirpated, and removed from the teachers and the hearers the power of the grace of God.

In the third place, they treated the community of temporal and physical goods falsely and with great deceit, other than they at the first had stated and promised to me. They practiced respect of persons, granting to the rich their own little dwelling, Franz and his wife maintaining their manner of life just like the nobility. As to food the common brother must reckon peas and cabbage as good, but the elders and their wives dine on roast meat, fish, fowl and good wine, for I never saw any of their wives at a common table. Another person may not have shoes or smock but they have made good trousers, coats and furs in profusion.

Fourth, they taught that water baptism is a work of righteousness, whereas that should be faith; this, I have heard from their own mouth, from the elder Jakob, which I also reproved him for in the presence of his brethren at the time, for he said that his comfort and salvation rested on water.

Fifth, they say that those who have received holy [baptism], who have recognized the will of God and by the power of the Holy Spirit have transformed their lives, such persons may preach; they are the true ambassadors of God. But they did not wish to recognize me as such, contrary to their own word and work.

Sixth, they condemn the children to hell contrary to all truth and Scripture, which in response to our request they have asserted.

Seventh, they have set aside the Lord's Prayer without any foundation in truth, which I also contrary to their will have by God's grace re proved with the truth.

Eighth, they never wanted to pay Charles the blood-money and war tax, which my Kaspar also certainly heard, and the Lord of Austerlitz himself, with great animosity, paid money to the state for the brethren. But as soon as Kaspar arrived they became willing to pay this blood-money, apart from any necessity. [...]

Ninth, the young women are bound in marriage to the young men without the knowledge and consent of their heart, with much pressure and compulsion based on God's command. [...]

Tenth, the young children suffer from a lack of milk and are ruined by solid food; more than twenty are wasting away and have been ruined: a stone must [...] pity them. Many donate fifty florins to the congregation only to see their children suffer from hunger later. [...]

These articles I testified against them and revealed the truth before all the people, bringing it to the light by the grace of God. I said therefore: Since this is true and undeniable I will withdraw from you as impure, false, misleading prophets and liars, together with all those who fear God out of a pure heart and love him, according to the command of God our Lord. I spoke further to them: Since you received from two purses four hundred gold pieces in four weeks you should make clear what you have dispensed to my brethren and sisters from their money which they submitted to you. The treasurer replied that they did not have one cent; and they had expended twenty florins for grain. That was all the account which they could bring to light of all that large sum of money. [...]

Therefore trusting in God and his grace, and for the sake of the truth, we left Austerlitz on the eighth day of January, departing from the false brethren and shaking the dust off our shoes against them. [...] We numbered 250 apart from children as we departed on a single day. Jews and heathen were moved to pity and sympathy by this sight at Austerlitz. We had to leave behind approximately forty sick persons in a small cottage, because they could not follow us, but we provided them with servants and supplies according to their need. Let everyone think for himself how delightful such a

journey was in such poverty, with but little money and many children, in wintertime. [...]

Through a noble lady in the market at Auspitz God provided for us a place of freedom to settle on, without any compulsion in matters of faith, to work at hand trades, to plant crops, to build, to purchase houses and to possess them, [...] a village called Starlitz, a parish-estate, where we now have fifty brethren and sisters. [...]

Here therefore you now have briefly an account of what has happened to us in the past. And do not estrange yourself from me because God led me as a sick man from Strasburg to Moravia. I would prefer peace but arrived in the midst of unrest. May God be praised forever and eternally, Amen.

Dearly beloved Brother Pilgram, I entreat you to show my letter quickly to all the dear saints and brethren for the sake of Christ and his holy righteousness, so that no one may be deceived through the false brethren at Austerlitz and through their messengers and thus as we have indicated to you, be led astray. [...]

[**Source:** "A Letter from Wilhelm Reublin to Pilgram Marpeck, 1531," *Mennonite Quarterly Review* 23 (1949), 67–75. Translated and edited by J.C. Wenger from C.A. Cornelius, *Geschichte des Münsterischen Aufruhres. Zweites Buch* (Leipzig, 1860), 253–259.]

Kasper Braitmichel (d. 1573)
"Conflict at Austerlitz in 1531," ca. 1570

At this time [in 1529] a man named Wilhelm Reublin came to Austerlitz, claiming to be a teacher or servant, but as nothing was known about him, he was not permitted to teach.

Meanwhile the devil—who does not rest but prowls around the house of God like a roaring lion, seeking every opportunity to cause division, destroy the unity of spirit, and stamp out what God gives—made an attack at the critical place, namely, at the elders of the church, who were responsible for the whole life of the people, as the devout Judith testifies in her book.

At that time they had no place where everyone could meet to hear the teachings, because it was winter and extremely cold. Therefore they decided to hold their meetings in three places, and for each place a particular servant was appointed to teach, exhort, and comfort his little flock.

Their teachings differed, however. One taught this and another taught something different. One of them

declared among other things that Christ had been a citizen of Capernaum and that therefore as citizens it was permissible to do civilian duties and swear oaths. Besides this, Jakob Wiedemann told several young sisters that if they would not follow his suggestions about marriage, he would have to give heathen wives to the brothers. He and some of his assistants alarmed the sisters with strange questions and gave them texts to learn. Those who could remember the texts and answer the questions clearly were highly praised, but the simple, unassuming sisters, although faithful and devout, were ridiculed and put to shame.

As there were so many people and their number increased daily, they were not all able to live in one house. Some of the servants who had learned more than one language—Franz Intzinger, Jakob Mandel, among others—came to think highly of themselves and supplied food and drink to one another, which was not in order. As is generally known, arrogance goes before destruction and pride goes before a fall. In that spirit some self-seeking members who had kept money in their pockets went to market to buy what they liked for themselves. All these disorders, and more, were noticed by those who fought against avarice, and this caused a great deal of complaint among the people. Especially those from Tyrol complained about the teachings and said they were not as comforting and instructive as they had been at home. Similarly, many were troubled and complained about church discipline and the children's education, saying that in these and related matters not nearly enough was done.

They reported these things to their particular servant, Georg Zaunring, who also became very disturbed about it and began discussing it with some of his assistants and servants, who all agreed with him, especially Burkhard [Braun] of Ofen, Bohemian David of Schweidnitz, and Adam Schlegel.

Early in 1530 Wilhelm Reublin began reading rather loudly one evening in one of the rooms. When people gathered around him to listen, he also expounded the Scriptures to them, although he had not been given the authority to teach. God cannot bear disorder in his church, so he seeks ways to change it even through unredeemed men, as we can see in this and other cases.

Wilhelm Reublin began to speak openly in the church against all the offenses committed by the servants. As Jakob Wiedemann, who was entrusted with the care of the whole church, was not at home, his assistants sent messengers to him without delay. As soon as he came, he summoned all the elders, from wherever they lived, and placed the whole matter before them in the presence of Georg Zaunring and the other servants who supported him. This took place in private at first. Reublin, however, persisted in what he had said and by scriptural proof tried to convince Jakob Wiedemann and all his followers that they were neither teaching nor standing rightly. Jakob Wiedemann and his supporters did not accept this but called the church together. He told the people how, in his absence, Reublin had pushed himself forward, teaching things that were opposed to what Jakob and his assistants taught, which could not be tolerated. At the end of a long speech that Jakob made before the church, he said that whoever acknowledged his teaching to be right and had changed his life through it should come and stand next to him.

Wilhelm Reublin then asked them, for the sake of God, to give him a chance to answer. Likewise Georg Zaunring, Bohemian David, Burkhard of Ofen, and Adam Schlegel unanimously requested all the people to hear Reublin's reply, since they had heard Jakob Wiedemann's charges. The church could then decide which side was right and which was wrong, as would only be fair before God and man. But their request was rejected outright.

Now most of the people went over to Jakob Wiedemann's side, many of them without knowing why, since not all of them had heard Jakob's accusations. About forty or fifty persons remained standing with Zaunring and Reublin, eager to hear Reublin's reply in order to be fair. But the others would not give in.

Thereupon Jakob Wiedemann called several of his followers and sent them to Georg Zaunring to inquire why they had gone over to the other side. They replied that, having heard Jakob Wiedemann's accusation against Reublin, their request now as before was for God's sake to let Reublin's answer be heard as well. This would enable the church to decide what was right before God, for no one should judge a matter that had not been given a hearing. But, as before, this was unjustly refused them. In other words, they attacked the flock with their horns.

Jakob Wiedemann warned his people that they should have nothing to do with the others. As a result, many who had previously followed Wiedemann now felt impelled to go over to Zaunring and Reublin. When the time came for Jakob Wiedemann's people to be called to a meal, the others were treated as though they were excluded. They had handed in what little they had, and if there had been fairness, they

would have been glad to remain. But they had to leave empty-handed.

Zaunring and Reublin and their people gathered outside the house, sick at heart. Reublin shook the dust from his shoes as a testimony against the high-handed action of Jakob Wiedemann and all who stayed with him. Then they set out, first finding lodging for their children and sick people in the town and leaving a servant, Burkhard of Ofen, to care for them and comfort them.

Zaunring and his assistants, with about 150 other people, made ready to move to Auspitz. Once outside the city of Austerlitz, the servants named above spoke very earnestly to the people, saying that whoever wanted to go with them should be ready, with them, to face the poverty of Christ and possibly even death. All the money they, had between them amounted to only a farthing per person. Therefore anyone who did not feel the courage to suffer hunger, great need, misery, and poverty for the sake of truth should rather return to the city or to his home. But all of them wanted to dare it, trusting in God. Not one turned back.

It was in this way that God again brought about a purification, separating the true believers from the unbelievers. Those who remained with Jakob Wiedemann are therefore still known today as the Austerlitz Brethren.

[**Source:** *The Chronicle of the Hutterian Brethren,* Volume 1. Translated and edited by the Hutterian Brethren. (Ulster Park: Plough Publishing House, 1987), 86–89. Used by permission.]

ANNO 1536   JAKOB HUTTER

Kasper Braitmichel (d. 1573)
"The Great Schism of 1533," ca. 1570

The Great Schism of 1533 secured Jakob Hutter's position as *Vorsteher*, and marks the beginning of the "Hutter"-ites as an identifiable movement.

The conflict centred on Jakob Hutter's status as a leader at Auspitz. Hutter had been one of the main leaders in the Tyrol and had organized the migration of hundreds of refugees to Moravia. As such, he felt he deserved to play a role in leading the community of predominantly Tyroleans. When he came to Auspitz, he found that he was no longer accepted as a leader. The *Chronicle* records his sense of vocation in this way: "How would you feel if you had gone on a journey, entrusting the people to someone else, and then had to stand back when you returned home?"[1]

When a series of events called into question the integrity of a number of the existing leaders—Reublin, Zaunring, Schützinger—Hutter emerged as the main leader.

Jakob Hutter was in the mountains of Tyrol, proclaiming the Lord's Word and doing the Lord's work. He traveled around, visiting those who were eager to hear the truth, helping them, and setting them on the right path. He sent one group after another down to Schützinger in Auspitz since the intense persecution made it impossible for them to remain in Tyrol. Everywhere they were spied on and betrayed, hunted down, and seized by the constables.

Not long afterward, Jakob Hutter, too, came to Auspitz with several others, arriving on August 11, 1533. The elders and the whole church welcomed him with great joy, and he himself rejoiced from his heart that God had led him safely to them. He told Simon Schützinger and the other elders and brothers and sisters that he had not come to strangers but to his dear brothers, his little children. Schützinger and all the others echoed his words, ask-

---

1   *The Chronicle of the Hutterian Brethren*, vol. I, translated and edited by the Hutterian Brethren (Ulster Park: Plough Publishing House), 101.

ing Jakob to help them care for the people, and he promised to do so. Jakob had also brought them a temporal gift, a sweet sacrifice, a small sum of money to repay the nuns of Brünn (who owned the land at Auspitz) for their help in a time of need.

On the following Sunday, Jakob Hutter shared news of the church in distant lands, telling of the believers he had left behind in Tyrol, who were suffering harsh persecution. He delivered their greetings and told about the wonderful deeds God had worked in spite of many tribulations. Then he announced publicly that he had heard there were some in Auspitz who hoped that when he came he would move with them to a different place. As far as he knew he had challenged and admonished all of them, making it clear that he had no such intentions. But he would help punish according to God's Word any fickle, selfish people who still wanted to go somewhere else. And since God had sent him to the church, he would put all his efforts into overcoming any faults he found in the house of God.

Now I want to tell further what happened in the church: the enemy always mixes weeds among the wheat; the Lord humbles the mighty; and nothing is so hidden that it will not be revealed. Each one can judge for himself from the following account how God separated the devout from the hypocrites. But this is how it began.

As reported above, Simon Schützinger and the elders had asked Jakob Hutter to help them care for the people, so a few days later Jakob was about to start improving certain things in the church. But Schützinger resisted and tried to stop him. Then Jakob wanted to know if he was wanted as a shepherd or not. He felt that he could not remain silent and fail to exercise his service. If he was not needed, he would move on and serve wherever the Lord led him. So he went to Rossitz and explained the situation to Gabriel [Ascherham], saying he did not know whether the people wanted him or not. He said he was willing to bring the matter before the church and do whatever the people of God asked of him. Gabriel agreed but said, "Do it humbly."

While Jakob was at Rossitz, Schützinger spoke with the two servants for temporal affairs, Leonhard Schmerbacher and Wilhelm Griesbacher. He said he intended to continue in his service and not give Jakob much chance to speak. The two brothers were not in agreement but said he should remain in his service and Jakob should serve with him. But Simon did not want this.

When Jakob returned home from Rossitz and wished to pass on greetings from Gabriel and his community to the church, Schützinger forbade it. He admonished Jakob and asked him what he was trying to do. Thus Schützinger revealed his own intentions against Jakob.

In reply Jakob told Schützinger and the elders, including Kaspar, a servant from Rossitz, that he wanted to know whether or not the church needed him. To sit around and not fulfill his service was something he was not free to do, and he would not know how to answer for it before God. Simon answered that through the drawing of lots God had entrusted this people to him and made him their shepherd and therefore he intended to continue in this service. If Jakob had anything to say, he should do so briefly, for he could not allow him to speak very long. Even though the elders who were present opposed him, he insisted on being the one to teach the people. The elders, including Kaspar from Rossitz, said they should both care for the people together, but still Simon wanted to be the only shepherd.

The elders wished to gather the church the very next day but had to postpone the meeting until Sunday, because a number of brothers were away. Meanwhile Simon sent to Rossitz for Gabriel, who set out immediately but stopped in at Philip's community. Simon Schützinger joined them and complained to Gabriel and Philip that Jakob was pushing to be a shepherd over the church. So they sent for Jakob, who came without knowing what they wanted. Later in the night, Kaspar from Rossitz, Leonhard Schmerbacher, and Wilhelm Griesbacher were also called. When they arrived, Gabriel accused Jakob of putting himself above Simon Schützinger in the shepherd's service. Jakob said that it was not so; he only wished to serve the church. "I have been sent here after earnest prayer to God. The people have been entrusted to me and to Schützinger. All I ask is to be able to continue in my service. "

Philip retorted, "If you want to do that, Jakob, then you are the most wicked devil who has ever come into this country. "

But Jakob stood firm, adding, "How would you feel if you had gone on a journey, entrusting the people to someone else, and then had to stand back when you returned home?"

After much talking, Philip said Jakob and Simon should work together, faithfully caring for the people, "Just as Blasi [Blasius Kuhn] and I do."

When he asked Jakob what he thought of that, Jakob replied, "I want nothing more than to serve with Schützinger. May God be praised."

Then Gabriel said, "No, I don't see it that way. I command you, Simon, to continue in your service as shepherd to this people. If you now were to lose courage for your service and allow it to be weakened because Jakob is more gifted and a better speaker than you, God would punish you. The same would happen to you as happened to me with the Swiss Brethren. "

Simon quickly replied, "Yes, yes, my brother. Praise the Lord! It is true, my brother Gabriel, it is true!"

Leonhard Schmerbacher objected, "But Philip said first that both should care for the people together, and now Gabriel says something quite different."

Philip replied, "I feel exactly like Gabriel. Even though what I said may have sounded otherwise, that is what I meant in my heart." After much talking (which does not need to be recorded here] Jakob again desired to hear what the church felt about him. This they could not refuse, but they told him to be willing to adapt himself and not push himself forward.

On the following Sunday Jakob spoke to the gathered church, explaining the reason for his coming and that for a time he had had to stop the work God had entrusted to him. With restraint he told about his talks with the elders and with Simon, Gabriel, and Philip.

Then Simon spoke, reminding the people of his election and saying that he was going to stand by it. Gabriel supported him in a long speech, describing how Simon had originally been chosen by lot. However, if they were going to insult him and preferred Jakob because he was a better speaker, or if they placed Simon and Jakob in the service together, then he, Gabriel, would have no part in it and would go back by the road he had come. He pointed out that in Jerusalem there was only one shepherd, namely James. Here Jakob contradicted him.

Nothing could stop Gabriel. He warned the people, using the terrible example of Korah: if they looked down on Simon's simplicity and preferred Jakob's fine speaking, God would punish them as he did Korah and his company. He warned the people to guard against making an idol of Jakob, who to him seemed proud and arrogant. After many words, he declared that Jakob did not have the gifts to serve the people as a shepherd but only as an apostle.

The church was then asked to make a decision. Two or three spoke to the effect that Simon should continue in his service and Jakob should assist him. But Peter Hueter said that to him neither seemed higher or lower, greater or smaller; one seemed to him as good as the other. Schützinger cut him short, calling him a stupid man—he had thought him a great deal wiser. Gabriel spoke against him in the same way, but with little basis of truth. Then Leonhard Schmerbacher declared that he was unable to put one before the other, for the people had been entrusted to one as much as to the other, but for the sake of peace, love, and unity, Jakob should give the honor and precedence to Simon. Everybody said, "Yes, yes." However, one brother added that he had nothing against the decision, "but Simon would do very well without having Jakob there."

Gabriel asked Jakob if he would accept the decision to give Schützinger precedence. Jakob replied that he wanted first to consider it before God, taking counsel with the elders and servants. Gabriel retorted, "I have nothing more to say to you; I will be on my way." The brotherhood separated in great anguish of heart. Some went to comfort Jakob, who was deeply distressed; others who saw this presumed that he wanted to win the people over and take them to a separate place. One said this, another that. In short, everyone was overcome with grief.

On the following Tuesday the brotherhood was again called together. Jakob announced to the church that he had taken counsel with God and talked with the elders, and he could only acknowledge that God, in his providence, had appointed him and sent him to this people. "But the brothers did not understand me," he added, "so there is nothing to be done. For the sake of love, peace, and unity, I will accept the decision of the church, but not for the sake of righteousness."

Gabriel retorted, "You say we did not understand you—but we speak German too. There was no need for you to say anything at all." The brotherhood, though very distressed, kept up their spirits and trusted that with God's leading everything would work out.

Two weeks later the Lord struck Simon Schützinger so severely that he lay seriously ill in bed. So Jakob Hutter proclaimed the Word of the Lord to the church, according to the grace he had been given.

The next Sunday, September 28, at the repeated request of the elders, he held a meeting in which he admonished and taught in the power of God, exhorting the people to the true community of Jesus Christ. At that point several began again to mutter against Jakob.

Just then Georg Fasser of Rattenberg in the Inn Valley placed his earthly goods at the disposal of the church. As head of the family, he ordered his wife and children to submit willingly to the Lord and his people by doing the same. They agreed, and he lost no time in bringing his bed and chests into the communal storeroom. The servants examined all his things and made careful inquiries, and it was found that without her husband's knowing, his wife had kept money that had belonged to her and the children and had hidden it. She was admonished and disciplined by the servants, her husband, and Schützinger.

Since this woman had deceived her husband and hidden money from him, it occurred to Jakob that Simon's wife, too, might turn out to be another Sapphira, for God had given Jakob the gift of discernment. He brought his concern before the elders and said, "If you will support me in the strength of God, we will take the matter up and look into it thoroughly." The elders readily agreed and told him he should simply do it; he should start with his own room and continue with the rooms of the elders, including Simon's.

When they came to Simon and asked him to let them take a look in order to set their hearts at rest, he was perfectly willing. As they were looking through a chest, they found a too-plentiful supply of bed linen and shirts and four pounds in Bernese money, all in small coins. Jakob pleaded with him in the name and power of the Lord, asking him to unburden his heart, to tell whether he knew anything about the money, and not to conceal anything else that was there. Simon then confessed that he had known about it. So saying, he reached under the roof and brought out forty gulden. Jakob and the other servants were appalled. They could hardly believe that he would knowingly have done such a thing: he taught full surrender and community to others and yet did not hold to it himself. Jakob pointed out his dishonesty and sent immediately for Philip [Blauärmel], but he was not at home.

Since Simon had been found guilty of such great deception, they could not postpone dealing with it. Early the next morning, on October 5, they called him before the brotherhood, and Jakob informed them of his faithlessness, greed, and treachery of heart. The whole brotherhood was horrified. The brothers and sisters began to lament and weep loudly in pain and heaviness of heart. But, as was only right and just, he was excluded in the power of Christ, according to the Word of the Lord, and given over to Satan. He confessed before the whole brotherhood that he deserved this but longed for grace and mercy. Jakob faithfully urged him to repent, and he promised to do so with all his might. Georg Fasser's wife and other unfaithful members were also separated from the church.

The whole brotherhood had previously chosen Schützinger as elder in preference to Jakob. Now that Schützinger was found to be a deceiver, Jakob exhorted all the brothers and sisters to consider how they had talked and acted and what sort of decision they had made. Also it had been said that he, Jakob, did not have the gifts to be a shepherd to such a people; instead they had chosen Schützinger as shepherd, a man whose wickedness was now revealed. And so, he said, they were once more completely without a shepherd, for as they had had so little respect for the Lord's Word, he was no longer certain about serving them. He challenged them, however, to pray earnestly, calling on God to raise up a faithful shepherd and servant for them.

For eight days and nights they prayed earnestly to God. They sent two brothers to Gabriel [Ascherham] at Rossitz to tell him of their need and to ask his advice about what they should do. He, too, suggested Jakob Hutter.

As they persevered in prayer, God gave them all a united heart and mind. They accepted Jakob as a gift from God to be their shepherd, and were all united in great love.

On October 12 the whole church rejoiced in spite of all their troubles. They also confessed before God and to Jakob that they had done wrong in giving precedence and honor to the deceiver. They admitted that Simon had not been the servant of God they had believed him to be. But because he was known to God, who knows all hearts, he had been revealed to God's own people. They asked earnestly and unanimously for forgiveness for this sin of ignorance. God forgave them because this had been done in blindness, and he blessed them. The Word of God grew in power among them; peace, love, and the fear of God increased daily; the wicked were separated from the church and the devout were accepted.

But when love, justice, and true judgment according to God's commandment increased—when the entire church lived in true peace—the devil, that ancient serpent, could not rest. He strove day and night to destroy this work by his cunning and to tear apart the bond of love.

On October 26 of this same year, 1533, the church was gathered to hear the Word of God when Philip Blauärmel appeared with Gabriel Ascherham and his assistant Peter Hueter. They had slipped in quietly before dawn, like wolves in sheep's clothing. The people were very startled to see them and feared that the devil would bring disaster, and indeed disaster soon followed. Nonetheless the servants and elders received them in peace, for at first they gave the impression of being very friendly, but Jakob asked them to explain why they had come. In response, Philip began by asking, "On what grounds did you exclude Bohemian David? He received a good testimony among you earlier, and yet you refused to receive him back. Second, why did you exclude Bernhard Glaser? Third, we understood you to say that the decision for Simon Schützinger's election did not come from God." Then Philip said it was and is from God and would remain valid forever in his sight. There was so much talk for and against on both sides that the brotherhood was unable to arrive at any clarity or true judgment.

After all manner of things had been said and one called the other a liar, the brotherhood was in deep distress. Many were heard to groan, and the faithful were shaken to the depths. No one knew what the outcome would be, who was right or who was wrong, and which side was to blame, until finally Philip and Gabriel came out with their malice, which could be concealed no longer. When Jakob Hutter spoke to them in the strength of God, saying, "You have made accusations against me and the brotherhood, and if your accusations were true, we would be the greatest scoundrels that ever lived," Philip shamelessly denied it and called Jakob a liar. But Jakob replied, "The lie will come back on you."

Then Philip said, "I have always said you are an idol and the people worship you. That is the plain truth." At this there was a great turmoil among the people, who cried out, "That's a lie!"

As soon as Philip was recognized as a liar by the entire brotherhood and was admonished for his blasphemy, he tried to gloss it over and take back what he had said. But after pouring out abuse for a long time, Philip and Gabriel stood up and said, "Dear brothers and sisters, we have nothing against you, only against your servants." They proposed that the brotherhood should delegate a few men, and they would do the same in their communities, and these brothers should judge the matter among themselves. As this was received in silence, they left.

On the following Monday the brotherhood appointed eight men to report to the other two communities what had taken place, informing them where the brotherhood stood in relation to them and their servants. The brotherhood sent four of these eight to Philip and his people to say, "We would like to come to you tomorrow or whenever it suits you to report about our brotherhood's actions."

But Philip received them as if they were children of the devil, not children of God. Because they represented the brotherhood, they were harshly accused of making an idol of Jakob and worshiping him, of excluding Simon Schützinger out of envy and hate, and of accepting Georg Fasser for the sake of his money. "And Bernhard Glaser," said Philip, "who was excluded by the church for lying, is more upright than any of you. I would rather believe him than I would all of you put together." The four men contested these accusations, but Philip and his followers reviled them on many other matters which are omitted here for the sake of brevity.

When the four men described the response they had received, their whole brotherhood was still more horrified. Philip had so recently acknowledged them as children of peace (as reported above], and now his heart was set against them.

The very next day eight men came from Rossitz, saying that Gabriel and Peter Hueter, their servants, had brought news that distressed them very much. The brotherhood at Rossitz had therefore sent them to find out what had happened. They expressed the wish of the group at Rossitz that all three brotherhoods should meet while Jakob, Philip, and Gabriel were to stay outside. Then Jakob's brotherhood should give an account to the other two, who were not involved, and let them judge the matter.

That same night, however, the enemy put a new idea into their minds. In the morning, when Jakob's brotherhood agreed to the Rossitz brothers' proposal, these eight brothers denied everything they had agreed to before and did not want Jakob's group to be present when the matter would be judged. (They thought no one would notice the reason for their change of mind.) But the answer was that Jakob's brotherhood wished to consider this before God and would let them know what they decided. At this the eight brothers went back to Rossitz, apparently in peace.

Jakob's brotherhood decided in great fear of God that they would prefer both communities to come to them and bring along Philip and Gabriel or anyone else they wished, and then they would give a full account. This decision was reported to the other two communities by the eight brothers from Auspitz, but it was rejected. The others wanted to know only one thing from Jakob's brotherhood: were they willing to meet without their servants or not? At this the brothers returned home and talked to Jakob and the other servants. They were all ready to stay away from the meeting, provided they were convinced through the Word of God and true testimony. The eight men conveyed this to Gabriel's representatives, who would not accept it but wanted an answer from the whole brotherhood. To avoid more trouble, it was agreed that they

should meet with the brotherhood. They would be called the next morning when the brotherhood was gathered. But that same night they crept in secretly to listen while the brotherhood was meeting to discuss the matter.

As soon as Jakob Hutter noticed them, he announced them publicly. When they came forward, they were informed by the brotherhood of the same decision the delegates had told them before. But they refused to accept it, saying, "Dear brothers and sisters, dear children of God, we have no authority to accept it, and we undertake nothing outside our own brotherhood. We will part from you now in peace, as from brothers and sisters, and will announce your views to our people. Then we will let you know what our brotherhood thinks." With this they took leave of Jakob and Leonhard Schmerbacher and the other servants, embracing and kissing them. They gave the greeting of peace to the whole brotherhood, and everyone said, "Amen, Amen."

Everybody rejoiced, hoping that the Lord might still provide a peaceful way out.

After all this, just as they were leaving, one of them asked, "Did you exclude Gabriel?"

Jakob replied respectfully, "We do not regard him as a brother or as a servant of God." Now the wolf could no longer stay in sheep's clothing. One of them, Hans from Strasbourg, jumped up and called Jakob a liar and a false prophet. Although they had been hypocrites for so long and taken leave in peace, he now poured it all out with such a flood of slander that everyone could see what the devil was trying to do. But God would no longer tolerate such lying and hypocrisy.

The brothers and sisters were in great distress, and God in heaven might well pity them. Then Jakob Hutter asked the brotherhood to pronounce its judgment on these men—who they were and whether they had come seeking peace or not. One brother began to speak with deep feeling, saying that they had seemed to come in peace and had said in the hearing of many that they would not undertake anything without their brotherhood, and now they had undertaken without their brotherhood to slander, revile, and tell lies. They had made a lie of their peace and their kiss, like Judas. Since they had behaved with such deceit that a blind man could see it, he would consider them the same as Gabriel and Philip.

When Gabriel's men heard this, they hurled abuse at this brother and rushed out of the door. But the brother continued to speak, comforting the brotherhood, for people stood trembling and full of pain but still trusting in the Lord. A few irresponsible souls, however, banded together and would gladly have made a commotion. Yet the Lord stood by his own and did not allow it.

The following Sunday the brotherhood sent the same eight representatives to Philip and his community to tell what had happened and warn them about Philip. But no one would listen to them or let them speak to the people. They were treated harshly and sent away with many abusive words.

On Thursday the brotherhood sent six members to Rossitz to advise the brothers there to exclude Gabriel and other evildoers and to explain the reason. Here again no one would listen or allow them to have a meeting, for Gabriel had so bewitched his people that not one said, "For the sake of fairness we should hear them." The six messengers then said that if the brotherhood was not ready to banish evil, they would be treated like Gabriel.

When the messengers returned to Auspitz, they told the brotherhood there was little hope of these people changing since they all agreed with Gabriel. May God protect the simple and innocent from suffering for this and redeem them from all error through Jesus Christ our Lord. Amen. […]

This is a short but truthful record of what took place at Auspitz in Moravia when the three communities split apart, and of the great distress and hostility provoked by Satan, which the church named after its shepherd, Jakob Hutter, had to suffer.

Anyone who reads this report should take care lest reading of rebellion and false spirits becomes a stumbling block for him. There must be stumbling blocks to reveal the chosen people who withstand the test, but woe to those who make stumbling blocks. And you, innocent and honest reader, rejoice in the Lord your God.

The struggle ended on November 22, 1533; fulfilling the Lord's words that two-thirds of the people shall be wiped out while a third of them shall be refined by fire like silver and gold.

[**Source:** *The Chronicle of the Hutterian Brethren*, Volume 1. Translated and edited by the Hutterian Brethren. (Ulster Park: Plough Publishing House, 1987), 98–110. Used by permission.]

"*Das große Glück*" detail showing Jakob and Anna Stainer's house at Klausen where Jakob and Katharina Hutter were arrested, Albrecht Dürer, copper etching, 1501. [Deutsche Nationalbibliothek]

JAKOB HUTTER (ca. 1500–1536)
Letter to the Moravian Governor, Jan Kuna of Kunštát, 1535

In 1535, the Hutterites were expelled from their community at Schakwitz due to mounting pressure put on the local lords by the emperor. The ruling authorities were especially nervous about any unusual activity at this time because of the attempt by revolutionary Anabaptists to take over the city of Münster (1534–35) in northern Germany. Together with the Peasants' Wars (1524–25) this unfortunate episode gave Anabaptists and Hutterites a bad reputation, not least because the Münsterites also practiced community-of-goods. The Hutterites were forced to break into small groups and roam the countryside looking for food and shelter. Rumours had spread that the Hutterites were armed, so the governor sent his men to check out the situation. Jakob Hutter was asked to put into writing what he told the governor's men.

Jakob Hutter was burned at the stake only a few months after this letter was written. The letter powerfully expresses the early Hutterite commitment to justice and non-violence as well as Hutter's strongly critical, prophetic voice.

Written from the open heath in Moravia
to the governor of Moravia, 1535

We, as those who are brothers and devotees of God and of his divine truth, and as authentic witnesses of our Lord Jesus Christ, have been driven out of many countries for the sake of God's name and his truth. We came here to Moravia, where we have been gathered into a fellowship and are living together under the lord marshal through the care and protection of the Almighty, to whom alone we give praise and honour and declare his glory, forever.

We want to let you know, dear governor of the land of Moravia, that we received the order and message delivered by your servants, as you well know. We already answered you by word of mouth, and now

Jakob and Katharina Hutter on the flight from Moravia to the Tyrol, artist and date unknown.

want to do the same in writing, as follows: We have fled the world and all its unjust and godless nature. We believe in God the Almighty and in his son, our Lord Jesus Christ. He will protect us from all such evil for evermore. We have given and devoted ourselves to God, the Lord, to live by his divine will and keep his commandments according to the example of our Lord Jesus Christ.

Because we serve him, do his will, keep his commandments, and leave behind all sin and injustice, we are therefore persecuted and despised by the whole world and robbed of all our goods. The same was done to all the saints, to the prophets, and also to Christ himself. Especially King Ferdinand, the prince of darkness, that cruel tyrant and enemy of divine truth and justice, mercilessly put many of our innocent brothers and sisters to death, murdering and

killing them. He has also robbed us of house and home, all our goods, driven us out, and persecuted us terribly. But through God's grace and assistance we were able to travel or move here to Moravia, and have lived here for a time, recently under the lord marshal. We have not troubled or harmed anyone and have lived faithfully by hard work in the fear of God. Everybody will confirm this. But now even the marshal has given us notice and forced us to leave our houses and property.

So we now find ourselves out in the wilderness, in a desolate meadow under the open sky. This we accept patiently, praising God that he has made us worthy to suffer for the sake of his name. But for your sakes we feel pain and heartache, that you treat God's devout children so cruelly. We cry to him about your hardheartedness and about the enormous wrongs and injustice that increase daily. Day and night we plead with God, the Lord, to protect and keep us from evil, commending to him our cares, so that he might lead us through, according to his divine will and his fatherly mercy. And he will surely do so; he is our captain and protector and will go to battle for us. The holy prophet Isaiah and the devout prophet Ezra foretold that all who turn away from and abandon evil and all injustice, all who love and fear God from their hearts, who serve him and keep his commandments, are bound to be robbed and driven and cast away from their homes.[1] This shows that we are children of God and that he is our father, that we are fellow heirs of his glory,[2] that we love him and are pleasing to him, as are all the saints. Therefore, we gladly suffer such things with great patience, and our hearts are comforted by his Holy Spirit.[3]

Behold, woe and double woe[4] to all who would persecute, exile, and hate us without cause, simply because we stand for God's truth! Their demise, punishment, and condemnation is approaching and will overtake them with terror, here and in eternity. According to his holy prophets, God wants to, and also shall, terrifyingly call them to account for all the innocent blood and all the tribulations of his saints.[5]

Now since you have commanded us to leave without delay, we give you this answer: We know of no place to go, and what burdens us especially is that we are surrounded by the king's lands. In every direction we would walk straight into the jaws of robbers and tyrants, like sheep cast among ravenous wolves and ferocious lions.[6] Besides, we have among us many ailing widows and orphans, many sick people and small, uneducated children who cannot help themselves and are unable to walk or travel. That godless tyrant Ferdinand, that prince of darkness, an enemy of divine truth and justice, had their fathers and mothers murdered. He also robbed them of their goods. These very same widows and orphans, sick people and small children, are entrusted to us by God the Almighty, who commands us to feed, clothe, and house them, and in every way to serve them from our hearts in all matters. So we cannot, and nor do we want to, abandon them or send them away—truly, may God protect and keep us forever from doing that![7] We dare not disobey God's commands for the sake of human commands, though

---

1   Isa 59:15; 2Esd 16:70–75.
2   Rom 8:17.
3   Acts 3:18; Heb 12:2.
4   Cf. Rev 8:13.
5   Deut 32:35–43; Joel 3:21; Jth 8:16–23.
6   Mt 10:16.
7   Acts 5:29.

Jakob Hutter,
unknown artist,
etching, 18th century.
[*WikiCommons*]

because of the sick, the widows and orphans, and also the small children. Praise God, there are not just a few but many of these helpless ones among us, about as many as there are able-bodied people. Now we are out on the open meadows, with no one being harmed, as God wills. We do not want or desire to cause anyone suffering or wrong, not even our worst enemy, be it Ferdinand nor anyone else, great or small. All we do, our words and deeds, our conduct, our way of life, are there for everyone to see. Rather than knowingly wrong anybody to the value of a penny, we would let ourselves be robbed of a hundred guilders. Rather than strike our worst enemy with our hand—to say nothing of spears, swords, and halberds such as the world uses—we would die and let our own lives be taken.

As anyone can see clearly, we have no physical weapons, neither spears nor muskets. No, all in all, what we preach is what we speak, and how we live and behave: that one should live in peace and unity in God's truth and justice, as the true followers of Christ. Our words and our way of life are transparent for all to see; we are not ashamed of giving an account of ourselves to anyone. It does not trouble us that many evil things are said about us, for Christ foretold all this. Such has been the lot of all believers, of Christ himself,

it cost us life and limb, for we must obey God rather than humans,[8] as Saint Peter says.

We have not had time to sell our homes and possessions, which we earned by hard labor, by the sweat of our brows,[9] and which rightly belong to us before God and man. These properties are yet to be sold (though we desperately need them), and in addition, we also need time

---

8   Acts 4:19.
9   Gen 3:19.

and of all his apostles, from the beginning.[10]

It is rumoured that we took possession of the field with so many thousands, as if we were going to war, but only someone who has no knowledge of us, or someone who is up to no good, a lying scoundrel, could talk like that. We lament to God that there are so few devout people (such as we truly are). We declare our wish that all the world were like us. We would like to convince and turn all people to this faith, for that would mean the end of warfare and injustice.

Next, as a further response, we would like to say that at this time we do not know where we could go to leave the country. May God, the Lord in heaven, provide and show us where to go! We simply cannot be denied a place in this country or on earth. For the earth is the Lord's, and all that is in it belongs to our God in heaven. Besides, if we agreed to depart and planned to do so, we might not be able to hold to that, for we are in God's hand and he does with us whatever he will. Perhaps God wills that we remain in this country to test our faith. This we do not know, but we trust in the eternal and true God.

On the other hand, we state as follows: although we are being persecuted and driven out, if almighty God in heaven showed us enough cause or gave a sufficient sign to depart from the country and move somewhere else, that he willed such, then we would do it gladly, without waiting for an ordinance. Once God's will concerning where we should go is clear to us, we will not hesitate. We pray fervently to God day and night to lead us where he will. We will not and cannot disobey his divine will. Neither can you, even if you try to hinder it. God the Almighty may suddenly reveal to us, even overnight, that we should leave you. Then we will not delay but would be prepared to live according to his will—whether to depart or to die. Perhaps you are not worthy or meritorious as to have us among you any longer.

Therefore, woe and double woe to you Moravian lords for eternity, because you have approved of, and assented to, Ferdinand, the awful tyrant and enemy of divine truth, and agreed to exile those who are devout and God-fearing from your lands: you fear a mortal, useless man more than the living, eternal, almighty God and Lord, and you are willing to expel and ruthlessly persecute the children of God, old and young, even the ailing, and afflicted widows and orphans, delivering them up mercilessly to plunder, anxiety, deprivation, with much pain, tribulation, ailment and extreme poverty. It is as if you strangled them with your own hands. It would be more considerate and preferable for us to be killed and murdered for the

---

10   E.g., Mt 5:10–12; Lk 6:22–23; Jn 16:2; 1Pet 4:13–14.

Lord's sake than to witness such misery being inflicted on innocent, God-fearing hearts. You will have to pay dearly for it, and you will have no excuse, even less so than Pilate, who also did not really want to crucify and kill the Lord Jesus.[11] Yet it was out of fear and dread of the emperor when the Jews threatened him (by God's direction), that Pilate condemned innocent blood. You do the same thing, using the king as your excuse. But God has made it known through the mouth of his holy prophets that he will avenge innocent blood in a terrifying and horrific way, against all who stain their hands with it.[12]

Therefore, great misfortune, misery and distress, deprivation and great tribulation, pain and heartfelt sorrow will come upon you, even including woe, hurt, and martyrdom for this reason, and they are ordained for you by God in heaven, in this life and forever. We state and proclaim this to you in the name of our Lord Jesus Christ, that you will certainly not be spared. You will soon see and experience that we have spoken to you the divine truth in the name of our Lord Jesus Christ

as a testimony against you and all who act or sin against God.

We wish all of you to turn to the living God so that you could escape such a fate. How we wish and desire that you and all people might be saved with us and inherit eternal life. So we plead with you for the sake of God to accept his Word and our warning amicably, and in the best way possible, and to take them to heart. For we speak and testify to what we know, which is the truth before God.[13] We do this out of the pure, divine fear and divine love, which we feel toward God the Lord, and toward all humankind.

With this we entrust ourselves to the care and protection of the eternal Lord. May he be gracious to us and be with us forever, through Jesus Christ. Amen. As for you, may God the Lord allow you to recognize his fatherly warning and chastisement, and may he be merciful to you through our Lord Jesus Christ, according to his divine will. Amen.

From us brothers and fellow sufferers in the suffering of Christ, driven into the fields for the sake of the Word of God and the witness of Jesus Christ.

[**Source:** Emmy Barth Maendel and Jonathan Seiling, editors and translators, *Jakob Hutter: His Life and Letters* (Walden: Plough Publishing, 2024), 94–100. Used by permission.]

---

11   Jn 19:6–12.
12   Joel 3:19; 2Esd 15:5–17; Jth 8:14–17.
13   Jn 3:32; Acts 4:20.

Jakob Hutter (ca. 1500–1536)
"A Prayer for the Persecuted Church," 1535

This prayer, excerpted from Hutter's seventh extant epistle written less than a year before he was captured and executed, provides a window into the spirit of the early Hutterite leader. As in many of Hutter's writings, one can sense the urgency of his calling and the lived reality of persecution. The apocalyptic energy of the early Hutterite movement is also evident: they were a people on the run; exiles without a home; a people living in daily dependence on God. This is why the early Hutterites saw themselves as the direct descendants of the New Testament Church. Notice how this prayer has similarities to the Psalms of lament.

O God of heaven, curtail the days of great tribulation for the sake of your chosen ones.[1] Protect and preserve, guard and shelter, and provide for your holy people. Release, redeem, and rescue them from their sins, enemies and adversaries who pursue them day and night seeking their souls.

O God from heaven, have compassion on the hardship, the pain, the great tribulation and the profound heartache of your afflicted little children from the heights of your heaven.

Come, O merciful God, make haste and delay no longer with your aid and mercy[2] for the sake of your child, Jesus Christ, and for the sake of your holy name. Have mercy on your holy people, and let them be commended unto you.

Give them and us your divine counsel—the knowledge and wisdom of your Holy Spirit from above—so that we may know what we are to do and what we are to leave undone, and what is pleasing to you, God in heaven, that we may act and proceed and work and

---

1   Mt 24:22.
2   Cf. Ps 70.

live according to your will and good pleasure, judging all things and exercising authority in your fear, to your praise and glory.

Guide and lead us with your divine, eternal light and by your gracious Holy Spirit, and with your holy angels in all truth and wherever you want, that we may bring you glory and much fruit and serve you and your people most diligently.

God of heaven, come down and stand by your people and accept them, God, as your own in all things, through Jesus Christ and his great mercy.

This is our prayer for you, beloved and chosen of the Lord, and this is what we ask of God day and night without ceasing, with great earnestness and diligence. God, hear our prayer through his holy name and through his child, Jesus Christ. Amen.

[**Source:** Translated by Kenny Wollmann from *Die Hutterischen Episteln 1527 bis 1767*, Volume 1 (Elie: James Valley Book Centre, 1986), 45–46. Used by permission. An alternative translation can be found in Emmy Barth Maendel and Jonathan Seiling, editors and translators, *Jakob Hutter: His Life and Letters* (Walden: Plough Publishing, 2024), 128–139.]

GABRIEL ASCHERHAM (d. 1545)
Lost Chronicle Fragment, ca. 1540s

Gabriel Asherham led one of the three communal groups—the Gabrielites—that settled in Moravia in the early 1530s. In 1531, his group along with the Philipites created a loose alliance with the community at Auspitz with Ascherham serving as the *Vorsteher*. Following the Münster debacle in 1535, all Anabaptists were expelled from Moravia. While some returned and formed congregations, the Gabrielites were not able to find their way together again. Many later joined the Hutterites. Little is known about Asherham after the expulsion.

When discussing the conflicts that led to the Great Schism of 1533, the Hutterite *Chronicle* portrays Asherham in an unfavourable light. There are, however, at least two sides to every story. The following fragment, in which Ascherham writes very critically about Jakob Hutter, is from a lost chronicle written by Asherham in ca. 1540. The sole surviving remnant of this chronicle appeared in the polemical text, *Der Hutterischen Wiedertauffer Taubenkobel* by Christoph Andreas Fischer in 1607. Fischer claimed this quotation was "transcribed word for word, faithfully and without falsification, from the…chronicle by Gabriel [Ascherham] the Furrier."

What transpired among the brethren who were expelled from all the German nations for reasons of faith and came to Moravia at that time to take up residence from 1528 until 1545. I will write what I personally saw, heard, and learned from reliable witnesses without overstating what I can say in good conscience.

First of all, this Jakob Hutter was a conceited [*auffgeblasener*] and arrogant [*ehrgeitziger*] person. This is why he cast [Simon][1] Schützinger aside and was chosen as an elder in his place. But, before he was chosen, he could not conceal his presumption and arrogance as he rose up in fury and attacked the people [saying], "Am I not also an apostle and shepherd? Must I also be pushed aside by you?" The chief fruit that

---

1   Sigismund.

Title page of *Der Hutterischen Wiedertauffer Taubenkobel* by Christoph Andreas Fischer. [Ingolstadt, 1607] In English the full title reads, "The Hutterite Anabaptist Pigeoncote: In which all their Waste, Shit, Dung, and Filth, that is, their false, stinking, filthy, and abominable teachings that they believe regarding God, Christ, the Holy Sacraments, and other articles of the Christian faith are articulated—briefly and faithfully from their own publications, both printed and handwritten—with citations to indicate where everything can be found. Also, [an account] of the great cock pigeon Jakob Hutter's life, after whom the Anabaptist Hutterites name themselves, appended."

Der Hutterischen
Widertauffer Tauben-
kobel: In welchem all ihr Wüst / Mist / Kott
vnnd Vnflat / das ist / ihr falsche / stinckende / vnflätige
vnd abscheuliche Lehr / was sie nemblich von Gott / von Christo / von
den H. Sacramenten vnd andern Artickeln deß Christlichen Glaubens halten /
werden erzählet / alle kürtzlich vnd treulich auß ihren eygnen Büchern /
so wol gedruckten als geschribnen / mit Anzeygung deß Orths /
wo ein jedliche zufinden / verfasset.

Auch deß grossen Taubers deß Jacob Hutters Leben /
von welchem sich die Widertauffer Hutterisch nennen / angehenckt:

Durch CHRISTOPHORVM ANDREAM Fischer D.
Pfarrherrn zu Velsperg:

Mit Röm: Kay: Mayest: Freyheit.
Getruckt zu Ingolstatt / in der Ederischen Truckerey
Durch Andream Angermeyr.

ANNO M. DC. VII.

resulted from his office and his establishment of community was his destruction of love and unity; the people who were previously united he caused to be disunited.

Now you can sing and say whatever you want about this Jakob Hutter, but I say this: based on my close acquaintance with him, Jakob Hutter was a bad man. Even if he let himself simmer and sizzle, I still do not know [any good] to say of him for he didn't demonstrate it in this land.

Indeed, he took revenge on all those who even spoke with Schützinger[2] and descended upon the community with his raging spirit [*Poltergeist*] and said threateningly, "Now do you see whom you praised, namely this scoundrel, whom you regarded as faithful while belittling me by saying, 'Schützinger should carry on in his position.' In this you have made a false judgement and you must repent for that!"

That is what you call a true raging spirit [*Poltergeist*]; a man who seeks his own honour. That is not the spirit of Paul, but rather it is a spirit of Balaam's descendants [*kinder*], that is, fools' children.[3] When Jakob flaunted his pride and boasted he had the spirit of Paul, a woman said

to him, "You have the spirit of the devil."

At the time, however, that the king [Ferdinand I] sought to expel the communities from Moravia, the abbess of Brno[4] sent her servants to Auspitz and drove Jakob and his people from their homes. When the governor sent his servants to present him with the royal proclamation Jakob let loose, saying, "Oh the bloodhound, the murderer! In the upper regions [in the Tyrol] he drove us from home and yard, took our possessions, and murdered our people [*die unserigen*], and now he wants to drive us out here, too!" He then said to the servants of the governor, "Tell your master this: We are going nowhere! If the bloodhound wants our blood, then let him come for it. We'll be here waiting."

The servants, however, said, "We cannot verbally convey such a message," because there was so much rambling and ranting from Jakob that they couldn't keep it straight [...].[5] [Jakob] wrote this in a letter with much scolding and slander against the king [Ferdinand I]. The main point of it was, "We will wait for the king here."[6]

---

2   James Stayer translates this as, "on all who spoke up for Schützinger." Given the lack of clarity of the original, it could be interpreted either way.

3   Num 22–25, 31:16; cf. Rev 2:14.

4   German: Brünn. Located in the modern-day Czech Republic.

5   The remainder of the sentence appears nonsensical. In James Stayer's translation this is omitted without indication.

6   An alternative account of this event that favours Hutter can be found in A.J.F. Zieglschmied, *Die älteste Chronik der Hutterischen Brüder: Ein Sprachdenkmal aus früeneuhochdeutscher Zeit* (Ithaca: Carl Schurtz Memorial Foundation, 1943), 151–152.

When this letter was delivered, people sought this Jakob, but he quickly fled and would not let himself be found. Perhaps the business of waiting for the king became too much for him. From this it can be concluded that he was merely a man of words and there was no truth in him. Meanwhile, other people in the land had to pay for his ranting and raving. This Jakob, however, fled up into the Etsch region [of south Tyrol], but the king sent out notices about him. When he finally captured him, he had him burned [at the stake] in Innsbruck.

This is how this Jakob perished, under the pretext that it happened for the sake of the Gospel, but, in this case, that was not the reason. Rather, he would have had to die because of his harsh lambasting, even if he had twenty lives.

[**Source:** Translated by Kenny Wollmann from Christoph Andreas Fischer, *Der Hutterischen Wiedertauffer Taubenkobel...* (Ingolstadt, 1607), 55–57. This fragment is freshly translated here, but carefully compared with and informed by James Stayer, *The German Peasants' War and Anabaptist Community of Goods* (Montreal: McGill-Queens University Press, 1994), 168–170.]

Testimony of Katharina Prast Hutter, 1535

Katherina Prast was born in Taufers, South Tyrol around 1500. Within months of her baptism by Jakob Hutter in 1532, she was arrested. She recanted under torture, but quickly rejoined the Anabaptists and was arrested again two months later. Following several months of daily beatings along with three other women in prison for refusing to recant, Katrina escaped from prison and fled to Moravia, where she married Jakob Hutter—possibly in May of 1534. She accompanied Hutter on a trip to South Tyrol and gave birth there in mid-October 1535, shortly before they were both arrested in the Pustertal on November 30. It is not known what happened to the baby. Katherina was imprisoned for several months at Gufidaun, and interrogated on December 3, 1535. She was able to escape once more, but was caught again and executed at Schöneck, probably by drowning. Most of what we know about Katherina is based on the following court testimony following her final arrest.

KLAUSEN, December 3, 1535

Katharina, daughter of Laurence Prast, confessed:

It was about three years ago when she was serving as a maid in Paul Gall's house in Trens that she was convinced to join the Anabaptist sect through Paul Gall and also Paul Rumer and others, some of whom have been executed and some who have moved to Moravia. Jakob Hutter, the leader, who is now her brother in marriage and her husband, baptized her there. After that she moved down to Moravia. Around this past Pentecost she married Jakob Hutter in Moravia. Hans Tuchmacher [Amon], who is also one of their brethren and a leader, married them.

Around Saint James' Day [July 25] she and her brother in marriage or husband and another brother named Jeronimus, the schoolmaster, who was also baptized by Jakob Hutter, came up from Moravia over the Tauern to Taufers. They camped out in the woods in Taufers for a while. Then they went to Waldner's in Ellen [Pustertal, St. Lorenz, South Tyrol, Italy], but he had recanted and became a destructive person.

"This portrait of Katharina Hutter shows her as she leads a group of Anabaptist families fleeing from persecuting government forces. The scene is viewed through the eyes of the child she is leading. Both are in contemporary garb as a reminder that Katharina is not a figure of distant history but rather lives on as a sister in the faith." Katharina Hutter, Jason Landsel, 2014. [Plough Publishing House. Used by permission.]

From there they went to Ober's in Hörschwang. He is a dear brother, as is his wife, their daughter Dorothy, also two servants (both called Martin), a young man Hans Wolf, and his wife, Else. Her husband Jakob Hutter baptized and converted all of them. Hutter also baptized Waldner in Ellen, mentioned earlier, but he has recanted and become a destructive Christian.

From there they went several times to Prader and Praun in Lüsen. Prader is not of their opinion or faith, but his wife and son, Melchior are. They often found accommodation and food there, with Jeronimus (mentioned above) who was with them. Those whom her husband Hutter baptized in Lüsen were baptized in the woods.

About fourteen days ago in the house of a wagoner named Schaffer or Schacher in Trens by Sterzing (the man was not home, and he is not an Anabaptist), Hutter baptized seven or eight people in a cellar; she doesn't know exactly how many but she thinks they were miners.

From there she and Hutter and Stainer's daughter Anna went back to Ober's in Hörschwang. They stayed there for a while but then realized that they were being hunted and left. They went through the woods and on the roads at night, until they got to Klausen. They passed the watchman's hut, crossed the bridge, and walked through the town. Then they crossed back over the bridge and came to the sexton's house around midnight. They wanted to leave immediately, but didn't know where to go. Her husband and brother Jakob Hutter said they should go to Niclau or Jörg Müller in Villnöß or wherever God would lead them.

Niclau's wife is her dear sister, but he is not dear to her; likewise with Jörg Müller and his wife in Villnöß. They were baptized by Hutter last fall, but Müller is good for nothing.

Further: She thinks nothing of Mass or the sacrament of the altar, which monks and priests raise above their heads; nor does she have regard for the piled up walls of stone [i.e., churches]; nor of infant baptism, which is nothing but a dirt-bath. Mass is an abomination and a stench before God. All of this is from the devil.

Niclas Niderhofer in the Schöneck district and a girl named Ulian, who was a maid in Kiens, and another person whom she doesn't know, were baptized by Hutter on Saint James' Day. They also took lodging with them a few times.

Regarding her husband Jakob Hutter's assets, or what money he has, he shares it with poor widows, poor little children, and other poor brothers and sisters who need it.

As far as she knows, there are no leaders or brethren in this land. They are all in Moravia.

[**Source:** Emmy Barth Maendel and Jonathan Seiling, editors and translators, *Jakob Hutter: His Life and Letters* (Walden: Plough Publishing, 2024), 236–237. Used by permission.]

JERONIMUS KÄLS (d. 1536)
Daily Prayers, ca. 1535

Jeronimus (Hieronymus) Käls was born in Kufstein in the North Tyrol. Before joining the Hutterites, he was a travelling student, spending time at the universities in Vienna and Leipzig, making him one of the most well-educated early Hutterites. He served as the first Hutterite schoolmaster from 1532–1535 and wrote influential morning, evening, and table prayers for children, some of which are used in some Hutterite communities to this day. Several of these prayers were later incorporated into Book 12 of *Ein Handbüchlein wider den Prozess...* as part of a defence of Hutterite schools (see *Handbook*, 215).

Käls accompanied Vorsteher Jakob Hutter to Tyrol in 1535, returning to Moravia with Hutter's last letter later that year. He and Michael Seifensieder and Hans Oberecker from the Adige Valley were again on the way to Tyrol in early 1536 when they were arrested in Vienna. While they had been eating in an inn, several men had recognized them as Anabaptists; one of the men wrote a note and sent for the bailiff. Although Käls could read the Latin note which read, "Here are three persons who I think are Anabaptists," the three men decided to stay and accept their fate. They were arrested, interrogated at length over a number of weeks, and eventually produced a concise confession (see Käls, 175). The men were burned at the stake in Vienna on March 31, 1536.

Käls also wrote 11 letters to the community and his wife and at least three songs. According to Werner Packull, "Jeronimus Käls, more than any other of the prison authors, provided a model of style and content for this important communication genre [epistles] and reservoir of community values."[1] Käls had a reputation for being a loud prisoner who could be quite confrontational with his interrogators. (See 209 for his remarks about singing in prison and 127–128 for an account of his capture.)

---

[1]   Werner O. Packull, *Hutterite Beginnings: Communitarian Experiments during the Reformation* (Baltimore/London: Johns Hopkins University Press, 1995), 258.

Table Grace

O Lord, almighty, eternal, and merciful God and father, we, your children, whole-heartedly praise, glorify, and thank you, and extol your holy, mighty, and glorious name and the vast and inexpressible grace and mercy you have demonstrated and proven through Jesus Christ, and that you constantly care for us so faithfully and fatherly as for your children. You nourish [*speist und tränkest*] us, both physically and spiritually, with generous sustenance. Therefore, we praise and honour you, and give thanks to you in your heavenly heights through Jesus Christ with all our hearts, forever and ever, amen.

A Morning or Evening Prayer

O almighty, gracious, eternal, and merciful God who has created as holy and good all things in heaven and on earth, and the sea and all creatures within it, and also graciously created humans according to your image; we thank you, O heavenly father, and praise your holy name for your vast and indescribable grace and mercy.

We all pray wholeheartedly that you, O beloved father, would gaze on us poor and wretched orphans from heaven with your gracious countenance; let us be pleasing to you and give us your blessing and divine wisdom.

O gracious God and merciful father, place [*pflanz*] us according to your divine will and let us be brought up from youth on in obedience, your truth and righteousness, so that we learn to serve, praise, honour, and glorify you together with your holy people which you have chosen for yourself from all the earth [*Erdkreis*]

and called them out from all nations, who are therefore spurned, persecuted, and despised by all people.

O Lord, strengthen and comfort your holy people; keep them in your truth so that we remain steadfast in your favour, holy and pure in the presence of your holy countenance.

O holy father, as young and developing [*kleinen und unmündigen*] children we wholeheartedly pray for our parents, which you have given to us out of grace and appointed them to discipline us. Give them grace, strength, understanding, and wisdom so that they can raise us according to your divine will, and that they would guard us from evil and teach us what is good.

O holy father, we also pray for our beloved brothers and sisters languishing in prison, enduring torture and martyrdom all over the world [*Erdkreis*] amid fear, anxiety, and distress. O Lord, strengthen and comfort them with the power of your Holy Spirit and keep them in your truth, holy and undefiled in your presence.

O holy father, we commend and give ourselves completely to your care; do with us as it pleases you so that your favour and mercy is never withdrawn from us and your people. This we pray and seek from you, o most beloved and only father, through our dear Lord Jesus Christ, amen.

O one, faithful, and gracious God, we also pray to you according to the pattern your child [Kind] Jesus Christ gave us and taught:

Our Father in heaven, hallowed be your name. Your kingdom come. Your will be done, on earth as it is in heaven. Give us this day our daily bread. And forgive us our debts, as we also have forgiven our debtors. And do not bring us to the time of trial, but rescue us from the evil one. For yours is the kingdom and the power and the glory forever and ever, amen.[2]

You are highly praised, honoured, glorified, and blessed in and through us and all your saints, together with all your heavenly hosts and through your dear Lord Jesus Christ, amen.

[**Source:** Translated by Kenny Wollmann from Rudolf Wolkan, *Geschichtbuch der Hutterischen Brüder* (Wien, 1923), 122–123.]

---

2   Mt 6:9–13.

JERONIMUS KÄLS (d. 1536)
Confession of Faith, 1536

Confessions of faith represent an important genre of literature produced by 16th century Hutterites missionaries. Peter Riedemann's confession of 1540 (see Riedemann, 195), originally addressed to Lutheran Prince Philip of Hesse, is probably the most well-known example because it was adopted very early on as the community's official doctrinal statement and is particularly comprehensive. There are, however, dozens of other extant confessions that shed light on how Hutterite *Sendboten* responded to interrogations in a variety of contexts. One of the earliest and shortest confession was written by school teacher Hieronymous Käls for the Catholic authorities at Vienna in 1536. The prisoners at Falkenstein (1539) also produced a confession, believed to be a composite of Käls' confession and the Schleitheim Articles.[1] Claus Felbinger's confession (see Felbinger, 219), written shortly before his execution in 1560 in Catholic Landshut, Bavaria was particularly highly regarded among fellow missionaries as being representative of Hutterite faith commitments.[2] Leonard Dax, a Catholic priest who witnessed the execution of Hans Pürchner and later joined the Hutterites in Moravia, produced a confession for his Calvinist interrogators while imprisoned at Alzey in the Palatinate. These are just some of the many confessions written at this time.

Protocols of confrontations between missionaries and various authorities were usually written down from memory at a later time, and thus are interpretations of the original cross-examinations rather than verbatim accounts.

The various extant confessions are evidence that Hutterites responded to representatives of a variety of traditions. In the last half of the sixteenth century rank and file members were encouraged to copy, read, and ponder confessions of faith as a way to internalize a theology of suffering and become equipped to give an account to outsiders themselves.[3]

---

1   Werner Packull, *Peter Riedemann: Shaper of Hutterite Tradition* (Kitchener: Pandora Press, 2007), 71.
2   Hans Georg Oswald, *Als die Brüder ins Land Zogen: Claus Felbinger und sein Bekenntnis zur Vollkommenheit Christi* (Oberlauterbach: Hallertauer Bienenhof, 2010), 25, 28.
3   Martin Rothkegel, "Books for the Church of God: Reading Materials and Manuscript Multiplication," Jacob D. Maendel Lectures, lecture 2, June 4, 2021.

Dear friend judge and all of you who have taken time for us and imagine that you can turn us from our holy Christian faith to return to the old shoes of our heathen life: We, bound and imprisoned for the sake of truth, wish you all the best, grace and eternal mercy from the almighty God and the true sight of your life, through Jesus Christ our dear Lord, Amen.

We have appeared before you four times and answered your questions truthfully (as we must answer to God); we still stand to what we said, and we will also endure to the end through God's help and grace. Therefore we plead with you, for God's sake, do not try further to change our minds, because we ourselves will stand, as all men must, each for himself, before the just judge Christ Jesus on that day. Each will have to bear his burden. Just as you refuse to turn away from the Babylonian whore, that is the pope and his train, so do we refuse to be turned away from Christ. But so that you do not sin more deeply against the innocent blood of the saints, we want to make a written account to you in short, truthful words. If you will see the truth differently, test and consider our innocence and your miserable life, whether you will also once turn away from the world, to a Christian, God-fearing life, and be saved. May God the almighty give you the humility to hear us who are small and despised by this world and accept you in grace, through Jesus his beloved son, Amen.

First, we believe in the one God, creator of heaven and earth, and all that is in and on it. Therefore we despise all idolatry, wooden, stone, silver, gold—in short, all painted or sculpted images, according to the Word of God,[4] of Christ,[5] of the apostles.[6] We read it in the Old and New Testaments, and through God's grace we will endure constantly.

We also believe in Jesus the Christ of God, that he was sent from the bosom of the heavenly Father from heaven to redeem all mankind. He took human form in the virginal pure vessel Mary. She conceived him through the Holy Spirit, without man's seed; she bore him and on the eighth day had him circumcised to fulfill the promise of the Father.

We testify in word and deed that what Christ demanded, taught and promised is the divine, eternal truth. We consider all those who believe him and his Word and follow him obediently to be worthy of his name as Christians. But all others, who say they believe in Christ but do not obey his words nor do what he taught and commanded, we say that they are anti-Christians, not Christians. By this we mean the papal church in which all things against Christ are done, yet they falsely claim to belong to Christ. They want to make Christ a cover for their

---

4   Ex 20.
5   Mt 4.
6   Gal 5; Jn 5.

prostitution.[7] All truth is testified by two or three witnesses.

In this is included Christian and truthful baptism of water.[8] Christ himself was baptized and afterwards baptized others.[9] It is also written clearly in his last farewell command.[10] We practice it as the dear apostle did.[11] Here the pope's infant baptism is negated, the first and greatest abomination in the eyes of the Lord, for by this every man beautifies his gruesome burdens and takes to himself, through this supposed baptism, the precious name of Christ—whether he is a whoremonger, thief, or murderer. A Christian should have the name of Christ, not of baptism. We want to hold to this through God's help, for we have already been buried with Christ through baptism.[12]

We confess to this Jesus Christ, our beloved Lord, and we testify that as soon as he gave the command of the Father, of true righteousness, and instituted baptism he was persecuted, despised, betrayed by Judas, and cruelly tortured under the authority of Pontius Pilot, who condemned him to death (although unwillingly), and crucified. With his bitter death and red blood he won salvation for all those who believe in him and follow him faithfully; to the others his suffering becomes a testimony to eternal death. For whoever does not suffer with Christ will not inherit with him, as Holy Scripture testifies.[13] All Scripture tells us that Christ and all the prophets [promise] nothing but persecution, cross, suffering, distress, abandonment, denying oneself.[14]

After he preached his comforting Word to the imprisoned spirits, he rose from the dead undecayed in a clarified body. He showed himself to his beloved disciples and commanded them, as mentioned above. Then he ascended to heaven in his body; and as he ascended, in the same way will he return. He sits at the Father's right hand.[15] From there we await him, according to Scripture, that he will come in the clouds of heaven, as the lightning strikes, and thousands of angels with him.[16] Here Scripture tells us that Christ is sitting in heaven with the Father and is not in temples built by human hands; neither does he want to be tended with human hands.[17] That is why we plead and admonish you not to serve the idol of bread [in communion] but rather to root it out.

---

7   In witness: Mt 12, Jn 15, Rom 8.
8   Mt 3.
9   Jn 3, 4.
10   Mt 28; Mk 16.
11   Acts 2, 8, 19.
12   Col 2.
13   Rom 8; Mt 20; Jn 5.
14   Isa 26; 1Pet 3; Mt 5, 26.
15   Ps 110; Acts 7.
16   Mt 24; Mk 13; Acts 17, 21; Rev 19.
17   Acts 7, 17.

We believe in the Holy Spirit, that he is the comforter of all depressed and sad hearts, and that he is and will be sent from the Father by Christ Jesus to all believing chosen people as Christ promised.[18] Anyone who does not have this Holy Spirit is not a Christian; anyone who claims he has the Holy Spirit and Christ but does works of the flesh is a liar, as Paul tells us[19] and in many passages Christ tells us.[20]

We also believe and know that there is a holy Christian church and a godly Christian fellowship. This church is the body of Christ, of which he is the head and rules his whole body. This Christian church is holy, without stain. But if a disturbing member should be found in the body which can be improved in no other way, it is excluded from the church and treated as a heathen. Other punishment is not practiced in the Christian church, as Christ forbade it: The worldly princes and lords practice violence but you should not.[21] Neither did Christ want to rule a temporal kingdom,[22] but said "My kingdom is not of this world."[23]

Regarding governing authorities, we stand as Christ taught us: to give taxes, tithes, rent and labour to emperor, king or governor as long as it does not serve war or execution. Paul teaches the same in Romans 13, and St. Peter in 1 Peter 2. Here Peter says one should submit to human institutions; by this we understand how he acted himself.[24] But laws that are against God he forbids us to obey, just like Daniel, Shadrach, Meshach and Abednego, and others in the Old and New Testaments.[25] We believe immovably, through God's help, that the Christian church has the key to loose and to bind sin, as Christ himself gave her this authority.[26] In 1 Corinthians 5 Paul also used this authority. It is given to the Christian church, not the papal.

We also believe the truth that all flesh will be awakened on the great day of the Lord God, and will be brought to judgment.[27] There the Lord will separate the sheep to his right and the goats to his left. There will be one shepherd and one fold, but hell will be the fold of the goats.

We believe that after this temporal life and death there will be an eternal life in the kingdom of God, and also an eternal life in the fiery pit.[28]

Here you have a short account of the basis of our Christian faith. May

---

18   Jn 14, 15, 16.
19   Rom 8; Gal 5.
20   Jn 8; 1Jn 3, 4, 5.
21   Mt 20; Mk 10.
22   Jn 6.
23   Jn 18.
24   Acts 4.
25   2Mac 7.
26   Mt 16, 18; Jn 20.
27   Ezek 37; Dan 12; Mt 22.
28   Mt 25; Rev 14, 21.

God grant that it is a testimony to eternal joy and not to the destruction of your souls. The other points, such as the salvation of children, mission, swearing of oaths we will not discuss; because, for the sake of brevity, we do not consider it necessary and because we have already said enough to you previously.

We think we have proved the faith of our hearts sufficiently with two or three witnesses. If anyone finds it insufficient, we cannot give him faith for that comes from God alone. The reason for our writing, however, is that we are not capable of speaking to you, nor are you able to hear us. We ask you to receive it well and make your judgment without being annoyed. Consider carefully beforehand what you are doing, in the fear of God, for he is still a judge over you before whom you, as well as we, will have to appear and give account for the innocent blood that will not remain hidden. Truly, we do not wish to fall into the stream, but if you throw us in we will suffer it patiently as Christians. We commend ourselves to God. We wish and desire to hurt nobody, neither pope, bishop, monk nor priest, neither king nor Kaiser, not a single creature. Our conscience is pure and free; we have done no evil nor had revenge in our hearts. Therefore we will suffer joyfully and with great patience whatever God allows through you. We know you can do no more than that to us. If the righteous Joseph had granted the whore her treachery, he would have been protected by her; but since he remained righteous he was thrown into prison by her false testimony, but the Lord turned his bonds and suffering to great joy. Thus, even if the whore has falsely accused us with her lies and brought us into prison, we have the certain hope and do not doubt that God will free us in his right time and help us out of this misery into peace, as Christ himself has promised.[29] But we feel sorry for you that you are sinning so deeply against the blood of the saints. Oh, if you are Saul, we wish you the grace to be a Paul but it is a great concern because the Word of the cross of Christ is despicable to you, although to us it is the strength of God. You desire to follow Christ and would gladly go with him to heaven, but you do not want to taste the eagerness to suffer with him and descend to hell. Whoever will not eat bitter salt will also not taste the Easter lamb in all eternity.

We commend ourselves to the protection of the highest. May he help us drink the cup of suffering, Amen.

Written in our miserable imprisonment under the authority of Ferdinand in 1536.

[**Source:** Emmy Barth, "For the Sake of Divine Truth: The Legacy of Jeronimus Käls, Michael Seifensieder and Hans Oberecker," *Mennonite Quarterly Review* 81 (April 2007), 249–253.]

---

29   Jn 16.

The ruins of Falkenstein Castle. [*WikiCommons*]

Kasper Braitmichel (d. 1573)
"In Captivity at Falkenstein in 1539," ca. 1570

The raid of the Steinabrunn community was a traumatic event that produced a significant amount of literary attention in the form of letters, songs (There is a *"Falkenstein Lieder"* section in *Die Lieder der Hutterischen Brüder*), a confession, and a narrative account in the *Chronicle*.

All of the community's men were taken captive and imprisoned at the nearby Falkenstein Castle; later, about 90 of the ablest were marched to Trieste on the Adriatic Sea to serve on galley ships. Most of the men were able to escape and return to the community.

When God wished to increase his glory and the welfare of the believers, he put those who had joined together in his name to a rigorous trial, as gold is tried in the fire. This was to test what was in their hearts so that the steadfastness of their faith would be visible in them as God's children. At the same time the malice of the old serpent showed up in his false prophets, who beset the Roman king Ferdinand (in the same way that Satan beset Job), filling his ears with unjust accusations against the church of God. They goaded him on until he finally did as they wanted and dispatched his marshal from Vienna with the provost and some mounted attendants, who arrived without warning at Falkenstein. Taking a reckless mob

with them, they attacked the Christian community at Steinebrunn in the late evening of December 6, 1539. They locked all the men they could find in one room, the women and girls in another. They posted guards and made a terrifying uproar, plundering whatever they could.

Most of all they wanted to capture the elders and servants of the church, hoping to get large sums of money and goods from them, thus robbing the poor without a thought that God would requite it with heavy punishment. Although the people they were after were in the house, God in his providence saved those brothers from the wanton rabble.

Unwilling to leave even a little food for widows and orphans, they searched every corner but could find nothing, for God frustrated all their plans and turned their efforts into sheer folly. During this infamous raid, the sick, the children, and the expectant mothers were overwhelmed with terror and fear for their lives. The brothers and sisters who were locked up prepared themselves to sacrifice their lives for God and die by fire or the sword.

That same evening, in the midst of all the distress, several men arrived from the Philippites to find out on what basis the church community at Steinebrunn was living. They were among the 150 brothers captured and taken under secure guard to Falkenstein Castle. Among the captives were some who had not yet been baptized and others who had fallen away from the truth and were seeking repentance.

When they had all arrived at Falkenstein Castle, the brothers met outdoors with those who were not committed to the faith and asked them what they were going to do in this predicament. With great love they explained that if for the sake of the witness they would put their lives in Christ's hands in this time of suffering, regardless of any fear or need they might have to face, the brothers would consider them as fellow heirs of God's kingdom, in the certainty that God would be merciful to them. The brothers added that if with God's help anyone of them should regain his freedom and return to the community, then

the church had the authority from God to consider the personal situation of each according to the church order. In the meantime the brothers would let the elders at home know what they all desired and then inform them of the church's decision. All the men expressed their heartfelt agreement. They were full of joy and thankfulness over the proposal and received it as a gift from God's grace.

Straightaway a written account was sent to the church, and a letter soon came back saying that all the believers agreed: Since those who had not yet become members of the church according to divine order (for reasons valid in God's eyes) were now of one mind with the church and ready to witness to the truth, to suffer with the brothers, and to endanger their own lives, they should be joyfully given recognition as fellow believers.

When the church's decision was made known to them, they readily entrusted themselves to the Lord and proved patient in all distress, giving good testimony in front of many witnesses, just as other believers did.

Meanwhile King Ferdinand dispatched his marshal, several scholars and priests, as well as the executioner as their "high priest" and assistant. They used the Christmas days (a thing rarely done anywhere) to begin their malicious treatment of the captive witnesses for the truth. Some they questioned under torture regarding their basic beliefs and hopes and where they kept their treasures. The believers confessed unanimously that Christ the Saviour was their only hope and dearest treasure, in whom they had attained the Father's mercy.

Their tormentors questioned them about many other points, with the intention of teaching and converting them. They especially stressed the eucharist and exalted it, trying to get the prisoners to believe that the flesh and blood of Christ was present in it, that it was "our Lord God." The brothers answered that it was a dumb idol and that they had an entirely different conception of the Lord's Supper than the twisted one used by their adversaries to deceive the world. After hearing this and many other statements of faith, the royal emissaries returned to Vienna, and the brothers remained imprisoned in Falkenstein Castle.

In 1540 the royal marshal came to Falkenstein accompanied by a mounted attendant known as *Lang Hans* (Tall Hans) and the provost and other armed riders. They questioned the imprisoned brothers one by one. All who refused to agree with them and held firm to the truth were bound in pairs with iron fetters, their hands chained together.

When word got around that the prisoners were to be sent to the sea, many sisters in the faith came to Falkenstein Castle. Some of them were wives of the brothers, others were friends and relatives. They

knelt down together and prayed fervently to their Father, the most high God, for protection from all sin and evil on land or sea and for steadfast hearts that remain faithful to the truth until death.

After they had prayed, the marshal's attendant *Lang Hans* gave orders for everyone to make ready for departure. They took leave with many bitter tears, encouraging one another to hold firm to the Lord and to the truth. Each one commended the other to God's merciful protection, not knowing if any would ever see the other again on this earth. Let each one judge for himself what a hard struggle that was for husbands to be parted from their wives and for fathers to leave their little children behind. In truth, flesh and blood cannot do it, but God will seek out those who cause such great distress and punish them severely.

The leave-taking was such a pitiful sight that the royal marshal and some of his men were unable to hold back their tears. When things were ready and the escort had arrived, the believers were marched through the gate two by two, firmly trusting that God would protect them. Ninety set out after being imprisoned for six and a half weeks.

The sisters had to stay behind in the castle. They climbed on the wall and, heartbroken with grief, gazed after their brothers, to whom they were bound by divine love, until they could see them no longer. Then they were sent away from the castle to return home.

Those brothers who were not taken to the sea because they were weak or sick or too young were held in the castle. Several of the young boys were given into the possession of Austrian noblemen, but nearly all of them returned to the church. The other brothers remained in Falkenstein Castle until God in his mercy led them out.

On that occasion the lord, Hans Fünfkirchen, vowed he would place an inscription above the castle gate, stating that since it was built, there had never been so many devout people in it as at that time, but it is likely that he forgot to do this. In spite of himself he had had to witness to the truth.

This great distress came upon the faithful because they testified against pope and priests, against their sinful lives and the whole idolatrous system, saying that God will punish them severely for their abominations and let them die in their sins. That is why King Ferdinand had empowered the bloodthirsty mob of priests to do as they pleased with the prisoners. The priests were quick in deciding that the brothers deserved to die, that they could not be tolerated on land but should be sent to sea to waste away in great suffering as galley slaves. They were to be handed over to the high admiral Andrea Doria for use in his fleet of warships that fought the Turks and other enemies.[1] Even as the brothers were being violently carried off and imprisoned, they warned the king's agents that they would not row a stroke to aid war and pillage. Whether on land or at sea, they refused to take part in evil and to sin against God because their hearts rejected all sin. God in his invincible power would protect them at sea as on the land and keep them in his grace.

Nevertheless the king's men received strict instructions that the prisoners be marched under guard from one courthouse to the next. So these witnesses to the truth were brought before the magistrates in towns and villages, where they had to suffer much hostility and hardship. But God always gives means of grace to his people. The brothers were able to pray to God every morning and evening without anyone stopping them. Any brother who was given words of solace or encouragement from God could speak without fear and so bring comfort to his brothers. The believers were deeply grateful for this special gift and mercy of God.

This among other things worked a change in people's attitude toward them in many places, with the result that they were regarded with sympathy instead of being taken for criminals as when they first arrived. As well as that, the soldiers who accom-

---

[1]   In 1528, Andrea Doria (1468–1560), the famous Genoese admiral, had placed himself and his fleet at the service of Emperor Charles V, using slaves as well as convicts on his galleys.

panied them frequently spoke on their behalf and encouraged them to witness to their faith in songs and other ways, instead of passing through the towns in silence.

In this manner the band of believers was driven like a flock of sheep through town and countryside to the sea at Trieste […].

All this time, the brothers endured hunger and great hardship; they were fed with the bread of fear and the waters of distress.

That was the way God chose to reveal his truth to peoples who were still in ignorance, to be heard like the sound of a mighty trumpet. God has always provided means of grace to draw men away from evil, as in this case. When the believers passed through the different places where strange languages were spoken and people had never heard the truth, they found some in southern Austria, Carniola, and northern Italy who were moved by their witness to seek it. A number of people embraced the truth and are serving God with sincere hearts to this day.

As for the ill-treatment the prisoners received in many places—how they were beaten and roughly handled, how they were tied to one another with ropes and chains—all this is unnecessary to describe. Everyone can imagine that what goes on in such places is far from pleasant. But although it was a dreadful experience, God always comforted the brothers in their hearts.

Even in times of greatest distress, God does not forget his own. He gave several of the prisoners inner promptings of hope and trust that God would show them a way to escape. They spoke of this together in the fear of God. Although they were determined to suffer and die for the truth rather than take part in wicked piracy, they had every reason to continue sighing and pleading that God might demonstrate his honour in them.

As they prayed, God showed them that they should agree among themselves how the strong were to take care of the weak and how one would help the other. Even though they had little food, they trusted that the Lord would provide for them so that they need not beg or search for bread. On the twelfth night in Trieste they all got free of their bonds. They walked out of the prison, and God showed them a place where within an hour they could all let themselves down from the city wall with ropes. The ropes that had bound them and by which they had been led into the prison now served for their escape. So whatever evil designs ungodly men have on the devout, God turns to good for his own people. Thanks to God's intervention they escaped from their enemies. With all the diligent watches the ungodly had posted on the city walls, God turned their precautions to folly: he showed the brothers a place right next to the sentry box on the wall. When all of them, sick and healthy, were over the wall, they knelt down to praise and thank him. The Lord also prepared the way for most of them to return to the church of the saints in Moravia, their hearts filled with joy and peace.

Twelve of them, however, were seized in the merciless pursuit that followed. They were handed over to Andrea Doria, the emperor's admiral for naval warfare, and taken to the galleys with the intention of using them at the oars. But the faithful were determined to risk their lives, to be flogged rather than to set their hands to rowing. We do not yet know exactly how each one met his end, but if they remained faithful to the Lord it is certain that they did not have many good days left. The brothers whom God had delivered returned to the church in Moravia on the fourth Sunday of Lent in 1540. They were welcomed with great joy and thanksgiving as a gift from God.

[**SOURCE:** *The Chronicle of the Hutterian Brethren*, Volume 1. Translated and edited by the Hutterian Brethren. (Ulster Park: Plough Publishing House, 1987), 187–196. Used by permission.]

Falkenstein Song: "*O Gott Vater vom Himmelreich / O Father God from Heaven's Realm*," 1539

The Falkenstein episode lived large in the Hutterite imagination and resulted in a flurry of literary activity, including songs. The "Falkenstein song" has traditionally been considered a joint effort by the Hutterite prisoners at Falkenstein, with 23 brothers contributed one or more stanzas. Composing hymns in prison is a practice we encounter several times in Hutterite history.

A beautiful song, composed by several imprisoned brothers in Falkenstein Castle

1. OSWALT FALGER.

O Gott Vater vom Himmelreich,
Ich tu dich fleisig bitten,
hilf deinen Kindern allgeleich
Nach väterlichen Sitten.
Steh ihnen bei, daß sie dich frei
Vor dieser Welt bekennen,
Die dich verspott't, spricht: Wo ist Gott?
Sie will dich nit erkennen.

1. OSWALT FALGER.

O God, Father from heaven's realm,
I earnestly pray to you,
help your children all
according to your paternal ways.
Stand by them, so that they freely
confess you before this world,
which mocks you, saying: "Where is God?"
It refuses to acknowledge you.

2. STOFFEL ASCHBERGER.

Ich bitt dich, lieber Vater mein,
Du wollest mich erretten,
In aller Angst jetzt bei mir sein
Wider die mich wollen töten!
Sie dringen auf mich ganz grimmiglich,
Tun mir ein' Gruben machen;
Aber du bist zu aller Frist
Mein Hauptmann, Schild und Waffen.

2. STOFFEL ASCHBERGER.

I ask you, my dear Father,
please rescue me;
be with me now in all distress
against those who seek to kill me!!
They press upon me fiercely,
digging a pit for me;
but you are at all times
my captain, shield, and weapon.

3. JOBST VON FILACH.

Stant auf, o lieber Herre Gott,
Und tu dein' Hand erheben!

3. JOBST VON FILACH.

Arise, O dear Lord God,
and lift up your hand!

187

O Gott Vater vom Himmelreich

Erzürn' dich nicht, o frommer Christ
Strassburg, 1530

O Gott Va - ter vom Him - mel- reich, ich
Ich bitt' dich lie - ber Va - ter mein, du
Steh' auf, o lie - ber Her - re Gott, und

tu dich flei - ßig bit - ten,
wol - let mich er - ret - ten,
tu dein Hand er - he - ben.

hilf dei - nen Kin - dern all - ge - leich nach
in al - ler Angst jetzt bei mir sein wi -
Ver - giss uns nicht zur Zeit der Not, schau

vä - ter - lich - en Sit - ten.
der die mich woll'n tö - ten!
dei - ner Ar - men Le - ben.

Steh' ihn - en bei, dass sie dich
Sie dring - en mich ganz grim - mig -
Die Got - lo - sen, die dich läs -

frei vor die - ser Welt be - ken - nen,
lich, tun mir ein Gru - ben mach - en,
tern, sprech - en in ih - ren Her - zen,

die dich ver - spott't, spricht: "Wo ist Gott?" Sie
a - ber du bist zu al - ler Frist, mein
dass du nicht siehst, was uns ge- schieht. Rett'

will dich nit er - ken - nen.
Haupt- mann und mein Wa - fen.
uns vor ew' - gen Schmer - zen.

Alexander Basnar,
*Von Trübsal, Schmerzen,
Elend groß: Die Falken-
steiner Lieder,* 44–45.
Used by permission.

Geketende weder-dopers in Oostenrijk nemen afscheid van hun gezinnen, 1540 / Austrian Anabaptists fastened in chains say farewell to their families, 1540, Jan Luyken, etching, 1685. [WikiCommons]

Vergiß unser nit zur Zeit der Not,
Schau deiner Armen Leben!
Die Gottlosen, die dich lästern,
Sprechen in ihren Herzen,
Du achtest nit, was uns geschieht.
Rett' uns vor ewigen Schmerzen!

10. KASPER BRAITMICHEL.

Christus hat uns aus seiner Gnad'
Sein Wort lassen verkünden.
Praise, Lob und Dank, Ehr' sei ihm g'sagt,
Rühmen zu aller Stunde!
Mit Wort und Tat hilf uns, o Gott,
Das Opfer dir zu bringen,
In Gerechtigkeit mit großer Freud'
Dich rühmen mit Lobsingen!

20. ANTHONY SCHUESTER.

Ich will den Herren rufen an
Mit Loben und mit Danken,
Daß er mir allweg woll' beistan
Und mich nit lassen wanken!
Er ist mein' Stärk', und ich sein Werk,
Mein Retter und mein Gotte,

Do not forget us in times of distress,
look upon the lives of your poor ones!
The godless, who blaspheme you,
utter in their hearts,
that you do not care what happens to us.
Rescue us from eternal pain!

10. KASPER BRAITMICHEL.

Christ has, out of his grace,
let us proclaim his Word.
Praise, honour, and thanks be unto him,
extoled at all times!
With word and deed, help us, O God,
to bring the offering to you,
in righteousness with great joy
to honour you with songs of praise!

20. ANTHONY SCHUESTER.

I will call upon the Lord
with praise and thanksgiving,
that he may always support me
and not let me falter!
He is my strength, and I am his work,
my saviour and my God,

Mein Hort, mein Schild, mein Helfer mild
In aller Angst und Note.

my refuge, my shield, my gentle helper
in all anxiety and trouble.

24. MATHES SCHUESTER.

Nun merkt, ihr lieben Brüder all',
Auf den ewigen Lohne,
Den wir nach diesem Jammertal
Beim Herrn werden hane!
Darnach will ich ganz ritterlich
Mit Herren Hilf' tun streben,
Nach seinem Will' ihm halten still,
Dieweil ich hab' das Leben.

24. MATHES SCHUESTER.

Now take heed, you beloved brothers all,
of the eternal reward
that we will receive from the Lord
after this vale of tears!
For it I will valiantly strive
with the Lord's help,
to peacefully follow his will
while I have life.

25.

Jetzund wir nun beschlossen han,
Miteinander zu sterben.
Gott' führ' uns auf der rechten Bahn,
Mit Jesu Christ zu erben!
Darumben wir befehlen dir,
O Gott, all deine Kinde,
Auf daß wir s' gleich in deinem Reich
Ewig in Freuden finden.

25.

Now that we have resolved
to die with eachother,
may God guide us on the right path,
to inherit with Jesus Christ!
Therefore, we entrust to you,
O God, all your children,
that we may find them
forever in joy within your kingdom.

[**SOURCE:** Prose translation by Kenny Wollmann from A.J.F. Zieglschmid, ed., *Liederbuch der Hutterischen Brüder* (MacGregor: Hutterian Brethren Book Centre, forthcoming).]

PETER RIEDEMANN (1506–1556)
[Double Honour] Letter from Prison to "Fellow Members in the Lord in Hesse, Swabia, and Moravia," 1540

Before Jakob Hutter became the main *Vorsteher* in 1533, there was significant turmoil around questions of leadership. It appears that from very early on, Hutterite leaders and their wives were treated differently than other members. They received privileges such as foods and drinks prepared by a special kitchen staff and ate separately from the rest of the people. Further, wives travelling with their husbands dressed in more fashionable "puffed sleeves." This was commonly defended by referring to 1 Tim 5:17, "You should count your servants worthy of double honour." Several people in the community resented these practices and complained that they violated the principle of equality. Others criticized the leaders for not standing by the people during the raid at Steinabrunn.

In 1540 Peter Riedemann addressed the issue of "double honour" in a letter he wrote while imprisoned at Wolkersdorf in Hesse. Several of the critics of the "double honour" policy, including Hermann [Schmid] and Hans Edelmaier, had been expelled from the community and had spread word about the inequality in the Hutterite community. The issue became serious enough that Riedemann felt a need to weigh in. He defends the practice of giving special treatment to leaders and his document played an important role in determining how Hutterites understood and practiced leadership.

Sixteenth-century Hutterites, like most Anabaptists, were anticlerical, which means they were very critical of the way the Catholic clergy conducted themselves, both in the luxurious lives they led and the way many neglected their office. Hutterites also emphasized equality within the church, against the strongly hierarchical structure of general society. It is thus somewhat surprising that Hutterites adopted the policy of double honour for their leaders.

To all in Hesse, Swabia, and Moravia who have found a common faith with us: my dear fellow members in the Lord. […]

From Peter, your brother and a prisoner of Christ as a witness to his name.

Dear brothers, I am not writing this to you as if you did not know it. You already know it well since you are children of the knowledge of God. I am writing it with the sole purpose of reviving your clear understanding in Christ so that you can share more diligently what you know and thus let your light shine out more and more. Then you will not let yourself be frightened off by opposition, grumbling, and slander from those who are falsely called brothers, but instead will let them spur you on to greater zeal, more love, wholehearted obedience, and reverence toward one another, most of all to your servants, through whom God grants his grace to you.

God is specifically telling you to do this, and because it is a pleasing service to him, the devil shrieks and rages against it all the more through those who serve him. He is trying to make you careless and suspicious of your servants so that you will dislike hearing the Word from them and the Word will bear no fruit in you. In this way the devil will be able to

scatter you and drag you into his kingdom.

At what point could he attack harder than here? What better way is there to demolish a house than to dig out and remove the pillars that hold it up? Now the servants are called pillars of the house of God. As Paul says, "They were recognized as pillars."[1] The devout Judith says, "You elders, on whom the lives of the people depend."[2] So he, the devil, seeks out the best place to attack and says, "A true shepherd lays down his life for the sheep; but when troubles come, your servants run away from you, so they are hirelings and not shepherds."[3] Furthermore: "They eat by themselves and of the best. They teach you community-of-goods but do not keep it themselves." With these and similar words the devil and his helpers try to deceive you and make you uneasy in your consciences and loath to do good. Woe to those who listen to them!

My dear children, I am not writing because I think you are negligent in this matter, for I know you yourselves are eager to do it. But to prevent any of you from being weakened by slander, I ask you, dear brothers, to consider God's severity to those people and his goodness to you, who have so far continued in what is good. Consider those who

---

1   Gal 2:9. All biblical references are absent in the original.
2   Judith 8:24.
3   Allusion to Jn 10:11–12. Riedemann is referring to criticisms directed against the leaders, for escaping "the wanton rabble" during the raid at Steinabrunn, while the women and children "were overwhelmed with terror and fear for their lives" and the brothers were led away to the Falkenstein castle (*Chronicle*, vol. 1, 188).

begrudged the servants what was given them by the church: is there a single one who has remained steadfast in the truth? Has God ever been pleased with a people who thought little of their servants instead of counting them worthy of the honour ordained for them by God? Haven't they all fallen into futility, and haven't some of them conformed to the world again? You who have held the servants in due respect have remained firm in the truth, and the Lord has been with you to this day. Why is that? It is because you have kept his ordinances and valued his gifts highly. [...]

Is it not true, dear brothers, that a man who opposes the Lord's order opposes the Lord himself? And the Lord's order is: "You should count your servants worthy of double honour because of their work."[4] Consider: Has the Lord ever given a task without appointing the wages so that the task can be fulfilled? If he has done this for other tasks, how much more for the task of preaching the Gospel? So Paul says, "If we have sown a spiritual crop for you, is it too much if we reap your material benefits?"[5] He says as well, "Who tends a flock without getting some of its milk?"[6] Do I say this from a human standpoint? Does not the Law say the same: "You shall not muzzle an ox that treads out the grain?"[7] Is it for oxen that God is concerned? Is it not said mainly for our sake? [...]

Paul shows in a clear and wonderful way that there is no validity in our opponents' interpretation. He says: "Do you not know that those who perform the temple service get their food from the temple, and those who serve at the altar get their food from the altar?"[8] So the Lord commanded that those who preach the Gospel deserve their living from the Gospel. Look into what Paul shows us here, dear brothers.

Did not God ordain the best of the sacrifice for the servants of the temple and altar, instead of letting them eat the same as those who brought the offering? All the fat was the Lord's, and after the Lord's portion the best was the priests'. The people took the rest to eat with their households. It was the same with the tithe and first fruits of their crops and flocks. This is the context for the Lord's words, "You shall not muzzle the ox that treads out the grain."[9] It means, "You shall not withhold or stint what is due to those who serve." These words state plainly that the servants have rights in temporal things, rights that must be heeded, and that they should enjoy the freedom of the Gospel. [...]

---

4   1 Tim 5:17.
5   1 Cor. 9:11.
6   1 Cor 9:7.
7   1 Tim 5:18 and Deut 25:4.
8   1 Cor 9:13.
9   1 Tim 5:18 and Deut 25:4.

From this, dear brothers, we see (if we are willing) that even if the servants themselves waive this freedom, you do not honour the church but dishonour it by accepting the situation, for that means you are neglecting the order and command of the Lord. Dear brothers, even if your servants are willing to give up this right, you ought not to let it happen, for it is a matter of your honour before God and his holy angels. I know well that your servants are willing to surrender not only what is due them but their very lives as well, for the sake of your salvation. […]

My dear brothers, I have written this to you because of the special love I bear you for the Lord's sake. I know that the dear brothers are afraid to broach this subject and would rather go without than say anything—in case someone should imagine they are self-seeking. Since I am away from you, a prisoner for the Lord, not knowing if I will ever see you again in this life or you me, no one can imagine I am writing this for my own sake or for any fleshly reason. I only want to carry out my service for you and show you the fitting way. […]

The reason I felt compelled to write this to you, dear brothers, was the amount of gossip among our enemies. They bring up all kinds of unjustifiable slander against the truth and use this on the simple-minded to confuse their consciences. Many try to defend their folly with this, which then leads to quarrels and heated words. The Lord rejects such foolishness and brings it to light. Be warned, then, and do not imitate their folly of heart lest you come to harm with them. My only concern is for you, since I see how other churches, on losing their zeal, have perished or been corrupted. If you lose your eagerness to serve and grow indifferent, then Satan, having won you over on this point, will soon attack you harder in another and will not give up until he has done the same to you as to others. Anyone who neglects or violates the Lord's command in one particular will soon be unfaithful altogether. […]

I wrote this letter also because I could not resist Kaspar's persistent urging that I do so. He says it is our duty as servants to step into the breach wherever division threatens and restore harmony by teaching what God says. Nowhere else is there more division, grumbling, ill will, and slander than in connection with that teaching, which is God's order and command. […]

May my heart, soul, and spirit be one with you always and the Spirit of Christ be with us all eternally. Amen.

Written from prison at Wolkersdorf in Hesse.

[**Source:** *The Chronicle of the Hutterian Brethren*, Volume 1. Translated and edited by the Hutterian Brethren. (Ulster Park: Plough Publishing House, 1987), 198–209. Used by permission.]

PETER RIEDEMANN (1506–1556)
Rechenschafft unserer Religion, Leer und Glaubens / An Account of our Religion, Teaching, and Faith, 1540–41

Peter Riedemann's *Rechenschaft*, written between 1539–1542 while he was imprisoned at Marburg and Wolkersdorf in Hesse, was addressed to Lutheran Landgrave Philip of Hesse. Philip was an unusually tolerant ruler and preferred the strategy of persuasion instead of executing heretics in his territories. The *Confession* was intended to clarify the principles of Hutterite faith and life to Philip and other rulers.

Riedemann makes the case that the Hutterite church is neither heretical nor sectarian, but based solidly on the traditional teachings of the Church, including Scripture and the Apostles' and Nicene Creeds. He rejects participation in warfare, and the union of church and state. He argues for the importance of community-of-goods (*Gütergemeinschaft*) by referring to the original design of Creation, as well as the witnesses of the Trinity and the apostolic church. The document has over 2000 biblical references, which means Riedemann likely had access to a Bible in prison. His frequent debates with Lutheran theologians at Marburg likely helped him refine his thinking.

The Hutterite church accepted the *Rechenschaft* early on as the definitive statement of their beliefs: When Ferdinand demanded the lords expel the Hutterites from their lands in 1545 they presented the first edition to the Diet of the Moravian Estates, drawing special attention to the sections concerned with obedience and submission to temporal authority. At the same time, they made it clear that in matters of conscience they would obey God rather than men. For example, they would not pay taxes that would be used for war or for executions.

The *Rechenschaft* is one of only a handful of books that was printed by 16th century Hutterites, and continues to be the official confession of contemporary Hutterites.

We Confess God

First, we confess that there is one God, who has being in himself and through himself, and who has neither beginning nor end. He possesses all power in heaven, on earth, and in the abyss. For this reason the word God is fitting and due to him alone. Although there are others called "gods," that is, "the mighty ones,"[1] there is but one God and mighty Power over them all. God is so much greater than all other powers, and there is no power except that which proceeds from him, or is bestowed or given by him. So great is God's power that he has brought into being and given shape to everything that exists.[2] Even today, all things owe their existence to God. As they have come into being through him, so they also have their end in him. Thus, all other gods or mighty powers ought truly to be ashamed and terrified before him, tremble and bow down, and honour him alone. His hand is strong. He shatters and creates again, humbles and exalts, kills and brings to life whom he will.[3] Therefore, he alone is rightly named God and given hon-

our. He himself says, "Hear, O Israel, the Lord your God is one."[4] Again he says, "I am the Lord your God,[5] and beside me there is no other."[6] Thus we acknowledge one God.

Our one great God, because he is so great, is in all places at once, and he fills everything in heaven and on earth with his glory.[7] This divine glory, unlimited power, and Godhead may be recognized in what he has created.[8] When the day dawns, which is a work of his hands, it gives light to every place. Air fills and pervades the whole Creation and is in all places at once.[9] Even so, and still more, the Creator shows himself faithfully and well in everything he has made, in each thing according to its nature. Therefore, this one, eternal, almighty God is the one, eternal, and unchanging truth, which has being in itself and remains eternally unchanged.[10] This truth pours itself into believing souls. It transforms us[11] so that we may live by it, and so our words and deeds may testify to the truth within us.[12]

---

1   1Cor 8:5.
2   Gen 1:1–2.
3   Deut 32:39.
4   Deut 6:4.
5   Deut 4:35.
6   Isa 43:11.
7   Ps 33:6–7; Isa 6:3.
8   Rom 1:20.
9   Gen 1:1–10.
10   Jn 14:1–14.
11   Ecc 7:7.
12   2Jn 1:4–6.

We Confess that Christ is Lord

We know that no one can call Jesus Lord except through the Holy Spirit.[13] We also know that all those who confess him in truth to be Lord must be children of his Spirit, that is, must have his Spirit. Since we experience his grace, which has been given us by God through him, we also confess him to be Lord. He is truly Lord because all power is given him by the Father, not only in heaven, but also on earth and under the earth.[14] For this reason all unclean spirits fear him and tremble in his presence.[15] He has overcome them, bound them, and taken away their power. Christ has delivered us, their prey, who were held captive in death, and set us free.[16]

No one may truthfully ascribe such glory and honour to Christ unless he has experienced this victory in himself. This means that Christ has overcome the devil in him too, has torn away his snare (his sin), set him free, and reconciled him with God.[17] Whoever confesses Christ on a different basis does not speak the truth but either labours under a delusion, pretends to have faith, or speaks from hearsay. They do not confess Christ as Lord.[18]

In the text mentioned above, Paul said that no one may call Christ "Lord" except through the Holy Spirit. The person in whom Christ is to become victorious must wholeheartedly surrender himself to Christ. That person must stand firm and allow Christ's work to be done in him. However, when this does not happen, Christ does not work in a person, and such a person remains in sin forever.

What the Church Is

The church of Christ is a foundation and a basis of truth. It is a lamp, a star of light, and a lantern of righteousness,[19] in which the light of grace is held up to the whole world,[20] so that its darkness, unbelief, and blindness may be illuminated, and people may learn to see and know the way of life.[21] So we see that the church of Christ is, in the first place, like a lantern completely filled with light, the light of Christ, which is then shed abroad to others.[22]

As the lantern of Christ has been made bright and clear by the light of the knowledge of God, so its

---

13   1Cor 12:3.
14   Mt 28:18.
15   Heb 2:12–16.
16   Mk 5:1–13.
17   1Jn 2:1–6.
18   1Cor 12:3.
19   1Tim 3:14–16.
20   Mt 5:13–20.
21   Eph 3:14–21.
22   Jn 5:14–15.

radiance shines out into the distance to give light to those who still walk in darkness.[23] Christ himself commanded this when he said, "Let your light shine before others, that they may see your good works, and praise God, the Father in heaven."[24] Now this can take place only through the strength of the Spirit of Christ working within us.

Just as a light, in accordance with its own nature, sends out a beam to give light to people, so also the divine light, wherever it has been lit in a person, sends forth its divine ray according to its nature.[25] The nature of this light, however, is genuine divine righteousness, holiness, and truth. It sheds its light abroad more brightly and clearly than the sun to enlighten all people.[26]

The church of Christ is a pillar and foundation of truth and continues to be that.[27] Truth itself is expressed, confirmed, and put into action in the church by the Holy Spirit. Thus, whoever endures and submits to the working of the Spirit of Christ, is a member of this church.[28] Whoever does not want this and allows sin to rule over them, does not belong to the church.[29]

Community of Goods

All believers have fellowship in holy things, that is, in God.[30] He has given them all things in his Son, Christ Jesus.[31] Just as Christ has nothing for himself, since all he has is for us, so too, no members of Christ's body should possess any gift for themselves or for their own sake. Instead, all should be consecrated for the whole body, for all the members.[32] This is so because Christ also did not bring his gifts for one individual or the other, but for everyone, for the whole body. Community of goods applies to both spiritual and material gifts. All of God's gifts, not only the spiritual but also the temporal, have been given so that they not be kept but be shared with each other. Therefore, the fellowship of believers should be visible not only in spiritual but also in temporal things.[33] Paul says one person should not have an abundance while another suffers want; instead, there should be equality.[34] This he shows by pointing to the law about manna. According to that rule, the one who

---

23   Jn 22:31–32; Jn 8:9–21; Mk 4:14–25.
24   Mt 5:14–16.
25   Jn 11:33–36.
26   Eph 3:14–21.
27   1Tim 3:14–16.
28   Rom 8:6–14.
29   1Jn 3:1–6; Ps 1:4–6.
30   1Jn 1:1–3.
31   Rom 1:16–17.
32   1Cor 12:12–27; Phil 2:1–8.
33   Acts 4:32–37; Acts 2:42–47.
34   2Cor 8:7–15.

gathered much had nothing extra, and the one who gathered little had no lack, since each was given the amount needed.[35]

Furthermore, the Creation still testifies today that at the beginning God ordained that people should own nothing individually but should have all things in common with each other.[36] However, by taking what they should have left, and by leaving what they should have taken,[37] people have gained possession of things and have become more accustomed to accumulating things and hardened in doing so. Through such appropriating and collecting of created things, people have been led so far from God that they have forgotten the Creator.[38]

They have even raised up and honoured as gods the created things which had been made subject to them.[39] That is still the case for those who depart from God's order and forsake what God has ordained. Now as has been said, however, created things which are too high for people to grasp and collect, such as the sun, the whole course of the heavens, day, air, and so forth, show that not only they, but also all other created things, were made common for all people.[40] Because they are too great to be brought under human control, they have remained common, and humans have not possessed them.

Otherwise, since people had become so evil through wrongful acquisitions, they would also have wrongfully taken possession of such things and made them their own.[41] […]

The more a person is attached to property and claims ownership of things, the further away he is from the fellowship of Christ and from being in the image of God.[42]

For this reason, when the church came into being, the Holy Spirit re-established such community in a wonderful way. "No one said any of the things they possessed were their own, but they had all things in common."[43] This admonition by the Spirit is true for us even today. In the words of Paul, "Let each one look not to your own interests but to the interests of others." In other words, "Let each one look not to what benefits yourself, but to what benefits many."[44] Where this is not the case, it is a blemish upon the church that should truly be corrected. Someone may say that this only applies to

---

35   Ex 16:16–18.
36   Gen 1:26–29.
37   Gen 3:2–12.
38   Rom 1:18–25.
39   Ecc 13:1–3; 15:14–19.
40   Gen 1:25–31.
41   Rom 5:12–14; Gen 3:2–6.
42   Gen. 1:25–27.
43   Acts 4:32–37; Acts 2:44–45.
44   Phil 2:2–4.

what took place in Jerusalem and therefore does not apply today. In reply, we say that even if it did only happen in Jerusalem,[45] it does not follow that it should not happen now. The apostles and the churches were not at fault, but the opportunity, the right means, and the right time were lacking. [...]

Warfare

Christ, the Prince of Peace, has prepared a kingdom for himself, namely, the church, and has won this kingdom by shedding his own blood. Therefore, all worldly warfare in this kingdom has come to an end. This is what was promised through the prophets: "The law will go out from Zion, the Word of the Lord from Jerusalem. He will judge between the nations and will settle disputes for many peoples. They will beat their swords into ploughshares and their spears into grape knives, pruning hooks, and scythes. From that time on, nation will not take up sword against nation, nor will they train for war any more."[46]

Therefore, Christians should not take part in war, nor should they use force for purposes of vengeance. Paul exhorts us not to avenge ourselves but to leave retribution to the Lord, who says, "Vengeance is mine; I will repay."[47] Since vengeance now belongs to God and not to us, it ought to be left to him and not be practiced by us. Since we are Christ's disciples, our lives should be examples of his nature. Jesus could have repaid evil with evil, but he did not.[48] He could, indeed, have protected himself against his enemies by striking down with a single word all who wanted to seize him.[49] But he did not, nor would he permit others to do so. He said to Peter, "Put your sword in its place."[50] This shows how our King, with a powerful army, sets out against his enemies, how he defeats them, and how he exercises vengeance! He restores Malchus's ear that had been struck off.[51] Jesus also says, "Whoever wants to be my disciple, let him take up his cross and follow me."[52] Christ wants us to act as he did. Therefore, he commands us in these words: "It was said to the people of old, 'An eye for an eye, and a tooth for a tooth.' But I say that you should not resist evil. If someone strikes you on your right cheek, turn and offer him the other one."[53] That makes it clear that you ought neither to avenge yourself nor go to war. Instead, as the prophet says, offer your back to those who strike and your cheeks to those who tear at

---

45   Acts 4:32–37; Acts 2:38–45.
46   Mic 4:1–4; Isa 2:1–4.
47   Heb 10:30; Rom 12:14–21; Deut 32:35.
48   1 Pet 2:19–23.
49   Jn 18:1.
50   Jn 18:10–11; Mt 26:51–54.
51   Lk 22:47–53.
52   Mk 8:34–35; Mt 16:24–25.
53   Mt 5:38–48.

the beard.[54] That means we should suffer with patience and wait upon God, who is just. He will requite the evil.[55] [...]

Taxes

Since the government and its authority have been ordained and commanded by God, the payment of taxes to the government is also ordained and commanded. As Paul says, "You must also pay tribute."[56] For this reason we willingly pay interest, taxes, tribute, or whatever it may be called, and do not oppose such payments in any way, for we have learned this from our Master, Christ. He not only paid it himself,[57] but he also commanded others to do so, saying, "Give to Caesar what is Caesar's, and to God what is God's."[58] Therefore, we, as his disciples, do our best to keep this command, and we do not oppose the government in this matter.

However, for taxes that are demanded for the specific purpose of war, executions, and bloodshed, we give nothing, not out of disrespect or obstinacy but in the fear of God. We thus do not partake in other people's sins.[59] One might say, "You ought to pay tribute where tribute is due, and you do wrong to refuse it."[60] We reply, "In no way do we refuse to pay tribute where and how it is due." God, as said above, has decreed that the government should receive taxes, which they have to collect yearly,[61] and we do not refuse to pay these. [...]

Buying and Selling

We allow none of our members to be traders or merchants, since this is a sinful business. The wise teacher says, "It is almost impossible for a merchant or tradesman to keep free from sin."[62] "As a nail is driven firmly into a fissure between stones, so is sin wedged between buying and selling."[63] Therefore, we allow no one to buy in order to resell, as merchants and tradesmen do. But when we buy what is necessary for the needs of our house or craft, and then use the materials and sell what is made—that is in order and is no sin.

What is wrong, however, is to buy an article and sell it for a profit in the same condition as one bought it.[64] This makes the article more expensive for the poor; it is stealing bread

---

54   Isa 50:6.
55   Joel 3:1–2; Deut 32:35–36.
56   I Sam 8:10–22; I Pet 2:13–17; Rom 13:1–7.
57   Mt 17:24–27.
58   Lk 20:20–25; Mk 12:13–17; Mt 22:15–21.
59   I Tim 5:22.
60   Rom 13:7.
61   I Sam 8:7–18.
62   Sir 26:29.
63   Sir 27:1–2.
64   Sir 26:29; 27:2.

from their mouths and forcing them to become nothing but slaves to the rich. Paul says, "Let the thief give up stealing."[65] Some may argue that the poor can also benefit if one takes commodities from one country to the other. Such people use poverty as a pretext while seeking their own profit first, and think only of the poor as those who have an occasional penny in their purse. Therefore, we do not permit our people to trade but say with Paul that they should labour, working with their hands at honest work, that they may have something to give to the one who is in need.[66]

Church Discipline

Paul says, "Put away the evil that is among you."[67] Therefore, in the fear of God we watch over one another, since we should protect and keep each other from all wrongdoing and from such evils as deserve exclusion. That is why we admonish one another, warning and rebuking each other persistently. Should anyone disregard or not accept the rebuke, the matter is brought before the church. If someone will not listen to the church, that person is then excluded and banned.[68]

A different method is used for major sins. Paul says, "If anyone who is called a brother is sexually immoral or covetous, or if he is an idolater, a slanderer, a drunkard, or a swindler, you must not even eat with him."[69] Such a person is separated from the church without admonition, since the judgment of Paul is already spoken. When a person is banned, we have no fellowship with him and nothing to do with him, so that he may become ashamed.[70] Yet the excluded person is called to repentance, in the hope that the sinner will be moved to return all the more quickly to God.[71] If that does not happen, the church remains pure and is innocent of his sin. It has no guilt and has earned no rebuke from God.[72] In all cases, however, a distinction is made. Whoever sins wilfully should be rebuked according to the weight of that sin, and the more wilful the sin, the sharper the discipline. If, however, one does not sin wilfully or maliciously but through weakness of the flesh, that person is disciplined without being completely separated from the church or excluded from all fellowship. Such a member is not, however, permitted to give or accept the Lord's greeting[73] of peace.[74] In this

---

65 Eph 4:28.
66 Eph 4:28.
67 1Cor 5:13.
68 Mt 18:15–17.
69 1Cor 5:11.
70 2Thes 3:14–15.
71 2Cor 7:8–11.
72 Josh 7:1–5.
73 Jn 20:19; Lk 24:36.
74 Mt 10:13.

way the erring member will humble oneself before God for the sin, and afterward guard all the more carefully against it.

[**Source:** Peter Riedemann, *Peter Riedemann's Hutterite Confession of Faith*, trans. and ed. John J. Friesen (Waterloo: Herald Press, 1999; Walden: Plough Publishing, 2019), 59–60; 66–67; 77–78; 119–121; 134–136; 149; 152–153. Used by permission.]

[PETER RIEDEMANN] (1506–1556)
Erklerung des Euangelisten Lucaum / Paraphrase on the Gospel of Luke, ca. late 1540s–1556

Early Anabaptists, very broadly speaking, can be divided into 'spiritualist' and 'biblicist' camps. For the spiritualists, the meaning of Scripture was 'spiritual' and could only be illuminated by 'inner' divine revelation. Spiritualists often favoured allegorical interpretations whereby biblical images or events are seen as representing spiritual realities.

For the biblicists, the meaning of Scripture was plain and clear and was to be found in the literal words of Scripture. This interpretative approach was central to the debates over infant baptism in Zürich. For the radicals, Scripture's lack of a clear command to baptize infants was enough to make them claim that the practice was unbiblical.

Hutterites of the sixteenth century placed great emphasis on reading the Bible; it was studied carefully, and there was an emphasis on making it accessible to all members. In contrast to a very literal approach, many early Hutterite writings tended to favour an allegorical approach to interpretation. Traditional Hutterite homilies (from the 17th century) frequently draw out the spiritual meaning of all sorts of biblical characters, events, images, or objects. For example, the traditional Easter homily on the Passover ritual goes to great lengths to spiritualize the different aspects of the Passover lamb.

Peter Riedemann's paraphrases of the Gospels, written during the final years of his life, are another striking example of allegorizing the biblical text, although his interpretations are more unusual. Riedemann equates certain biblical words and phrases (often based on the etymology or meaning of the name or word) with a specific meaning in his own Hutterite context. He is especially concerned with demonstrating the authority of the office of the Servant of the Word, and his interpretations often serve to bolster hierarchies and encourage submission to leadership. Very likely, only ministers had access to these esoteric writings. In writing his paraphrases, Riedemann was drawing on a tradition popularized by Erasmus of Rotterdam. Thus far, Riedemann's paraphrases have not attracted much scholarly attention.

Some of the allegorical interpretations Riedemann makes include:

- Males represent various types of teachers or ministers, i.e., servants of the Word;
- Females represent communities of believers;
- Marriage represents the relationship between a servant and a congregation;
- Parenthood represents making converts and the service of the Word;
- Nations, places, landscapes, and buildings represent various types of congregations;
- Angels represent itinerant servants;
- Devil and demons stand for evil teachers who seduce the faithful;
- Diseases stand for various types of sins;
- Healing represents forgiveness;
- Death stands for unbelief or mortal sin; life for faith and righteousness;
- Lakes, rivers, and the sea represent tribulation.[1]

In the text below, the equivalents from the biblical passage are inserted into Riedemann's paraphrase using square brackets. This indicates the allegorical interpretation Riedemann is making; for example, in the first verse, Riedemann equates "Herod" from Luke 1:5 with "the fiery dragon."[2]

An Explanation of Luke the Evangelist [1:5–8]

5ªAt the time of Herod, the King of Judea, there was a priest named Zechariah of the order of Abijah.[3]

At the time when *the fiery dragon* [**Herod**] intends to *take over the reign* [**King**] of *those who want to be considered confessors of God* [**Judea, i.e., Jews**], some are also found, especially amongst among *those who are appointed to God's service, and who are ordained by God* [**priest**] according to the *lineage and rule* [**order**] of the *Father of the Lord, or the will of the Lord* [**Abijah**], *whose name is from the Lord, who helps the Lord, or who remembers the Lord* [**Zechariah**].

---

1   Martin Rothkegel, "Learned in the School of David: Peter Riedemann's Paraphrases of the Gospels." In *Commoners and Community. Essays in Honour of Werner O. Packull*, edited by Arnold Snyder. Kitchener: Pandora Press, 2002: 233–55.
2   Cf. Rev 12.
3   The biblical passages are taken from the *Froschauer Bibel* and translated accordingly. Verse numbers were added based on modern translations.

⁵ᵇHis wife was from the daughters of Aaron, and her name was Elizabeth.

And the *community that is entrusted to them* [**wife**], also derives from the *community established by the Word* [**from the daughters**], *the strong mountain, or the mountain of strength* [**Aaron**], and is now called *the fullness of my God* [**Elizabeth**].

⁶They were both righteous before God and obeyed all the commandments and statutes of the Lord without fault.

Together, at the same time, both the servants and the community *enter into the piety and righteousness that is acceptable before God*[4] [**righteous before God**] to please him, and to walk diligently in all the *commandments, customs, and traditions* [**commandments and statutes**] of the *sovereign and ruler of all things* [**Lord without fault**], so that they may appear blameless to all.

⁷They had no children, because Elizabeth was barren, and they were both very old.

And although they were loyal in their righteousness, *no one was drawn in by them or born by the Word of grace, in which the inheritance of the children of God* [**They had no children**] is established, for although *the community, which is called the fullness of my God, has been lavished and supplied with every good thing by the promise* [**Elizabeth**], it has nevertheless been *humbled by God until a certain time, so that glorious things may break forth in due time and the power of God may be revealed in it* [**barren**]. And yet both the servants and the community have been *well sustained in the promised grace according to the expectation* [**very old**], and have laboured together many years to draw others in, but without success. Thus all hope of any improvement among humans is completely lost.

⁸And it came to pass that while he was performing the priest's office before God according to his order, following the custom of the priesthood, that it was his lot to burn incense.

In the same way it happened that *the servants carried out their duties before God* [**performing the priest's office before God**], faithfully performing them *at the time appointed and prescribed by God* [**according to his order**], that is, at the time when divine salvation begins to break in. For according to *the custom and precept of the office of divine service* [**custom of the priest-**

---

4   Cf. Rom 1:17.

hood], divine inspiration pertains to and prepares those who are to be *devoted to prayer and offer it to God especially on behalf of the entire community* [**burn incense**]. […]

[**Source:** Translated by Kenny Wollmann from [Peter Riedemann], *Erklerung des Euangelisten Lucaum*, Ms II 100, National Library of Romania (Batthyaneum Branch), Alba Iulia, Romania.]

Offrus Sebold (n.a.)
"Gottes Gnad' und Fried' allezeit / God's Grace and Peace Forevermore," ca. 1560–70s

Like other Protestant Reformers, the Hutterites produced many ballads, songs, and hymns. These songs remember and recount important events in Hutterite history such as persecution or martyrdom. For example, the song, "*O Gott Vater vom Himmelreich*," (see Falkenstein Song, 187) tells the story of the ninety Hutterites captured at Falkenstein. The songs don't merely recount history, but also function as prayers, interpret events in light of Scripture, and offer encouragement.

Around 385 such hymns are preserved in Hutterite manuscripts from the 16th and 17th centuries. It wasn't until the 20th century, however, that they were collected by Dariusleut elder, Elias Walter, in *Die Lieder der Hutterischen Brüder*.

The hymn below by Offrus Sebold contains a hidden message in the form of an acrostic using the first word of each stanza. These acrostics are common in Hutterite songs—particularly those written by prisoners—and can reveal authorship or encode some other message. Some songs would have been composed in prison and sung to fellow prisoners in adjoining cells. The following quotation from the imprisoned schoolteacher Jeronimus Käls (d. 1536) reveals important details about their context and how the songs functioned:

> [...] But praise and honour be to God, I rejoice with all my heart when I hear you singing in the Lord—especially you, my dear brother Michael. When you sing in the evening I can almost understand every word if I listen carefully and you are sitting right by the window. Please, my dear cherished brother, wake this sleepyhead [*mich schleffrigen*] more often with your songs in the Lord Jesus Christ.

> Often when I woke first because of Hans, I would begin to sing and then both of you sang together as well; I eagerly listened for each of you because it is a delight for me to hear the lines [*Rayen*] about Jerusalem sung, dear brothers, especially because it bothers Satan so

much. This is a sure sign that it is pleasing to God. They think they have prevented us from talking so we cannot comfort each other, but let us cry out until our throats crack [*last uns schreien, das uns der halss kracht*]!

I sang two songs that I badly wanted to give you, but the devil is more diligent than I ever imagined [*gmaint*]. I sang it in the Lord, and not otherwise, for when the godless begin to blaspheme and taunt [*lestern und zue schwätzen*] I begin to compose songs [*tichten*] as if I'm deaf, so that I don't hear their godless sneers. May the Lord teach you to sing his song.[1]

Three of Käls' songs are included in *Die Lieder der Hutterischen Brüder*.

Part of the significance of these songs is that they are traditionally thought to have been penned by Anabaptist forerunners or Hutterite martyrs such as Felix Manz, Peter Riedemann, Peter Walpot, and others. Many of the hymns are set to a limited number of melodies where the fit between music and words is frequently awkward. The hymns can also be very lengthy, some running over one hundred verses!

These songs or ballads might be compared to ancient epic poetry which tell of great deeds of heroes of the past and play an important role in the historical memory of a community. In a similar way, these hymns remember the deeds of those powerless heroes—the martyrs—and preserve their witness in the memory of the community.

**The second song composed
by our dear brother Offrus Sebold.**

1.

GOTTES *Gnad' und Fried' allezeit
tu sich in dir vermehren;
des Vaters Lieb' und wahre Freud'
durch Christum, unsern Herren,
der alle Ding wohl geordnet hat
nach sein' göttlichen Willen,
der brauch' dich selbst nach seinem Rat,
sein Werk durch dich zu erfüllen!*

2.

GEIST, *Kraft, Weisheit, christlichen Leben,
dich selbst auch überwinden!
Der Herr vermehr' in dir sein' Segen,
zu Trost all' seinen Kindern,*

1.

GOD'S grace and peace forevermore,
may they within you grow;
the Father's love and true joy,
through Christ, our Lord,
who has ordered all things well
according to his divine will!
May he use you according to his counsel,
his work through you to fulfil!

2.

SPIRIT, strength, wisdom, Christ-like life,
Self-master yourself as well!
May the Lord increase his blessing in you,
for the comfort all his children,

---

1   Rudolf Wolkan, *Geschichtbuch der Hutterischen Brüder* (Wien, 1923), 120 n1, translated.]

die er ihm auserwählet hat,
durch sein Wort neugeboren,
sie ihm zub'reit't nach seinem Rat,
zur Wohnung auserkoren!

whom he has chosen for himself,
born anew through his Word,
prepared by him according to his counsel,
chosen as his dwelling!

3.
***SEI** wohl getröst't, du frommer Held,*
laß dich die Feind' nit irren!
Der Herr hat dich darzu erwählt,
sein Völklein einzuführen
in das verheißne Vaterland,
das ewig zu b'sitzen schone,
die sein' Volk nachgefolget hane
und auch darnach getane.

3.
BE well consoled, you faithful hero,
let not the enemies lead you astray!
The Lord has chosen you for this purpose,
to lead his small flock
into the promised homeland,
to be possessed eternally
by those who have followed after his people
and also acted accordingly.

4.
***MIT** dem bewähten Schwert des Geist'*
helf' er die tapfer fechten
und stärk' dich' daß du sieghaft seist
wider all' Teufels Knechten,
die allezeit mit falschem List
am Frommen tun hantieren!
Drum sich fürsicht ein jeder Christ
und laß sich keins verführen!

4.
WITH the proven sword of the Spirit
he helps the brave to fight,
and strengthens you that you might be victorious,
against the devil's minions,
who ever employ false wiles
to mock the faithful!
Therefore, let every Christian be vigilant
that nothing lead them astray!

5.
***DIR** steh' des Herren Engel bei,*
helf' dir das Volk vermahnen,
allweg dein treuer B'leitsmann sei,
bis ans End' bei dir wöll wohnen
und auch bei allen Frommen schon,
die Gott fürchten von Herzen,
um die ganz G'mein fein sich legen tan,
sie behüten vor ewigen Schmerzen!

5.
YOU have the Lord's angel by your side,
to help you to instruct the people;
in all ways to be your faithful companion and guide,
And dwell with you until the end.
And also among the faithful,
who fear God from the heart,
and seek to join the entire community,
may he protect them from eternal pain!

6.
***HERZ,** Mut und Sinn in Ewigkeit,*
im Glauben unzerspalten,
im Geist und Fried', auch Reinigkeit
wöll' euch Gott all' erhalten!
Er geb' euch sein Wort zu aller Stund'
gar lauter zu verkünden,
daß ihr allsamt aus einem Mund
dem Herrn viel Frucht mögt bringen.

6.
HEART, soul, and mind remain
undivided in faith for eternity;
in spirit and peace, also purity,
may God preserve you all!
May he give you his Word in every hour,
to proclaim it clearly,
that you together, with one voice,
may bear much fruit for the Lord.

7.

LIEBER sei dir auf Erden nicht
denn nur das G'setz des Herren;
darzu du dein G'müt fleißig richt',
weisheit tu' es dich lehren,
wie man in Haus des Herren fein
recht' Ordnung halten sollte!
Das wird dir viel köstlicher sein
dann viel' tausend Stück Golde.

8.

BRUDER, ich erkenn' dein' Lieb' und Treu'
und deiner Mitgenossen,
die ihr täglich an uns beweist
mit Treuen unverdrossen.
Der Herr, der sie gepreiset schon
um all sein' Gnad' und Gaben;
der helf' uns all' in seinem Thron
dir ewiglich lobsagen!

9.

PETRUS, ein wahrer Fels und Grund,
den Christus selbst tät legen,
der bleibet fest zu aller Stund',
der Höllen Port nit bewegen.
Ein Baumeister zu predigen schon,
bist du draufg'stellt mit Namen,
all', sie sein Wort recht nehmen an,
sollst du führen zusammen.

10.

WALD, Graben, Berg in Wind und Regen,
in den Steinklüften tiefe
die Fromm um der Wahrheit wegen
müssen darin umschliefen,
bis dass sie Gott erfreuen tut,
eifrige Menschen finden,
da Gott erneuert Herz und Mut,
zu werden Gottes Kinder.

11.

BOT[1] mit Befehl des Herren g'sandt,
der Welte zu verkünden,

7.

BELOVED, let nothing on earth be dearer to you
than the law of the Lord;
direct your mind unto it diligently.
Let wisdom teach you
how to maintain proper order
in the house of the Lord!
This will be more precious to you
than many thousand pieces of gold.

8.

BROTHER, I acknowledge your love and faith
and that of your companions,
which you prove to us daily
with tireless devotion.
The Lord be praised now already
for all his grace and gifts;
may he help us all from his throne
to praise [him] forever!

9.

PETER, a true rock and foundation,
placed by Christ himself,
remained steadfast at every hour;
the gate of hell will not prevail.
As a master builder, to preach
you are appointed by name;
all who accept his Word aright
you must gather together.

10.

Forest, ravine, and mountain, in wind and rain,
in deep rock clefts—
for the sake of the truth the faithful
must in these places hide
until God fills them with joy,
fervent hearts to behold,
where God renews heart and mind,
to become children of God.

11.

A messenger sent by the Lord's command,
to proclaim to all nations,

---

1   The original contains the acrostic, "*Gottes Geist sei mit dir, herzlieber Bruder Petrus Wald-bot.* / God's spirit be with you, dear brother Peter Wald-bot [Walpot]." It was not possible to fully maintain this acrostic in translation.

daß sie abstehn von Greuel und Schand,'	that they turn from abomination and disgrace,
Buß' tun von ihren Sünden.	repent from their sins.
Welche nun folgen Gottes Rat,	Those who now follow God's counsel
den' wird die Sünd vergeben;	will have their sins forgiven;
und hilft aus dem ewigen Tod,	they will be delivered from eternal death
führet s' ins ewig Leben.	and led into eternal life.

[**Source:** Prose translation by Kenny Wollmann from A.J.F. Zieglschmid, ed., *Liederbuch der Hutterischen Brüder* (MacGregor: Hutterian Brethren Book Centre, forthcoming).]

Gottes Gnad' und Fried' allezeit

Ton: Sohn David

Got - tes   Gnad'_ und   Fried'   al - le - zeit
des   Va - ters___ Lieb'   und   wahr - e   Freud'

tu   sich   in   dir___   ver - mehr - en;
durch   Chris - tum,   uns - ern   Her - ren,

der___   al - le   Ding wohl ge - ord - ner   hat
der___   brauch' dich   selbst   nach   sein - em   Rat,

nach   sein'   gött - lich - en   Wil - len,
sein   Werk   durch   dich___   zu er - füll - en!

Portrait of Philipp
Melanchthon, Lucas
Cranach the Elder,
painting, 1543.
[*WikiCommons*]

Ein Handbüchlein wider den Prozess zu Worms am Rhein gegen die Brüder so man die Hutterischen nennt / A Handbook in Opposition to the Trial at Worms on the Rhine…, 1557

In 1557, about thirty years after the first Hutterite communities were established in Moravia, a group of Lutheran theologians led by Philip Melanchthon met in the German city of Worms. Together they drafted a document entitled, "*Prozess wie es soll gehandelt werden mit den Wiedertäufern [...]* / *Legal proceeding on how Anabaptists should be dealt with [...]*," urging the authorities to deal severely with the "heretical" Anabaptists, whose "damnable doctrines and practices" they considered to be blasphemous and therefore warranting the death penalty.

The charges were primarily directed against the Swiss Anabaptists living in territories where Lutheranism was the official religion following the Peace of Augsburg in 1555. Yet the Hutterites were the only Anabaptist group to respond to these allegations in writing. This is significant and also surprising because Worms is located in south-western Germany and the Hutterites were settled about seven hundred kilometres to the east in Moravia, which was on the margins of the Holy Roman Empire and where Lutheranism was not the official religion. The Hutterites probably chose to respond because of a brief but severe criticism aimed specifically at the treatment of children in the Hutterite boarding schools.

The medium-sized booklet of 12 "books" or chapters produced by the Hutterites was entitled *Ein Handbüchlein wider den Prozess zu Worms am Rhein gegen die Brüder so man die Hutterischen nennt.* The following topics are addressed:

1. concerning worldly authority and whether such an authority can be a Christian;

2. concerning the use of law courts and lawsuits;

3. concerning the taking of an oath;

4. concerning the Anabaptist claim that whoever does not belong to their church (*Gemeinschaft*) is condemned and not saved;

5. concerning infant baptism;

6. concerning the Lord's Supper;

7. concerning original sin and whether children have it;

8. concerning the necessity to preach and to hear the Word of God;

9. concerning the Holy Trinity, whether Christ was the Son of God;

10. concerning whether rebirth prevents any backsliding hereafter;

11. concerning justification, whether man is justified through Christ or by his own endeavour;

12. concerning the upbringing of children in communal establishments.

Seven of these books are related to charges in the 1557 document and five relate to an earlier Lutheran work. *Ein Handbüchlein* was written between 1558–1560 likely under the direction of Peter Walpot. It is worth mentioning that the earliest *Schulordnung* was written in 1558, around the same time as *Ein Handbüchlein*.

Ein Handbüchlein is a significant historical text for several reasons. It is one of the earliest detailed descriptions of the faith commitments of the South German Anabaptists. It is also the earliest extant description of Hutterite schools, making it a valuable source for understanding early modern educational practices. In this publication we get a glimpse of the great historical and biblical knowledge of at least some Hutterites at this time, as well as their preparedness to engage the ideas and accusations of their contemporaries. They are conversant with the writings of Church Fathers such as Origen, Jerome, Augustine, various Church councils, and contemporaries such as Luther and Zwingli. Further, in 1756, when the crypto-Protestants from Carinthia encountered the Hutterites in Transylvania—who had ceased to practice community-of-goods around 1690 and had dwindled to a single community at Alwinz—they were persuaded to revive *Gütergemeinschaft* and join the old Hutterites through reading *Ein Handbüchlein* and Riedemann's *Rechenschaft*. Thus, one could say that the very existence of Hutterites today owes something to this document.

Book Twelve

Concerning the upbringing of young children, regarding which the Lutherans make unsubstantiated accusations.

TRUTHFUL RESPONSE: It must be said: if one would consider his words according to the truth and write based on solid experience, many a liar's words would be spared and trampled underfoot. Lies come about when people don't sufficiently fear God while speaking and don't consider that they will have to give an account for each unnecessary word that they speak. Therefore, dear Philipp Melanchthon and Johannes Brenz, you should have spared your words and feather, instead of writing lies and slanders about our child-rearing practices. In your *Prozess*-booklet you write that the Church of God in Moravia crams and crowds together their young children so that many do not survive childhood.

A short description from the church community and all the faithful concerning our child-rearing practices:

You Lutherans need to know that our children are near and dear to our heart in truth before God [*vor Gott nach der Wahrheit*]. God will be our witness on Judgement Day, and all others will recognize that they have unduly slandered and defamed the Church of God for their child rearing practices. For everyone should know that the Church established schools for the children in simple [*reiner*] fear of God, wherever it was possible—by God's grace—to do so. As soon as we discern a need, we lovingly serve our children with utmost diligence and as much as possible in heavenly and earthly matters. Thus, they are not crammed to the ceiling, as you Lutherans think, for we seek to please God as much with our child rearing as with other matters pertaining to salvation. Therefore, we know we are innocent before God and that your accusations are groundless. We nonetheless confess that when the holy and blameless God comes and, despite all the diligence, ser-

vice, and care that we provide our children, takes them to a blessed rest in his kingdom through a physical death, that it is a profound grace, for then that the evils of the world may not steal the children's innocence. For this reason, they have died prematurely and yet still fulfilled a lot of time [*haben doch viel Zeit erfüllt*], for their souls are pleasing to God and that is why he quickly took them away from the wicked. [...]

Yet, we do not want to hide from anybody the rules and regulations with which the church community seeks to raise its children in heavenly and earthly discipline. The faithful consider it to be appropriate that they guide their children in the proper fear of God and with holy diligence, by leading them to the Lord. Our goal is for them to cultivate and practice proper habits, virtues, and the commandments of God, so that Adam's evil seed, the inclination toward evil, will be rooted out of the hearts of our youth, giving good and holy things room to grow according to godly counsel. [...]

Now, everyone should take note of how the schools are managed in the Church of God:

FIRST: When a child is brought to school by his biological parents, which happens after the second or third birthday, depending on the strengths and weaknesses of the child, it learns first of all the holy [Lord's] Prayer.

SECONDLY: When the child has learned this prayer and is mature enough and is able to work with his/her hands, we give the girls and boys the opportunity to create something useful. The boys learn to read and write, the girls spinning and sewing. Thus, the inclination toward evil is avoided, an evil which the spiritual fathers and mothers discourage through ongoing reminding, teaching and disciplining.

THIRDLY: Besides the appointed sisters and spiritual mothers the children also have schoolmasters, who monitor them, and provide whose advice and oversight guides the children's eating, drinking, sleeping, waking, coming and going, so that everything happens in an orderly way. For God's honour is required from young and old alike.

FOURTHLY: When the children receive their food, the parents ensure that they raise their hands in prayer and thanksgiving before and after the meal. At school, a boy stands up and leads the prayer.

Table-prayer: [See Käls, 171.]

FIFTHLY: It is routine in our community that before the children are put to bed in the evening and after they are woken in the morning, the schoolmaster gathers all the boys and girls in the school and outside the [boarding] house and prays with them. Approximately once a week, the community's schoolmaster conducts religious instruction. He teaches the children how to lead an obedient and God-pleasing life. Following this teaching, which takes place either in the evening or early morning, the children kneel and pray with raised hands, united in spirit and trust to God. A boy prays the following prayer out loud:

Morning and evening prayer, when the children wake up or go to sleep: [See Käls, 171.]

SIXTHLY: A God-fearing sister is responsible to watch and care over the children, along with a helper when necessary. They must watch over the children the whole night and provide them with the necessary care. The spiritual school fathers and mothers and the appointed school sisters are required to treat and serve all children equally, supplying them with clothing, washing, bedding, and other provisions. This is not done in order to please humans, but to bring God joy and favour, so that the Lord's honour is promoted in all things, in the young as well as the old, and that everything is conducted in an orderly manner in the house of God.

I hope that by now the God-fearing reader is satisfied with how we have defended ourselves with the truth about our children and recognize the Lutheran slanders as falsehoods. [...]

[**SOURCE:** Translated by Jesse Hofer from *Ein Handbüchlein wider den Prozeß [...]*, Bodo Hildebrand, editor, unpublished, 1991.]

Claus Felbinger (d. 1560)
Confession of Faith, 1560

Claus Felbinger wrote his *Rechenschaft* while he was imprisoned and interrogated by Catholic authorities near Landshut, Bavaria in 1560 shortly before he was executed. His confession was especially popular among Hutterite *Sendboten* (i.e., missioners) for its clear and succinct summary of Hutterite convictions. Felbinger writes movingly and confidently about Christian freedom, true repentance, hope, the nature of the church, and the importance of Christian community.

Introduction

Dear Lords and Magistrates of this town of Landshut, God who does nothing without a cause, has so disposed that we have been arrested for the sake of divine truth, and handed over to you as prisoners. Although we have already been questioned twice in Neumarkt by the county sheriff and his assistants, and several times here by the lord's men regarding our way of life, yet I feel in my heart that I have not fully disclosed my mind in such a way that you might understand the foundation on which we stand.[1] [...]

The Witness of Suffering

My lords, first, as you also are servants of God, though outside the perfection of Christ (namely, to take vengeance on evildoers, to punish the evil, and to protect and shelter the devout),[2] God has given the sword into your hand.[3] He has granted you such honour and dignity as is meet, that you may be rightly obeyed in that which is not against God.[4] And we say to you: "He who withstands the authorities in just matters withstands God's ordinance, for the authorities hold their office in order that disobedience might be punished."[5] This is the reason, you servants of God, that I

---

1   1 Pet 3:15.
2   Rom 13:3–4.
3   Pro 8:15–16.
4   Acts 5:29.
5   Rom 13:2.

wanted to remind and exhort you to consider your office—not that we were dismayed at having to suffer for what we have done for the sake of our confession. Oh, no! For we do not count ourselves worthy or able or good enough to suffer anything for the sake of God's Word; but we praise God with all our hearts that in his providence he has ordained that we, unworthy men, be true witnesses of his holy truth. And that we have also vowed and promised him in the covenant of true Christian baptism, namely, where need be to lay down our lives for his name, and after recognizing the truth, never to act against God consciously and wilfully, in word or in deed, but with his help rather to suffer death than do so, to follow his holy Word unswervingly, and to adorn our faith with work pleasing to God. For he has given us, who believe his Word, grace and strength to do his divine will joyfully; this, however, was impossible to us until we had given ourselves utterly to him. God has promised from the beginning that he would, in all things, make it possible for those who truly believe to do what he demands of them, and what is right in his eyes; for he would confirm their faith with the strength of his Holy Spirit, who would lead and guide them into all truth and strengthen their spirit, so that they may know for certain that they are children of God and coheirs (*Miterben*) with Christ, in so far as they suffer with him.[6] […]

6   Rom 8:17.
7   Ps 24:1.

Theology of Mission

We have been asked by sundry people why we have come into the prince's [of Bavaria] land, and draw people away. My answer is, we do not go only into this land, but into all lands, wherever our language is known, for where God opens a door for us and shows us zealous hearts that truly seek him, hearts that are discontented with the godless life of the world and would gladly do what is right—there we go, for we have divine cause to do so. For heaven and earth are the Lord's and all men are his;[7] but we have given, surrendered, and sacrificed ourselves wholly to God. Where he sends us and will use us, there we go, in obedience to his divine will, regardless of what we must suffer and endure.

Governmental Authority and Nonviolence

Further they have asked us: "As governmental authority is ordained by God and has its power from him, therefore all should fear and honour it—now, why do you not do so?" Mark the answer! The government is not given for the just to fear, but only for the evil, for the government should be a shield to the just. For this reason the Lord has placed a sword in its hand, and its annual income in taxes, interest, duties, etc., that it may be able to execute its office and protect the just. If it does not do so, God will punish it the harder. Therefore we are gladly and willingly subject to the government for the Lord's sake, and in all just matters we will in no way oppose it. When, however, the government requires of us what is contrary to our faith and conscience—as swearing oaths and paying hangman's dues or taxes for war—then we do not obey its command. This we do not do out of obstinacy or pride, but only out of pure fear of God. For it is our duty to obey God rather than men.[8]

That is the reason why we refuse, namely, that we fear God. Christ forbids those whom he loves, those who are meant for Life, all carnal wrath and vengeance. Thus they are forbidden to kill, and are told to leave all vengeance to God.[9] Therefore we do nothing to promote bloodshed, for such does not befit a Christian who is taught of God in his Son, since we should be like young children, without resentment or bitterness, and like a dove, guileless.[10] To the men of old it was indeed said, "Thou shalt hate thine enemy and love thy friend." "But I say unto you," said Christ, "love your enemies, do good to them that hate you, pray for them that spitefully use you, that ye may be children of your Father in heaven."[11] Therefore one must distinguish between the Old and the New Testaments. "It was indeed said to the men of old, an eye for an eye, a tooth for a tooth, a hand for a hand, and a head for a head;[12] but I say unto you that in all things ye resist not evil."[13]

On Swearing Oaths and Christian Freedom

That we do not swear an oath nor promise an oath, as is the way of the world, has its origin in the words which Christ speaks to those who are his: "To them of old it was said, 'Thou shalt not swear falsely, but perform unto the Lord thy oath.'[14] But I say unto you, swear not at all, neither by heaven, for it is God's throne, nor by the earth. But your yea shall be yea, and your nay, nay. What is more than these cometh of evil."[15] Therefore, dear men, consider this when we oppose you in anything; do not think that we do it in pride, but only because we fear God, who is indeed to be feared. For the apostles also did not let themselves be driven by the Jews or by any authority from what they had recognized as right before God, but rather laid down their lives.[16]

And that I, too, with God's help, hope to do, and will let no one stop me from speaking of that which is

---

8   Acts 5:29.
9   Deut 32:35.
10   Mt 10:16.
11   Mt 5:21–22.
12   Ex 21:24.
13   Mt 5:38–39.
14   Lev 19:12; Num 30:2; Deut 23:21.
15   Mt 5:33–37.
16   Acts 5:29.

right before God, especially of what I have seen and heard and sensed in my heart, through the renewal of the Holy Spirit, of the resurrection of Christ Jesus, who has established new life within us who believe in him and honour his name, who give ourselves wholly to him and are quiet before him.

And we say freely and confess openly that among you there is no godly life, as your works also bear witness; but that which the devil has planted grows, yea, all manner of unrighteousness gains ground, so that it is as though your sin can no longer be opposed. For the world has run wild and is so sunken in sin that it knows nothing of God. And now the very teaching of the Gospel is to men a new teaching, a heresy and a false teaching. For when God awakens for them a messenger of salvation who proclaims to them the divine Word and shows them the way of blessedness, they do not believe him but count him a fool, and so regard those who are rich in the Spirit as mad and foolish, and their malice has blinded them to such an extent. They kick, as it were, their salvation from them and make themselves unworthy of eternal life. For they do not believe that one can serve God without sin, in true piety, as though it were not possible to leave the sinful, evil nature which is the work of the devil.

Then Satan would be stronger than God—but far be it! For Christ has been sent by the Father into this world to take away the power of the devil,[17] the old serpent, tread upon his head,[18] destroy his work, and banish sin—that is, from all who gladly let their sins be taken away. These are they who listen to his holy Word, believe it with all their hearts, and keep it in a sensitive, pure, and good heart.

Now, does Christ compel people with the stocks to hear his teaching, as is the manner of those who think they are Christians?

Oh, no! On the contrary, he speaks only to those who thirst for his justice, who have ears to hear, who are heavy of heart, who would gladly be set free from their sins—who are urged and drawn by God. Know well that faith is not a matter of course but that it is a special gift, given only to those who love God.[19]

God wants no compulsory service. On the contrary, he loves a free, willing heart that serves him with a joyful soul and does what is right joyfully.[20] [...]

True Repentance and the Wisdom of God

How incomprehensible a thing it is to the worldly-wise when one shows them the narrow way! The Word of the cross of Christ is, of course, fool-

---

17　1Jn 3:8.
18　Gen 3:15.
19　Eph 2:8.
20　2Cor 9:7.

ishness to them that are lost.[21] They declare that we mount far too high; that Christ has paid and has already done what is necessary for us; that one need do no more than believe this firmly, and simply confess himself a sinner, for God is merciful and gracious. They say not a word either of the new birth, without which no one can be blessed, or of true repentance. For true repentance is "to sin no more,"[22] to begin a new and holy life with God, and to conform no more to the world.

Thus the worldly-wise flaunt their high knowledge before us and say, "We find it in the Old and New Testaments. As we see things, you are aiming far too high. Were none to be saved except those who act as you do, the whole world would have to be condemned at once." To this we answer that we believe the Word of God utterly: the Word that stands and that cannot lie. It does not conform to the world. Men have only to act in accordance with the Word. The worldly-wise, especially the monks, clergy, and scribes think that because they have read books and are well practiced therein they can be found wanting in nothing. Oh, foolish men! The wisdom of God is neither to be gleaned from books nor learned in universities—

far from it! For the fear of God is the beginning of wisdom, and a good understanding have all they who do accordingly.[23]

Thus one sees that only those have the secret of the kingdom of heaven who faithfully follow Christ: the others having eyes see not, and having ears hear not.[24] David said that the secret of God is only with them that fear him, and he will show them his covenant.[25] They that continue in Christ's teaching will understand the truth, and the truth will make them free.[26] Knowledge only puffs up, but love improves and builds up.[27] For the Word of the cross of Christ repels all the wise. Reason advises not to come under the yoke, for the way of the flesh is enmity to God.[28]

Condemning Others

We are accused also of condemning all who are not of our mind and who act not as we do. That we deny. We condemn no man, but we show to men their reprobate life and warn them of condemnation, and this we do in accordance with the Word of God that cannot lie. For we believe this Word, and that it will come to pass, and for the sake of loyalty to it we are often forced to lay down our lives. No human being can condemn

21   I Cor 1:18.
22   Jn 5:14; 8:11.
23   Ps 111:10.
24   Mt 13:13.
25   Ps 25:14.
26   Jn 8:31–32.
27   I Cor 8:1.
28   Rom 8:7.

another. Judgment is in the hand of the Lord;[29] but sinful, evil works are what condemn man, when he has not left them in accordance with the Word of God and brought forth honest fruits of repentance.[30]

Baptism

Further I was asked with regard to baptism, how often I was baptized. I said, "Once, as God has commanded." They then asked if I had not also been baptized "by the brothers." I answered, "The devout brothers who baptized me in accordance with the command of Christ first taught me repentance and faith in the name of Jesus Christ.[31] Then, at my request, they baptized me on confession of my faith; which faith, God, according to his promise, also sealed and strengthened with his Holy Spirit,[32] who has until now kept me in the way of truth. And it is my hope in God that he take him not from me until my end."

But infant baptism I regard as simply nothing. It is conceived by men for the sake of money, that the parsons may by its means enrich themselves; it is a plant which the heavenly Father has not planted; therefore it must be rooted out.[33] For they find not a single word in the Old or in the New Testament about infant baptism, not

a word that shows either that Christ commanded or that his disciples practiced it. […] To sum up, it is a foolish and blind affair. Through it all manner of evil and infamous men get the precious name, in that they call themselves Christians, which thus but becomes a cloak for their knavery. For a Christian has not received his name from baptism, but from the conduct of his whole life.

Shepherds

As Paul said clearly to Timothy and Titus, [shepherds] should be men who are blameless, the husband of one wife only, vigilant, sober, of a right mind, of good behaviour, given to hospitality, apt to teach the doctrine of faith, not lovers of wine, not strikers, not greedy of filthy lucre, but kind, not brawlers, not covetous, one that conducts his own house well, that he may have believing children.[34] He must, however, also have a good testimony.[35] They should likewise be courageous, not double-tongued, but sober, just, holy, devout, and bear in a clean conscience the mysteries of the faith.[36]

Hold your clergy up to this mirror to see if there be in them a vein of such virtue! Is not the opposite every-

---

29　Jam 4:12.
30　Mt 3:8.
31　Acts 2:38.
32　Eph 1:13.
33　Mt 15:13.
34　1 Tim 3:2-5; Tit 1:6–9.
35　1 Tim 3:7.
36　1 Tim 3:8–9; Tit 3:8–9.

where reflected? For this reason no one is improved by their teaching. It brings forth no fruit. Why? They do not speak as the mouth of God, but only their own thoughts, the deceit of their own hearts, and do but destroy themselves and all who listen to them, holding them in what is evil. Their word has no strength: it makes no one free from sin and devout, it renews none. They remain the same old sinful wineskins, that are unable to hold the wine of divine sweetness.[37] The Holy Spirit will not dwell in men who are the vessels of sin. He enters no heart that wills to do evil.[38] Therefore they are blind guides.[39]

Communion and Community

I was also asked what our attitude is to the holy sacrament. I said, "The sacraments of the clergy I regard as naught, for their blessing is a curse in the eyes of God, since they despise his Word. But I think much of the Supper of Christ and of his memory, and of him who holds it and can do so worthily—but this involves much."

Then they asked me if I do not believe that Christ is essentially present in the bread and wine as the very body and blood in which he suffered for us on the cross. I answered,

"No! Christ has ascended to heaven. There he sits at the right hand of God, the heavenly Father.[40] He does not let himself be conjured thence into the hands of sinners, that they may afterward sell him for money. He is the enemy of all evildoers. The mad shall not appear before his eyes. Thus, also, the mad, drunken clergy may not come before his face."

"But," say they, "He has clearly said, This is my body and my blood." Yes. We know also, praise be to God, the interpretation of this high mystery which he wanted to disclose to his loved ones in this comforting supper—namely, by means of bread and wine he has shown the community of his body.[41] Even as natural bread is composed by the coming together of many grains, ground under the millstones, and each giving the others all it possesses, they have community one with another, and thus become one loaf; and as, likewise, the wine is composed of many grapes, each sharing its juice with the rest in the wine press, so that they become one drink. Even so are we also, in that we become completely of one nature with him, in life and death, and are all one in Christ: He the vine and we his branches,[42] he the head and we his members.[43]

---

37 Mt 9:17.
38 Wis 1:4–5.
39 Mt 15:14.
40 Mk 16:19; Heb 1:3.
41 1Cor 10:16–17.
42 Jn 15:5.
43 Eph 5:30.

But the branches must bear no other fruit than that which it is the nature of the vine to bear. For all unfruitful branches are cut off and cast into the fire.[44] On the other hand, the limbs of Christ's body seek not earthly goods, and regard nothing else but what the head, Christ, wills through them and inspires in them by his Spirit. He who has not his Spirit, however, is none of his.[45] But they who have given and surrendered themselves wholly to God, with body and soul and all their members, let themselves be ruled by his Holy Spirit,[46] led in faith by him in true confidence in the Lord, quietly suffering him to work and keeping his Word in a pure, good heart, such are able to bring forth fruit in patience. Only they who have the Word of God, which is spirit and life, within them (the flesh is of no profit) eat the body of Christ and drink his blood. He who acts otherwise deceives himself.[47]

For no sinner who has not yet cleansed his heart through obedience to truth in the spirit of sincere brotherly love may sit down at this Supper. [...]

The Nature of the Church I Joined

I have also been asked why I have left the "holy Christian Church" and given myself up to a "sect" that is no-

where tolerated and is obnoxious to the emperor, king, princes, and all men. Thereupon I answered, I have not left the true Christian Church; I have but joined her and let myself be incorporated into her by true Christian baptism. I have no doubt that I am in the true community and fellowship of the saints, in which there is forgiveness and remission of sins, to which the power and key is given and committed by the Holy Spirit to bind and to loose, both in heaven and on earth.[48] I feel in my heart that through no other doctrine could my heart and soul have reached peace with God and true calmness. For at the moment I answered God's voice with an obedient heart saying "Here am I!" my soul revived, and is now waiting in blessed hope and true confidence for his salvation. Praise and thanks be to God for the love, grace, and mercy he has shown me, unworthy man! And I have no doubt that God has removed my sins farther from me than the East is from the West, and that he will neither behold them any more nor think of them.[49] If I continue to walk faithfully before him he has promised to take from me all sin and bury it in the innocence of Christ. Of this I am certain.

Now where previously in my blind, unconscious infant baptism was I

44   Jn 15:2, 6.
45   Rom 8:9.
46   Rom 8:13.
47   1Cor 11:29.
48   Mt 16:19; Jn 20:23.
49   Ps 103:12; Is 43:25.

able to have such faith and certainty in God? Thus I have not left the true Christian Church, but the so-called "Christian" congregation of sinners and the unjust, prostitutes, adulterers, gamblers, slanderers of God, gluttons, winebibbers, liars, covetous men, and idolaters who do not cease to rouse God to wrath.[50] I have indeed come out from among all these, for I will have no fellowship with such unless they leave their godless nature and repent truly by coming to a true recognition of their sins. For God has still a devout people on earth, whom he has shocked and startled into leaving sin through his living Word, whom he has called from the world to his holy name and gathered by the Holy Spirit. These he has chosen to be his own, to the praise of his glory, that they might walk according to his nature, proclaim his strength and virtue, adorn their faith with works pleasing to God, put on the garment of innocence and the cloak of justice and righteousness, and always bear before them the breastplate of right action; that the world may see what is pleasing to God and have occasion to consider its ungodly life, to leave it and turn from sins to God.[51] For God has never left himself without a witness, in words and works, so that no one can excuse himself before him. [...]

Is Blessedness to be Found Only in Moravia?

They who do not know God likewise say, "Now why do you not stay here? Can not one also do right here and become blessed? Or is blessedness confined to Moravia?" Now note the answer. One can do good just as well here and become blessed—if one would only do it! But men not only do not do it themselves, but they hinder those who would gladly do good. Here men are compelled to idolatry with the stocks and robbed of their goods. As Paul wrote to Timothy: "All those that will live a godly life in Christ Jesus shall suffer persecution."[52] For a devout soul that fears God cannot keep silent but speaks and witnesses against their abominable life, saying they cannot please God, much less become blessed. Whereupon hate is roused and from that hour they say, "Away with these rogues! They want to be better than we are: it is not right that they should live!" Then the devout man must flee with Jacob, who was beloved of God, before the unstable Esau and his children, and go to Mesopotamia to his friends and fellows in faith.[53]

Therefore, as is said above, blessedness is not confined to any land or place; for the Word of God does not suffer itself to be bound. He that fears God and does right is pleasing

---

50   I Cor 6:9–10; Gal 5:19–21; Rom 1:29–32.
51   I Pet 2:9; Eph 4:24, 6:14; I Pet 2:12.
52   2 Tim 3:12.
53   Gen 27:41–45.

to God, wherever he may be; but the true children of God come together in zeal for God and do not remain apart from each other, that each may be a comfort to the rest. For a devout man is never happier than with his dear brothers and fellows in faith, where each can show the others love and good, yea, faithfulness and honour, as divine love has a way of looking upon itself as the neighbour's debtor and is diligent to help him with all its strength, and to do so with joy. For one devout heart refreshes the other with the gift it has received from God for the good of the body of Christ, which is his holy church, all believing, devout hearts that have bound themselves together in God's love. There one sees holy examples, good patterns of the devout fathers in word and deed, provoking one to emulation.[54] That is the most pleasant of all to the lover of God, as it is written, "Wisdom is a golden jewel to the obedient ear."[55] [...]

Therefore also is it written: "With the devout thou wilt show thyself devout, with the pure wilt show thyself pure, and with the upright thou wilt show thyself upright—but with the evil one thou becomest evil, with the froward thou dost act frowardly."[56] Therefore Sirach said: "Birds of a feather flock together."[57] So is

it also with man. He seeks those like himself. For woe to him that is alone when he falls! Who will help him up?[58]

Complete oneness [*Einigkeit*], separation from the world, and fellowship [*Gemeinschaft*, i.e., communal life], is only to be found in the perfect kingdom of Christ, for one sees how Christ separates all those whom he has ordained for life, how he has now confirmed the new covenant of divine grace with his death and has won from the Father the promised Spirit who shall lead all true believers into truth.[59] He began communal life among them. As one finds in the Acts of the Apostles, in the first five chapters. [...]

And God still has such a church on earth, which acts according to his law and walks in true community of spiritual as well as of temporal gifts and goods. For God wills to have children who are of his nature, who are not false; who let themselves be ruled by his Holy Spirit, through whom they are gathered and kept at one. That I testify of them with truth.

Having [Original] Sin Versus Committing Sin

They say furthermore: "You are but justifying yourselves. Now none is just—none save the one, God. We will wait with the obvious sinners

---

54   Heb 13:7.
55   Prov 2:10.
56   Ps 18:25–26; 2Sam 22:26–27.
57   Sir 27:9.
58   Ecc 4:10.
59   Jn 14:17, 16:13.

in the temple until he tells us we are just." Yes, would they but do so and come into the "Temple" in which there is remission of sins! But the Temple is the true Christian Church, the true community of saints.[60] Therein, however, they will not go— how then can God justify them? But we have come into this Temple and confessed ourselves obvious sinners before God and his Holy Spirit. Then we were set free through the justification of the saints and their earnest prayer (to God be praise!), and can and will, with God's help, hold to justification with the obvious sinner, and sin no more, that nothing worse need overtake us! For this reason you do not understand this saying at all, but are even like the hypocrites who think they can please God without repentance. You go and sin, building on God's mercy, and at the same time you will not leave sin and evil that God may establish a new life within you.[61] If Christ has set you free from sin, as you boast, why do you still act so ungodly? You are just as free as a prisoner lying bound, who says he is free and is walking, while his hands and feet are in the stocks. All would rightly laugh at such. For he that sins is not yet free but the servant of sin, and the servant will be no heir, but the Son and such as the Son makes truly free.[62]

Then they continue: "I do not believe that one can serve God without sin, for sin always goes with one." Yes, but one must discriminate between having sin and committing sin. To have sin and to commit sin are very different things. No man who is born of a woman and the seed of man is without sin. For they all share in the original sin that comes from Adam.[63] […]

And therefore, as has been said above, much is said in the world about sin without discrimination— as though Paul, John, or James were also sinners, since they confessed that they were not without sin.[64] Now note, original sin, the rising urge in flesh suggesting sin, the inclination or desire, evil occurrences and sinful thoughts through which man is tempted to do wrong—from these the devout are not exempt. The devout man is tempted by this. This is all sin, and still rouses itself in the body. That fills a devout lover of God with fear and trembling. He would gladly be free of it. It often appals him, troubles his heart, and makes him sad. He cries to God, beseeches that he might take it away from him, pleads that he has indeed pleasure in true devoutness, as Paul had when he said,

> The messenger of Satan buffeteth me as a warning to my flesh. For this thing I besought the

---

60   I Cor 3:16–17.
61   Rom 6:1–2.
62   Jn 8:34–36.
63   Rom 5:12; Ps 51:5.
64   I Jn 1:8; Rom 7:19-20; Jam 3:2.

Lord thrice, that it might depart from me, but the Lord said unto me, 'Paul, be content with my grace, for through thy weakness is my strength seen and felt more strongly.'[65]

And again Paul said:

I delight in the law of God after the inward man: but the law of sin in my members striveth against the law of God in my heart. O wretched man that I am! Who will deliver me from the body of this death? I thank God, however, through Jesus Christ our Lord, who hath given me the victory.[66]

Just so have devout men lamented unto the grave over this sin, but they were not sinners after conversion, after they had once received grace. As Paul said to the Galatians: "But if, while we seek to be justified by Christ, we ourselves also are found sinners, is therefore Christ the minister of sin?"[67] God forbid. How could we want to live in sin, when we have died to sin?[68] But the world calls all who have sin "sinners" without discernment. A child in the cradle also has sin, but is no sinner. The man also who truly repented, was forgiven by God in his divine goodness, and God has passed over all the sins which he has done, and will never more think of them.

But original sin remains: from it he is not set free. As long as man is in the flesh, he must fight against it. In this God will preserve him if he has a horror of sin and hates his own flesh. For one who truly fears God, who does not sin consciously and intentionally, knows that formerly he roused God, his Lord, to wrath and betrayed him; therefore he refuses this harm to his inner being, he gives no place to the temptation and does not follow sinful thoughts, but fears God and is master of his own heart. Thus one must not sin but withstand sin when one seeks to punish the cunning of the flesh, to "take reason prisoner under the obedience of Christ."[69] Therefore we must make a distinction. Because a devout man does not consent in his heart to sin and does not stretch out his limbs to do wrong, he is no sinner. Though he has indeed sins that stir themselves powerfully within him, he fears God and overpowers himself and crushes the sinful suggestion through the strength of the Spirit. When this is the case, sin must be melted and the work of the body must be killed through the Spirit, that sin may not be living and active but cease its work.

[**Source:** Robert Friedmann, "Claus Felbinger's Confession of 1560" *Mennonite Quarterly Review* 29 (April 1955): 141–161. Used by permission.]

65   2Cor 12:7–9.
66   Rom 7:22–25.
67   Gal 2:17–18.
68   Rom 6:1–14.
69   2Cor 10:5.

The "Golden Years" Period
(1565–1592)

During the Golden Years, the Hutterites in Moravia developed a thriving medical practice which included notable physicians such as Georg Zobel and Balthasar Goller. These doctors served not only the Hutterite community but also the nobility and even imperial courts. Barber surgeons and folk practitioners, collectively known as *Bader* or *Wundärtze*, occupied a lower class than university-educated physicians and were responsible for most hands-on, "dirty" work. They produced and administered various medicines including salves, oils, poultices, enemas, purgatives, and performed blood-letting. Additionally, they managed some of the famous Moravian bathhouses. Hutterite critic Christoph Andreas Fischer laments that on Saturdays, many Catholics flocked to the Hutterite baths for treatment. Leonhard Gagasser, a senior *Bader*, wrote and compiled numerous manuscripts containing detailed recipes and remedy instructions for apprentices. The title translates as "Book of Wound Medicine, including a Basic Antidotary. All necessary points for complete wound treatment included. Intended as a initial or teaching guide." [Courtesy of Jason Stahl.]

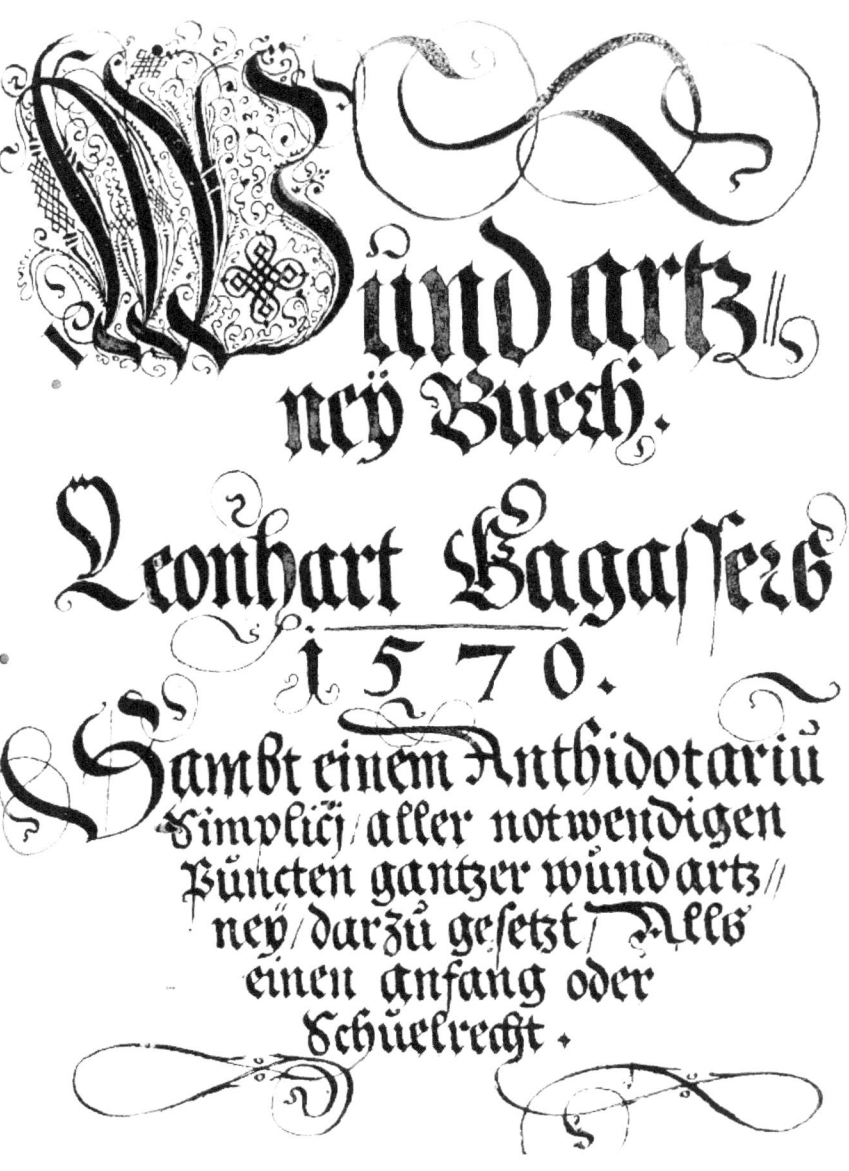

Peter Walpot (1521–1578)
Schulordnung / School Ordinance, 1568

Sixteenth century Hutterite schools were remarkable because they prioritized literacy for both boys and girls some three hundred years before universal education was introduced across the Western world.

Schooling took place in a boarding school context, which means children attended school from age 2–12 and slept in school dormitories. The schools offered basic religious instruction and taught both boys and girls to read and pray, as well as skills related to the workplace. Formal schooling beyond this level was viewed as unnecessary and even dangerous.

In the second half of the 16th century, there were a number of serious problems within the Hutterite schools. Discipline was harshly applied. Diseases spread rapidly among the student population. Neglect by caretakers led to malnourishment, injuries, and fatalities. Parents were not happy with the attempt to break family ties by having the children stay at the schools all the time. We can infer that these problems persisted, because of the regular updates and revisions to the *Schulordnungen* (Lanzenstiel, 1558; Walpot, 1568; Kräl, 1578; Braidl, 1588 and 1596). The 1568 *Schulordnung* issued during Peter Walpot's tenure as elder is representative of these efforts.

The *Schulordnungen* were addressed to the schoolmasters and school mothers who instructed the children and cared for their overall needs. Besides providing best practices for health and hygiene, they demonstrate awareness of child psychology, counselling moderation and discernment when disciplining.

Herein are recorded several necessary points which the brethren and sisters who are appointed to supervise the schools, together with their assistants, are to observe in the care and discipline of the youth.

In the first place they must constantly keep in mind that they are, appointed over the children by the Lord and by his people.

Further, the school masters and school mothers, since they are the ones who are responsible for the good character of the discipline of the school, are to be peaceful and trustful in their relations one to another. There should be a willingness to assist each other with good advice and to maintain a strict and regular order in all phases of the care of the youth, for to be dutiful and peaceful is conducive to good discipline, while discord and indolence are conducive to disorder.

They shall also take proper care in directing and supervising their assistants according to the adopted discipline.

They shall take care that no disunity, strife, or boisterous speaking is heard by the children, but rather by a peaceful, cheerful, good-natured, and sober life and quiet walk they shall inspire the youth likewise to quiet and sober living and give them a good example.

They should avoid vain and idle words so that the children shall not have occasion to gossip.

The school masters and sisters shall admonish and ask the boys and girls in their later teens to be diligent in prayer. And it would be well if when the school masters speak with the children once or twice a week, the sisters be present if possible, and thus testify by their example and pattern to their desire to inspire the youth with ideals of piety; the sisters should not absent themselves to go to other places but should give due consideration to the honour of the

Lord and the welfare of the youth. Yet the school master should not occupy the time of the children with long preaching and with much reading of many quotations because the children can understand and grasp but little.

When one or more children are guilty of something, either of unbecoming conversation or other foolishness—likewise the girls when they spin—it is ordered that not every sister should at once step in and punish but should take care in the fear of God so that the youth should not be hastily disciplined.

For this reason, in order to be better able to give account before God and man, it is believed best that the sisters should report the matter to the brethren in the school or to the school mother and should not be too severe, seeing that the Lord does not deal with us elder ones always according to our deserts, but according to grace.

The [older] boys are to be punished by a school master and not by a sister, but the middle-sized boys may be punished with the rod by a school mother if the school master is absent and the boy is stubborn and will not submit to the sister's words. But if it is a larger boy, it should be noted and reported to the school master when he comes home.

Likewise, the [older] girls are to be disciplined by a school mother and not by a brother.

Stealing, lying, and other gross sins, whether done by boys or girls, shall not be dealt with by a sister alone, but shall be disciplined with the approval and advice of a brother.

If punishment with the rod is necessary in the case of a larger boy or girl, it shall be done in the fear of God and with discernment. In case of knavishness, lying, thieving, and unchaste conduct, severity shall be used according to desert. This shall not be done secretly or in a corner, but in the presence of all the children, so that they may learn thereby to have fear of wrongdoing.

The children shall be trained not to resist the rod, but willingly accept punishment. In this way it will be possible to always deal with them in a free manner, more than if they resist, which one shall not and cannot permit them.

A school master shall permit the boys to go out once to the lavatory mornings and evenings, and shall himself watch, but shall not refuse the children permission to go out in between times, for the natural processes cannot be controlled by law and it is harmful to obstruct nature too long. The same applies to the girls.

It should also not be difficult for a pious school mother and her assistants to counsel with a brother in the school and to enquire when one wishes to take the children out and let them go home.

Likewise a school master shall have sympathy and cooperation for the sisters and shall yield in matters which do not interfere with the honour of God and good discipline. The bread and meat [sandwiches] may and shall be handed out to the larger children by the school master, except if he does not have time or lacks the food. In that case the school mothers may do this or appoint another sister to do it.

If something special is to be given to the children, such as apples, pears, and other fruit, it shall not be done on the individual decision of anyone, but shall be done on the counsel of several at a proper time. The children's clothing shall not be had in excess; what is necessary shall be kept on hand and be kept clean. The boys' clothing shall be handed out by a brother himself.

The linen cloths shall be in the hands of a school mother and shall be given out by her, but as far as the table cloths for the children are concerned, she shall give it to the table sisters and not to the girls.

The sisters shall exercise diligence that they lift the little children out and into their beds mornings and evenings, and not leave this to the girls so that they themselves may know how the children get in and out of bed. However, the girls may help them in carrying the children to and from the beds. They shall likewise clean and wash those who are dirty.

In the morning the girls shall be called at five o'clock in winter time to spin. Then at six o'clock the boys are to be awakened and during the time that the latter are clothing, combing, and washing themselves, the smaller children are to be taken out, dressed, and washed, so that they will be quite ready for prayer and be able to sit at the table. Then the babies are to be taken out, dressed, washed, and after they have had a bit of exercise and have been walking about they may be taken to their meals, so that they are not fed at once after awakening from sleep, which is unnatural.

At evenings one should take particular care not to put the children to bed too soon after eating, which is unnatural for them, but to lead them about for a time after the meal or let them run around, small and large, in the winter time until six o'clock, and in summer time until sunset. And since it is often warm and moist in bed in summer, they shall be allowed to stay up longer at such warm times, but when it is cool they should for this reason be put to bed a little bit earlier.

During the night the nurse [*Wachterin*] shall take care that the children, both small and great, sleep well and are well covered, so that they may not become cold. Also one of the sisters should help the nurse to watch for a while when the children are going to sleep until the children are all asleep, and the children shall not be given anything to

eat in bed or anything to suck except that a sick child may be given something to drink for his sickness. The children that are well shall be allowed to sleep without interruption for it is unwholesome to be feeding the children night and day. Likewise the sleeping children shall not be forced to arise during the night but shall be allowed to sleep, for if anyone has need, nature will of itself awaken them. But if a boy or a girl has some particular unclean habits, such a one may be awakened in order to be cured of such unclean habits, according to good discipline. If it happens once or twice that someone wets the bed, possibly in a dream, it shall be overlooked, with the hope of improvement, but if it occurs frequently the child shall be punished for the same.

The nurse shall likewise not at once begin to strike the child with the rod if a child begins to cry at night, but shall use other methods to quiet it.

When the innocent little children make the bed unclean they shall be diligently dried and one shall not economize with bed clothing and layettes. They shall not be left to lie because they cannot ask for help or cannot understand. The nurse shall also take good care to notice when a child cries or screams to hold it for a while over the vessel and cover it well so that it should not get cold from being without cover.

But when the little children who have begun to talk, still make a bed unclean, it may be overlooked two or three times and the children instructed with words, but if this does not help, finally they shall be punished lightly so that they shall learn to keep clean.

But the sisters shall take especial care with the little children, that they be not harsh with them but rather be sympathetic and long-suffering with them on account of their innocence and lack of understanding, just like mothers do with their own children. They shall be concerned in so training the children that they shall not be allowed to become self-willed but shall be gradually trained to love the Lord and as soon as they begin to talk they shall be taught to pray at the proper time.

Further, the brethren and sisters in the schools shall take especial care to avoid giving offence by discipline and punishment in the presence of brothers and sisters from other places who come to visit the school and observe the children. They shall be careful in this matter.

The boys and girls shall not be depended upon to take care of the little children either by day or by night, nor to take them up or lay them down, but the sisters shall be careful to be present, especially when the children get up, so that no one shall be injured.

The brethren in the schools have already been instructed by the elders that they shall not manifest wrath toward the children and shall not strike the children on the head with the fist nor with rods, nor shall they strike on the bare limb, but moderately on the proper place. It is necessary to exercise great discretion and discernment in disciplining children, for often a child can be better trained and corrected and taught by kind words when harshness would be altogether in vain, while another can be overcome by gifts. A third however cannot be disciplined without severity, and does not accept correction. Therefore the exercise of discipline of children requires the fear of God.

One should show sympathy to the little folk who have just started attending school and should not undertake all at once to break the self-will, lest injury come therefrom. For the children who are a bit larger one must also exercise very diligent care so that one can always have a good conscience.

The bed clothing shall be kept clean and shall be regularly changed, and when the little children arise in the morning a sister, or two or three girls, must always be at hand to take care on the stairways that no one falls.

When the children are brought to the school they should be carefully examined and if anyone is found to have a contagious disease such as scurvy or French disease [syphilis], the same should be instantly separated from the rest in sleeping and drinking and in particular in washing. Also special brushes and combs shall be used in taking care of the hair of those having skin eruptions. Those who have such eruptions shall be put together and not kept with those who are clean. Likewise those who have head diseases. If a child suffers or receives an injury on account of carelessness of whatever sort it may be, the injury shall not be concealed, but help and counsel shall be sought as soon as possible before greater injury comes of it.

And when the school mothers examine the children for bad mouths and reach into a bad mouth with the fingers, they shall be careful that they do not at once with unwashed fingers reach into a healthy mouth and thereby contaminate it, but shall always beforehand cleanse the fingers with a clean cloth and water before they examine and cleanse mouths. They shall likewise demonstrate to the sisters with them how to heal scurvy of the mouth, and not withhold this from them that others also may be able to attend to such things if they are appointed for it.

Brushing shall not be turned over to the girls to do.

In the case of diseased heads and bad mouths the school mother shall take especial care, in particular about contagious diseases, and shall arrange for a separation in all matters, as in part already stated, as for instance in the matter of beds, washing, eating, drinking, using spoons and cups, also in the matter of examining the mouth and sitting on stools.

Once a week the clothes of the children shall be examined for lice, likewise the clothes of the children when they come to school. The new children shall have their heads and clothing examined for lice.

When boys and girls are used outside of school for help in tending the cattle or driving the horses, care shall be taken that they do not go astray since they often like to absent themselves or hide. Therefore they shall appear twice weekly on brushing day.

One should not let the shoes of the children become too hard so that they cause blisters and the parents may have occasion for complaint. Therefore care should also be taken that the clothing and everything else is regularly repaired.

The new children whose parents are still on probation shall not at once be clothed in new clothing, but shall for a time be given the old clothing until their parents have proved themselves worthy members.

The nurses [for sickness] shall diligently stay with the sick children, faithfully care for them, so that no one climbs over the bed or falls on the stairs, and it shall be earnestly impressed upon the mind of the girl in charge that they shall take good care of the children, but shall not be away from them long in case they must leave the bedside.

The food which is to be given to the children they shall not be forced to eat. Drinking shall also be attended to so that drinking is not postponed too long or refused so that the thirst does not become so great that they drink to excess, which is harmful.

And for the sick children especially one should be free to ask the cook for that which they may need; yet this should be done orderly and not each sister run to the cook on her own account, but the request should be made on advice of the school mother.

When children are sick one should not be too severe with them if they ask for this or that, but should in true faithfulness as unto God be diligent in waiting upon them, in lifting and laying down, in cleaning and washing.

And where there are two schools, the small and the large, the two shall be conducted as though they were one, and not separately. The sisters in the two schools, in whichever they may be, shall be in the proper attitude and love toward each other and shall faithfully assist one another in combing and brushing; in bathing and washing, as is necessary. That is, in everything the children of the two schools, whether sick or well, shall form a unit, and fellowship shall be exercised with open heart, without vanity or selfishness.

If the parents who are visiting a school desire to take their children home to themselves for a visit, per-mission may be given for a definite time by a school master or school mother but such permission shall be given with caution in the fear of God as the circumstances dictate, and those in authority shall have a definite understanding as to whither the children have been taken.

They shall also take care in super-vising the larger children who serve as bread cutter, water carrier, bed-room maid, sweeper, dish wash-er, children's maid, sick nurse, etc., since they have often been found to be inconsiderate, mischievous, thieving and frivolous. Wherefore, those who are older shall take dili-gent care to supervise and watch over them so that no one shall be found guilty of permitting such con-duct and have to be disciplined.

Neither brethren nor sisters shall of themselves undertake or order something without the counsel, knowledge, or will of the elders. Even though someone knows a bet-ter method, it shall not be followed without good counsel.

When the sisters go out into the field or into the garden with the children, they shall be careful, as many of them as find it possible, to stay with the children so that the children do not get into trouble. The school master shall also be along as much as possible.

The larger boys or girls should not by any means be allowed to bump or pull or hit the children.

The sisters shall take special care that the small children shall be kept clean.

The sisters shall also not go away to their rooms on their own business too much but the one shall tell the other.

They shall not carry hot water into the rooms so that no one may be injured.

They shall not bathe the children in too hot water for that is harmful.

They shall not let them sit too long on the stools lest they take cold or do themselves harm.

The wash woman shall be careful in making the fire and in heating water and shall not depend too much upon the girl who is helping her.

The night nurse [*Wachterin*] shall take good care of the light at night and shall frequently go about among the children to look at them and cover them.

The school mother shall not arrange matters for the sisters or for the girls without the counsel of the school master.

If a child will not keep quiet during the admonition it shall be taken out so at the other children may not become restless, for sometimes one child is shy, another one thirsty, a third has some other need which one does not know. For this reason it is not possible to bring everything in order by using the rod.

During the day in school one should not attempt to settle everything with blows, but moderation should be used.

Also, no sister shall show disfavour to a child under her care or another child, nor show partiality against one that would prefer not to stay with her.

Neither brothers nor sisters shall show favouritism to particular boys or girls or send them to special places for they soon are overcome by the flattery and become proud.

Likewise the school masters shall not for any reason of their own or on account of business, without the counsel and consent of the elders, seek occasion to be absent from or leave the school. They shall not engage in work outside the school, such as planting or building or working on trifling things and thus neglect their work in the school. They must not by any means go to the markets here and there and buy according to their pleasure but rather they shall ask for the things they need at the place where these things are provided. They shall not occupy themselves with writing and reading and shall not let others take their place who often deal wrongly with the children out of favour or disfavour but they all themselves supervise the children.

The sisters likewise shall not look after their own interests whether in sewing and mending or such work and shall not depend too much upon the girls and shall not go about too much outside the building and then when they come into the school accept a complaint from a boy or girl and then without proper consideration proceed to deal out punishment. Therefore we instruct them, faithfully to remain in the school and take care of the children since by such diligence discipline frequently becomes unnecessary and can be avoided.

No one shall unwillingly with complaint or impatience serve the needy ones of the Lord in the schools, for there would be no blessing in such work and the children would in consequence have to suffer from violence and rudeness in discipline. For where good will is lacking, there are often unkind words. Such expressions as these may then be heard: "You bad children; one must be continually occupied with you, one cannot do anything for himself," or similar improper things. By such conduct all who hear it would be grieved and the Lord, who hears all things, will take notice and he will punish it in his time. Therefore each one should willingly and gladly do his part to please the Lord.

It is therefore the appeal of us as elders to all of you who have the youth in charge, brethren and sisters, and especially you who are appointed as school masters and school mothers, that you perform your duties faithfully with all diligence as far as is possible by the grace of God, so that this and similar rules of order shall be observed by you and your assistants faithfully and harmoniously so that in these and other necessary points which would be too long to write and possibly also not necessary, a peaceful discipline may be kept in all your care and supervision of the youth, since you must give an account for the same. May you do it with joy as to the Lord in heaven who will also be a faithful rewarder of your diligence.

In conclusion, let each one deal with the children by day and by night as if they were his own, whether in the matter of giving them to eat and drink or taking up or laying down, or leading about or carrying, or cleaning and washing, whatever is necessary, so that each one may be able to give an account before God and may have a conscience void of offense before the godly and the ungodly.

All this which has been here written and told at some length is a pattern of how counsel should be given to those who are concerned with the schools. At times more should be said and at times less, just as is necessary at each place according to the circumstances. By this each one will know how to conduct himself so that the honour of the Lord may be promoted.

The kitchen help and the waiters shall be told that they shall prepare and distribute with good will the food and drink which has been ordered for the children according to their need whether sick or well, young or old, and they shall not make many words about it.

And if it is necessary to ask for some particular food for a sick child, out of the usual order, they shall avoid using rough words. If what is asked for cannot be given, there should be a clear explanation, so that no one give occasion for complaint to another.

[**Source:** Harold S. Bender, "A Hutterite School Discipline of 1578 and Peter Scherer's Address of 1568 to the Schoolmasters," *Mennonite Quarterly Review* 5 (1931): 231–41. Used by permission.]

Dirk Willems saves his pursuer in 1569, *Martyrs Mirror*, 1685, etching. [*WikiCommons*]

[Peter Walpot][1] (1521–1578)
Ein schön lustig Buchlein etliche Hauptartikel unseres Glaubens betreffend / [The Great Article Book:] A Very Delightful Little Book Concerning Several Key Articles of our Faith, 1568

In their encounter with various confessional groups, including other Anabaptists, the Hutterites produced not only confessions, but a larger collection called *Das große Artikelbuch* that organized their position on a number of key issues. The five topics addressed are infant baptism; the Lord's Supper; the true inner surrender (*Gelassenheit*) and Christian community-of-goods; the sword; and separation between believers and unbelievers. A condensed form appears in *Das große Geschichtsbuch*.

For each of the five topics, a series of "articles" or points argue for the correctness of Hutterite beliefs. Typically, these are biblical proof texts and examples. Each section can be categorized as follows: Old Testament, New Testament, "Questions the World Asks," and "Further Considerations," which include arguments from Church Fathers and other ancient authorities.

The occasion for the writing of this text may originally have been the discussion leading to the readmission of the remnant of the Gabrielite Brethren in 1545. It was likely also used to prepare Hutterites to engage with non-Hutterites, whether rival groups or officials that had the authority to interrogate and imprison them.

---

1   The authorship of this apologia is currently undergoing scholarly debate. The possible compilers include *Ältester* Peter Walpot, or the missioner, Hans Zuckenhammer.

[The First Article:
On Baptism]

1.

Christ says: "[…] Go and teach all nations and baptize them in the name of the Father, the Son, and the Holy Spirit."[2] […]

Here the correct order of baptism is indicated for us, and it is established that teaching should precede baptism. For [Christ] says, "teach all nations," and then adds, "and baptize them." We see that baptism is based on teaching. He calls baptism a water-bath in the Word[3] because those who are to be baptized must first be taught the mystery of baptism, the rules of faith, and what they must know and do as Christians. […] Like faith without works is dead,[4] so are works that do not proceed out of faith as nothing.

'To baptize' basically means dipping or plunging into water, and to be baptized is to be plunged or sprinkled with water; it is not the act, but the understanding, substance, and meaning of the act that counts. Baptism is a cleansing, denial, and dying to the self[5] and a yielding to God; it is like a signature, union, or marriage of the believer with Christ.[6]

Baptism is not and cannot be of any benefit to somebody before they understand it, and no one understands it unless they are instructed and taught. […] How could the apostles have been able to move the people if they had not taught the people beforehand and given them instruction regarding baptism, and to what end they should or want to accept baptism. Therefore infant baptism is in every respect contrary to Christ. One cannot teach infants or preach the gospel to them, for it would not be Christian but foolish. Also, they are unable to keep what Christ has commanded them. For this reason there is no ground whatever given here for baptizing infants.

2.

Mark 16 says, "Go into all the world and preach the gospel to every creature. […]"[7] Here you see further that baptism is based on preaching and on faith.

[Christ] again commands the disciples to preach first. But to whom? Not to wood, stone, or mountains, nor to uncomprehending beasts or uncomprehending children. […] If one preached to a child for a whole

---

2   Mt 28:[18–20]. All scriptural references included in the text have been converted to footnotes for ease of reading. References in square brackets are editorial additions.
3   [Eph 5:26.]
4   [Jam 2:14.]
5   [1 Cor 6:11; Rom 6:4.]
6   Isa 44:[5].
7   Mk 16:[15–16].

week, if he believes in Christ one has won. If not, and it is still baptized, that baptism is no baptism but a curse before God. The one who is to be baptized in accord with Christ's command must believe first. With infants that is impossible; hence infant baptism cannot be considered and shall not be practiced. [...]

6.

Christ our example was personally not baptized until he was about thirty years old and about to begin his work; this is an example that we should not be baptized as children, but when we have come to mature years and good understanding, able to begin the work of God. [...]

8.

Infant baptism is simply monkey-business [*Affenspiel*]. It is as if you sent a troop of infants from their cribs to the emperor as soldiers into a camp against the enemy. And if you set up a day-old or week-old child to swear submission and obedience to the government, yes, if you commanded a child to manage the business of citizens, make purchases, to sow and to harvest, that would be highly ridiculous. Likewise infant baptism is ridiculous, a mockery and disparagement of the true baptism of Christ. [...] Again, those to whom earthly matters cannot be entrusted, to them divine matters cannot be readily entrusted either.

28.

At the time when Noah was building the ark in which a few [...] were preserved through the water or flood (which is a [...] picture of baptism, as Peter says), there was no child in the ark. Therefore they are not to be baptized. And just as no one entered the ark unless he believed first, on the strength of this figure also no one is to be baptized in water unless he has first the understanding and knowledge of faith. [...] By baptism one enters the community and church of God which is the true ark in which the obedient are preserved by the Word.

123.

If one wants the testimony of the ancient teachers—although there is no need of it because Christ and his apostles are sufficient testimony—hear what JEROME, writing on Matthew, has to say about baptism [...]: "He commanded his disciples first to instruct and teach all nations, and later instruct them in the sacrament of baptism on faith or immersing in water." [...]

BEDE, on Acts 19, says: "All who came to the apostles to be baptized were instructed and taught by them." [...]

AUGUSTINE says to Seleuciana: "People should repent before baptism, as Peter told the Jews in Acts 2."

Of the modern teachers [...] [ERASMUS OF ROTTERDAM] in his *Annota-*

tions on Mark chapter 16 says: "The apostles were commanded first to teach, then to baptize. The Jew is led to knowledge by ceremonies, the Christian learns first." One could easily find more like this, but it is not necessary to waste time on it. […]

Pomeranus, in the pamphlet concerning unborn children, says, the church has been in error some twelve hundred years with respect to children, whom we cannot baptize, but would so dearly love to. […]

[The Second Article:]
Concerning the Supper of Christ […]

[1.]

During the night of his betrayal the Lord Jesus knew that the time had come when he would depart from this world amid suffering and death. Because he would leave his followers to return to his Father, he gathered them together.

He took the bread:[8] The antichrist takes the host or oblation. Christ did not do that, but took bread. […] This earthly bread points us to the true bread of heaven, which is Jesus' body given for us on the cross.

And gave thanks: The antichrist consecrates, blesses or hallows it. Christ, however, gave thanks; he praised and honoured God to show that we should also do the same. Eating this bread is a special feast, by which we proclaim the Gospel; it is a feast of thanksgiving.[9]

And broke it: As though he would say, "Look, even so will men treat my body—just as bread which one wants to eat is broken in pieces, so will my body be broken and killed for you, that your souls may enjoy salvation. When the soul is separated from the body we call this a departure. Therefore, we also break the bread with our own hands, for we, ourselves, are to blame that he was crushed and bruised like this. […]

And said, 'Take, eat.' These two words still apply to the bread he offered to be eaten […]. It is as if he wanted to say, 'As a constant, ever-to-be-renewed memorial and remembrance of my love, that I have won eternal salvation for you, and, like the grains of wheat are ground and made into one loaf, you have been made communitarians, members of my body, suffering and eternal kingdom. You are redeemed, ransomed and set free from the power of death and the devil,[10] not with corruptible silver and gold[11] or through the sacrifice and bodies of beasts, oxen, calves, and rams, as in the Old Testament, rather:

---

8   Lk 22:19.
9   Heb 5.
10   1Pet 1:[18f].
11   Heb 9:[12].

'This is my body, which is broken for you.'

These words do not apply to the bread, but to his actual human body sitting there among them. God has prepared him to come to do his will; his body was given to death on the cross and slain for our sake.[12] It was not bread that was broken or sacrificed on the cross for us [...].[13] These words, "This is my body" do not have such strength that we should understand that the actual body, with flesh and bones, with skin and hair, with hands and feet, is in the bread or that the actual blood is in the wine. No, but that we should not regard and use it simply as any other food and drink, but also as something intended as a great sign and indication pointing to Christ and his most holy observance. With it we remember the Lord and proclaim his death. Other suppers are meant for the maintenance of the natural life, but the Lord's supper for the remembrance of Christ. [...]

In the same manner he took the cup, which represents his new covenant [...] and testament of his last will, which [...] brings with it the suffering Christ.

And said, 'Drink of it, all of you,' savour and use this growth of the vine as a true reminder and encounter with the glorious grace[14] I have given you all [...]. Even as grapes all give their juice to one drink, in the same way have I led you into true fellowship of saints and grafted you onto the vine of Christ.[15] This does not happen with the blood of oxen, goats and calves, as in the old covenant, which without the shedding of blood there was no forgiveness, but,

'This is my blood of the new covenant, which is shed for many for the remission of sins.' [...]

"Do this in remembrance of me," write Luke and Paul.[16] This explanation is added: namely, that ever as the Israelites ate the lamb in remembrance of their redemption from Egypt,[17] we must also eat of the bread and wine, as a holy memorial, remembrance and exhortation, yes, as a feast of thanksgiving and refreshing reminder of his great deed, when he, with suffering, death and the shedding of his blood, redeemed and reconciled us, who but for this were lost, through the sacrifice of his body and blood on the cross.[18] [...]

2.

Therefore in the supper we remind ourselves, firstly, of his love and of his suffering and death for us: that he has brought us, who were lost,

---

12   Lk 22:[19]; 1Cor 11:[24]; Heb 10:[7].
13   Rom 8:[32]; Eph 5:[2].
14   1Cor 12:[13].
15   Jn 15:[1ff.]; Heb 9:[12].
16   Lk 22:[19]; 1Cor 11:[24].
17   Ex 12:[14].
18   Heb 10:[12].

back once more and redeemed us. And we do this in remembrance of him, for what is more precious to God than his only Son? What greater thing could the Son have done for us than to give himself in death for us, even though we did not deserve it? Yes, we are loved by him with a greater love than we can love ourselves. [...]

Secondly, we confess and demonstrate to one another that we are all of one mind in our heart, and members of the body of Christ. [...] We are ground together by the Word of God into one church and fellowship of God's people. Whoever insists on living with personal property, greed, self-will and obstinacy cannot observe it in all honesty. [...]

3.

"I say to you," said Christ after keeping his supper, "I will not drink of this fruit of the vine from now on until that day when I drink it new with you in my Father's kingdom."[19] With this he sufficiently demonstrates what the wine and the bread are. Previously, what he called the wine after his blood, he here he still calls wine. Yes, with clear words, by means of a subtle statement, he calls it a fruit or growth of the vine. If he had changed the wine present at the supper into his blood, or if his blood

had been therein, he would not have called it a growth of the vine anymore, for blood is not wine. [...]

18.

The Lord's Supper was not ordained for the sake of physical eating, but rather for the purpose of thanksgiving and calling to remembrance. Those of old [...] called it the *Eucharist*, that is 'the thanksgiving,' and it is an instrument of Christian unification. [...]

19.

There are three things to be noted regarding the Lord's supper: substance, reality, and practice: [1.] In accordance with nature, the physical substance [...] is and continues to be bread and wine. They are not in substance the body and blood of Christ, but in remembrance and implication. [...] [2.] The reality is the setting free, i.e., the washing away of sin, which has taken place for us through Christ. [...] [3.] The practice is that those who have already come together as one loaf through faith and holy baptism, place their confidence in the death of Jesus Christ, gather together to consider this and to break bread with one another. [...]

---

19   Mt 26:[29]; Mk 14:[25].

[The Third Article]: Concerning GELASSENHEIT AND CHRISTIAN COMMUNITY-OF-GOODS [...]

He who will have the one,
must let the other go.

As gold is tried in the fire,
so are men in the
furnace of surrender.[20]

Not hard the Word of God would be
if from self-interest men were free.

I.

The Lord commanded Israel, "There shall be no poor among you."[21] The people of the new covenant fulfil this on a higher level in perfect community, for if the old covenant had been fulfilled and sufficient, another covenant would not have been sought.[22]

19.

When people asked the forerunner of Christ, John the Baptist, what they should do, he instructed them to hold things in common, saying, "He who has two coats, let him share with him who has none; and he who has food, let him do likewise."[23] Note how clearly he puts it!

21.

The Lord Jesus called his disciples [...] and said to them, "Follow me!"

[T]hey left their net, boat, and father behind and followed [Jesus].24 See how he calls his own away from their property and how they let it go and leave their parents and friends and follow him on the way of *Gelassenheit* and community.

37.

The Lord said to Peter, "Go and cast a hook into the sea, and take the first fish that comes up, and when you open its mouth, you will find a shekel. Take that [...] and give it to [the tax collector] for me and yourself."[25]

The deeper meaning of this is nothing else than that they, as fishers of men, are to catch, by preaching, from out of the world those that believe, and give their possessions over to true community to be used for the needs of all, as in the Church in Jerusalem. [...] [T]he sea must bring forth gifts to the name of the Lord, as Isaiah says.[26]

58.

"A new commandment I give to you: that you love one another, even as I have loved you. By this all men will know that you are my disciples, if you have love for one another."[27]

---

20 Ecc 2:[5].
21 Deut 15:[4].
22 Heb 8:[7].
23 Lk 3:10–11.
24 Mt 4:18–19; Mk 16–20; Lk 5:11.
25 Mt 17:26–27.
26 Isa 60:5, 9.
27 Jn 13:34.

The new commandment of love has a special essence, namely that we must have and demonstrate fellowship toward one another in all the gifts and goods we have from God, so that they are equally available to all. [...]

63.

When the Holy Spirit came down, he brought about Christian community in its perfection, so that the three thousand[28] and five thousand[29] at Jerusalem, indeed, all that had come to believe, were together and had all things in common. They sold their goods and possessions and distributed them to all, as any had need.[30] The Apostle therefore calls it a "community of the Holy Spirit,"[31] because where the Spirit truly dwells, this is the result.

65.

Ananias and his wife sold their property and, with treachery in their hearts, embezzled some of the money, laying only part of it at the apostles' feet. [...] Undoubtedly, they did this in order to have something in hand in case they [...] fell away again. Both of them had

to die a sudden death. Peter said, "[...] You have not lied to men but to God."[32] [...] Now if community did not have its ground in Christian doctrine and in the Holy Spirit, [...] Peter would have had to say to Ananias, "You have not lied to God and the Holy Spirit, but to men."

86.

"Love is patient and kind; it does not envy; [...] love is not self-seeking,"[33] hence it only seeks community. That is why true community arises among those who have love and are sound in love.[34] Nothing is so strongly enjoined on us as love,[35] for it is communal by nature and seeks the common good. It contains the whole law and all the prophets.[36] But there is no love in a man who pursues his own interest and property. [...]

141.

God does not want his children to live like cattle during their time here on earth[37]—like cows, donkeys, or oxen, with everybody just thinking of, and filling, their own belly. Much less does he want them to be like dogs, which never have enough,[38] or

---

28   Acts 2:43.
29   Acts 4:4.
30   Acts 2:44–45.
31   Phil 2:1; 2Cor 13:14.
32   Acts 5:1–5.
33   1Cor 13:4–5.
34   Tit 2:2.
35   Jn 13:34.
36   Mt 22:40.
37   Ps 32:9; 49:20.
38   Isa 56:11.

like sows, which want to be the sole owners of the trough and leave the others only with what they cannot handle. Rather, he desires that his own should live here on earth as newborn[39] people and as members of one body.[40]

143.

Property has no part in the Christian Church, but rather, belongs to the world; it belongs to paganism, to those that do not have the love of God; it is appealing to those who live according to their own will. If there were no self-will, there would be no property.

True community-of-goods, on the other hand, is appealing to believers, because, by divine right, says AUGUSTINE, all things ought to be common, and no one should take to himself what is God's, any more than he would the air, rain, snow, or water, as well as the sun, the moon, and the elements. Just as these things may not be divided up, so earthly goods, too, which God has evenly apportioned and measured out for common use,[41] should and may not be taken for one's own use. [...] Whoever fences off and appropriates what is and should be free, does so against the one who made and created it as free. This is a sin, says the THEOLOGIA GERMANICA. [...] Unfortunately, this has gone so far that, if they could grab hold of the sun and the moon and the elements, they would appropriate them and sell them for money.

[The fourth article: CONCERNING THE SWORD]

1.

Early on, God said to Noah, "For your own lifeblood I will surely require a reckoning: from every animal I will require it and from human beings [...]."[42]

God did not ask for a blood sacrifice, indicating that if the blood of unreasoning beasts is so precious, how much more is that of a human!

17.

"The wolf and the lamb shall feed together, and the lion shall eat straw like cattle, but the food of the snake shall be dust. No one shall harm or kill another in my entire holy mountain, says the Lord."[43] So where there is beating, lashing, stabbing, shooting, injuring one another, destruction, quarrelling, fighting, killing, and shedding blood, that is the

---

39 1Pet 1:23.
40 Rom 12:5.
41 Deut 4:19.
42 Gen 9:[5 f]; Mt 26:[52]; Rev 13:[10].
43 Isa 65:[25].

devil's ungodly and unclean mountain and the place of Lucifer. Just as one recognizes the kingdom of Christ and his disciples by their love, peace, and unity, so also the devil's kingdom by the wrangling, quarrelling, and warring of those who take after Cain.

26.

Christ, the Prince of Peace,[44] teaches us this Gospel, saying: "Blessed are the meek, blessed are the merciful, blessed are the peacemakers, blessed are those who are persecuted for righteousness' sake."[45] From this it follows that the arrogant and surly are unchristian and not blessed, the unmerciful are not blessed, the war makers and those who quarrel are not blessed, those who cause persecution are not blessed. For that reason, whoever exercises the office of the sword cannot be in Christ. Whoever carries the sword at his side is not a peacemaker, but a combat-maker.

49.

Christ refused to condemn to death or pass judgment on the woman caught in adultery[46] although the law upholds such a judgment. Neither can a Christian do so with God's approval, even though the office of the ruler demands it. For "just as the Father sent me into the world,"

says Christ, "so send I you." Christ was not sent into the world to reign as a worldly king, prince, or lord, or an authority using force, sword, and power. [...] He says, "the servant shall not be greater than his lord, nor the messenger than he who sent him;"[47] it is enough if they are like the master.

88.

Initially, the Patristics [*Alten*] also believed that Christians may not go to war or serve as secular judges, and those in office were not regarded as Christians. Here are several primary documents and references that speak against their own practices:

CANON LAW specifies that it is not fitting for them to kill anyone. Their code puts no one to death, but places excommunication on the wicked. The reason why these are not to be so punished is given in their decree, namely that those who are foreordained to salvation may better their lives. [...]

CHRYSOSTOM, who lived in 390, was strongly opposed to warfare and taking revenge because they committed themselves to the one who taught peace. Read his exposition on Matthew and John.

The COUNCIL OF ELVIRA decided that magistrates should not be admitted into the church during the year they are in office. Indeed, many

---

44　Isa 9:[6].
45　Mt 5:[5, 7, 9, 10].
46　Jn 8:[11].
47　Jn 13:[16].

other decrees and many ancient teachers are opposed to the participation in war of those who are [true Christians]. [Margin:] Note, neither do they consider worldly rulers to be Christians.

In the COUNCIL OF TOLEDO, [...] at the time of Honorius and Arcady, it was decided that whoever is a soldier after baptism shall not be made a deacon even if he has not participated in a specific war. [...]

In his *Hauspostille*[48] on Matthew 13[49] LUTHER speaks of the tares: The church or the office of preaching does not wield the sword, but whatever it does it does solely with the Word. [...] If Matthew, when he was still a tax collector, and Paul, when he was persecuting the Christians, and the thief on the cross had been sentenced and executed as wicked men (which they were) immediately after the deed, then the wheat that grew from them afterward [...] would have been uprooted. [The Church] is to ban and exclude [the wicked] as heathen so they recognize their sin and mend their ways, and that others may be warned by their example and be watchful. ([Margin:] Just listen, you Lutherans, how well you follow him!) [...]

[The Fifth Article]:
CONCERNING SEPARATION IN MARRIAGE BETWEEN BELIEVERS AND UNBELIEVERS

1.

According to the laws of Israel [...] no one was permitted to have or marry an unbelieving wife.[50] The Lord said through Moses, "Do not give your daughters to their sons or take their daughters for your sons, for they will turn your children away from following me to serve other gods [...]."[51]

3.

The Lord said to Israel, his former people: "If your [family member] [...] entices you secretly, saying, 'Let us go and serve other gods,' [...] you shall not yield to him or listen to him [...], but you shall kill him [...]."[52]

If they had to kill and stone their wives who wanted to turn them away from the law of God, how much more should and must we now rightly separate ourselves and depart from the same, and refuse

---

48   A bible commentary for devotional reading.
49   [24–30.]
50   Ex 34:[36].
51   Deut 7:[3].
52   Deut 13:[6–10].

to put a carnal marriage [...] above surrender to God.

10.

Christ says, "If your hand or your foot cause you to stumble, or if your right eye makes you stumble, tear it out and throw it from you, for it is better for you to lose one of the parts of your body, then for your whole body to be thrown into hell."[53]

He does not mean that we should physically sever our external body parts, but speaks parabolically about how we must let our members be cut off when they cannot be healed and do harm to the other members. [...] (By foot and eyes, he means those that are placed closest to us. [...]) Even though we have such great love for and friendship with them, and they are bound to us and as necessary and useful as feet and eyes, nevertheless we cut them off because they are a hindrance to our salvation.

Therefore, if the wife or the husband are a hindrance, a stumbling-block, harmful or an evil influence it is better to leave them behind, in accordance with the Lord's Word, that at least one partner be saved. An unbelieving marriage partner can cause more harm and damage than twenty hands, feet or physical eyes, and neither medicine nor perseverance can help.

12.

Christ says, "Whenever they persecute you in one city, flee to the next; for truly I say to you, you will not finish going through the cities of Israel until the Son of Man comes."[54]

This freedom, given by Christ, extends to a Christian marriage partner that has been converted from among unbelievers in the same way it applies to a marriage where both partners are Christian. [...]

20.

"I am convinced that neither death nor life, neither angels nor demons, neither the present nor the future, nor any powers, neither height nor depth, nor anything else in all creation, will be able to separate us from the love of God that is in Christ Jesus our Lord."[55] Therefore nothing should separate us from God and his love, and if there is anything on earth, no matter how grand, that wants to sever us from it, we should leave it behind and flee.

28.

[The People of the world may] say, 'But even Christ says, "What God has joined together, humans should not separate."'[56]

Response: Yes, my dear friend, but I must first ask if God joined them together or if it is done according to

---

53   Mt [5:29]; [18:9]; Mk 9:[47].
54   Mt 10:[23].
55   [Rom 8:38–40.]
56   [Mt 19:6; Mk 10:9; 1Cor 7:10.]

the ways of the world where people do not marry in reverence to God. […] People are getting married as in the first world which God destroyed with the flood; "They saw that the daughters of men were beautiful; and they took wives for themselves, whomever they chose."[57] Who would want to say here that God joined them together? People of the world often come together as prostitutes and johns [*Huren und Buben*] and the priests (who is often such a one) officiate. Is this joined together by God? Much rather, it is Satan who has joined them together where people are married for the sake of money or property, as is the general trend in the world where they often cannot even look at each other through a fence. Should God have joined this together? Avarice and greed has joined them together! Because of this, the marriage and wedlock of the world is not truly joined together by God.

[…] Even if a believing partner leaves such an unbelieving partner—and they must—it has been previously mentioned that this does not happen according to human words. Rather, Christ, his Word, and will part it—he separates this marriage and not we. He came to divide people and to separate household members with his Word.[58] […]

The Word of the Lord endures forever.
And this is the Word that was preached to you.[59]

[**Source:** Translated by Kenny Wollmann from Lydia Müller, ed. *Glaubenszeugnisse oberdeutscher Taufgesinnter*, vol. 1. (Leipzig, 1938), 238–256.]

---

57   Gen 6:[2].
58   Mt 10:[35].
59   1Pet 1:[25].

Gründliche kurtz verfaste Historia.

Von Münsterischen Wi-

dertauffern : vnd wie die Hutterischen Brüder
so auch billich Widertauffer genent werden / im Löblichen
Marggraffthumb Märbern / deren vber die sibentzeben taufent sein
sollen/gedachten Münsterischen in vilen änlich/
gleichformig vnd mit zustimmer sein.

Durch.

Christoffen Erhard Theologum, auß der Fürstlichen
Graffschafft Tyrol/von Hall geborn.

Gedruckt zu München/Bey Adam Berg.
Cum gratia & priuilegio Cæf: May:
Anno M. D. LXXXVIIII.

Hans Kräl (d. 1583)
"Description of the Community," ca. 1570

Hans Kräl's idealistic account of the community during the Golden Years portrays a harmonious, well-ordered society where industriousness and a sense of purpose rule.

During these years God gave his people quiet times. In honour of his name we must record this in detail, for after the Lord had purified his church in various ways, allowing it to experience all kinds of tribulation and poverty for years (as can be found above in this book), God granted his people quiet times and rich blessings, as he did to the devout Job after his temptation. This he did to see how they would prove themselves in such times and to make sure that his work and plans would be publicly carried out and become known to all people far and wide. God did this and gave his people peaceful times, contrary to the intentions of the whole world, with the result that for twenty years or more there was no general persecution (as will be seen in this chronicle), except for a few incidents now and then.

However, in these times many accusations were made and decrees issued by the emperor and the king at the Imperial Diets, as well as in the Provincial Diets, which were made up of various Estates and faiths. Although they were otherwise quite disunited, in this they all agreed: that these people should be exterminated and not tolerated anywhere. But the Lord prevented this in many ways and at many times. On one occasion he gave the persecutors something else to worry about. Another time he made them lose courage to carry out their plans, for he can trim the sails according to his own wind.

Many resolved not to lay their heads on a pillow until they had expelled and exterminated God's people, and they received power (but not from God) for this purpose. But the Lord destroyed them before they could begin. Many intended to inflict suffering on our people but only brought harm to themselves.

There was a great deal of discussion. One counselled that they [the believers] should all be hanged; another wanted to burn them; a third to seize their elders, thereby destroying them at the roots. A fourth wished he had the power to deal with them as he pleased and wipe them off the face of the earth. But most of these people did not live long, and the years of their lives were cut short by death. This we have experienced. We could even give names.

As usual, wherever possible, the tribe of priests kept stirring up the powers that be. But the Lord our God stood in the way. The Archangel Michael stood watch over his people; otherwise they would long since have been swallowed up and devoured like bread. But as a hen gathers her young under her wings, protecting them by pecking at all that want to attack her own—indeed, as an eagle hovers over its young— this and much more God did for the sake of his people. Even the unbelievers often had to acknowledge that God refused to let this people be driven away or annihilated.

They lived in the land God had provided especially for them. They were given the wings of a great eagle and flew to the place God had prepared for them, and they were sustained there as long as it pleased him. Thus they gathered in peace and unity and preached the Word of God

publicly. Twice a week, sometimes more often, they held meetings in which the communal, united prayer was offered to God, asking him for all the needs of the brotherhood and giving joyful thanks for all the good things they enjoyed. Likewise, intercession was made for emperor, king, princes, and worldly authorities, that God might make them think about the office entrusted to them and conduct it properly, so as to govern peacefully and protect the faithful.

Furthermore, the Christian ban was used against the wicked when they were discovered in the brotherhood. The brotherhood banned and punished, each according to his sin. When they showed true repentance, they were re-accepted into the church.

In accordance with the Lord's command and the practice of the apostles, Christian baptism was given to adults who could hear the Word of God and could understand, accept, and believe it, infant baptism being the complete opposite and totally false.

The people met and celebrated the Lord's Supper to remember and continually refresh the holy memory of the suffering and death of Jesus Christ: through his death he redeemed us who were otherwise lost and brought us back, making us of one mind as members of his body. It was a celebration of thanksgiving for his love and unspeakable kindness in what he has done for our sakes; this we in turn should do for his sake in thanksgiving. Such a celebration of the Lord's Supper is the opposite of the idolatrous sacrament of the priests.

They practiced Christian community-of-goods as Christ taught it and lived it with his disciples and as the first apostolic church practiced it. No one else dared to join them. Those who earlier had been rich or poor now shared one purse, one house, and one table—the healthy with the healthy, the sick with the sick, and the children with the children.

Swords and spears were forged into pruning knives, scythes, and other tools. There was no musket, sabre, halberd, or any other weapon of defense. Each was a brother to the other. They were a thoroughly peaceful people who never took part in any war or bloodshed by paying war taxes, much less by active participation. They did not resort to revenge—patience was their weapon in all strife.

They were subject to the authorities and obedient to them in all good works, in all things that were not against God, their faith, or their conscience. They paid their taxes, annual dues, interest, tithes, and customs, and they did their compulsory labour. They honoured the governing authorities because of their divinely ordained office, which is as

much needed in this wicked world as daily bread.

In conclusion, all twelve articles of the Christian apostolic faith and all things founded on Holy Scripture were confessed and observed.

Christian mission was carried out according to the command of the Lord: "As my Father has sent me, so I send you." Also: "I have chosen and appointed you that you go out and bear fruit." Therefore each year servants of the Gospel and their assistants were sent out into the lands where there was a call. They visited those who wanted to change their lives, who sought and enquired after the truth. These they led out of their land by day and by night at their request, heedless of constable and hangman, with the result that many lost their lives for the sake of this cause. Thus they gathered God's people in a manner befitting good shepherds.

They separated themselves from the world and its evil, unjust life. They shunned especially the false prophets and false brothers.

The kind of cursing and profanity without which the world cannot speak was never heard among them. No oaths were sworn or promises made. There was no dancing, gambling, or carousing. They did not make fancy, slashed, fashionable, or immodest clothes; such things were done away with. They did not sing shameful, immoral songs, which the world is full of, but Christian and

A postcard image of Alinkov from 1935.

Archaeologist Jiří Pajer of Strážnice, Czechia, has devoted his career to studying 16th-century Hutterite settlements in southern Moravia. In 2014, his team discovered a former Hutterite settlement at Alinkov (Čermákovice), which was active from 1595 to 1622. This site is unique because it is the only one from that era with mostly intact buildings. Pajer claims 100–150 people lived there, focusing on winemaking, pottery, tanning, and milling. The preserved architecture and layout offer valuable insights into the daily life of Hutterites at the turn of the 17th century.

Pajer's vision is to transform the site into a "Memorial to Moravian Anabaptists." His plan includes reconstructing one building to showcase 16th-century Hutterite life, restoring others as guest houses for visitors, and creating an interpretive center or museum to tell the Hutterite story. However, a major challenge is securing the necessary funding to make this vision a reality.

A row of farm buildings at Alinkov, 2014.

Main residential building at Alinkov, 2014.

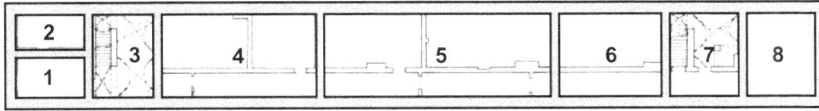

FIGURE 1

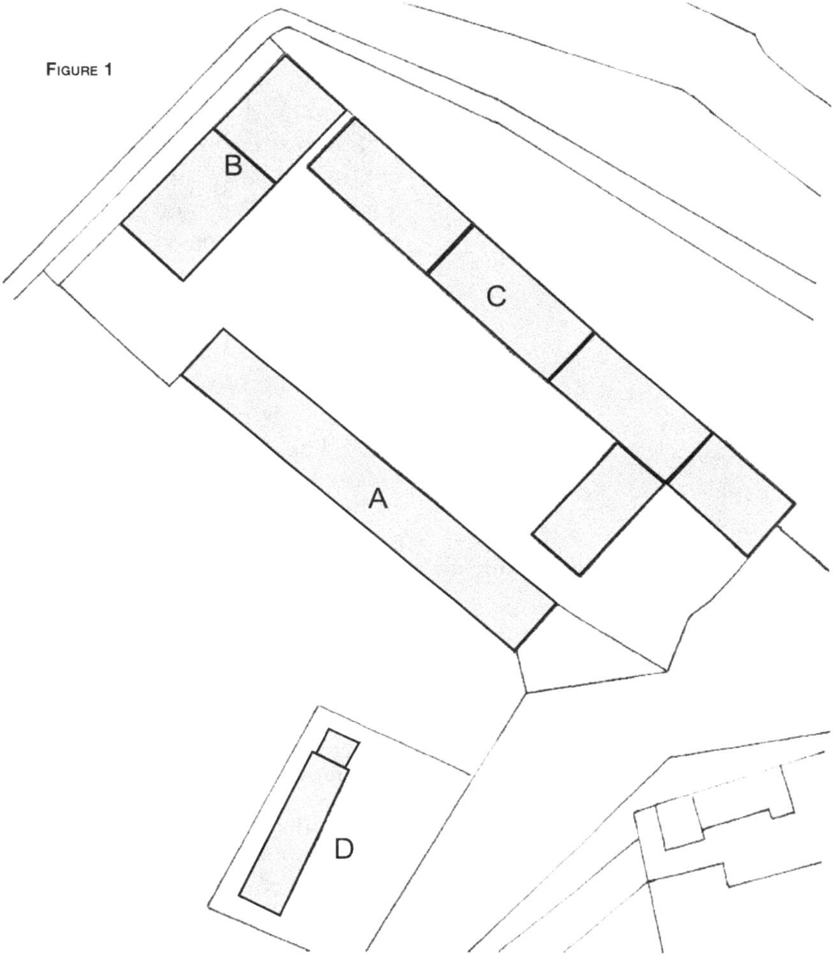

B

C

A

D

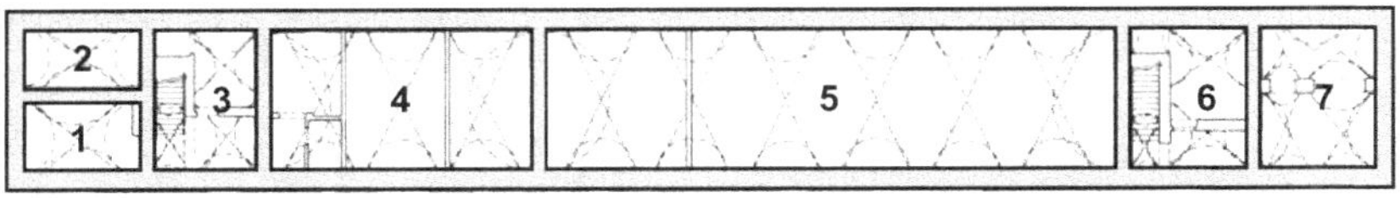

Figure 1: The layout of the buildings part of the Alinkov *Hof*: A. Main residential building; B. Adjacent residential building and mill; C. Row of Farm buildings; D. Cellar.

Figure 2: The first floor of the main residential building: 1, 'office' for public relations; 2, room for the steward; 3, hall; 4, hospital and hospice; 5, prayer room; 6, common dining room; 7, washroom, 8, guestroom for the nobility.

Figure 3: The ground floor of the main residential building: 1 and 2, chambers; 3, hall and main staircase; 4, small barn; 5, large cattle shed; 6, hall and work staircase; 7, communal kitchen and bakery.

FIGURE 2

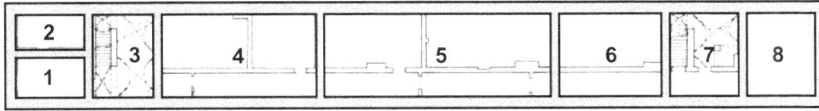

FIGURE 3

[**SOURCE:** Jiří Pajer, "Newly Discovered Anabaptist Settlement at Čermákovice (Alinkov Farmstead, Municipality of Horní Kounice, Znojmo District)," *Acta Ethnographica Hungarica* 60 no. 2 (2015): 329–285. Used by permission.]

spiritual songs and songs of Bible stories.

Leadership was entrusted to the elders, men who guided the people with the Word of God by reading, teaching, and exhorting them through Scripture. They practiced admonition and reconciliation, putting right any mistakes and wrongdoings.

Some men were carefully chosen to take charge of the management of temporal affairs. They made and received payments, provided for food and supplies, and did the buying and selling.

Others were in charge of organizing the work and sending each one to the job he knew and could do well, in the fields or wherever necessary. These were the work distributors.

There were brothers charged with serving at table. The meals began with prayer and thanksgiving to God, and thanks were given at the end before returning to work. Thanksgiving and prayer were offered at bedtime and again in the morning before going to work.

Certain brothers were responsible for the school. Together with the sisters, they looked after the children and their needs in all areas.

There was no usury, no buying and selling for gain. There was only honest labour to earn a living through the daily toil of those who worked as vine-dressers and farmers in the vineyards, fields, and gardens. Car-

penters and builders went out within Moravia and as far as Austria, Hungary, and Bohemia to build many large mills, breweries, and other buildings at fair wages for the lords, nobles, and other citizens. A brother was especially assigned for this purpose, an experienced builder who organized the carpenters, accepted work, bargained, and made agreements on behalf of the brotherhood.

Many of the brothers were millers, and there were many mills in that area whose owners asked the brothers to take them over and look after the grinding for a third or a fourth share, which was a fair deal according to current practice. So the brotherhood appointed a brother to oversee the mills. With the advice of the elders, he made, all the agreements, assigned the millers, and saw to it that the mills were staffed and functioning well.

For a long time the lords and noblemen (especially those on whose land we lived) employed our people to run their farms and other work departments, some for a third share, some for wages, or whatever was acceptable to both parties. A brother was responsible for taking on such farms as the community could manage, often after repeated requests by the landlords. He made the arrangements and saw to it that enough people were available to staff them.

In short, no one was idle; each did what was required and what he was able to do, whatever he had been before—rich or poor, aristocrat or commoner. Even the priests who joined the community learned to work.

All sorts of honest, useful trades were represented: those of mason, scythesmith, blacksmith, coppersmith, locksmith, clockmaker, cutler, plumber, tanner, furrier, cobbler, saddler, harness maker, bag maker, wagon maker, cooper, joiner, turner, hatter, cloth maker, tailor, blanket maker, weaver, rope maker, sieve maker, glazier, potter, beer brewer, barber surgeon, and physician. In each work department one brother was in charge of the shop, accepted orders and planned the work, then sold the products at their fair value and handed the proceeds over to the church.

Everyone, wherever he was, worked for the common good to supply the needs of all and to give help and support wherever it was needed. It was indeed a perfect body whose living, active members served one another.

Think of the ingenious works of a clock, where one piece helps another to make it go, so that it serves its purpose. Or think of the bees, those useful little insects working together in their hive, some making wax, some honey, some fetching water, until their noble work of making sweet honey is done, not only for their own needs but enough to share with man. That is how it was among the brothers. So there has to be an

order in all areas, for the matters of life can be properly maintained and furthered only where order reigns— even more so in the house of God, whose Master Builder and Establisher is the Lord himself. Where there is no order, there is disorder. There God does not dwell, and the house soon collapses.

The brotherhood became widely known through those servants of the Word and other brothers imprisoned in different places for the sake of their witness to Jesus Christ and his truth. In many different ways, they were closely questioned about the basis of their faith. This happened all over the German-speaking lands, wherever brothers were imprisoned, some for long periods of time. In word and deed, by their life and their death, they testified that their faith was the truth.

Moreover, emperors, kings, princes, lords, and those at their courts, especially in the German-speaking lands, became acquainted with the brotherhood's religion, teaching, faith, and life. They often came to see for themselves, and commoners came too, and learned that the communities were harmless and that the evil reports about the brothers were untrue. Many were convinced and praised them as a devout people that must have been established by God, otherwise it would have been impossible for so many to live together in unity, whereas among them, when only two, three, or four live together in one house, they are constantly in each others' hair and quarrel until they have to part company.

Some preferred to have brothers rather than anyone else working for them and serving them, so there were not enough brothers in the land, since—because of their reliability—everyone wanted them for his own benefit. But because of their religion they were always thought to be too many.

It was a remarkable situation: Some lords were angry and ill disposed toward the brothers because of their faith, and they did not want them to be tolerated in the land. Others were angry that not more brothers were assigned to work for them, although they had kept asking for many years. In short, some wanted to have them accepted, others wanted to have them expelled. Some said the best about them, others the worst.

The world did not want to tolerate them but had to. God divided the sea—the raging nations of this world—so that people could be gathered from all lands and dwell together in great numbers, fearlessly doing the work of the Lord against the devil and the world. Indeed, it is a wonderful handiwork of God, when you think about it. Some people thought it was right for those who had the strength. Others wished they, too, could live like that. Still others, the majority, in their blindness saw it as error and seduction or as a human undertaking.

Yet all the world so hated and envied them that they might have said with David, "We have more enemies than hairs on our head." As soon as they stepped outside the door, they were abused and called Anabaptists, re-baptizers, new baptizers, schismatics, agitators, and all kinds of insulting names. People everywhere disparaged them and taunted them with gruesome lies, accusing them of eating children and other horrible things that would have shocked us deeply had we even dreamed of them, much less done them. Many slanderous accusations of things that are not human, let alone Christian, were brought against the brotherhood to lay it open to suspicion and hatred.

The world hated and persecuted us solely for the sake of Christ's name and his truth, because we followed him, and for no other reason. And this was a sure sign: If someone traveled with only a staff in his hand to show that he did not mean to harm anyone, or if he prayed before eating, he was called an Anabaptist, a heretic. Such is the stupidity of the devil. But if someone became unfaithful and walked according to the ways of the heathen, a sword at his side and a musket at his shoulder, from that moment on he was welcome to the world and "a good Christian" in their eyes.

A man who wore no ruff round his neck or other signs of vanity in his attire, who declared that gambling, haughtiness, gluttony, drunkenness, and carousing are evil and against God, and conducted himself in a quiet way with patience and other qualities befitting a disciple of Christ—such a person was reckoned by the world to be a heretic, a sectarian, a deceiver, or a fool. He was hated and despised by people who had never seen him before and could accuse him of no wrongdoing, since he had harmed no one and had no wish to do so. This just shows what the world has come to.

But as soon as someone was unfaithful, returned to the world, and stepped into the inn saying, "Boys, let me treat you to a drink," singing immoral songs, drinking wildly with others, and sticking a plume in his hat like a fool; as soon as he indulged in gambling and dancing, wearing a huge ruff round his neck, baggy breeches, and clothes with ornamental slits, making a show of their thousand and one much-honoured sacraments, spreading syphilis and other dreadful diseases, and swearing and blaspheming God—from that moment on such a person was befriended by the world and acknowledged again as one of them. They approved of him and said, "Well done! You were right to leave the brothers and be converted and become a good Christian. Now that you have the true faith never let yourself be led astray from our church again. You did well to leave the brothers and separate yourself from their sect"—as they call us. Wherever he went, he found good

friends. People liked him and accepted him, even if they had never seen him before. They could see all his wicked deeds and vices, and still he was liked by the world because he had forsaken the truth of God. From all this it is clear that they hate and persecute us simply because we are zealous for God. Envy, stemming from the old serpent, is behind their hatred of God's truth. No one wants to admit it, but there is no denying it.

Eventually even the people living in our area began to hate and envy us, as Esau envied Jacob, on account of the blessings God poured out on us over and above what we earned with the toil of our hands. We had what we needed in house and home and—thank God—food, while they for the most part had to make do with very little because they spent it all on drink. They wasted their time and often squandered their money on drinks before they had even earned it. They loved to be idle and lazy.

What shall we say, then, about the false brothers and communities who complained about God's brotherhood more than about anyone else? They found fault with the brotherhood on every point. They hated us and resented it when we admonished them about their deviations. That verse in the Gospel is indeed true where Christ says about his own, "You will be hated by everyone for my name's sake." Because the Lord's Word truly applies to us, all this simply reassures and strengthens us all the more.

The Lord also strengthens us, his church, through those who forsake the truth and return to the world. Many of them—however long they live outside—have no peace in their hearts day in, day out, waking or sleeping. No matter what they set themselves to do, their consciences smite them constantly and their hearts pound with fear because of their unfaithfulness. They return deeply convicted, and in tears they repent and confess their sins, seeking peace with God and his church, ready to die rather than forsake the truth again.

Indeed, the number of such experiences gives us a deep certainty. It caused us great pain and shock to see for ourselves the despair of those backsliders who had once confessed and accepted God's truth but then deviated from it. Then God struck them down with sickness, and death hovered over them (a time when all things are revealed to a man). But too late and in vain they were overcome with remorse because they had turned away from the truth and had to die in their apostasy.

Some saw their punishment before their very eyes and carried on frightfully, crying out, "Woe is me!" and seeing themselves as beyond help. Others said that with their own feet they had kicked the door of heaven shut in front of them. Still others admitted that if only they had remained brothers and had repented, they would gladly die and part from this life. Many prayed in fear and trembling and pleaded with God to restore their health just once more. Then they would repent and return to what they had forsaken. Those who recovered did just that without a moment's hesitation. Many, however, were never able to experience such a reconciliation but, as already stated, died with a burdened conscience and in deep dread because they had mocked God too many times. When God had called them, they did not want to listen. Now, when they pleaded, the Lord turned a deaf ear.

Here we will end this part of the account and return again to the description of other matters. […]

[**Source:** *The Chronicle of the Hutterian Brethren*, Volume 1. Translated and edited by the Hutterian Brethren. (Ulster Park: Plough Publishing House, 1987), 402–410. Used by permission.]

"*Allgemeine Dienstordnung* / Rule for Supervisory Positions," 1580

The "*Allgemeine Dienstordnung*" of 1580 is one of the most comprehensive early ordinances. It defines the roles and responsibilities of a number of positions in 16th century Moravian communities, including those of the vintners, wine stewards, meal servers, housekeepers, kitchen workers, nurses, and laundresses.

What is to be presented to those in positions such as Vintner, Wine Stewards, Meal Servers, Stewardess, Kitchen Workers, Nurses, and Laundresses.

First, each one should consider why they have been appointed to their position, for what purpose, what is required of them, and whom they serve, namely, the Lord in heaven and his people. God has designated them by the counsel and discernment of his people. Because of this, each should preside over the matters of the household in their position in such a way, that above all, they are united amongst themselves, agreeable, and peaceful, not loud, disrespectful, nor ridiculous—whether in the kitchen, at the table, or anywhere else—but calm, disciplined, and with respectable conduct, as a good example and model for the community [*Geschwister*].

Secondly, that they are not appointed to dominate, bluster, or rule by force over the inheritance of the Lord,[1] but rather to be unassuming, friendly, and gracious towards everyone. For what is entrusted to them does not belong to them, but to the Lord and all the devout, and therefore they shall deal and behave knowing they will have to answer for it to the Lord.

In the first place, the community is commended to our [the Servants of the Word] care with the Word of God and in all godly counsel; our helpers are the servants of necessities [*Notdurft*], and all the stewards who are responsible for the community's property.

I   Cf. Deut 4:20.

Steward

His office is to oversee all aspects of the household, to see how it is running, and to ensure that all necessities are delivered to the household and purchased in due time. Also, to see that [the necessities] in the kitchen, the cellar, and all other areas are faithfully looked after and distributed for the common good, so that the people are provided for. Therefore, he shall attend to all members with responsibilities [*Amtleuten*] in the household and diligently ensure that each department fulfils their obligation, duty, and vocation to satisfaction.

He is to periodically go to the kitchen in person to taste the food prepared for workers, the healthy, and the unwell, diligently ensuring this is not ignored so that he can give an account of this. Also, [he is to] take care and diligence that the sick are provided with bedclothes and their necessities.

He is to inspect the lights and hearths to see how they are cared for and see that good order is maintained everywhere, and that the law is observed.

The steward shall direct the children to school at the proper time, as it is appointed, and diligently ensure it happens according to his instructions; he should not tarry in this.

The steward shall also collect the money from the craftsmen every fourteen days, not leaving too much to accumulate.

The steward shall also take heed of the bakers, lest they distribute soft bread at their pleasure and whim; it is not for them to distribute, but to bake. [...]

He shall diligently record all debts and credits—or have them recorded—so that disputes, be it with lords or other people, can be dealt with on good grounds knowing that nothing is done unjustly.

[Ensure] that [we do] not work too much on credit so that no large debts are accumulated.

Diligently guard against borrowing—whether it be money, grain, flour, or other things beyond that—for much effort and work is required before it is returned, and a portion of it [usually] remains unaccounted for.

Therefore, a great deal depends on a steward, for the benefit and also for the harm of a household. [...]

Vintner [*Weinzierl*]

His responsibility is to direct the people to the various tasks and to see that they proceed, and the work completed with diligence.

Also [ensure] that the people are dutifully given work for their money.

[Ensure] that not too much freedom is taken in the vineyards with fruit, grapes, and various other things.

The vintner and the steward's assistant shall do everything with the good counsel of a steward, carefully enquiring and advising one another, so that one doesn't send the people here and the other there, whereupon much gossip will ensue.

[Margin: This is not necessary.] Neither shall they accept work by themselves without the prior knowledge of the steward, nor release labourers, as if he, and not a steward, were responsible for the labourers.

That he deals meekly, kindly, and brotherly with the people, without partiality or favouritism.

In addition, take heed of the vulnerable and the young with brotherly instruction and forbearance, so that no one may be distressed or become fainthearted because of contempt, scorn, or mocking words.

He shall also see to it that the work is carried out peaceably, and that where there is any controversy, grumbling, impatience, or loud, unseemly behaviour, or any other lewd discourse, he shall soberly rebuff and admonish it.

That the Vintner [inserted: -or assistant] should not let it be noticed by the brothers if he and the steward are opposed to each other in organizing the work.

[Margin: This is not necessary.] That he neither borrow nor incur debts. He shall also diligently write down and record his dealings.

[Margin: NB.] If greater necessity in the vineyards or fields do not demand it, he should not take sisters away from spinning too often, for spinning is also of great importance to the community, and it is very expensive if it has to be bought.

Wine Steward

His duty is to diligently attend to the wine—filling, washing, cleaning, and [ensuring] that the barrels are cared for, so that no harm comes to the community.

He shall be diligent in gathering the dregs, to prevent the wine from becoming cloudy.

Before going to sleep, he shall diligently inspect the cellar at night and in the morning as soon as he rises, so that no damage occurs.

He shall work in good faith with the steward's advice, and not tap [a barrel] by himself.

To be generous [*geschmeidig*] with the wine. Also, to periodically enquire to whom the meal-bearers serve wine.

Diligently remain in the cellar, so that others do not take cause to run off with the wine. And also, not to sit too long at the table, or otherwise presume to chatter.

Neither should he always have wine at the table or immediately give wine to just anybody. If, however, he recognizes a need to give a drink of wine to someone, he shall fetch it from the cellar [himself] or otherwise leave it be so that no one else has to run for it.

Before he goes to sleep, he shall carefully wash the vessels he used during the day, hang them up, [and] then turn out the light and lock the doors.

Meal Server

He shall diligently attend to his duties, and diligently serve the people in the [dining] room, bringing bread, drink, and salt, and the food from the kitchen to the table with good will.

They shall not presume to perform other work, but remain faithful to their task in the dining hall and in the store room [*Kammer*] so that they do not need to be sought out at length.

[Ensure] that he be diligent in providing the elderly with bread and butter.

[Ensure] that the guests are not neglected or have to sit and wait for a long time, but that they are addressed in a friendly manner, and promptly given food, as is proper and orderly [...].

After the meal, the bread is to be stored in its proper place by the meal server, not left lying in the [dining] room or on the tables.

[Ensure] that the bread is handled properly. Keep the bread bowls dry and clean, and avoid cutting the loaf too thickly. Cover the bread diligently so that no vermin or other insects get into the bread or into the bowls and cause annoyance and regret.

And see that nobody takes large chunks of bread from the table after the meal [...].

Neither should he permit anybody to cut bread on their own and carry it off. Nor shall they be allowed to take as much bread as they want, but rather they shall be given what they need.

Wherever one can help another—vintners and servers—they should do so with diligence and not hiding themselves. And in this way, vintners and servers shall see to it that they diligently supply the necessities for all the faithful entrusted to them.

[Margin: This is no longer necessary.] Do not let the washing of foreign guests fall into neglect.

A server should pay heed to the people, and also admonish them frequently if they are noisy.

Be very humble with the brothers and sisters. [...]

Extinguish the light in the [dining] room and store room at the proper time.

Stewardess [*Haushalterin*]

She should (as a mother to all the sisters) also act in accordance with the good counsel, knowledge, and wishes of the steward, as far as housekeeping is concerned, [...] not letting anything go to waste through carelessness.

She shall not distribute lard or anything else without the knowledge of the steward, nor present it as a gift or give it away as a favour, either afield or at home, but rather according to necessity.

She should go to the kitchen frequently to ensure that the food is varied or alternated as often as possible, and give wise counsel to the head cook, providing what is needed in good time.

She should see to it that the lard is used well for the benefit of the people [Insert: so that the cook doesn't use it wherever she wants to].

Also that food is properly provided and distributed, so that there is not a surplus in one place, but a shortage in another—be it with lard or other things—but rather that a balance is maintained.

The stewardess shall also supervise the water bearer [*Wasserträgerin*], the laundress, and the baker [*Bäckerin*], so that each of them performs according to their responsibilities. [...]

She should also pay attention to how the young women responsible for the cattle are housed, how the cattle are cared for and fed, and that they have food in the winter.

She is to keep the sisters spinning, and not permit them to leave without good reason.

She should also use the children's mothers as necessary, so they do their part [*Fleiß*] in spinning and all other things.

She should therefore (as a housemother) supervise all the sisters in the household, so that good order and diligence are maintained.

Also, if the young sisters are too frisky and chatty, or want to stay up too late in the evening, they should be admonished and quieted.

And what she has to give, must be given freely. If someone requests something she is responsible for giving, she must do so diligently. But if it cannot be given, she should still respond in a kind and friendly manner. [...]

Head Cook

She should diligently consult with the stewardess.

[She should] not be excessive with frying, and ensure that the food is prepared in a safe and practical way.

Also, fairly give, distribute, and dispense [food] faithfully and diligently, not with favouritism, but according to what is needed. And, for our sake, not too much. [...]

Kitchen Nightwatch

She must diligently do her part with the sick during the night, looking in on them, bringing them refreshment, so they are faithfully supplied with what they need.

[She must] be devoted to the other things she is instructed to do.

She must take care of the fire and light. And also, be diligent in keeping watch where the sick are cared for at night, so that the light is carefully and diligently kept and maintained. [...]

Spinstress

That she be diligent and keep the sisters spinning.

No one has the authority to take sisters out of the [spinning] room without her counsel, because she knows best which ones are suitable and would rather work outdoors than spin.

Nurse [*Beterin*]

The nurse and stewardess are to be diligent in preparing beds for guests.

The nurse must be especially diligent with the sick, when one is so ill they need a cover [...], especially if they are in mortal distress.

When the sick are lying down, they are to be given what is needed, and diligently cared for. In this instance, especially, it is proper before God to be diligent and compassionate, not showing impatience or impudent words towards them.

That they do not give out beds according to their preference that somebody might with time claim as their own. [...]

In Conclusion

It is our petition and exhortation that they all [the brothers and sisters in these positions] work together, and that each one in his own department and position, give the brothers and sisters good counsel, good responses, and direction; be friendly with them and do not overpower any of them. In addition, what must be and is necessary, should not be left hanging.

They are not to oppose one another in the presence of the people, or favour one over another in order to please somebody, but speak to the best of their ability in every situation. If somebody has anything against another, they must settle it on their own and honestly, without gossipping, and not in the presence of the people.

No one should overreach the other in their position without good cause or necessity, so that everything happens with the counsel and consent of the others.

Nor should they be attached to each other in carnal camaraderie, seeking to be good companions to each other, but rather be faithful in their service. By this it may be seen that they love the Lord and his order and are of value to him. Each will have to give account and answer before God as to how their service in the community is conducted and performed. For this reason, each one should take it seriously, so that no one has just cause for complaint.

[**Source:** Translated by Kenny Wollmann from EAH-165, Bruderhof Archives, Walden, NY.]

ADOLF MAIS (1914–1982)
Anabaptist Legends, 1964

Legends are not standard historical sources. They are stories that mix historical details with fantastical elements from folklore, and are often exaggerated for effect. So why include stories of dubious historical veracity in a collection of historical sources? While legends are not completely reliable from a historical perspective, they clearly include kernels of truth, in this case about beliefs and attitudes held by Hutterite neighbours in Moravia. Through these legends, which have been told and retold, shaped and reshaped across many generations, we can still get a sense for how the Hutterites in Moravia were viewed by their contemporaries. This is significant because we have very few sources that give us this kind of information. Read alongside internal Hutterite sources such as *Das große Geschichtbuch* and anti-Hutterite texts such as the Catholic priest Christoph Andreas Fischer's polemical writings, these legends can illuminate and enrich the historical record in a unique way.

Adolf Mais has collected 26 legends dealing with the following topics related to Hutterites in Moravia: the considerable wealth of the Hutterites; the caves [*Löcher*] used by the Hutterites during times of persecution; the Hutterites' reputation for quality craftsmanship, particularly in producing quality pottery, knives, wine as well as their fame as *Bader*, midwives, wet nurses, etc.; cultural peculiarities such as marriage practices; and associations with the occult (devil, merman, etc.). Six of these folk tales are presented here in English for the first time.

Besides shedding some oblique light on Hutterite life in Moravia in the latter half of the 16th century, the following etymological legend seeks to explain the origin of the nickname "*Habaner*," a designation used in many of the folktales for the Hutterites in Moravia, even though it was a nickname only applied to them in Slovakia after 1760, when many Hutterites became Catholic:

> Along with their unique customs and traditions, the Hutterian Brethren brought with them a particular language, a kind of Low German, a mixture of the various German tongues spoken in the different lands

they had resided in and where their members hailed from before coming to Hungary. In this language, which is not spoken any longer, the word "*Haban*" refers to a ball, a toy commonly used by boys. Now, a Hutterite *Prediger* once urged his congregation to stand firm in the faith despite the fact that they had been fatefully tossed about like a ball [*Haban*] in the hands of boys and could easily experience further adversity in the future. This was picked up and came to refer to a wandering people who "bounced" around from place to place, whose identity remained difficult to pin down. This name stuck over time, but lost its insulting meaning. When they converted to the Catholic faith, the community had to give up the Hutterian Brethren name and took the name *Habaner*. They have kept it to this day, even though few of them are aware of the origin and meaning of the name they bear.[1]

Adolf Mais considers this explanation to be unreliable in terms of explaining the origins of the term *Habaner*. Yet the legend does draw attention to a historical fact: the Hutterite experience in the 16th century and beyond was unsettling and unpredictable.

The Legend of the Golden Apples

When the Hutterites left Landshut [in Bavaria, southern Germany] they had to leave behind all their property and possessions. They buried as much as they could in their cellars. It is said that when they were preparing to leave, they asked for permission to at least take along some apples. This request was granted and so they took along several wagons filled with apples.

They travelled into Slovakia and had to cross the March River. Since they had no money, they hoped the ferryman would take them across for free. They waited several days until the ferryman finally brought them across. As payment they asked him to take as many of the splendid apples as he wished.

At first, the ferryman declined [*stand auf sie gar nicht an*], but finally took two apples. The Habaner travelled on to Brodské, the first Slovakian community. To relieve his thirst the ferryman took a hearty bite out of one of the apples and nearly broke his old teeth on a golden ducat hidden in the apple. When he broke open the second apple, he found another golden ducat. Then he ran yelling after the Habaner, hoping that they might give him several more apples. But they did not hear him.

The Habaner Basement in Landshut

The Habaner basements are very interesting, and above all, enshrouded in a certain mystery. They are found practically under all of Landshut. What were these dark,

---

1   A. Freihr. v. M[ednyanszky], *Nachrichten über die Habaner*. (Brünn: Hesperus, 1810, 211).

winding passages used for? As hiding places in times of persecution? Some sources among us say that the Habaner lived their real life in these underground passages. There they were in league with the devil, to whom they dedicated their souls.

The Habaner Treasure in Landshut

In a house in Landshut there is a steel door which leads to the Habaner cellars. Behind this door an eternal fire burns and a cock sits on a barrel of pitch [*Pechfaß*] guarding the Habaner treasure. Whoever tries to take the treasure but does not know the password, is bewitched by the cock. The cock is only powerless on Christmas Day.

To this day, the Habaner come to Landshut on moonlit nights to carry off their treasures, which still remains undiminished.

The Habaner and the Cardinal

Once the King of Hanover came to Groß-Schützen, where he visited Cardinal Kollonitseh. The Cardinal gave his esteemed guest Habaner cutlery and a set of Habaner knives as gifts. The knives were so sharp, they could cut a feather in flight. The Cardinal was so impressed with the quality of the knives that he let the Habaner remain in the area.

The Merman and the Habaner Midwife

In the brook which flows through Klein-Schützen lived a merman who was on good terms with the Habaner. He often came into the village and visited the taverns. One could recognize him immediately by his green pants and red jacket, as well as the fact that water flowed from his boots. And he helped the villagers.

Once he brought a Habaner midwife to assist his wife. She went with

During the Golden Years, Hutterite society mainly consisted of artisans. They were famous for their pottery, also known as Habaner faience. [Courtesy of Jan Gleysteen]

him into his home on the bottom of the stream to attend to his wife. And she left the underwater world with a handsome reward and she gave the heavy golden coins over to the community.

My father saw this kind of coin in my grandfather's possession.

The Clever Habaner Wet Nurse in Vienna

The Habaner were well-regarded wet nurses among the nobility and were frequently brought to Vienna. And so it came about that a young wet nurse served a high-ranking nobleman at his Vienna residence. Once a party was held where the baby was shown off to the visitors. As the party was wrapping up, the wet nurse returned the child to its bedroom. And as she was putting the child into bed, she noticed that a man—likely a robber—was hidden under the bed. Now what? If she screamed, the man might kill her. But the clever nurse chose a different approach. She carefully laid the child into the bed and then pinched the child, so that it started screaming. She continued to pinch the child until the whole house gathered in order to see what was causing the terrible screaming. In this way the robber could be arrested without anybody getting hurt.

This incident came to the attention of the emperor, who asked the Habaner nurse to come to him so that he might reward her for her decisiveness by granting her a request. The girl was not in the least intimidated by the emperor and requested that he free the Habaner from compulsory military service. The emperor fulfilled her request and since then the Habaner have not been required to join the armed services.

[**SOURCE:** Translated by Jesse Hofer from Adolf Mais, "Die Wiedertäufer Sagen," *Österreichische Zeitschrift für Volkskunde* **67** (1964), 125–155.]

THE 17TH CENTURY

Title page of *Ein Send=Brieff an alle die jenigen so sich berühmen ... daß sie ein abgesündertes Volk von der Welt seyn wollen, ... Brüderliche Gemeinschafft, das höchst Gebott der Liebe betreffend* [A Circular Letter to all those who Boast ... that they wish to be a People set apart from the World, ... Concerning Brotherly Community, the Highest Command of Love], 1652. This volume represents one of the few Hutterite writings printed in its own time. A copy is held at the Leipzig University Library, Leipzig, Germany.

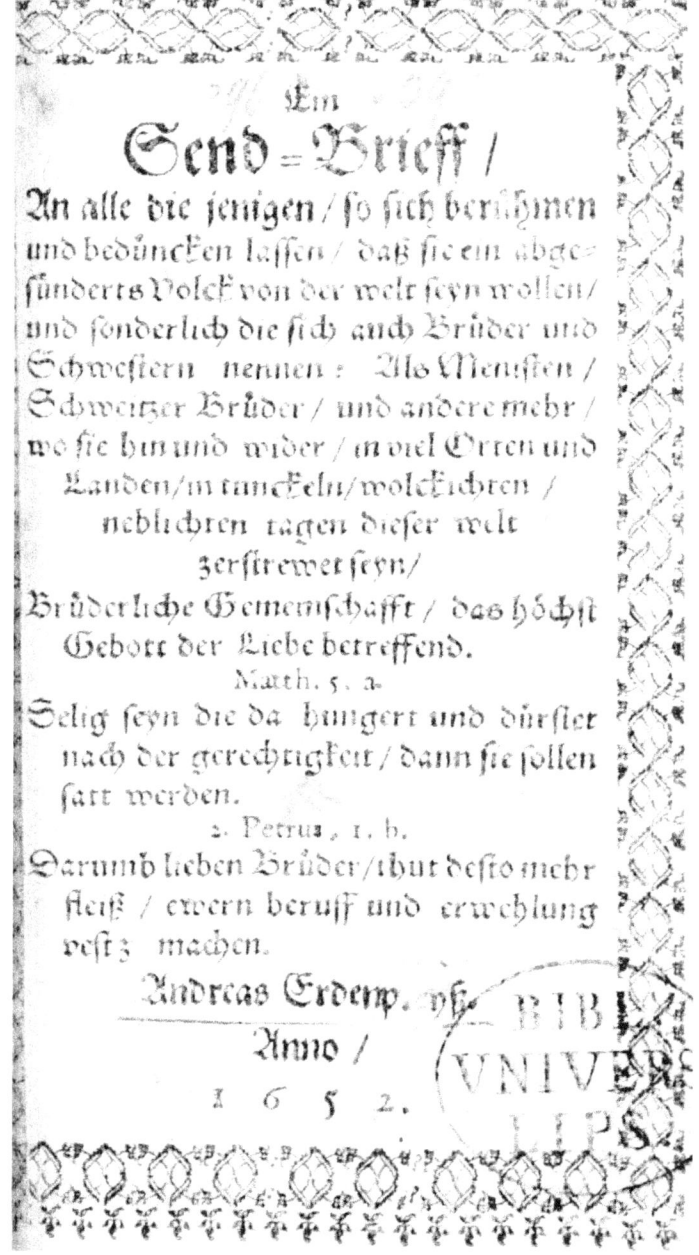

278

ANDREAS EHRENPREIS (1589–1662)
Ein Sendbrief… Brüderliche Gemeinschaft betreffend / An Open Letter on Brotherly Community, 1652

Andreas Ehrenpreis was appointed *Vorsteher* (i.e., elder) in 1639, nine years before the end of the Thirty Years' War. During his tenure as elder, the Slovakian communities were in sharp decline, both economically and spiritually. Part of Ehrenpreis' strategy to reinvigorate the movement was to send out missionaries—as was the practice during the 16th century—and the *Sendbrief* was designed to equip them. Ehrenpreis emphasizes the importance of love expressed in a life of surrender, discipline, sharing, and fellowship. The *Sendbrief* was one of the few books printed by the Hutterites at the time.

Grace, salvation, mercy, and divine blessing to all whose souls hunger and thirst, wherever you may be scattered under heaven. Amen.

I want you to know that in reading the history of our community I found that our forebears searched seriously for a way in which our communities could be united and, while no great differences appeared, nothing fruitful came of it. Yet I did note two reasons: namely community, that is, giving up of material possessions; and obedience, that is, giving up one's own will [into that of the community]. Since we are accustomed to having our own things and doing as we please from our youth this is very difficult and painful to human nature. But if we truly enter into the holiness of God we find that perfection cannot be achieved without it.[1]

They who would enter into life must come through love, the highest commandment; there is no other way through the narrow gate.[2] Hundreds of Scriptures and many witnesses make it very clear that whoever wishes to have the precious and hidden jewel must go and sell everything, yes, hand over everything they possess.[3] Different interpretations of these texts have been

---

1   Mt 19:16ff.
2   Mt 22:34–40; Jn 14:1–14.
3   Mt 13:45–46; Acts 2:43–47.

given because people want to keep what they have, but we cannot deny the work and power of the Holy Spirit, by which the apostles set a firm example in the first church in Jerusalem and three thousand were added.[4]

Therefore no one can think otherwise of this truth, or prove that the people did not understand what they were doing, or that they acted wrongly, or that it was not necessary to sell their houses and land to have community. They laid the proceeds at the feet of the apostles; no one said that anything belonged to them; they had everything in common. That is a clear light to the world, a city on a hill that cannot be hidden.[5] Think of our Lord Jesus Christ in his poverty; surely servants are not above their Master.[6] Or think of sailors in a storm at sea, who throw their cargo overboard, however precious it may be, to save their lives.[7] And yet their lives endure only a short while, for no herb has yet been grown against death.[8]

Moses also worked for true community in the wilderness, instructing the people of Israel to gather manna only for their daily needs.

Those who gathered much had nothing left over next day, and those who gathered only for their needs also had enough.[9] There is little difference before God between poor persons who hoard their meagre possessions and the rich who hoard theirs; both are rich enough for disobedience. Our Lord Jesus Christ said in several instances that those who love something more than himself, and do not renounce everything, note everything, cannot be his disciples.[10]

There are many witnesses who testify that we cannot be a people of God without these articles.[11] From among all animals God chose sheep, from all birds the dove, and from all wood the grapevine to show that by nature they want to be together.[12] This is also true of people: with the pious we become pious, with the crooked we become perverted.[13] A glowing ember soon dies if it lies alone. Peter said to Jesus: we have left everything and followed you, and Christ did not respond by saying that that would not have been necessary, but rather that their reward would be a hundredfold.[14]

---

4   Acts 2; 4:32–37.
5   Mt 5:14.
6   Mt 10:24–25.
7   Acts 27.
8   Ps 49.
9   Ex 16.
10   Mt 10:37–39; Lk 14:7–14.
11   Heb 12.
12   2Esd 5:21–30; Jn 10:1–18.
13   Ps 18:25–27.
14   Mt 19:27–30.

The wise man Sirach used bees to illustrate community. They all work diligently together, keep nothing for themselves, and maintain true community.[15] Where this does not take place love is tinted and community a sham, as others in the world also do. There is no doubt that if only love of possessions and self-will did not exist, and if we loved the poor life of Christ and his obedience as much as our wealth, the cross of Christ would not seem foolishness to us,[16] but rather a clear illustration and example of love and community.

Community Cannot Be Coerced

It is completely wrong and mistaken when we are accused of forcing people into community. That is far from us. Nor does the Lord or we compel anyone to it.[17] Those who are moved by the Spirit of God are children of God. We believe the words of our Lord God when he said that we cannot serve two masters.[18] We enter community not with subdued obedience, but as Christ wants us to, with happiness and great joy, as having lost a small thing and gained a great treasure.[19] This treasure brings eternal health, life, joy, and good days.[20] Therefore they who find it, but cannot commit themselves, should leave it and stop talking about their love for God and the poor. It would be better never to have known the way of truth, than to walk it halfway, or cause others to stumble.[21]

In an attempt to justify themselves some use fig leaves to conceal the truth, saying that living in community leads to disunity and strife, as though Christ, and the apostles, and the Holy Spirit did not know or understand what would happen. They take the saying of the world as an example, that husband and wife love each other best when they are away from each other, but this is not true in a good marriage. If this is true here, how much more so in the spiritual life among the people of God who relate to each other in love, forgive each other, and do not leave anyone alone because of human weakness. I take as example Abraham, Jacob, and Job who had serious quarrels with their wives, even being troubled unto death, but they did not, on that account, leave them but remained true to them until death.[22] Christ and the apostles also had difficulties. When Peter rejected the coming of Christ's death the Lord said, "Get behind me, Satan,"[23] nor did he want the Master

---

15 Sir 11:3.
16 1Cor 1:18.
17 Rom 8.
18 Mt 6:24.
19 Mt 13:44–50.
20 Acts 7.
21 Mt 18:6–7.
22 Gen 21; 30; Job 2:9–10.
23 Mt 16:23.

to wash his feet,[24] and they argued about who was the greatest among them.[25] That is why the Lord gave us the Our Father with a prayer for forgiveness.[26]

Therefore we do not reject a whole people because of their failings, nor pour the baby out with the bath water.[27] Those who are concerned for their salvation have true love for the house and church of God, they become spiritual building stones who give their possessions together with themselves as a living, holy offering pleasing to God.[28] This is also the true worship of God. Giving a penny is not enough. No, those who want to be a light in the world must give themselves and, in giving light to others are themselves consumed.[29] That is what Christ did, but he also admonished the young man to give what he had to the poor and to come and follow him.[30]

Whoever claims to belong to Christ in love, but cannot give their possessions to the community for the sake of Christ and the poor, cannot deny that they love worldly goods, over which they have only been placed as caretakers for a time, more than

Christ. Therefore Christ says, blessed are the poor in spirit, for theirs is the kingdom of heaven.[31]

Yet Christ does not ask this simply for the sake of the poor, but also that his followers may be free and surrendered [gelassen = yielded, at peace] and not have a treasure on earth to which they tie their heart, about which he warned.[32] Let everyone seek the welfare of others. Love does not seek to meet its own needs.[33] Why does Christ denounce selfishness so and imply that it might be a mortal sin to invite the rich, and others who can invite you in return, except for the sake of the poor? You will be repaid in the resurrection.[34]

Working for Others Is a Blessing

All this can lead to where people wonder whether they might as well cease serious work if there is no profit in it for them. But is this the answer, that only personal profit is the goal of our work? Is it not much more that we should work for the common good, and that if it is blest thirty, sixty, or one hundred times we shall hear the well done, faithful servant, from our Lord.[35] The Lord

---

24   Mt 13:8.
25   Lk 22:24.
26   Mt 6:5–15.
27   Mt 18:15–18.
28   Rom 12:1–2.
29   Mt 5:14–16.
30   Mt 19:16.
31   Mt 5:3.
32   Lk 12:22–34.
33   1Cor 13.
34   Lk 14:12–14.
35   Mt 25.

also reminds us that not everything in life should be done for the sake of reward saying: truly, they have received their reward, if it is done for praise.[36]

Many thousands think it is impossible to give up their possessions and self-will, as God and Christ have commanded. But we have enough examples to the contrary in Abraham, who left his home and country;[37] in Moses who left the royal palace;[38] and the apostles, who left father, boat and nets, and everything they had.[39] Paul left everything for the sake of Christ;[40] and a thousand times more, Christ himself left the heavenly glory, even so that the foxes and birds were richer than he.[41]

The Lord himself established community with his disciples. Only one controlled the purse. They had not yet received the Holy Spirit and Jesus could not tell them many things because they would not understand;[42] now the Spirit of truth has come, with many signs and wonders.[43] Since that time many thousands have also come to us, disposing of their property, others coming to us with empty hands, rejoicing that God had given them this insight.

That the much discussed community is considered as divine righteousness by all those who call themselves Christians, and is called for by them, comes from the Holy Spirit, for they remained steadfast in fellowship, in breaking bread, and in prayer.[44]

Community and the Lord's Supper

We note that the Lord's Supper was instituted by Christ with bread and wine, primarily for the establishing of unity and community. The faithful thereby testify that we, though many, are all one bread and one body, partaking of one loaf. In this the Lord Christ wants us to understand that even as the seeds on the field needed to die in the ground, then form roots and sprout, enduring the cold and heat of summer and winter to reach maturity, so also those who want to follow Christ must deny themselves, and endure suffering, taking the cross upon themselves.[45] As the grain of wheat needed to be ground and broken, so also those who eat the Supper must first be ground by the millstone of God's Word; kernels that are not ground up are thrown out and useless.[46] In the same way the grapes must be crushed before they can become wine, each giving

---

36   Mt 6:1–4.
37   Gen 12.
38   Heb 11.
39   Mt 4:18.
40   Phil 3.
41   Jn 16; Lk 9:57–62.
42   Jn 16:12.
43   Acts 2; Lk 24.
44   Acts 2:42.
45   Mt 16:24.
46   1 Cor 9.

itself up for the whole. This message of the kernels and the grapes, the bread and the wine in the Lord's Supper, is the example Christ sets before us to achieve community.

In a similar way in the Lord's Prayer, which Christ taught his apostles, we say when we pray, "Give us this day our daily bread," meaning that it is no longer mine or yours but ours, belonging to everyone.[47]

The apostle Paul knew about the dangers of wealth. Therefore he wrote that those who want to become rich fall into many temptations, and he adds that we brought nothing into this world and can take nothing out of it when we die. And further that there is great gain in godliness with contentment, saying finally that the love of money is a root of all kinds of evil.[48]

Christ said, "This is my commandment that you love one another as I have loved you;"[49] and how did he love us? By leaving his Father and dying for us.[50] How then, we read in 1 John 3:17, is God's love in us if we see our brother or sister in need but do not help them?

It follows then that where the love of Christ does not bring about com-munity to give help and counsel to the neighbour, there the blood of Christ does not free from sin. And Peter teaches us to love one another, for love covers a multitude of sins.[51] What does the apostle want to say to the Hebrews except that in sharing what we have and in doing good we reconcile [?, rather "please"] God.[52] Do we not all have one Father, has not one God created us all? There-fore those who love their brother and sister remain in the light, there is no darkness in them.[53]

Without love nothing can exist nor be acceptable before God. This is the message we have heard from the beginning.[54] Where does this leave riches and earthly possessions? Yet not these alone are meant. Paul writes that if eating meat causes someone to stumble, he will not eat it.[55] Or the example of the rich fool who wanted to build bigger barns and was told that his soul would be required that night.[56]

Now God the Lord only requires faithfulness and the possessions of both rich and poor, only that one be surrendered [to him, *gelassen*, yield-ed]. But the reward will be great: do you not know that the saints

---

47   Mt 6:11.
48   1 Tim 6:6–10.
49   Jn 15:12.
50   Phil. 2:6–11.
51   1 Pet 4:8.
52   Heb. 13:16.
53   1 Jn 2:8–11.
54   1 Jn 3.
55   1 Cor 8:13.
56   Lk 12:19–21.

shall rule the world?[57] To those for whom *Gelassenheit* is difficult, Paul writes the comforting words that earthly suffering is only momentary.[58] Therefore the thoughts of the pious should not be in their treasure chests and boxes. They remember Paul's encouragement: if then you have been raised with Christ, seek that which is above, where Christ is, seated at the right hand of the Father.[59]

Greed Is the Same as Other Evils

Those who did not come to the wedding banquet because they had bought an acreage, or a yoke of oxen, or had just been married, did not commit a mortal sin by not coming but simply gave priority to their own affairs. They were not worthy of the invitation.[60] We see this in the fig tree. It was not cursed because it bore bad fruit but because it could bear good fruit yet did not.[61] Bearing good fruit means I was hungry and you fed, clothed, and served me;[62] it means growing in our spiritual life, showing virtue, modesty, patience, and communal love, thus being fruitful in prayer and building the community of the saints.[63]

In this way we are to be resurrected with Christ, and through the perfect law of love seek that which is above. People should not be like animals with their heads set toward the ground in search of food. God created us to walk upright with our heads at the top. Our kingdom is not an earthly kingdom or a land filled with milk and honey. We have died to our old self and can no longer be found with our former possessions, even as a dead person is no longer found in his or her house. We are imitators of God as his children,[64] writes Paul, by which he means that we keep order in our household, living together in a community of love.

Here we can see why the apostles so often talk about greed, adultery, and other sins in the same context.[65] Before God these are all equally works of the flesh.[66] Yet few people realize or recognize this dangerous poison. In their desires most people are like the rich, only regretting that they have not achieved it for themselves. In any case, greed is the root of all evil, driving the world to disasters, war, strife, murder, robbery, arson, and the destruction of land and people, the shedding of innocent blood. Yet nobody wants to be

---

57   1Cor 6:2.
58   2Cor 4:17.
59   Col 3:1.
60   Lk 14:15–24.
61   Mt 21:18–22.
62   Mt 25:31–46.
63   2Pet 1:3–15.
64   Eph. 5:1–2.
65   1Cor 5:9–10.
66   Gal 5:19–21.

known as greedy. Still, the worst of all is that this evil penetrates life so ingeniously and artfully, even in the guise of virtue, that people who think they are no longer worldly do not notice it. Yet in comparison to their splendour Christ and his disciples would look like beggars and slaves in their simplicity and humility.

Idolatry is the first commandment God placed on the tablets,[67] and in Colossians 3:5, the apostle says greed is idolatry which brings the wrath of God upon the disobedient, warning us to have no more to do with this than with lepers. He adds further that we should not even eat with those who are immoral or greedy or an idolater, drunkard, or robber. Yet some love their possessions so much that they do not hear the apostles, though it is clear that greed is idolatry.

Menno Simons, a wise and learned man, wrote many good and useful teachings in his *Foundation* Book[68] and other writings. He came so near to perfection in writing about pride, greed, and other things, yet he neatly avoided, undoubtedly intentionally, to focus on community when he talked about the rich young man, as also about the first church in Jerusalem which had all things in community under the leading of the Holy Spirit.[69] He passed by the story of Ananias and Sapphira, and did not often refer to it.[70] He praised Zacchaeus and wrote harshly about the lust for riches, but in directing his reprimands against his enemies he lulled his own people to sleep. Perhaps, if he had truly explained in his writings the fruit of love [as community], he would have had fewer followers, for those who have chosen the narrow way have always been few.[71]

[**Source:** Cornelius J. Dyck, *Spiritual Life in Anabaptism* (Scotdale: Herald Press, 1995), 120–127.]

---

67   Ex 20:4–6.
68   Menno Simons, *A Foundation and Plain Instruction of the Saving Doctrine of Our Lord Jesus Christ*, 1539.
69   Acts 2, 4.
70   Acts 5.
71   Mt 7:13–14.

ANDREAS EHRENPREIS (1589–1662)
Baderordnung / Barber-Surgeon Ordinance, 1654

Hutterite barber-surgeons (*Bader*) provided mineral baths for members and as a service for non-Hutterite clients. They also cut hair, and practiced blood-letting and cupping. The occupation of the *Bader* presented a challenge to community leaders, since the barber-surgeons were often away from the community, had opportunities to pocket money they collected for their services, and often amassed a formidable, esoteric assortment of books and equipment to support their work. The *Ordnungen* cautioned the *Bader* not to abuse privileges such as traveling on horseback outside the community and attempts to put limits to their unusual work.

The barber-surgeons are charged:

1. To be more mindful of their vocation, of their own souls' salvation, and the good and welfare of the brotherhood;

2. To be an asset to their profession and to their faith by showing honesty, faithfulness, industriousness, and sobriety in their work within the brotherhood and for people of whatever class outside the community;

3. To pray faithfully to God, that he will give them grace and bless them and their medication and treatment;

4. To diligently study in the Holy Scriptures and the books of pharmacy;

5. To rise promptly in the morning at reveille, and to retire in good time at night and to avoid all disorderliness;

6. Not to leave their "shop" without previous notice;

7. To go where they are sent and faithfully carry out their instructions;

8. To gather roots and herbs as instructed, and not to come home empty-handed, because their time was spent in sloth or wine drinking.

9. Not to loiter around in the house or in the workshops, gossiping or socializing, and causing annoyance; likewise not to sit and drink with the people of

the world and to show approval of this, as some have been doing. It is not right to be so deceitful!

10. To befriend all people and not to give curt answers and make sarcastic remarks. The latter is exceedingly disgraceful for us.

11. NB. NB. Also, do not dress in the style of the world lest you be—as has already happened—not recognized, but greeted and welcomed as a stranger. (NB. disgraceful headdresses and hair.) When people joined the community, they were ashamed of their worldly clothes. Now, some are ashamed to wear the garb of the community. They want everything to look different, be it hats, ribbons, trim, skirt or jacket, belt with either an enormous buckle or just a band, buttons in the back; it is not altogether in the style of the world, yet it must be about half and half.

12. The same goes for manners and speaking: worldly and pompous, hair looking like bristles, scraping with their feet, and other frippery. What a mockery! Certainly the noblemen have enough courtiers around them. (The barber-surgeons must cut the brethren's hair in the proper way, and not according to each individual's taste, such as halfway down to the shoulders and parted in the middle. That is the style of the soldier, and puts our

men on the same level with the world. Some of our people have recently shown such disobedient behaviour.)

13. The apprentices must not be led to such arrogance in pompous appearance and other things, lest they be hardly able afterwards to serve the simple peasant with a haircut or washing.

14. The barber-surgeons must keep their instruments immaculately clean and sharpened, so that the peasants would not have to shed tears during a haircut, bloodletting or cupping.

15. In the bath-house the barber-surgeons are to be friendly and take good care of the people. They are not to make people sit and wait. They must not leave the bath-house or barbershop and gossip, while the customers leave in dissatisfaction, as has been happening these days.

16. They are not to avoid work as if they were too good for it or not made for it.

17. They are not supposed to have their own pharmaceuticals and make profit from them.

18. They are not allowed to have their own chickens and pigeons, etc.

19. All money, be it a gift or tip, or be it earned income, must be faithfully handed over to the supervisor.

20. All buying, exchanging and trading must cease and is forbidden, as it always has been in the community.

21. The barber-surgeons must not take money or gifts from those of their clients who belong to our communities, for this is not right!

22. They must diligently care for our elderly invalids, so that these do not have to sigh and complain.

23. They must not bring their superiors into disrepute or talk behind their backs when conversing with clients, intimating that they could help if only the supervisors would let them have certain medicines.

24. Extreme care must be taken in the administering of medicine, lest they have the patients' blood upon their hands.

25. No barber-surgeon is to set up his private business or independently seek the employment of a nobleman.

26. No one must leave his master [employer] for unjust reason.

27. The barber-surgeons should go regularly to the common dining room along with all the other brothers and sisters. These instructions were also given to the alchemists in Nikolsburg [Mikulov] and to Stophel Eckstain and Nathaniel Hamer. Also, the barber-surgeons must not get too dependent on riding or driving, especially those men who are still young and healthy.

28. They must not become greedy for all sorts of things, like coats and other clothing for themselves and their wives.

29. The older barber-surgeons are to instruct the young ones diligently and to keep them disciplined and respectful. They must not beat the boys, tussle with them or scold them with coarse insults. Likewise, they must not be silly with them and joke with them. The same goes for the barbers' attitudes toward newcomers.

30. If a brother is told of his bad behaviour, he should not immediately want to get up and leave, but accept the reprimand graciously.

31. The barber-surgeons must not collect a lot of superfluous equipment to gratify their own vanity, for they can hardly load all this on their wagon. The barber-surgeons have always had their ordinances! Today, their attitude mocks their honourable fore-bearers who gave these ordinances and who had decided that the barbers must not travel with too much baggage from one place to another, and must not have more than one wagon-load. What is this leading to? It cannot be tolerated! Suppose a purchaser, householder, man

in charge of the dairy, or miller would want to travel around like this; how many wagons would they have to take with them? And what they [the barber-surgeons] cannot take along they sell, even their domestic animals!—well, well, what a miserable reputation this gives the community!

32. And when they find that they have situated themselves comfortably, they no longer want to travel, but hang on to their noble employers [*Herrschaft*]. They obtain positions of power and thus exercise their own will which is totally in contrast to their calling and commitment.

The fact that the young people are so spoiled, bold, disobedient and insubordinate has not a little to do with this situation.

[**Source:** John Hostetler et al, *Selected Hutterian Documents in Translation, 1542–1654* (MacGregor: Hutterian Brethren Book Centre, 2013), 113–116. Used by permission.]

Hutterite Homilies, 1600s

Hutterite homilies originate primarily from the middle of the 1600s, although the earliest date back to 1566. Andreas Ehrenpreis, elder from 1639 to 1662, gathered the few teachings from the early Hutterite period, but also commissioned the writing of many more. Because of the centrality of these teachings to Hutterite faith, Rod Janzen and Max Stanton comment that "modern Hutterites are perhaps more the 'children of Ehrenpreis' than they are the children of Jakob Hutter or Peter Riedemann."[1]

Hutterite teachings are divided into two types: the primary type, *Leadn/Lehren* or sermons, are structured exegesis of biblical texts. The second type are *Vorredn/Vorreden* or prefaces, which serve as an introductory meditation. The *Vorredn* are not organized around a biblical text, but rather pick up themes related to the Christian devotional life, struggles within the community, or a specific holy day such as New Year's Day.

Seven writers have been identified: Hans Fredrich Küentsche, Kasper Eglauch, Mathias Binder, Johannes Milder, Tobias Bertsch, Benjamin Poley, and Andreas Ehrenpreis. It is thought that these texts originally functioned as sermon outlines or as aids for sermon preparation.

A large portion of Hutterite homilies originated at a Bruderhof near Kesselsdorf in Slovakia, which was the seat of the elder and housed an archive and scriptorium where these texts were reproduced. Writing continued up to 1677 at a slower pace, and then ceased completely. Following the primary period of generation, the homilies fell out of use during the Transylvanian and Hungarian era.

In the late 1700s, elder Johannes Waldner sought to revive "the old and genuine spirit of the Hutterites as it had been at the time of the great bishop Andreas Ehrenpreis."[2] Waldner's renewal efforts included an *ad fontes* effort

---

1   Rod Janzen and Max Stanton. *The Hutterites in North America* (Baltimore: John Hopkins University Press, 2010), 24.

2   Robert Friedmann and Richard D. Thiessen, "Johannes Waldner (1749–1824)," *GAMEO*, May 2007. https://gameo.org/index.php?title=Waldner,_Johannes_ (1749–1824)&oldid=143783.

of gathering and re-copying earlier texts. Eventually Hutterite pastors began reading these texts verbatim, a preaching tradition of serving up "ready-cut bread" that has largely continued into the present. The collection of homilies—while likely not intended to function this way—has essentially become a closed canon, with additional texts only very occasionally being added. (The Hutterite funeral teachings, for example, originate from the North American period.) This body of teachings provides Hutterites with theological unity and a lens through which to interpret Scripture. However, we could ask if this has come at the cost of spiritual vitality and renewal.

Preface on the Resurrection

Beloved brothers and sisters, we are assembled in the precious name of our God, as is our custom, and gathered under his paternal care and protection, solely for divine purposes, that we may be earnestly admonished and call to mind the great mercy and love of God which has come to us from God the Lord in this time through Jesus Christ our Lord.

He [Christ] was born not only according to the promises of God, but also completed his life's journey and pilgrimage in great suffering, struggle, and conflict accordingly, to accomplish our salvation through his bitter suffering and dying on the cross.

Thus, he redeemed us from the fall of Adam and Eve who sinned in Paradise and violated God's command. This has been sufficiently dealt with elsewhere [in the preceding Easter teachings], namely that without this [redemption], we would all have to suffer eternal death and be deprived

of the kingdom of heaven along with our primordial parents, and would have to say with David:

> Can anybody redeem his brother,
> or give to God a ransom?
> The redemption of their souls
> is so costly,
> that he must let it stand
> for eternity.[3]

In summary: We were all lost with no claim to blessedness at all, with not even the faintest hope to obtain it through human effort. Everything was futile and in vain until the promise of God was fulfilled and the serpent-crusher came, which God had promised our mother Eve when he said to Satan: I will put enmity between…your seed and her seed; he shall bruise your head, and you shall bruise his heel.

All this had to unfold and come together and not one word could go amiss, rather, it had to proceed according to the counsel and will of God, just as he had spoken. The love

---

3   Ps 49:7–9, translated.

of God towards humanity extends to such heights, which is a glorious comfort to us, that his beloved and only begotten son in heaven was not secure for humanity's sake, but had to come to earth when nothing else would suffice.

This was the arrow lying hidden in the quiver of whom the prophets of God spoke and prophesied centuries earlier. He would come and surrender his life for the human race, thereby rescuing us from sin, death, hell, and damnation. [...]

[T]his precious remaining arrow in the quiver of almighty God, yes, in the bosom of his mercy from eternity on, was destined and reserved for this purpose and released in these final days of the earth for us all, as previously mentioned, to free us from the bonds of death and hell. [...]

Therefore, even to this day, the faithful have good reason to rightly reflect upon and embrace the vast love, grace, and mercy of God. [...]

Paul says, "Therefore God has highly exalted him and bestowed on him the name which is above every name, that at the name of Jesus every knee should bow, in heaven and on earth and under the earth,"[4] "who has gone into heaven and is at the right hand of God, with angels, authorities, and powers subject to him,"[5] and "all God's angels [shall] worship him."[6]

Today, what was prefigured with Jonah is accomplished, [namely] that he came out of the belly of the whale and from the depths of the sea without injury.[7]

Today, Daniel came out of the lion's den, hale and hearty.[8]

Today, Sadrach, Mesach and Abed'-nego came out of the fiery furnace unsinged.[9]

Today, the grain of wheat that fell on the earth and died, germinated and bore much fruit.[10]

Today, Joseph is released from prison and made prime minister.[11]

Today, Samson placed the city gates with both its posts and latch on his shoulders and carried it away.[12]

Today, the Cherub with flaming sword before the gates of Paradise is removed.[13]

Today, the host of angels of God rejoice over the great healing of the nations.[14]

---

4   Phil. 2:9–19.
5   I Pet 3:22.
6   Heb 1:6.
7   [Jon 1–2].
8   [Dan 6].
9   [Dan 3].
10 [Jn 12:24].
11 [Gen 41].
12 [Jud 16:3].
13 [Gen 3:24].
14 [Rev 22:2].

Sixteenth century Hutterites wrote at least 16 commentaries on books of the Bible, including one on the gospel according to John. Its title page reads, "John the Evangelist Explained across all Chapters, by Br[other] Hauprecht Zapff in the Year of Christ 1597. Copied Word for Word by H[einrich] H[artmann] in the Year of Christ 1630." These books were likely used by pastors as a resource when preparing a message (*Lehr*) for worship. Over time, some sections were excerpted and used as a homily that was read aloud from the pulpit. Only one of these comentaries has been published: Hauprecht Zapff, *Johannes der Evangelist über alle Kapitel erklärt: Ein täuferischer Bibelkommentar von 1597*. Edited by Martin Rothkegel. MacGregor: Hutterian Brethren Book Centre, 2017.

Today, Goliath, the great and mighty enemy of Israel, was overcome, so that we can sing, dance, and be merry.[15]

Today, Joshua defeated his thirty-one kings and conquered the city of Jericho.[16]

Today, the arrogant and hostile Haman, who wanted to exterminate all the Jews in one day, was executed.[17]

Therefore, let us observe this joyful feast for seven days, indeed, our whole lives through.

As pitiful, agonizing, and sorrowful as the suffering of Christ may have been, just so consolatory, joyous, and festive is his laudable and rich in grace resurrection. Amen.

[**Source:** Translated by Kenny Wollmann from "*[Auferstehung] Vorrede*," Sarah Waldner, Evergreen Colony, copyist, Feb. 23, 1986.]

An explanation of several chapters from the Old and New Testament, to be presented at Pentecost, concerning the sending and outpouring of the Holy Spirit, what he has done and how his power and effect is still to this day evident and revealed in the hearts of all who believe and are faithful.

[Acts 2:1a] When the Day of Pentecost arrived...

When the symbolic feast of the seven weeks, or the fiftieth day [after the Passover], was at hand, when the harvest began or was about to begin, that is when what will be reported here happened.

Israel had to observe three particular feasts each year in addition to the regular Sabbath, as God commanded them through Moses. First, they had to observe the Passover [...]. The [second] feast was the feast of Pentecost, which was also called the Feast of Weeks, or the Feast of Harvest, or the Feast of First-fruits, because the first fruits of the harvest were gathered in with the sickle. This symbolized the new fruits of the Holy Spirit, which are now to grow from the soil of the earthly humans. The third feast was the Feast of Tabernacles [...].

At Pentecost, however, the fruit of the Holy Spirit is shown to believers, which all true followers and disciples of Jesus Christ should receive and exhibit if they have truly departed from Egypt and the world. That is what we must learn from this.

We must observe and celebrate Pentecost in honour of the Holy Spirit of God, whom Jesus Christ,

---

15 [1Sam 17:49].
16 [Josh 12:7–24; 6:20].
17 [Est 7].

the Son of God, prayed for us from his dear Father in heaven, that he might lead us, teach us, and guide us along the way that leads to heaven, and that we may come to where he, the Son and the Father himself, dwell, and that he should struggle and strive for us, give us courage, reconcile us to God, present our praise and thanksgiving—along with the petitions of our hearts—to God, and bring us a response from him, so that we may always know how our affairs are ordered with God and the Lord Jesus Christ.

Without this spirit we would be completely defenceless and unprotected against every attempt of the enemy; we would stand naked and bare, without a sword and could not resist, protect, or defend ourselves, and it were as Solomon says, "like a breached city, one with no walls."[18]

This can be seen in the disciples of the Lord Christ. Although Peter carried an outer sword and struck with it, he lacked the sword of the Spirit within, and denied Christ three times. The other [disciples] fled like hares from hounds.

Therefore, whoever does not have this invisible sword, that is, the Spirit of God, cannot endure in the army of heaven, but will be rejected as unfit for battle. Christ does not say in vain: "He who has nothing, let him sell his garment and buy a sword."[19] […]

[Acts 2:1b] … they were all together in one place.

Now this must be so, dear brothers and sisters, for being of one mind and dwelling together is pleasing and acceptable to God, the Lord.

Christ also affirms this when he says, "If two of you agree on earth about anything you ask, then my Father who is in heaven will do it for you. For where two or three are gathered in my name, I am there with them."[20]

And the Holy Spirit dwells where there is such unity, and its sound and smell is sweet and pleasant; all Christian fruits and virtues grow and flourish there, as David says:

Look at how good and pleasing it is when brothers live together as one! It is like expensive oil poured over the head of Aaron, running down onto his entire beard and onto his robes. It is like the dew on Mount Hermon streaming down onto the mountains of Zion, because it is there that the Lord has commanded the blessing: life everlasting."[21] […]

Oh, dear brothers and sisters, how good, wonderful, and praiseworthy

---

18   Pro 25:28.
19   Lk 22:36.
20   Mt 18:19–20.
21   Ps 133:1–3.

it would be if we permitted this to penetrate and took up the cause of unity in a noble and heartfelt manner. For even if we had not a single [other] example in this world, we would see well enough the great benefit and joy that arises from unity between harmonious marriage partners, and in contrast, the great harm and heartache that arises from the disunity between quarrelsome ones.

When husband and wife are united, what a diverting life they have!

Many wives have said: I have been with my husband so and so long—twenty, thirty or more years—I truthfully say, it hardly seems six or seven years to me. There peace and unity have been the best garment—better than a thousand ducats—for one as much as the other wanted love and peace [...].

[**Source:** Translated by Kenny Wollmann from a manuscript copy by J.D.W., Neumühl, Alberta, 2008.]

Three etchings from a series of 18 images by Lorrainian artist, Jacques Callot (1592–1635), titled, "*Les Grandes Misères de la guerre* / The Great Miseries of War." Callot's intent was to portray the horrors the Thirty Years' War unleashed on civilians.

Top image: plate 11, "*La pendaison* / The Hanging;" middle image: plate 4, "*La razzia* / The Raid;" bottom image: plate 7, "*Pillage et incendie d'un village* / Looting and burning a village," Jacques Callot, etchings, 1633. [*WikiCommons*]

"Plundering of the Communities following the Thirty Years' War," 1664

During the Thirty Years' War (1618–1648) and for significant stretches of the 17th century, Hutterite communities in Hungary were regularly plundered by armies from a number of countries. Early modern armies lacked effective supply lines and relied on anything they could find along the way to feed soldiers and horses. In Transylvania, the community of Alwinz was caught in conflicts between the Ottoman Turks and the local princes. The upheaval brought by these raids are essential for understanding the Hutterite *Sitz im Leben* during this period.

In the spring of 1664, the imperial field marshal Count de Souches advanced to Neutra and opened fire on the town. The perennial foe surrendered the city and fled into the castle, but the imperial forces attacked so strongly that the Turks asked for free passage to withdraw, which for some reason was granted.

So the Turks left Neutra and ceded it to the Christians. They had to abandon the ammunition that was in the castle but were escorted to Neuhausel with all their goods and people, even their camp followers. The same happened at Lewenz, also taken by Field Marshal de Souches. He opened fire and stormed the place, and when the attack went in his favour and the enemy saw he was in earnest, they agreed to surrender the town.

In March and April there was still hope of getting something into the ground and seeding the fields at Dechtitz. Then the marauding hussars returned and took two of our horses straight from the plough in the field.

In spite of the great danger and loss, our people managed to sow and raise some field crops until harvest time, though in these months they had to flee from their houses several times, not from the Turks but from the imperial troops. Just at harvest, when they were looking forward to enjoying some of it and most of the hay and grain had been carried home, the imperial forces again invaded the country.

First of all a regiment came through Dechtitz and stole whatever they found. They stripped and beat up any brothers they caught. They carried off a mass of booty, threw the sick people out of their beds, and stole the bed linen. Our people had to abandon Dechtitz for the summer and autumn, and the little they had left in house, garden, field, and vineyard was stolen from them day after day in countless raids.

Even the two cows still left after the Turkish raids were now seized and carried off by the Germans.

On June 30, Neu Serinwar in Croatia was stormed and taken by the Turks. From the seventeen thousand men in the fortress not five hundred escaped with their lives.

On August 13, a force of about five hundred Saxonian infantry arrived at Senitz and camped on the Branc estates for eleven weeks. They were a great drain on our community at Sabatisch and caused us much trouble.

On September 28, when the imperial camp was moved near Dechtitz, a thousand German and French soldiers suddenly came into the village of Gutwasser, robbing and plundering at will, taking grain, hay, and whatever else they could find. They emptied people's underground store places and drove off with loads of hay that the community at Dechtitz had hauled to this village. Five of our horses were stolen from behind the castle, where we had thought they would be safe. The soldiers beat the waggoner cruelly and carried him off for some distance but then let him go again.

From this time on until almost winter, our community at Dechtitz was continually being plundered, and no one dared be seen by the Germans. There were so many instances of cruelty that it is impossible to remember them all now. Afterward, our poverty-stricken people came back to the empty, burned-out, and ruined houses. Those who survived the enemy suffered bitter hardship and great hunger.

On October 11, Colonel Nikolaus and Sergeant Major Stang took up quarters in our place at Vel'ké Leváre with fifty-five horses and a large number of people. We had to give them twelve pecks of oats daily and enough hay and straw too. We had to buy old wine for them, paying twenty pennies the half measure. This went on for a week. Counting all the extra gifts, it cost the community over a hundred gulden.

On October 17, no sooner had the Germans left than the French arrived. The people in Vel'ké Leváre were preparing to hold the evening prayer meeting but had to break off and flee. When the soldiers found hardly any of our people there, they plundered and did a lot of damage in the community, amounting to several hundred gulden.

On October 18, the Saxon artillery horses were stabled at Sabatisch,

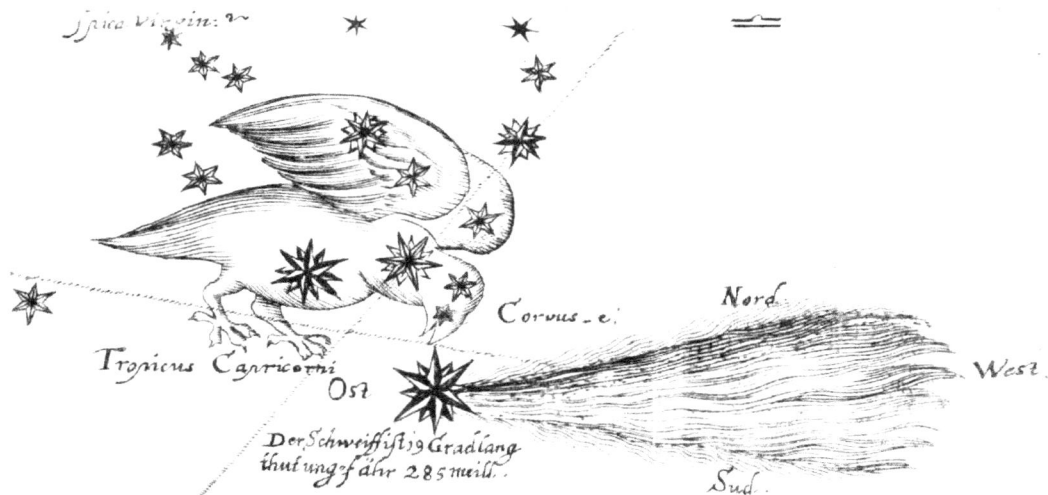

costing us a great deal. Seven stable hands with fourteen horses stayed at our place for seventeen days.

The same day a cavalry regiment arrived under the command of Count von Nassau. They remained until October 22 but were no particular burden to us, praise God, except for the gifts we gave them out of good will. Then they went on to Schossberg.

On November 6, the Rabicksh regiment came to Vel'ké Leváre. No one was quartered with our people except one cavalryman as a bodyguard, but that cost the community more than twenty-three gulden.

On November 5, the Saxonian soldiers left the country and returned home. We had to pay the sergeant major twenty-five gulden and fifty pennies for the lieutenant colonel's lodging, since he did not lodge with us. We also had to pay the quartermaster three gulden for the seven stable hands and fourteen artillery horses. With the food, drink, and fodder that was used, the cost came to nearly forty-six gulden.

One hour before midnight on December 24, a comet was seen that was visible for several nights afterward. It had also been observed earlier in various places for many nights. Its significance is known to God alone.

Anonymous depiction of the comet of 1664. This comet was one of the brightest of the time, visible all across Europe and reported in many publications. [*Wikicommons*]

[**Source:** *The Chronicle of the Hutterian Brethren*, Volume 1. Translated and edited by the Hutterian Brethren. (Ulster Park: Plough Publishing House, 1987), 789–791. Used by permission.]

HANS JAKOB CHRISTOFFEL VON GRIMMELSHAUSEN (1621/22–1676)
Simplicius Simplicissimus / The Simplest Simpleton, 1668

Hans Jakob Grimmelshausen's novel *Simplicius Simplicissimus* presents a rare, if idealistic, outside portrait of a 17th century Hutterite community in Hungary. The book is a coming-of-age novel (*Entwicklungsroman*), in which a naive boy, Simplicissimus, embarks on a journey of self-discovery in the midst of the chaos unleashed by the Thirty Years' War. His encounters with various people and places help him develop a more sophisticated, informed view of the world. One of his encounters involves a Hutterite community in Hungary.

It is unclear whether Grimmelshausen actually visited a community or whether he was relying on word of mouth. The community he is describing must have existed in the first half of the 17th century, because later on the communities were in decline.

A brief diversion concerning Hungary's Anabaptists and the way they live

Back home, I kept myself to myself. My favourite occupation was burying my head in a book. I collected huge quantities, covering a wide range of topics, notably books that really made me think. What grammarians and schoolmasters have to study soon wearied me, which meant that arithmetic, for instance, quickly went back on the shelf. As for music, before long I hated the subject like the plague, going so far as to smash my lute to smithereens in consequence. Maths and geometry I still enjoyed a bit, but as soon as they strayed into astronomy I gave them up as well, preferring astrology. For a while astrology was my delight. Yet eventually it too began to sound false, imprecise, and simply not worth bothering with any longer. I tried Ramon Llull's *magnum opus* instead. However, finding it all guff and little substance and in any case a monotonous rant, I dropped that too and immersed myself in the Jewish kabbalah tradition and Egyptian hieroglyphics. In the end, all my reading led me to one conclusion and one alone: when it came to subjects there was no beating theology—but theologia that led to the love and service of God. Taking that as my guiding principle, I worked out a lifestyle capable of raising mankind to the level of the angels. It involved folk coming together to form a community of marrieds and singletons (i.e. both men and women) who, like the Anabaptists, strive to meet every physical need with the work of their hands alone, operating under a knowledgeable superior, and who spend their entire lives praising and serving God and pursuing the salvation of their souls. I had already (in Hungary, in Anabaptist communities) seen examples. Which is why, provided that such well-meaning folk neither held nor were committed to other wrongful and (in the eyes of most Christian Churches) heretical and hence repellent views, I had decided of my own free will to follow their example or at least look upon their way of life as the most blessed in the world. Their everyday conduct put me in mind of how Josephus and others described the Jewish Essenes. In the first place they had plenty of treasure and more than enough to eat. However, they wasted none of it, nor did a single curse or murmur of displeasure leave

their lips. I never heard a superfluous word uttered among them. I saw only craftspeople working away as if earning their livelihoods. In schools, teachers instructed not classes of youngsters but so many adorable children—quite as if they had been their own. Nowhere did I see menfolk and womenfolk bundled in together. The sexes occupied separate premises, each separately performing their appointed tasks. I found rooms set aside for perinatals, who were looked after not by their husbands but by other members of their sex. They themselves and their newborns received all necessary care unstintingly lavished upon them. Other rooms contained only large numbers of rocking cots, whose tiny occupants had their nappies changed and other attentions provided by dedicated female nurses. The mothers were required only to come along at set hours three times daily with breasts swollen with milk to feed their respective sprogs. All the looking-after of both perinatals and infants was performed by widows. Elsewhere I saw females doing nothing but spin, in rooms that might contain up to a hundred wheels. Or one might do the laundry, another make beds, a third see to the animals, a fourth wash the dishes, a fifth wait at table, a sixth be in charge of table linen. Of the others, too, each knew what to do. And just as the various jobs were neatly distributed among the womenfolk, each man and boy had his particular function. If one person (male or female) fell ill, he or she was assigned a personal medical attendant as well as a general doctor and apothecary of the appropriate sex. In fact, though, so good was their diet and so excellently ordered their existence that they seldom did fall ill. I saw many a fine figure hopping about in the best of health at a ripe old age, which was something not often seen elsewhere. Each had specific mealtimes and a specific bedtime—but no time at all for playing or going for walks, except for the young, who after each meal would be taken by their teacher for an hour's healthful stroll. However, prayers and spiritual singing were compulsory. Of anger there was no sign, nor was there of agitation, animosity, jealousy, hostility, care for secular interests, arrogance or any regret. In sum, all was loving harmony, everyone one's sole concern (apparently) that of increasing the human race and extending the kingdom of God in all modesty and respectability. No man saw his wife except when, at a set time, they together withdrew to his bedroom, which contained his made bed and nothing else except a chamber pot and ablutionary equipment (a washbasin, jug of water, and white hand towel) for him to wash his hands prior to retiring for the night and after rising in the morning to go to work. For the rest, they all addressed one another as "sister" or "brother," not that such wholly decent familiarity prompted the least impropriety. The religious life as practised by those Anabaptist heretics was one I should gladly have lived myself; to my mind, it topped that lived by monks and nuns. How many times did I tell myself, "If you could achieve such noble Christian conduct under the aegis of your own authorities, you'd be a second St Dominic or St Francis. Ah, and if you could persuade the Anabaptists to teach their way of life to their fellow believers here, what a saint you would be! Or if you could make your own comrades in the faith lead so evidently Christian and virtuous a life as those Anabaptists do, what might you not have achieved?" I replied, of course, also speaking to myself, "Fool! What business is it of yours how other folk live? Become a Capuchin— you've had it with women anyway!" I wondered, though: "But tomorrow's another day. Who knows what you'll need to follow Christ's way correctly? Today you feel like keeping your trousers but toned; come morning you could be on fire."

Such thoughts and others like them preoccupied me for some time. I couldn't stop thinking about turning over my whole farm and my entire fortune to setting up a united Christian community of some kind. However, dad said straight out: he doubted I'd ever get a bunch of lads like that together.

[**Source:** Hans Jakob Christoffel von Grimmelshausen, *The Adventures of Simplicius Simplicissimus*. Translated by J.A. Underwood. Penguin Random House, 2018), 440–442.]

THE 18ᵗʰ CENTURY

Johannes Waldner (1749–1824)
"Infant Baptism Introduced at Vel'ké Leváre," 1725

By the early eighteenth century, Vel'ké Leváre was the first community to succumb to the Jesuit pressure to have their infants baptized. It was soon followed by Sabatisch, and from 1733 on, all babies were reluctantly baptized in the Hungarian communities. According to the *Chronicle*, "When the children baptized as infants were old enough to understand, they were baptized on confession of their faith. The baptism was in a private room, however, and no longer in public, in front of the congregation of the church."[1] The following account describes the tactics used by the Jesuits to realize their goals.

It is highly probable that disunity, quarrelling, and strife went on growing until there was an open break. Dear brother Andreas Ehrenpreis had been afraid that this would happen, as he said in his last words to the church. Several circumstances make us conclude that community-of-goods came to an end about the year 1693 or 1694. But the date cannot be fixed conclusively.

I ask anyone who finds out about this to write an account on these empty pages.

A little information has been gleaned by talking to old people who once lived in community-of-goods. One or the other still remembered enough to tell where the common kitchen and this or that workroom had been. Pieces of equipment were still about that were said to come from the days when there was a common life.

The descendants of the church community founded by Jakob Hutter had become unfaithful in many ways and were not living steadfastly in the light of divine truth. Therefore, in the end, God withdrew his light and grace and plunged them in darkness. They fell from one wrong into the next, until in the course of time they lost their name, too, and had no way out but to accept the popish religion, as we will recount in the appropriate place.

---

1   *The Chronicle of the Hutterian Brethren*, Volume 2. Translated by the Hutterian Brethren. (Ste. Agathe: Crystal Spring Colony, 1998), 313.

In 1725, child baptism was introduced at Vel'ké Leváre. This was how it happened. On March 6, two Jesuits came to the lord's castle, Vel'ké Leváre. They asked for the Elder, whose name was Jacob Polman. When he came to them they soon began disputing with him on questions of faith. The Elder held his ground, however, and answered their points, so that this time nothing happened to him, and they went away.

The following day they returned, bringing other priests, judges, and jurors with them. They again made every attempt to force the brothers to deny their faith, and finding no success, they wrote down the names of all the people, both men and women. For a few days nothing happened, but on March 10 the Jesuit sent a message to the community that several brothers should come to him since he had something important to tell them. The brothers went to him in his room. With many smooth and hypocritical words, he proceeded to present his demands: they were to attend church and to have their little children baptized. The brothers replied that they could not do this, for it was against their faith and divine truth.

After a short delay, the godless Jesuit took the matter up again on March 13. He sent for Jacob Polman, intending to imprison him. But the brothers at Vel'ké Leváre realized it would be dangerous to obey the summons. They consulted togeth-

er and agreed to go in their Elder's place. The Elder slipped away to Sabatisch and the whole community took his place in front of the Jesuit and the nobles. This infuriated the Jesuit, who at once had sixteen brothers chained hand and foot and locked into a dark cellar. Then he gave a lying report of the incident to the Bishop of Vienna, who was the actual lord of the manor for Vel'ké Leváre. He slandered the church, declaring that the brothers had tried to storm the castle and had forced him from two rooms into a third. The bishop was very angry about it.

The church took up the brothers' cause and made every effort to have them released. Two brothers rode to Modern and Pressburg to their old protector, Count Adam, and complained to him of the injustice done to them. The count advised them to pluck up courage and go to their real manorial lord, Kollonitsch, who was a bishop at the imperial court in Vienna at the time. They followed this advice and arranged that the young servant of the Word, Johannes Mayer, and two other brothers should go. The three traveled to Vienna to complain of the unjust treatment they had received in contradiction to the privileges previously granted, and they begged the bishop to release their brothers.

The bishop refused to give them audience because he was extremely angry with them. They had to return home with nothing accomplished. To make matters worse, the bishop believed the Jesuit and gave him permission to punish the brothers for their violence.

As a result, the whole community was driven out of Vel'ké Leváre. A godless rabble came by night, seized the place and began breaking down the doors and stealing whatever they liked. They carried the booty back to the castle. The people at Vel'ké Leváre had to leave the place empty and move over to St. Johannes and Sabatisch.

The Jesuit refused to release the imprisoned brothers unless the whole congregation signed an agreement to attend church and have their small children baptized. In the end the people signed, and the brothers were set free. That is how easily they gave up true Christian baptism, signing against their own hearts and consciences because they were not willing to suffer for God and his truth.

[**Source:** *The Chronicle of the Hutterian Brethren*, Volume 2. Translated by the Hutterian Brethren. (Ste. Agathe: Crystal Spring Colony, 1998), 308–10. Used by permission.]

Johannes Waldner (1749–1824)
"Rationale for Writing Church History," 1793

The Austrian historian Johann Loserth (1846–1936) once suggested that "Johannes Waldner was the only true historian of the Hutterites." While this claim is debatable, it does draw attention to the fact that Waldner—despite not receiving any formal education beyond grade school—had a gift for grasping and communicating the history of his people.

Waldner is a skilled story teller, but also capable of insightful historiographical reflection. In the context of writing about internal conflict, he thoughtfully considers why it is important to document both light and shadow in church history.

I would much rather have passed over these quarrels in silence. I have found it hard and distressing enough to revive for posterity the memories of these old faults and failures in the church, for perhaps as people died these things might have been forgotten. But my heart and conscience compelled me to write against my will, for the following reasons:

First, in order to present the whole truth about our history and keep back nothing important that took place, both praise-worthy and un-praiseworthy acts are recorded, just as in Bible stories about the God-fearing people of old—patriarchs, kings, and prophets.

Second, to serve as a warning, for while quarrels and divisions arise all too often among believers, no one should reject community and the sharing of a common life because of faults and weaknesses. No one should copy the opponents of community and true surrender, the self-seekers who exaggerate such things and say that community and a common life only multiply reasons for quarrelling and division. We must not let such difficulties frighten us away from the Lord's work. We need only look back to earlier times to see that they were never free of similar weeds which the enemy tried to sow among the wheat. What confusion and divisions there were in the church in Jakob Hutter's day!

But brothers and sisters did not give up because of them. They put things right and reunited.

Third, to warn against any of us presuming to introduce a new practice he has invented himself and: thereby alter, disturb, and displace the old, well-proved order of the church. This applies particularly to articles of faith and interpretations of Scripture.

No one should have too great a confidence in himself and rely on his own understanding and insight. Such fabricators and hair-splitters, who try to know and understand everything better than anyone else, have never at any time led to anything good. This can be seen clearly enough from our experience with Mathies and others. For however good his intentions may have been, he went too far and erred to the right.

[**Source:** *The Chronicle of the Hutterian Brethren*, Volume 2. Translated by the Hutterian Brethren. (Ste. Agathe: Crystal Spring Colony, 1998), 494–95. Used by permission.]

Johannes Waldner (1749–1824)
"Account of How and Where Our Church Began," 1793

In this excerpt from the *Klein-Geschichtsbuch*, Waldner recounts the circumstances that prompted the crypto-Protestants from Carinthia to emigrate to Transylvania, where they came into contact with the Hutterites at Alwinz and eventually revived *Gütergemeinschaft*.

In particular, how God delivered our forefathers from the gross error, blindness, and darkness of popery and led them to the recognition of divine truth; a description, too, of how the church began to gather and be built up; how the enemy of divine truth tried by every means to hinder it, stirring up fierce persecution against the believers; and how God rescued his people from this oppression by leading them out of the country from near Kronstadt over the Transylvanian Alps into Wallachia.

Next, the community's sufferings in Wallachia during the Turkish wars, their journey by God's will and leading through Moldavia and the Kingdom of Poland into the Ukraine, and all other noteworthy events in the church up to the present day are carefully recorded in a very simple way for the benefit of all who come after us.

In 1752, in the archduchy of Carinthia, a great awakening was stirred by the books and teachings of Dr. Martin Luther. This area was out-and-out Roman Catholic, however, and no one belonging to the Lutheran, Calvinist, or any other religion was allowed to remain there. All the ceremonies and usages of the Roman Catholic Church were diligently performed and strictly observed with fasting, many prayers, and the invocation of various patron saints; worship of images, especially of Mary; the purchase of many masses, and making the sign of the cross; wearing rosaries and scapulars; pilgrimages, confessions, and innumerable other idolatrous practices. The poor, ignorant people in their blindness and error were zealous in such observances, since they had been taught nothing better. They knew of nothing else because common people never had a copy of the Holy Scriptures in their hands. Peasants were strictly forbidden to possess a Bible. The common people had to believe what the priest preached to them from the pulpit and whatever might have been written in Roman Catholic books by Augustine, Ambrose, Bernard, and other old church fathers.

The Roman Catholic catechism contains these words: "I believe what is commanded by the Holy Roman Catholic Church, whether it is written in the bible or not."

At the beginning of this book, we have recorded that when Martin Luther brought to light all the deceit and trickery of the Roman Catholic church, he wrote a great deal against the papacy. Not only he, but other scholars such as the renowned Johann Arndt, Joseph Schaitberger, the fugitive Father Christof Fischer, and more beside, wrote in sharp opposition to the terrible blasphemies, the sale of indulgences, the worship of images of dead saints, and praying to the mother of God. With many proofs from the Holy Scriptures, both the Old and the New Testament, they made plain that these things are against the Word of God and they rejected such Roman Catholic ceremonies as human inventions, accursed and condemned to hell.

These books and writings were introduced into Carinthia in the mid-18th century. Although they were brought in secretly, they produced a great ferment and revival. Many peasants stopped attending church and read the Bible and other books in their homes instead. They also began holding secret meetings at night. For the joy of hearing God's Word, many often went long distances through the dark in rain, snow, and wind. In these meetings they prayed, read from the Bible and other books, sang, and talked together. This was happening not only in one place but had spread to nearly every judicial district in Carinthia, for instance to the areas around Gailtal, Paternion, Himmelsberg, Spittal, and other places.

The Roman Catholic clergy could not tolerate this, for what they represented was being belittled and despised. They therefore used energetic measures to stifle the fire. All who were suspected of contamination by Lutheran teachings were summoned to the priest's house, closely questioned whether they had forbidden books, and given strict orders to reveal and hand them over. Anyone later found with a Bible, New Testament, or any Lutheran book was to be fined 12, 18, 20, or 24 gulden, according to the size of the book.

Reading such books therefore became very dangerous and could be done only with the greatest secrecy. There were many constables and spies who crept by night to listen at the doors and windows of houses to discover if people were reading and singing from the forbidden books. As soon as these children of Judas found anything suspicious, they betrayed people to the authorities. The homes were then visited and searched. Any books that were found were confiscated, and the house-holder had to pay a heavy fine. This happened to Johannes Hofer from St. Peter when some traitor told the sheriff that Johannes had a Bible.

Next the authorities ordered everyone to bring all books to the priest's house. Here the books were examined. Those which were not Roman Catholic were confiscated; the Roman Catholic books were stamped with a coat of arms on the title page and returned to the owner. Little was achieved by this, as the people did not bring all the forbidden books; mostly they brought only the Roman Catholic ones. They hid the Bible and the Lutheran books all the more carefully, and this was especially the case in Gailtal.

When this was brought to the notice of the authorities, they made another house search. Anyone found in possession of a book without a stamp was ruthlessly beaten and heavily fined as well.

It is said that one man was executed with the sword for holding Lutheran beliefs. This is what happened: At a major church holy day, crowds of people were carrying out their idolatrous practices according to Roman Catholic custom, making offerings, praying and so on in front of the crucifixes and other images set up for the purpose. One man from the Lutheran side said to another, "Why ever is there such a crowd?" To which the other replied, "Why should it surprise you? Christ says in the Bible that where there is a dead body the vultures will gather." Someone overheard and reported him. He was at once arrested, brought before a court, and asked if he realized what he had said and if he intended to keep to his statement. He replied that he could not say anything else, for he regarded their idolatry as nothing but loathsome carrion. The papists considered his words a terrible blasphemy, and they condemned him to death.

In every town and village, priests and chaplains shouted from their pulpits against the Lutherans; they cursed Martin Luther's teachings and damned them to the lowest depths of hell. One of them complained in his sermon of how much the peasants were swayed by the blasphemies of Luther's books and expressed his opinions as follows:

Nothing is kept in its proper place anymore. Many people have the effrontery to meddle in matters not fitting for them. A farmer or head of a family should have a plough, whip, or oxgoad in his hands, not the Book. His wife should have a cooking spoon and household keys, not the Book. A farm labourer should have a hoe, woodcutter's axe, flail, or manure fork, not the Book. A servant girl should be at the spinning wheel, feeding the pigs, or similar work, not occupied with the Book. But now no one is content with his rightful station and work; everyone wants to be a priest.

I cannot go further into this, however, but must return to my narrative.

In spite of the strong measures used by the Roman Catholics, resistance strengthened and more and more people fell away from the papacy. As a result, open persecution began against all who accepted the Lutheran religion or the Augsburg Confession. The sheriff from Spittal, Johannes Turteltaub, was appointed as commissioner of religion and received instructions from the imperial court to purge the archduchy of Carinthia of Lutheranism. This led to decisive action.

Johannes Turteltaub sent his couriers or constables to summon all who were suspected of Lutheran beliefs to assemble in the market town of Spittal. He questioned them individually, warning them to recant and return to the Roman Catholic religion, and threatening the young people in particular that he would have them held down and whipped. He ordered the flogging block to be brought out to show how it would be, and he kept some of them imprisoned for several weeks to intimidate them.

Those who remained firm and refused to revert to Roman Catholicism were immediately informed that they could no longer be tolerated in the country. They were to be driven from their homes, their farms and property, and deported to Transylvania. To frighten them still more, they were told how they would be treated in that country: they would be forced to live in destitution for the rest of their lives. The little children would starve, for there would be no bread, far less anything else to give them.

Their friends and relatives begged and pleaded with them to stay in their homes. Why should they go away? God the Lord was everywhere, and they could believe whatever they wished in their hearts even if they had to attend church and observe the Roman Catholic faith.

Some gave way when it came to the point of leaving their worldly possessions, wife, child, brother, sister, and other relatives and friends. They could not overcome and give up worldly goods for the sake of their faith. These subsequently had to make a public recantation and confession of faith in church.

Most remained firm, however, and left their farms and houses and all their property. Many prosperous, respected heads of families left everything they had.

Many young, unmarried men and women left parents, relatives, and everyone they knew and declared publicly that the Lutheran doctrine was the truth and the way to eternal life. They refused to be intimidated by mockery, threats, bonds, or imprisonment. A good part of them did not wait to be summoned, but went of themselves to the commissioner of religion to have their names added to the list.

Our own forefathers were among those who held firmly to the Lutheran doctrine, namely:

JOHANNES KLEINSASSER from Amlach, his wife Barbara, his three brothers and one daughter: Stephanus (20) Mathies (17) Joseph (15) Christina;

GEORG WALDNER with his Anna and three children, also from Amlach: Christian, Johannes, and Maria;

PETER MÜLLER from Unteramlach; Michel and Mathies Hofer, also from Amlach, left father, mother, and a brother;

ANDREAS WURZ from St. Peter with his Margareta and five children: Christian, Magdalena, Elisabeth, Anna, and Christina

CHRISTIAN GLANZER, also from St. Peter, with his Maria, his three brothers Martin, Paul, and Veit and two children: Christian, Anna;

JOHANNES HOFER from St. Peter with his wife Anna, five sons and two daughters: Johannes, Michel, Christian, Paul, Jacob, Anna, and Barbara;

CHRISTIAN NÄGELER from Stockenboi in the jurisdiction of Paternion with his Dorothea and three daughters: Katharina, Christina, and Maria;

JOSEPH MÜLLER from Lentsach with his wife Elisabeth and two children: Joseph, Barbara;

JACOB EGERTER from St. Peter and his two sisters, Christina and Anna;

JOHANNES PLATTNER from St. Peter and his sister Elisabeth;

GEORG GURL with his Lena from the Himmelberg jurisdiction; JOHANNES AMLACHER from Oberamlach; VALENTIN RESCH; CHRISTINA AND ELISABETH WINKLER from Oberamlach; and ROSINA BICHLER from St. Peter.

The commissioner of religion gave orders that all who would not recant must prepare for the journey. They, their wives and children, and the little bedding they were allowed to take with them, were loaded on wagons provided by the authorities.

Constables or couriers drove them from Spittal to Klagenfurt. The movable and immovable property left behind was listed and its value assessed. The exiles were promised that it would be sent after them. Nothing was done, however, and very few ever received anything from their previous possessions.

On their arrival in Klagenfurt they were put in the penitentiary in the fort and well-guarded by soldiers. They had to work there carrying stone, sand, and mortar, and giving other help to the masons working in the penitentiary. This lasted for about two months. From Klagenfurt they were taken through Styria in Austria to the town of Ybbs on the Danube. Here they were locked in the barracks and closely guarded. They had to wait two months until more emigrants had arrived and 270 were assembled. In September 1755, they were moved on from Ybbs by boat. This part of the journey lasted three weeks. They were taken to Vienna in Austria and on down the Danube into Hungary, via Pressburg, Komorn, Gran, Buda, and Peterwardein. From Peterwardein they had to haul the transport boats through the canal that had been dug there, until they reached Temesvar, the capital of Banat. Here they left the boats and were taken by wagon into Transylvania. After two weeks' traveling they arrived safely at Szaszvaros. The following day they were brought to a village called Rumes. They were lodged with neighbouring farmers, and the authorities said they were to settle in the place. This was in October 1755.

After a few days, a Lutheran councilman came to Rumes from Szaszvaros. His name was Kraft. He and the Lutheran pastor of the place called all the immigrants together and assembled them in a large room. The Lutheran pastor read out a letter sent in the empress' name with the following contents:

Because they had declared their adherence to the Lutheran religion while in Germany, namely in the Archduchy of Carinthia, where only Roman Catholicism was allowed, the empress had ordered their removal at her own expense to Transylvania, where the Lutheran religion was tolerated. Here they could have the Gospel, which had been their desire in Austria. "But since Her Imperial Majesty has shown you such especial favour, she requires each and every one of you to swear an oath assuring her of your future loyalty. She will then continue to be gracious to you, and will have houses built for you at her expense and will give you fields, meadows, and other necessities."

The immigrants were both astounded and dismayed when they heard they must swear allegiance to the empress. They refused, for they had left their native land in order to have the freedom to live according to the gospel and now they were to be forced to swear an oath, which was directly against the Gospel.

Mathies Hofer was the first to voice his opposition. He said to the councilman and the Lutheran pastor, "How can you demand that we do something Christ has forbidden?" And he quoted in full from Matthew 5 and James 5. The councilman said, "You may be able to read well, but you don't understand what you read. Why haven't you read Romans 13 as well: 'Whoever resists the authorities, resists the ordinance of God?'" A great deal more was said, but the exact words are no longer known.

Valentin Resch and others then expressed their refusal to take the oath. It became impossible to conclude the matter immediately.

The Lutherans were not content to leave affairs like this, however. They persisted in their demand until most of the immigrants had taken the oath of allegiance to Her Imperial Majesty. Once the newcomers had sworn, houses were built for them, fields, meadows, and other necessities were given them, and they were promised that the goods left behind in Carinthia would be forwarded.

Although our forefathers (whose names are recorded above) had also accepted the original *Augsburg Confession*, they were not to be coerced into acting in plain opposition to the Gospel. Through God's grace they soon realized that the Lutheran churches did not follow Gospel truth nor at all justify the expectations they had formed while still in Carinthia. They found a great deal of wrong and injustice within the church, especially the insatiable greed of the pastors, oath-taking, abusive talk, lying, deceit, fornication, adultery, drunkenness, and similar sins, all of them against the Gospel.

Deeply troubled and dissatisfied at heart, they did not know what to do. During the first winter they attended the Lutheran church and allowed their children to be baptized.

[**Source:** *The Chronicle of the Hutterian Brethren*, Volume 2. Translated by the Hutterian Brethren. (Ste. Agathe: Crystal Spring Colony, 1998), 367–76. Used by permission.]

Catherine the Great of Russia (1729–1796)
Manifesto for Settlement in Southern Russia, 1763

Catherine II of Russia (Catherine the Great) was born in Stettin, Pomerania, Prussia, and was raised in an environment of German culture and traditions. In 1745 she married Peter III who stood in the line of succession to the Russian throne. Catherine became Empress of Russia in July 1762 following the assassination of her husband. Her rise to power came at the end of the Seven Years' War, a religious and political struggle that left much of Western Europe in dire economic and social conditions.

Russia has a long history of recruiting Germans with skills needed to develop their country. For decades, they had attempted to productively colonize its empire to the south after winning territory from the Ottoman Empire. The government felt that the area along the lower Volga River was unstable and bands of roving bandits made settlement impossible. Catherine and her government wanted to solidify this region as Russian territory and she needed free settlers who would turn the land into productive farms and serve as a model for native people living in the area.

Catherine's second Manifesto was issued on July 22, 1763, at the end of the Seven Years' War. This Manifesto was perfectly timed to appeal to the war and tax weary European populace. Copies of the Manifesto were printed in newspapers and on leaflets that were distributed throughout Europe, but with a focus in the German speaking lands where much of the war had been fought. The Manifesto of 1763 had great appeal to many who were seeking a better life. Over 30,000 people began their migration to Russia between 1763 and 1766.

By God's Grace

we, Catherine the Second,

Empress and sole ruler of all Russians
in Moscow, Kiev, Vladimir, Novgorod, Czarina of Kasan,
Czarina of Astrachan, Czarina of Siberia, Lady of Pleskow and Grand
Duchess of Smolensko, Duchess of Estonia and Livland, Carelial, Tver,

Yugoria, Permia, Viatka and Bulgaria and others; Lady and Grand Duchess of Novgorod in the Netherland of Chernigov, Resan, Rostov, Yaroslav, Beloosrial, Udoria, Obdoria, Condinia, and Ruler of the entire North region and Lady of the Yurish, of the Cartalinian and Grusinian czars and the Cabardinianland, of the Cherkessian and Gorsian princes and the heiress and sovereign of many others.

Since the vast extent of the countries in our empire are sufficiently known to us, we noted among other things that no small number of these territories lie uncultivated and, for their best use, could most conveniently and advantageously be settled and populated by humankind. Most of these areas have an inexhaustible wealth of all types of valuable ores and metals hidden in their depths; and as they are provided with woods, rivers, lakes, and seas well situated for commerce, they are exceptionally suited to the development and increase of various factories, manufacturing processes, and enterprises.

This occasioned the issue of the manifesto to the profit of all our faithful subjects on December 4 of the past year, 1762. However, our desire has been conveyed only in brief outline to foreigners who may wish to settle in our empire; to clarify our statement we have decreed the following terms which we now establish with all solemnity, commanding that they be put into effect.

1. We permit all foreigners to enter our empire and settle in whichever province they please.

2. After arrival, these foreigners can report not only in our city of residence to the office specifically instituted for foreign colonists, but also, as each finds convenient, to the governor in any of the border towns of our empire, or, if there is no governor, to the highest authority in the place.

3. As some of the foreigners desirous of immigrating into Russia may lack the means necessary to pay for the journey, these can apply to our ministers and embassies in other countries, who are to send them to Russia without delay, providing the fare as well as paying for all other necessaries for the journey.

4. As soon as the said foreigners arrive at our city of residence and report at the Aliens' Supervisory Office or at one of the border cities, they shall be required to state their precise wishes and intentions: whether they desire to register as merchants or tradesmen and to become citizens, and, if so, in which city; or whether they wish to settle as whole colonies and villages on unoccupied, productive land in order to engage in

Von GOttes Gnaden

Wir Catharina die Zweyte,

Kayserin und Selbstherrscherin aller Reußen,
zu Moscau, Kiow, Wladimir, Nowgorod, Zaarin zu Casan,
Zaarin zu Astrachan, Zaarin zu Sibirien, Frau zu Plescau und Großfürstin zu Smolensko, Fürstin zu Esthland und Liefland, Carelen, Twer,
Jugorien, Permien, Wiatka, Bolgarien und mehr andern; Frau und
Großfürstin zu Nowgorod des Niedrigen Landes, zu Tschernigow, Resan, Rostow, Jaroslaw, Beloeserien, Udorien, Obdorien, Condinien,
und der ganzen Nord-Seite Gebieterin und Frau des Iverischen Landes, der Cartalinischen und Grusinischen Zaaren und des Cabardinischen
Landes, der Tscherkassischen und Gorischen Fürsten und mehr andern Erb-Frau und Beherrscherin.

Da Uns der weite Umfang der Länder Unsers Reiches zur Gnüge bekannt; so nehmen Wir unter andern wahr, daß keine geringe Zahl solcher Gegenden noch
unbebauet liege, die mit vortheilhafter Bequemlichkeit zur Bevölkerung und
Bewohnung des menschlichen Geschlechtes nutzbarlichst könnte angewendet
werden, von welchen die meisten Ländereyen in ihrem Schooße einen uner-
schöpflichen Reichthum an allerley kostbaren Erzen und Metallen verborgen halten; und weil selbige mit Holzungen, Flüssen, Seen und zur Handlung gelegenen Meeren gnug-
sam versehen, so sind sie auch ungemein bequem zur Beförderung und Vermehrung vielerley Ma-
nufacturen, Fabricken und zu verschiedenen andern Anlagen. Dieses gab Uns Anlaß zur Erthei-
lung des Manifestes, so zum Besten aller Unserer getreuen Unterthanen den 4ten December des
abgewichenen 1762sten Jahres publiciret wurde. Jedoch, da Wir in selbigem denen Ausländern, die Verlangen tragen würden sich in Unserm Reiche häuslich niederzulassen, Unser Belie-
ben nur summarisch angekündigt; so befehlen Wir zur bessern Erörterung desselben folgende
Verordnung, welche Wir hiemit aufs feierlichste zum Grunde legen, und in Erfüllung zu se-
tzen gebeten, jedermänniglich kund zu machen.

1.

Verstatten Wir allen Ausländern in Unser Reich zu kommen, um sich in allen Gou-
vernements, wo es einem jeden gefällig, häuslich niederzulassen.

2.

Dergleichen Fremde können sich nach ihrer Ankunft nicht nur in Unserer Residenz bey
der zu solchem Ende für die Ausländer besonders errichteten Tutel-Canzelley, sondern auch in den
anderweitigen Gränz-Städten Unsers Reichs nach eines jeden Bequemlichkeit bey denen Gouver-
neurs, oder, wo dergleichen nicht vorhanden, bey den vornehmsten Stadts-Befehlshabern melden.

3.

Da unter denen sich in Rußland niederzulassen Verlangen tragenden Ausländern sich
auch solche finden würden, die nicht Vermögen genug zu Bestreitung der erforderlichen Reise-
kosten besitzen: so können sich dergleichen bey Unsern Ministern und Residenten an auswärti-
gen Höfen melden, welche sie nicht nur auf Unsere Kosten ohne Anstand nach Rußland schi-
cken, sondern auch mit Reisegeld versehen sollen.

agriculture or various useful trades. All these people are to be promptly granted their wishes and preferences. [...]

5. As soon as any foreigner has arrived in our dominions with the intention of settling, and for this purpose has applied to the Alien's Supervisory Office or at any border city of our empire, he has first of all to declare his exact intentions as stated above in paragraph four and then swear to be a loyal, obedient subject, taking the oath according to the rites of his own religion.

6. In order that the foreigners who desire to settle in our dominions may perceive the extent of our gracious concern for their advantage and profit, it is our will that:

    1. We grant the foreign immigrants to our dominions free and unrestricted practice of their religion according to the rules and customs of their church; to those who do not settle in cities, but in unpopulated sections, especially in colonies, we grant the freedom to build churches and bell towers and to maintain the necessary number of priests and church officials; the sole exception is the construction of monasteries and convents. But warning is hereby given that in no circumstances may any person persuade or entice a Russian national who also holds the Christian faith to accept or pledge himself to that person's faith and church, this on pain of the utmost rigour of our laws. An exception is made for all the nations on our frontiers who belong to the Mohammedan religion. We not only permit them to be influenced in a right way to the Christian religion but also to be made our subjects.

    2. None of the foreign colonists who immigrate to Russia are to be forced to pay the smallest sum into our treasury, or to give customary or extraordinary labour services, or to quarter soldiers or other people; in short, there is freedom from all dues and taxes with the following distinction: those who settle in colonies of many families together on virgin territory shall have thirty years' exemption; those who settle in cities and register as craftsmen or merchants, either in our capital, St. Petersburg, or in the neighbouring cities in Livonia, Estonia, Ingermanland, Karelia, and Finland, no less than in Moscow, are to be given five years' exemption. In addition, all who enter Russia for more than a short stay, in order to settle and live in the country, are to be lodged at no expense for half a year.

    3. A helping hand is extended to all immigrants to Russia who wish to grow grain, engage in handicrafts or manufacturing, or build factories and installations. In proportion to the need for the proposed

Catherine II of Russia,
Fyodor Rokotov,
oil on canvas, 1763.
[*WikiCommons*]

factories and installations and to their future usefulness, especially such as have not been built in Russia before, each immigrant will be provided with more than adequate support and whatever advances he requires.

4. Each shall receive from our treasury, interest free, the advance necessary for building a house, obtaining the various types of domestic animals required by his household, likewise everything for agriculture, and the tools, accessories and material for a trade. The advance is to be repaid only after a ten-year interval and then over a three-year period in equal annual instalments.

5. Where the immigrants settle in complete colonies or villages, we permit them to administer their internal affairs according to their

own ideas. This means that our own appointed officials will not concern themselves with their internal organization. In all other respects, however, such colonists are under obligation to submit to our civil law. Yet their wishes will be met if they themselves desire us to provide a particular person, with a company of well-disciplined soldiers, as guardian or overseer of their safety and defense until they have become known by the neighbouring population.

6. Every foreigner who wishes to settle in Russia may bring his goods, of whatever description, into the country duty-free, with the one restriction that the goods are for his own use and requirements and not for sale. Any who bring possessions beyond those required for personal use, and with the intention of selling them, are permitted by us to import three hundred roubles' worth of such goods duty-free per family, but only on condition that these immigrants remain ten years in Russia. In all other cases, customs dues will be collected both on incoming and outgoing goods.

7. While domiciled in this country, the foreign settlers in Russia shall not be taken against their wills for military or any other service apart from the customary labor services. They are to be exempt even from these services on the land until the expiration of the duty-free years granted above. However, if anyone chooses to become a soldier and volunteers for military service, he will receive on enlistment a bonus of thirty roubles in addition to his regular pay in the regiment.

8. On registering at the Bureau of Guardianship or at a border town, and after stating their intention to enter Russia as settlers, the immigrant aliens will immediately receive journey money and free transport to their chosen destination.

9. To any immigrant into Russia who starts a factory or enterprise for producing goods not previously made in Russia, we grant ten years' exemption from any kind of customs dues on the sale and export of his goods by inland water transport or across borders.

10. For foreign capitalists who start factories and enterprises at their own cost, we hereby grant permission to buy the serfs and peasants necessary for such factories and other enterprises.

11. To all foreigners who have settled as a group in their own colonies and villages, we also grant permission to arrange market days and fairs as they deem best, without paying the smallest fee into our treasury.

7. The privileges and arrangements listed above are to be enjoyed not only by those entering and settling in our country, but also by their surviving children and descendants even if born in Russia; the period of exemption to be reckoned from the date their forefathers entered Russia.

8. When the period of exemption is over, all foreign settlers in Russia are obliged, like all our other subjects, to pay the customary dues and taxes, which are in no way burdensome.

9. To conclude, if any such settlers, who have become our subjects, should afterwards wish to leave our empire, we give them complete freedom to move at any time, with this exception: that each is obliged to pay into our treasury a portion of the profits earned in our dominions: those who have lived here between one and five years must pay one fifth; those here from five to ten years and more are to pay a tenth; thereafter, each is allowed to move freely wherever he wishes.

10. In addition, if some of those desiring to settle in Russia are motivated by concerns and interests not cited above and wish to obtain other conditions and privileges, such aliens should apply either in person or by writing to the Bureau of Guardianship for Foreign Colonists. This office will present all the facts to us, and after the circumstances are examined, each applicant may rest assured that in our love of justice we will not hesitate to issue an exceedingly favourable resolution from the highest quarters.

Issued at Peterhof on the 22nd day of July in the year 1763, the second year of our reign.

The original was signed by her Supreme Imperial Majesty with her own hand as follows:

CATHARINA

Printed by the Senate on July 25, 1763.

[**Source:** Adapted from *Chronicle of the Hutterian Brethren*, Volume 2. Translated by the Hutterian Brethren. (Ste. Agathe: Crystal Spring Colony, 1998), 835–840. Used by permission.]

Testimonies of the Carinthian
crypto-Protestants, 1764

In the middle of the 18th century, there was a Protestant revival in the Habsburg province of Carinthia (*Kärtnen*) ruled by Catholic Empress Maria Theresa. Many people began to meet privately in their homes to read the Bible and Protestant (Lutheran) literature instead of attending Catholic services and practicing the Catholic faith.

Fearing a repeat of the Reformation in the early 16th century, official orders were given that any reading of non-Catholic literature was illegal. Books needed to be brought to the local clergy and given a stamp of approval. Those who refused to submit to the new measures were exiled to the easternmost reaches of the Habsburg empire, to Transylvania, where the Protestant faith was tolerated.

From Carinthia about 1000 people refused to accept the Catholic faith and opted for exile instead. When they reached Transylvania, they were asked to swear allegiance to the Empress before receiving land to settle on. Among those who refused due to their religious convictions were the Hofer, Kleinsasser, Waldner, Wurtz and Glanzer families. Without land, they were condemned to work as day labourers in the area near Alwinz where the old Hutterites lived. About 60 years earlier, in 1690, the Hutterites in Transylvania had given up community-of-goods but they still read much of the earlier literature.

When they came to Alwinz in search of work the Hutterite brothers hired them. Through conversations and by reading Peter Riedemann's *Confession of Faith* as well as the *Handbüchlein wider den Prozess...*, the Carinthian transmigrants became acquainted and impressed with the Hutterite faith. They were persuaded not only to join the old Hutterites but to rekindle and revitalize the practice of community-of-goods in 1756. Eleven years later, they were again forced to relocate to Wallachia to escape the intense campaign led by the Jesuit Delphini to force them to become Catholic.

The following court transcript reveals the questions the representatives of each of the communities (Stein, Kreuz, Alwinz, Hermannstadt prison) faced from the Lutheran interrogators several years after they settled in the area. The questions are based on the articles of the Augsburg Confession, the founding Lutheran confession presented to the Diet of Augsburg in 1530.

The Carinthian transmigrant Anabaptists answered the individual questions as follows:

11TH QUESTION: Of what faith [*Glauben*] are you? Are you Protestant Lutherans like we are?

> **Kleinsasser:** We confess to being Protestant, but we do not know anything about Luther. We do not want to be called Lutherans.
>
> **Glanzer:** They are Protestants, but not Lutheran Protestant Christians.[1]
>
> **Hofer:** No, I am Christian; I make no claim to follow any man because the Apostle Paul said that [the Corinthians] should not claim to follow Paul [*paulisch nennen*].[2]
>
> **Amlacher:** Yes, Protestant, but not Lutheran.
>
> **Strauß:** We call ourselves Christians.
>
> **Wurtzy:** Protestant, certainly, but not Lutheran!

12TH QUESTION: Are you not from the Moravian Church [*Herrnhuter*], or members of the Bohemian [*mährischen*] Brethren?

> **Kleinsasser:** We don't know much about the Moravians and do not associate with them.
>
> **Glanzer:** They were neither. They used to gladly read Moravian literature because they were in accordance with holy Scripture; they are, however, no longer accepted.
>
> **Hofer:** I am a member of [the body of] Christ, but I am not ashamed of the Moravian Church's teachings; as much as you have heard, they have the correct doctrine.
>
> **Amlacher:** Yes, we hear from external sources that we are Moravian.
>
> **Strauß:** We do not know anything about other groups.
>
> **Wurtzy:** Yes, we belong to and are considered part of the Bohemian Brethren.

13TH QUESTION: Why do you separate yourselves from our co-religionists?

> **Kleinsasser:** Because they do not live out the Gospel they have received.
>
> **Glanzer:** They separate themselves because our co-religionists no longer live out what the Gospel commands.
>
> **Hofer:** Because they do not lead a Christian life.

---

1   Glanzer, a 33 year old mason, spoke on behalf of the group at Stein. Throughout this transcript his responses are given in a third-person point of view.

2   1 Cor 1:12.

Amlacher: Because they do not teach the teachings of Christ.

Strauß: Because you do not have the right doctrine.

Wurtzy: They separate themselves because the Lutherans no longer hold to what the Gospel commands.[3]

14TH QUESTION: Why do you not come to our public assemblies to sing, pray, and hear the preached Word of God?

Kleinsasser: Because it is not taught pure and clear!

Glanzer: Because the Lutherans do not agree with their religion.

Hofer: Because the Lord has commanded us to separate from our relations: Come out [...], so that you do not take part in their sins.[4]

Amlacher: Because they do not leave the Gospel pure.

Strauß: Because it is not a Christian assembly.

Wurtzy: Because the Lutheran teachings are not in harmony with their religion.

15TH QUESTION: Why do you not observe holy baptism in the same way we do?

Kleinsasser: Because it is not God's command to baptize in that way.

Glanzer: Because they do not accept it as right.

Hofer: Christ the Lord has forbidden children to be baptized.

Amlacher: Because it is not in accordance to the Gospel.

Strauß: Because it is not commanded in Scripture.

Wurtzy: Because they do not accept it as right.

16TH QUESTION: Why do you not observe the [Sacrament of the] Lord's Supper with us?

Kleinsasser: Because you do not observe it like Christ the Lord!

Glanzer: For the reasons given under questions 14 and 15.

Hofer: Because you do not observe it according to [Christ's] command. The Lord has not commanded that we should eat his flesh.

Amlacher: We observe it as Christ has taught it.

Strauß: Because you do not observe it as Jesus instituted it.

Wurtzy: We do not accept the teachings in the *Augsburg Confession* on baptism, and also not regarding the Lord's Supper.

17TH QUESTION: Why do you not make use of the ordained Protestant-Lutheran ministers or pastors?

Kleinsasser: Because their teaching is not pure and clear!

Glanzer: Because they were not given the right, in spite of wanting it; they were not permitted to have a [pastor].

Hofer: We do not consider them to be true teachers. They seek much for their own gain. [You] say in vain, "They have received it freely."

---

3 Wurtzy's responses to question 13–15 are recorded in the third person point of view.

4 Rev 18:4.

Amlacher: Because they are not faithful to the Gospel.

Strauß: Because they do not teach correctly.

Wurtzy: Because they did not receive this right when they requested [a minister].

18TH QUESTION: **Do you believe that our Protestant-Lutheran doctrine is erroneous?**

Kleinsasser: What else?

Glanzer: They believe this because the Protestant-Lutheran doctrine is not compatible with the Gospel.

Hofer: Yes, I believe this.

Amlacher: Yes, most of it is in great error [*großer Irrtum, nicht wenig*].

Strauß: Yes.

Wurtzy: We do not accept the teachings on baptism, swearing [oaths], and other things because they are not in accordance with the Gospel. [...][5]

IN CONCLUSION

1ST [QUESTION]: **Where and by whom have you been convinced of this erroneous belief?**

Kleinsasser: Refused to answer.

Glanzer: It occurred in Alwinz, through the residents living there, that they were enlightened.

Hofer: That we should not swear [an oath] we knew well already in our homeland, and also that here [in Alwinz] were priests with private property. [Our beliefs] regarding baptism were learned here in Alwinz.

Amlacher: Through Scripture, back home, and also here.

Strauß: Through the Word of God while we were in Alwinz; we do not want to reveal which books we have.

Wurtzy: They were enlightened by the residents in Alwinz.

Müller: We are no longer in error.

2ND [QUESTION]: **Will you let yourselves be dissuaded from these many and gross errors?**

Kleinsasser: We cannot let ourselves be led down any other path than what we have confessed because Christ the Lord has revealed it to us.

Glanzer: They are prepared to do so, if anybody can convince them with the Word of God.

Hofer: You can try, but I hope we will turn out to be right.

Amlacher: No.

---

5   The redacted portion of the transcript deals with questions specific to the Augsburg Confession.

Strauß: No.

Wurtzy: We are prepared to do so, if anybody can convince us with the Gospel.

Müller: No.

3RD [QUESTION]: **Will you sincerely accept the doctrine of our Protestant-Lutheran Church and enter into our church communion?**

Kleinsasser: No.

Glanzer: We do not want this for the reasons cited in question 18.

Hofer: O certainly not! We refuse to be coerced by human decrees.

Amlacher: We have no fallacies, but rather, the pure Word of God.

Strauß: We believe [*verhoffen*] we have the clear Word of God and refuse to depart from it.

Wurtzy: No, we do not want to do that!

4TH [QUESTION]: **Are you determined to live or die by your present Anabaptist convictions?**

Kleinsasser: Yes.

Glanzer: They are determined, by the grace and help of God, to live or die by their convictions.

Hofer: Certainly, according to the teachings of Christ and his commands.

Amlacher: You could not dissuade me, therefore we will stay with our teachings until death.

Strauß: Like Amlacher.

Wurtzy: Yes.

5TH [QUESTION]: **Who in Stein, Kreuz, or elsewhere in Transylvania belongs to your church or Anabaptist community?**

Kleinsasser: Refused to answer.

Glanzer: In Stein there are no more than those already listed by name on the register. In Kreuz no more than those mentioned before. From Bazna, those people found in the statement [*Specifikation*], and from Henndorf the seven people in addition to another daughter of Waldner, whose name he didn't know, that joined them.

Hofer: Even if I knew of anybody, where has God commanded that I identify him, so that he can be persecuted?

Amlacher: We don't know, but there are still some in Stein and Kreuz.

Strauß: Our stepfather is Andreas Wurtzy and he lives in Eibesdorf.

[**SOURCE:** Translated by Kenny Wollmann from Erich Buchinger, *Die Geschichte der Kärntner Hutterischen Brüder in Siebenbürgen und in der Walachei (1755–1770), in Russland und Amerika.* (Klagenfurt: Verlag des Geschichtliche Landeskunde von Kärnten, 1982), 200–211.]

Pyotr Alexandrovich Rumyantsev-Zadunaisky (1725–1796), was one of the foremost Russian generals of the 18th century and widely considered to be one of Russia's greatest military leaders. Unknown artist, painting, early 1770s. [*WikiCommons*]

Privileges to be Granted to the Colonists with the Intent of Settlement in Vishenka, 1770

In 1767, a remnant of sixty-seven Hutterites crossed the Carpathian Mountains to Wallachia to escape the Jesuit's intense efforts to claim them for the Catholic faith, which included book confiscations, imprisonment of leaders, and the last straw—a plan to seize Hutterite children and place them in a Catholic orphanage. After spending fewer than three years in Wallachia the Hutterites were forced to relocate once again primarily because the Russo-Turkish War (1768–1774) was raging in the area. They were able to negotiate a satisfactory contract with Count Pyotr (Peter) Alexandrovich Rumyantsev-Zadunaisky to settle on his estates at Vishenka northeast of Kiev.

1. They shall have full freedom to practice their religion: they are never to be compelled to swear an oath either in a court of law or elsewhere.

2. They are never to be employed for military service.

3. No one may prevent or hinder them from living in community, and they are permitted to work and pay taxes communally.

4. They will be given complete tax exemption for three years.

5. They will receive necessities on credit, including a bushel of flour for the whole group each day.

6. They will be provided with thirty rubles for their journey and with whatever is necessary on their arrival in Vishenka. In addition, they will receive money and wood for building on credit.

7. After the three years' exemption, they will pay a fixed rent on the land assigned to them for cultivation, hay-making, and raising garden crops, etc.

8. Each is free to work for his own livelihood. They are not allowed to form a guild. They are free to sell whatever they produce.

9. Their freedom may not be restricted in any way. If at any time the owner of the estate or they themselves should no longer wish the community

to remain on the aforementioned property, they shall be permitted to move away; but they must payoff all goods and money advanced, plus a tenth of the value of the resources they have acquired.

10. After the three free years, they shall pay taxes in cash on land and houses.

11. At hay-making, eighty wagon loads of hay shall be allotted to them for their cattle.

12. As they cannot complete the construction of the necessary buildings before winter, temporary housing will be provided for them.

IN CAMP BY THE PRUIT IN THE DISTRICT OF RABOG
June 1770

[**SOURCE:** *The Chronicle of the Hutterian Brethren,* Volume 2. Translated by the Hutterian Brethren. (Ste. Agathe: Crystal Spring Colony, 1998), 453–454. Used by permission.]

JOHANNES WALDNER (1749–1824)
"Vishenka Mavericks," 1770–1802

The Hutterites lived at Vishenka from 1770–1802, when they relocated to Radicheva. While the community at Vishenka faced few external threats, it encountered several internal challenges involving members who left. "Thus in a few years," lamented chronicler Johannes Waldner, "three of the most skillful and best-educated brothers left the church. They excelled many others in knowledge and intelligence, and they might have filled a useful place as brothers in the church if they had continued to use their gifts humbly and simply. Mathies Hofer and Johannes Hofer fell away to the right and Christian Wurz to the left,"[1] meaning that Mathies and Johannes lost their way in spiritual matters, while Christian was lured away by worldly pursuits. The following three accounts describe some of the challenges the community at Vishenka encountered when dealing with these three individuals.

The Account of Mathias Hofer

In January 1773, the Almighty God in his grace brought us all together for the first time: those from Kreuz, from Stein, from Alwinz, and from Hermannstadt. We had all longed to gather in the unity of the Spirit while in Transylvania, but had been prevented by the hostility, envy, and hatred of godless men. The brothers from Stein would gladly have moved to Kreuz when the brotherhoods united, but the villagers would not allow it. The Jesuit had had the Alwinz families forcibly removed from Kreuz by government authority. Some had been imprisoned in Hermannstadt the whole time we were in Transylvania (as is described in sufficient detail above). Until this year, it had never been possible for us all to gather in one place.

The whole church community of God rejoiced that he had led us together. We praised and thanked him from the depths of our hearts. All the believers were firmly re-

---

1   *The Chronicle of the Hutterian Brethren*, vol. 2. Translated by the Hutterian Brethren. (Ste. Agathe: Crystal Spring Colony, 1998), 548.

solved to live in true peace and unity, serving God and their brothers and sisters in Christian, brotherly love, one helping to strengthen another in faith, working zealously for Christian community in both spiritual and temporal matters (as the highest commandment of love).

Satan never rests, however. As Peter says, he continually prowls around the house of God like a roaring lion. He is always trying to cause confusion and to hinder the believers from carrying out the Lord's work and serving him. He strives unceasingly to sever the bond of love and peace. So the Enemy was hard at work now, but without success. Although he made his attack very subtly, in the guise of an angel, and as if it were deeply spiritual, he failed completely. This will be seen from the account of what took place. I will give a truthful and thorough report of how the trouble arose— not in every detail, but explaining the main points.

Soon after the brothers from Hermannstadt arrived; a sharp disagreement developed between the brothers from Kreuz and those from Stein, so that the little flock was nearly torn in two and would have divided if the Lord had not especially protected us.

The disagreement and division was caused by Mathies Hofer. He was, in many respects, a very zealous and deeply spiritual man who, to use a familiar phrase, knew the whole Bible as well as he knew the Lord's Prayer. He knew the entire book of Psalms by heart, as well as every chapter in the Old and New Testament that contained a prayer. At the beginning, before he went too far, he did much to establish the community, strengthening and encouraging us in many ways. During his time in prison he composed many spiritual songs, nearly thirty if all were counted. He had written out books which the brothers from Alwinz had sent us to copy, and we have a great number of copies in his beautiful handwriting. For all these reasons the brothers had a high regard for him and loved him very much, especially Hans Kleinsasser, the church Elder, who followed his advice in almost everything. As time went on, however, this did not turn out for the best.

In Psalm 119:62 it is written, "At midnight I will rise to give thanks," and in Psalm 134:1, David says, "Praise the Lord, all you servants of the Lord who watch by night in the house of the Lord." These verses led Mathies Hofer to introduce a new practice into the church community: Every night two brothers were to be on watch, one before and the other after midnight. At midnight the first had to waken all the brothers and sisters for prayer. Mathies wanted them to dress and gather in the meeting room, but as this was not fitting, people simply knelt up in bed. One of them led the prayer by speaking it aloud; the others participated in silence. All took turns to lead the prayer: the single brothers and sisters according to rules, the married people alternating with each other. If anyone was sleepy, the others roused him. This practice continued for some years in Russia, until about 1782, but now it has long been given up and forgotten. Each one is free to make his own judgment on this practice.

Prompted by Mathies' advice, Hans Kleinsasser also started the practice in the community for prayer to take place morning, noon, and evening, the married brothers in one group, the married sisters in another, the unmarried brothers together, and the unmarried sisters together. In the midday meetings there was not only prayer, but reading, too. Those present took turns to read as well as to lead the prayer.

In addition, there were two meetings a day. Early in the morning before breakfast, everyone was called to prayer. At this meeting there was simply the common prayer, led by the Elder, without any preface, reading, or singing. Later, when Joseph Kuhr returned, he read a short preface before the prayer. After the people rose from prayer they gave one another the greeting of peace. Brothers embraced brothers and sisters embraced sisters. Brothers and sisters did not embrace each other, but only shook hands when they greeted one another, as is directed in the church's Confession of Faith. This took place every morning. Then they had breakfast.

In the evening before supper, everyone was called to prayer again, and the servant of the Word read from the Psalms of David in the Bible. He began at the first and went through them in order, meeting by meeting. When he had reached the last, he began at the beginning again. After the prayer, one or two chapters from the Bible or passages from some other book were read. After this came a song. Then we sat down to supper. The community at Kreuz had begun this daily order of prayer meetings while still in Transylvania, and it was continued for some years in Russia. After Hans Kleinsasser's death (1779), the servant of the Word no longer used the Psalms for daily prayer. The early morning meeting was also discontinued and we made our common prayer only once a day, at the evening meeting, as we still do today.

This Mathies Hofer, after reading the story of Mordecai and Haman, also concluded that we should not remove our hats in the presence of magistrates, nor should we greet unbelievers. He supported his ideas with so many texts from Holy Scripture that not a brother in the church community could dispute with him. Everyone had to go along with his opinions. It was customary among people in general for a man to take off his hat when nobles were present and to greet neighbours in their homes or on the street. When Mathies and the other brothers in the community ceased this practice, they caused great offense. It was regarded as defiant, stubborn behaviour and certainly did little to honour God's name or to convince others that they should lead a better life. We continued the custom when first in Russia, but after we received our church chronicle from Transylvania, we read about our dear forefathers (whose faith, teaching, and religion we affirm as our own). We found that they had given greetings, and also that they had never caused offense to lay magistrates by refusing to take off their hats. It is certain that if they had refused, they could not have avoided provoking the lay officials. The offense they caused to priests and spiritual authorities is recorded in great detail. We therefore decided to keep to our old beliefs and practices on these points.

Mathies Hofer also began insisting on the basis of Holy Scripture that it is not right to work for an unbeliever in return for wages, because it helps him amass private property. This was why we stopped working for the villagers in Kreuz. They grew more hostile to us when we were no longer of any service, for the one thing they had liked about us was that we had worked hard for them.

As time passed, Mathies went so far as to write and speak against the church's *Confession of Faith*, especially against the brothers' way of observing Sunday. They had kept it as a day of rest, though not for the sake of a commandment. To avoid angering ignorant people and giving them reason to revile us, they had refrained from practical work and occupied themselves with the Lord's Word. Mathies wrote that, on this point, the brothers wanted to be better than Christ. Christ healed on the Sabbath although it offended the Pharisees. In the *Confession* it sounded as if Christ had not acted rightly because he had not avoided provoking them, etc. Mathies could sway brother Hans Kleinsasser to his way of thinking on every question, and now he managed to persuade the whole brotherhood to follow his ideas in this, too, and to turn away from our forefathers' confession of faith. Sunday mornings were devoted to preaching and instruction in the faith, but the afternoon was used for communal work. The village would not tolerate this, and we were forbidden to work on Sunday; but we continued nonetheless. The justice of the peace and other freemen from the village came and took our work away from us. The community still would not give in.

Many brothers were not happy about it. They believed we should keep to the church's statement of faith and not make innovations. But such opinions were discounted at the time.

While we were in Wallachia, serious disagreement arose on this point between the brothers from Kreuz and those from Stein. Brother Peter Müller was strongly opposed to the new arrangement and urged us to hold to the guidelines and confession of faith written down by brothers in earlier days. The brothers from Stein gave in for the sake of peace, united with the brotherhood, and again took part in Sunday afternoon work with the others. But Peter Müller would not be coerced into working; he sat reading the Holy Scriptures in the afternoon, too. This made him appear obstinate and opinionated. He was never reconciled with the brotherhood but held to his own convictions until he fell asleep in the Lord on December 8, 1769.

I will leave each God-fearing reader to decide for himself which attitude was right. Sunday work was gradually dropped in Russia, and now we do only what is absolutely necessary: herding cattle in summer, for instance, feeding stock in winter, cooking, working in the distillery, or in the mill.

These and other points not mentioned here were raised while the community was still in Transylvania. The longer Mathies went on, the more extreme he became. After the community had left the country, he started on the brothers and sisters imprisoned with him and wanted everyone to give up silent, personal prayer. Instead they were all to pray together. In his opposition to personal prayer in silence, he declared that it was idolatry, a sacrifice offered to the devil: people who prayed in this way were dumb dogs unable to bark. He compared it to the Roman Catholic mass, to burying talents, to the foolish virgins, to a dog in a manger that cannot eat hay himself but grudges it to the cow. Even when the others consented to pray together he was not satisfied unless they would admit that silent, personal prayer was devil's work. The brothers and sisters could not agree to this, so he separated himself and was no longer at peace with them. In 1768 when brother Joseph Kuhr and Paul Glanzer came from Wallachia to visit the prisoners in Hermannstadt, they found Mathies already disunited with the others. […]

When the brotherhood withstood him and would not accept his ideas, he ran away again and wandered around in the woods for days until he was faint with hunger. A few brothers went in pity and compassion to look for him, meaning to give him burial if he had died. They found him still alive but had the greatest difficulty in persuading him to come home with them. In the end he said he would be content if he might stay as a guest and stranger among them, having food and lodging from the community while left in peace to hold his own views.

The brothers were called to a meeting where his request was put to them. They agreed on condition that he apologized for his strong expressions. He was ready to take back his words and admitted he had spoken too loudly and roughly, not with love and kindness as he should have done. At the same time he defended his views and what he had actually represented. As the brothers could not accept his statement, it was again asked what should be done with him. Again each brother voiced his opinion.

Some felt great pity and sympathy for Mathies and said that if none of the brothers objected, they, for their part, would let him live in the community. But most said that he should be put out of the church, for he was the root of much evil and damage in the community, a self-willed man who brought disturbance and confusion. If he clung to his own ideas and refused to be corrected, we should not allow him to remain, following the example of the church of God in Moravia when dealing with such people. This was the answer made to him.

Mathies was given a few roubles to help him on his journey, and he set out. Before he had gone many miles he was arrested and taken to prison in Glukhov. Since he was unable to speak Russian, he was interrogated by a German to discover who he was and where he was going. When asked whether he belonged to the colony at Vishenka, Mathies denied it.

He was asked where he wanted to go. He said he was looking for his brothers. When questioned further about what brothers he meant, he replied that the Quakers were his brothers. Mathies was then given a man to escort him from one town to the next until he was out of the country. In this way he came to Elbing in Prussia. There he was given hospitality in Ellerwald by Gerhard Wiebe, a minister and elder of the Mennonite church. Mathies explained his situation to him. This chain of events brought us in contact with the Mennonites in Prussia, for previously they had known nothing about us, and we nothing about them.

In the following year, 1781, Gerhard Wiebe wrote a letter to the church in Russia. It is included here to clarify the situation.

Ellerwald near Elbing
March 5, 1781

My dear brother Joseph Kuhr, whom my soul loves! I wish you and the church in your house great grace and peace from God the Father and Jesus our Saviour, together with the comfort of the Holy Spirit, so that we may be united more fully in faith and love and more closely with Jesus, our true and loving Emanuel, and so become one in spirit. Amen.

I took the liberty of mailing a short letter to you on December 11 of last year. As I have not received a reply, I presume that the letter did not reach you. I will repeat what I then wrote. Some years ago, a Bohemian brother, a harness maker named Jan Schlerk, told us the tragic news that the community of brothers in Upper Hungary had been wiped out by severe persecution and that the community in Transylvania had been banished. But we were unable to discover where you were now living.

On December 5, 1780, however, a man from your community arrived here, very poor but in good health. His name is Mathies Hofer. I never took a more surprising guest into our home than this one! When I asked him why he had made such a long journey, he replied that he had been unable to find agreement with the brothers about public prayer at the Lord's Supper or breaking of bread, and they would not allow him to stay. His conscience had driven him to leave the church and his wife, and he was now looking for a congregation that agreed with his views and lived in community-of-goods. I advised him against going farther, as I do not believe he will find what he seeks. I am acquainted with the congregations in Germany and Holland, for I correspond with them, and I do not know of any that live in community-of-goods. So he is still with me, and I do not want to let him go farther, but advise him to return to you as soon as I have received your answer.

Well, dear brother, that is the reason for my letter: first, to get to know you and, as we cannot meet and talk face to face, to write from time to time so that we may cheer and encourage one another in the Lord as fellow pilgrims on a hard and wearisome road. And may God grant us his help until through grace we are brought where we may see one another in eternal love, and may rejoice and delight in one another before the throne of the Lamb. Amen.

Second, I would like to be a humble mediator between this exile and your dear congregation. So I am making a heartfelt appeal to you and the community on this brother's behalf. Forgive the poor man for Jesus' sake if he has gone against your convictions at any point. One can hope he did not do it out of malice, but either out of weakness or because his conscience compelled him. Forgive his fault if, as I gather from what he says, it is a matter of different opinions and does not involve opposition to sound doctrine.

What is best to do in this case? I think it best to bear with one another in love. He still seems to love the community and does not want to be separated from it. The Apostle Paul teaches us such forbearance. Whence he circumcised Timothy for the sake of the Jews, he gave us an example of how we should reach out to the weak. I hope, dear brother, that his Spirit will teach you that love is greater than all else, also greater than all knowledge.

I beg you to forgive me for my presumption. I am sure you will do so. I will look forward to receiving a charitable answer. My humble words are written with only the kindest intentions, and I am confident that you will let them weigh with you a little and will ask this poor brother to return. When this happens, I intend, God willing, to send with him a few writings of service in building up God's Kingdom. I believe this man came to us by God's especial leading to help us to get to know each other as we sojourn here. If my letter reaches you and I receive an answer, we will open our hearts more deeply to each other.

In closing, I commend you to God's protection and greet you and the church with the peace that Christ bought so dearly for us. Although we have never met, we are united in love, and I remain your brother and unworthy fellow servant of the Gospel of Christ.

[SIGNED:] Gerhard Wiebe

His letter was answered by the elders of the church, who explained on the basis of Holy Scripture the good and sufficient reasons for Mathies' expulsion from the church and why we could not re-accept him unless he changed his convictions.

After this, letters were often exchanged with Gerhard Wiebe. When we sent no invitation for Mathies to come back to us, he did not remain with the Mennonite elder but left Ellerwald for Brenkenhoffswalde near Driesen, another place where Mennonites had settled. There he stayed for a time with an elder named Ernst Voth, then went on to Hamburg and wanted to cross the ocean to America. Since he had no provision for his journey and could not pay fifty imperial talers to go by ship, he made his way to Holland. He reached the city of Groningen, but could go no further because he did not know the language. So he turned back to Altona and lived there for a time. In 1784, he returned to Brenkenhoffswalde, where he fell asleep in the Lord in 1786.

After brother Hans Kleinsasser had died and Mathies Hofer had left the community, the order of worship they had introduced began little by little to lapse and disappear. I do not mean to commend this neglect, nor am I glad for it. The gatherings for prayer and especially the reading at midday helped build up the young people's faith. As previously described, each read in turn and so each was involved, and it often led to a talk about the meaning of a passage of holy Scripture. At that time each one took pains to be able to read out the Scriptures fluently, and such a practice could still be used with a good conscience today. Now each young brother wants to have a good, well-bound Bible with big print, but many of them (always excepting the zealous) know little of what is inside. Paul taught in 1 Thessalonian 5:2, "Prove all things, hold fast to that which is good." It would have been possible to drop what was unnecessary and exaggerated and to keep what was good. But each can judge the matter as he sees fit.

[**Source:** *Chronicle of the Hutterian Brethren,*Volume 2. Translated by the Hutterian Brethren. (Ste. Agathe: Crystal Spring Colony, 1998), 466–505. Used by permission.]

The Account of Johannes Hofer

In this same year, 1784, Johannes Hofer left the church. Judging from the way he behaved, it was nothing but self-will, arrogance, misused intelligence, and overweening self-satisfaction that drove him away. I will give a short account of what happened.

This Johannes Hofer was a young man of 21, naturally quick and intelligent. While still a boy he had read diligently in the Holy Scriptures and other religious books. When he became a brother and was put to work in the smithy, he was even more diligent in his reading, and he began to make up songs and expound Scripture. Sometimes, he spent nearly the whole night in these occupations, so that the next day, when he was expected to do his work alongside the others, he was worn out, unfit for his task, and produced very little. As time went on, this led to trouble between him and the master smith, who sometimes admonished Johannes for getting so little done. Johannes replied to the effect that they were labouring for mere temporal things, which were not very important. Whenever someone tried to instruct him to explain how to do various tasks in the fields or elsewhere, he always knew better, began to contradict and quarrel, and always had to be in the right and have the last word.

According to him, the whole brotherhood and especially the elders and other responsible brothers were very far from what they should be. He often spoke contemptuously about them to those of his own age. Most of all he criticized and found fault with dear brother Joseph Kuhr as church Elder. Johannes was strongly of the opinion that not so much emphasis should be placed on temporal things—in other words, on work. There should be much greater zeal for spiritual concerns. Brothers should be sent out to convert people. In his view, a great church should be built up as in our forefathers' time.

In spite of his knowing so much, little virtue, dedicated obedience, or humility could be found in him—only self-conceit, which led to contempt for his neighbour, answering back, stubbornness, and disobedience. These faults gradually marred his good points until they ceased giving anyone pleasure. Many regarded him as headstrong and obstinate and avoided his company. Consequently, he was no use whatever in the church.

When he saw what he had brought upon himself and that nobody took notice of what he said, he made up his mind to go into Germany to proclaim the Gospel of truth and establish a community.

No one could dissuade him from this idea, although his cousins and other relatives, who still loved him, tried hard to hold him back. Once he had made up his mind, he would not alter it. He tried to talk other young brothers into taking his side and traveling with him, but he had no success.

Following his own set plan, he undertook the journey alone and arrived safely at Sabatisch. He made inquiries and heard from many people that they would gladly return to their earlier faith if they only had the freedom to do it. This encouraged him to go to Prussian Silesia to look for a place where he could start a community. He approached the royal government at Breslau and presented a petition promising that he would bring people into the country on condition they were granted religious freedom and a place to live.

The authorities readily agreed and sent him with an open letter and a sealed document to the district magistrate of Gross Strehlitz in Upper Silesia. The magistrate was instructed to implement his requests.

Johannes went to Gross Strehlitz, and when the magistrate had read the letter from the royal council and heard from the young man himself, he was delighted. He promised to obtain extensive privileges from the king if only such people could be brought into his district to build up a community—people like those in Moravia in earlier times who had been known as Anabaptists. Their reputation for honesty and trustworthiness was still remembered. Moreover, circumstances were very favourable, for the magistrate had previously had a colony of 32 houses built in this same district at the king's expense. He had settled a number of immigrants there, advanced money, and allowed a year rent-free. For all his effort, they were bad, slovenly people, for when the free year was over, many had moved away without a word, and now many of the houses were standing empty. He also had a manor house and a well-established farm at the same place. He promised to give it all to Johannes if he would only bring people to start a community. Johannes could not have wished for a better opportunity. All he lacked was the people. He took leave of the magistrate, who had provided him with a pass and money for the journey, and he returned to Sabatisch. From there he wrote a letter to the brotherhood in Russia, telling them what a wonderful opportunity he had found for establishing a new community. He urged them to send a servant of the Word with several other brothers to the place he described, and said he hoped and expected that in a short time many hundred people would flock to the faith, for wherever one went there were many seekers on fire for the truth. In addition, he admonished the brotherhood not to be so slack and lazy in doing the Lord's work of gathering the elect: We should not sit in our panelled houses, like a goose brooding on her eggs, while the Lord's house was left ruined and forsaken! Finally, he warned us in the strongest terms that if we did not comply with his request we would have to answer for it at the Last Judgment. His letter, still extant, deals with this theme at great length and is full of scolding and unedifying expressions.

When the letter reached the community, the elders met to consult about what should be done in the matter. They could not believe that God would use such a self-willed and self-appointed man to gather his elect. As no one felt urged by God, we did nothing at all, and nothing at all resulted from Johannes Hofer's wonderful plans. From time to time over a number of years, people brought us news of his doings in Sabatisch. He had stayed for eleven weeks in the attic of a woman named Dangler. In the end no one visited him anymore, and they grew so tired of having him that they asked him to move on. Since then, we have heard nothing of his whereabouts. It is quite possible, however, that he will reappear some time in the future, for strange things can happen with people.

I have written his story to warn each one of us against placing too much confidence in himself, in his own wisdom and understanding, thus deceiving himself and going overboard to his own ruin. We should rather remember what the holy apostle Paul teaches us, "in humility count everyone better (and thus also wiser) than yourselves."

Until now, 1819, we have received no news of him.

[**Source:** *Chronicle of the Hutterian Brethren*, Volume 2. Translated by the Hutterian Brethren. (Ste. Agathe: Crystal Spring Colony, 1998), 543–546. Used by permission.]

The Account of Christian Wurtz

At about the same time Christian Wurz began to weaken in faith and fall away from the church, although he was not completely separated until 1786. His story is as follows:

For a long time we had treated people in the community with home remedies only. In Transylvania and Wallachia and for some years in Russia, we did not use bloodletting or other medical treatment. After a time, we began to rely more on such measures for our people, and in several emergencies we sought the advice of doctors and surgeons. At last we came to a point where it was considered a practical necessity to have a brother in the church community who understood a little about medicine, even if only about bloodletting, so that we were not obliged to go out seeking help from the world for every medical problem.

About 1780, a good opportunity arose. Count Rumyantsev was living on his estate at Tschereschinka at the time and had with him a French doctor named Alphorus Francia. After we had met this doctor several times, got to know him, and indicated that we would be glad to have a doctor in the community, he offered to train one of our brothers if we would like to send someone to him.

The brothers talked over this possibility and Christian Wurz was chosen as suited for the task. He was 26 years old, had a wife and three children, and was trusted by everyone. He was endowed by nature with a good intellect and skillful hands.

So with the knowledge and permission of Count Rumyantsev, we let Christian go to Dr. Francia. We made an agreement that in dress and other points he should keep to the ways customary in the community and should not have to obey in any matter contrary to our faith.

For a time, this brother remained firm enough and did his best to defend our faith and the truth, so that the brotherhood expected he would soon become a help to them. They were disappointed, however, for as time went on he began to forsake the simplicity of Christ and to be attracted to the world. He had worldly clothes made for himself and later shaved off his beard; he swore an oath in order to be registered in the emperor's service. We let all this pass in the hope that when he came home he would once more act like a brother and submit to all the church's directions. But although he pretended he was still a brother, his heart had already turned away from God and the believers. As a result he fell into one sin after another and was no different from a worldly person with cursing, swearing, and other unseemly behaviour. He even began to speak contemptuously of several God-fearing brothers. Among many other things, he said that our forefathers' faith and church order were nothing but man-made inventions. Finally, when he asked to be allowed to wear a wig with a braid, we gave him a curt refusal; when he wore one all the same, he was excluded from the brotherhood. The church community was told he was an unfaithful member and should be avoided. He forsook the truth, his faith, God and the church, and his wife and children, too. Later he moved from Glukhov to Moscow, and for a short time he did very well according to the flesh, diverting himself with worldly pleasures and luxury. But his good time soon came to an end, for he died in January 1792 in Moscow.

[**Source:** *Chronicle of the Hutterian Brethren*, Volume 2. Translated by the Hutterian Brethren. (Ste. Agathe: Crystal Spring Colony, 1998), 546–548. Used by permission.]

THE 19ᵀᴴ CENTURY

Alexander I hands a decree to free serfs to Count Sergei Petrovich Rumyantsev, Bernard-Romain Julien, lithograph, 1803.

Alexander I of Russia (1777–1825)
Decree of the Governing Senate, 1801

When Count Pyotr Alexandrovich Rumyantsev-Zadunaisky passed away, his son Sergei Petrovich Rumyantsev became their new manorial lord. He refused to honour the terms of settlement negotiated with his father, especially the exemption from military service and the freedom to leave his estates. Over a period of about five and half years (1796–1802), the community at Vishenka was in limbo about its future. After considerable effort in negotiating new terms with the count and appealing to Czars Paul I and Alexander I to intervene, they were granted Crown land for settlement at Radicheva. Note that in official government documents, Hutterites were referred to as "Mennonites."

In ratification of the humble request for resettlement from the Mennonites resident in the Province of the Ukraine, domiciled at Vishenka, one of the estates belonging to His Excellency Count Sergei Rumyantsev; in consideration of the said Mennonites' request to move and settle on the crown lands they already hold on lease, also to receive the same privileges as are granted to all other Mennonite settlers in Russia; with due regard to the consent expressed by Count Sergei Rumyantsev, whose father concluded a contract on this point with the Vishenka Mennonites: we are pleased to command the Department of State Economy, which has the guardianship for all foreign settlers throughout Russia, to instruct these Mennonites to move to the crown lands for which they apply, provided that the said lands have not been granted to some other person. In the event that these lands are already assigned, the petitioners are to receive sections of land from properties lying untended or else available for lease in the Province of the Ukraine, allotment to be made according to the Charter of Privileges granted to the Novorosisk Mennonites on September 6, 1800: each family to receive 65 dessiatines [175 acres] for an annual payment of fifteen kopeks per dessiatine to the crown treasury, and the land to be no longer available for lease.

Furthermore, we graciously extend to these Mennonites all the rights and privileges, without restriction, which are granted to the Novorosisk Mennonites by the aforementioned Charter of Privileges, except for the years of exemption from all payments, not applicable in this case since the settlers have already been many years in Russia. As the Department for State Economy has an office in Novorosisk (now Yekaterinoslav) for the care and supervision of local aliens, and this office is nearer and more convenient, the Vishenka Mennonites are to be referred to this office for the practical execution of the Senate's decree.

St. Petersburg
May 22, 1801
[Signed:] Alexander I

[**Source:** *The Chronicle of the Hutterian Brethren,* Volume 2. Translated by the Hutterian Brethren. (Ste. Agathe: Crystal Spring Colony, 1998), 575–576. Used by permission.]

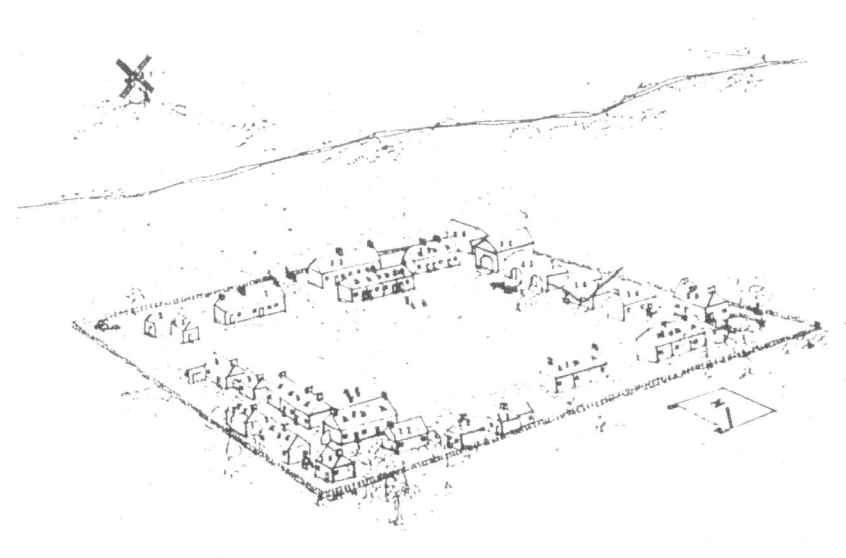

A drawing by W.P. Thompson of Radicheva according to a written description from 1818. [Paul Thompson, *Hutterite Community: Artefact Art,* Vol I, Part II, Thesis, Cornell University, 1977.]

Alexander Augustovic Klaus (1829–1887)
Official Report on the
Hutterites at Radicheva, 1887

Since they had settled on Crown lands at Radicheva, the government periodically sent officials to inspect and report on their welfare. One such report, provided by two Russian councillors of state and included in the second *Chronicle*, gives us a sense of how the community functioned.

Here [in Radicheva], Councillor Kontenius saw 'for the first time a family of two hundred living together on one farm and under the stewardship of the church.' He reports that in addition to working the land, the brotherhood was occupied in making pottery. They marketed a considerable amount of glazed ware and also practiced the following handicrafts: tanning, lock-making, carpentry, turnery, blacksmithing, hat making, and weaving. The fine linen made by the brotherhood was sold at one rouble, 10 kopecks for about ¾ m. and was 'in no way inferior to Dutch linen.' At that time, the community was enlarging their orchards and intended to make a 'mulberry plantation of 5,000 trees. They had already planted about 1000 two- and three-year-old trees.'

The members of the present brotherhood cannot, of course, take credit for the centuries-long suffering and testing by martyrdom that their forebears endured for the sake of their convictions, but they show their beliefs by their actions. By common report, they are conspicuous 'for their Christian virtues and unimpeachable morals in every respect.' Even in 1841 the governor of Chernigov confirmed that 'when the Radicheva [Hutterites] lived in brotherhood like one family, they conducted their affairs honestly and decently and lived quite prosperously.' He himself had spoken with several merchants who had done business with them and who 'to this day cannot give high enough praise for the dependability of the brothers' word and the punctuality with which they fulfilled whatever they had promised.' It is clear, therefore, that in both moral and material aspects their life met the standard necessary for them to thrive.

But in order to learn more about the structure and organization of the Radicheva colony we will take the liberty of quoting some interesting passages from a report that Assistant Councillor Bunin, Inspector of Colonies for St. Petersburg, wrote to the Minister for the Interior. Bunin was instructed to speak with the nobles in the Chernigov and other administrative districts about the settlement of foreign colonists on their land, and he visited the aforementioned colony on January 28 and 29, 1818. Bunin reports:

The brotherhood's houses are situated on a piece of land 490 feet square. It is surrounded by a fruit bush hedge with an entrance gate. They regard themselves as one family. The building where the members live and practice various handicrafts has six brick and two wooden wings of one story, built rather low. There are several small houses on the place as well. The roofs of the main building are high-pitched, and corridors have been built through the attics with small cells, or rooms, opening on either side. This is where the [Hutterites] have their dwelling quarters, each married couple with their own room. There are no stoves. In each room there is a bed, a table, and two chairs. The couples use them only for sleeping or for short stretches of time.

Similar but larger rooms for sleep and rest are provided for the unmarried, men from fifteen years old and upward, who have finished their school studies and received baptism. There are twelve to sixteen men in each room and a bed for every two of them. The older girls also have separate sleeping accommodation. In addition to the bedrooms there is still enough space in the attic to dry the laundry, etc.

The government is already aware that these [Hutterites] have a particular confession of faith, which they say is the apostolic faith. For worship services they set aside a separate room without any pictures of saints or crucifixes. Here they meet on Sundays and church holidays and also gather for prayer every evening before they go to supper. The service is taken by the Elder, Waldner, and his two helpers. During the service they sing appropriate songs, and the sisters are especially well-taught in singing.

The brothers' way of life appears to be humble and unassuming; they are well-mannered, friendly, eager to do their duty, hospitable, and ready to give any and every help.

Shortly before a baby is due in a family, the mother is brought into a warm room for the delivery. There she and other mothers nurse their children until the age of one and a half years. To help at the birth the community has capable though untrained midwives. Once the child is weaned, the mother rejoins her husband. The child is taken to another room (furnished with beds and cradles) and brought up with other children here until the age of four years. They are supervised by sisters chosen from among the older widows in the community. Here also the children have their meals, which are prepared in a special kitchen. At four years old the children of both sexes are moved to another room with similar teachers. Later, at seven years old, boys and girls are separated. The girls are trained and taught by sisters, the boys entrusted to a male teacher's guidance. From this time on, both sexes are taught reading, writing, and religion. When their school years are over and they are more mature, they are baptized and they move to the attic dormitories.

The mothers and fathers are not forbidden to come to their children during free time or to take their children to their rooms. In general the clothing is poor. All the children's practical needs are looked after by older women, and the beds are made by the unmarried girls while the boys are in class or at work. The young sisters take turns at the task. At dinner and supper, married and unmarried people and the young people who are already baptized gather in a room where men and women sit at separate tables. The mealtime begins with a prayer. Dinner is at half past eleven, and after dinner there is an hour's rest. The evening meal is at twilight.

In winter, they go to bed at nine o'clock and to work at five in the morning. In both cases, various members in turn have the duty of telling people when it is time for bed or for work. In summer, because of the increased workload, the people get up earlier and go to bed later.

Visitors to the community cannot be anyone's personal guests. They are the guests of the whole brotherhood, in whose name the Elder offers them hospitality.

In this way, the community lived and prospered in peace from the time they settled here until 1817, honouring God and the czar and stirring the admiration of their neighbours. Arable land and meadows were fertile and productive. The brotherhood preferred, however, to have them cultivated by hired labourers drawn from the neighbouring Ukrainians who received one to two hundred roubles for a year's pay. Cattle raising was done on a large scale, using good Hungarian stock. […]

The brothers kept bees, too, but they were mainly occupied in their own trades and crafts, including the cultivation of garden crops and silk production. They owned two stills for making spirits, one on the right and one on the left bank of the Desna with all the buildings necessary for work and accommodation. These stills produced up to 61,500 litres annually. On the Jessman river, some ten miles [16 km] from the settlement, the brotherhood owned a mill with three sets of millstones. Felt hats—mostly plain but some furred—were made in the community, and carpentry, turnery, tailoring, weaving, pottery, blacksmithing and lock-making were carried on as well, and produced no small quantity of goods for sale. There was, in addition, a workshop for making winter wagons and summer wagons, harrows, ploughs, cleaning machines, spinning wheels, etc., and a tannery which provided sole-leather and Russian leather.

All this goes to show that the brotherhood did not sit with their hands idle in their laps, and that although they lived simply and without luxury, they were nonetheless comfortably off."

[**Source:** A. Klaus. *Unsere Kolonien: Studien und Materialien zur Geschichte und Statistik der ausländischen Kolonisation in Russland.* Translated from Russian to German by J. Töws. (Odessa: Verlag der "Odessaer Zeitung", 1887), 61–65. This translation is taken from *The Chronicle of the Hutterian Brethren*, Volume 2. Translated by the Hutterian Brethren. (Ste. Agathe: Crystal Spring Colony, 1998), 606–610. Used by permission.]

Decline of the Community in Russia and Who is to Blame, 1850s[1]

The reasons for the decline of the community in Russia are not well understood by scholars because of few available sources. By 1842, the remaining Hutterites at Radicheva had relocated to the Molotschna in an attempt to revive their flagging morale, and address the collapse of their schooling and desperate financial situation. In 1819 the community at Radicheva had been dissolved due to differing commitments to communalism held by leaders Johannes Waldner and Jacob Walther.

In the Molotschna, Hutterites adopted a foreign mode of existence that chafed against their cultural and communal ethos. Their villages were organized in typical Mennonite fashion, and work relationships and governance structures changed drastically. These changes created significant friction among the new settlers. The following document was written by someone outside of leadership circles with a limited formal education and could be described as grievance literature. The author describes a number of incidents involving community leaders, Johann Cornies, and other village administrators in a highly critical tone. Johann Cornies was instrumental in coming to the aid of Hutterites in Radicheva, helping them finance the move to the Molotschna and arranging settlement, education, and employment opportunities among the local Mennonites.

A n account, for the leaders of the community, of the time when the community lived in the village of Radishchev in Russia, 1819, and what happened there, written by a brother with the help of God, inasmuch as God gave him strength and he knew and experienced in recent times.

In 1819 our temporal community[2] in the Chernihiv governorate of Little Russia *Grälwetz*[3] was dis-

---

1   The author and source of this document are unknown.

2   Throughout this document '*Gemein[de]*' is used for both a location and the practice of community-of-goods. This translation attempts to differentiate between the two.

3   Meaning undetermined.

solved. Nevertheless, its spiritual vitality was very robust with the *Schulzenamt* and existed until 1843. However, when Daniel Janzen arrived in Huttertal, he led them [i.e., the *Schulzenamt*] astray.

In 1842 we were transferred from Little Russia to Tashchenak, which is situated in today's Taurida Governate. We settled in Melitopolsky Uyezd, and Johann Cornies took charge over us and borrowed 15,000 rubles from the crown [on our behalf]; we are supposed to repay the money within six years.[4]

In 1842 we began construction and Cornies named the village "Huttertal." [...] We were originally brought from Wallachia to Little Russia by the field marshal, Count Sergei Petrovitch of Zadunaisky.[5] We settled in Vischenka [in 1770]. We lived in Vischenka in community-of-goods for 33 years and three months. In 1801 we moved from Vischenka to Radicheva, because the count wanted to make us serfs.[6] This cost our ancestors dearly.

Once, when [Johannes Waldner and Christian Hofer] were in St. Petersburg before Czar Paul I, the count betrayed our ancestors and said that whatever we want, we can rest easy: he would conduct himself according to the contract made by his father with our ancestors in Russia. He was, however, deceitful. The count had a *Belück*[7] German officer who said that we should not ease off. We are already listed twice in the [army and taxation] register. We would also have to pay *Päduschnä*.[8] [...] They were frightened and went to [St.] Petersburg a second time.[9] Johannes Waldner and Jakob Walter appeared before Emperor Alexander I and presented him with the petition.[10] God inclined his heart and mind towards us just as he did when Esther found mercy with King Ahasuerus when she and Mordechai freed their entire people; almighty God came to their aid (Esther 5:2).

And so, the Imperial Governing Senate said they would not press us for the money, nor use any violence against us. Cornies got along with us quite well, but we heard that he had said there will probably be beatings, but it will not come to a fight. We did not know what that meant [at the time].

[Selling Wheat]

In 1844, however, it changed. Cornies began using the *Schulzenamt* forcefully, and we had to haul the wheat into the city of Verdpaus;[11]

---

4   Cf. *The Chronicle of the Hutterian Brethren, vol. 2. Translated by the Hutterian Brethren.* (Ste. Agathe: Crystal Spring Colony, 1998), 637.
5   *Chronicle*, vol. 2, 453.
6   *Chronicle*, vol. 2, 568.
7   Meaning undetermined.
8   Meaning undetermined.
9   *Chronicle*, vol. 2, 568ff.
10   *Chronicle*, vol. 2, 574f.
11   Unidentified.

such brutality was used that many boys remained in the city. Each had to weigh how much wheat we had. I had to declare a value of 16 *tchetvert*[12] for my household, which was not enough. The *Schulzenamt* went to measure it themselves for all the fields and summoned [us] a second time. We were forced to give more; I then had to give an additional *tchetvert*. At that point an elderly brother by the name of Peter Hofer spoke up, saying "You should not coerce the brothers like this, and ought to believe what they are reporting to the officials."

The *Schulz's* name was Christian Waldner, and his assistant's name was Samuel Kleinsasser. One of them, Andreas Wollman, was very quick to [protect] Cornies' reputation. [He] became enraged and swore terribly and spat on [Peter Hofer] in the *Schulzenamt*, and said, "You have a beard to your belly button, and you are all liars!"[13] This was certainly the plain truth as it was spoken, and Wollman [was young enough to] have been Peter Hofer's son. Oh, [what a] wretched Christianity! That is no love for one's neighbor. "By contrast, the fruit of the Spirit is love, joy, peace, patience, kindness, generosity, faithfulness, gentleness, and self-control. There is no law against such things" is what Paul says to the Galatians (5:22–23).

As a result of this, they banned Peter Hofer from entering the *Schulzenamt*.

Dear reader, it is [also] not to be forgotten, that when a woman complained because they had written her down a *tchetvert* more than her husband, Benjamin Stahl, declared, the assistant *Schulz* Andreas Wollman cursed and said: "Go and shove your goods into your asshole." They punished Susanna Stahl by putting her in the *Schulz* on bread and water.[14]

Now winter is coming and what shall we eat? God has had mercy on us and provided a means for us to borrow bread from the surrounding Russian villages so we do not perish of hunger.

[In] 1845, the *Schulzenamt* could not haul any wheat or *Werdians*[15] and calculated how much each person had to give. Christian Waldner wanted to give Andreas Wollman forty Kopec per *tchetvert*. He [Andreas Wollman?] said it must be sold to another person because Christian Waldner wanted to haul it away himself and then bring the money to the *Schulzenamt*.[16] He was not permitted to do so and they wildly rampaged through his yard and again took it by force from the granary. As we were lamenting, we had to watch them prowling around in our granary in such a monstrous

---

12   Obsolete Russian unit of capacity: 5.95 bushels.
13   Regarding "bearded ones," see *Chronicle*, vol. 2, 644 and 645.
14   The *Schulzenamt* also served as a jail.
15   Meaning undetermined.
16   It appears the *Schulzenamt* was also a grain broker.

manner, emptying the granary. It would not be any different than if the Napoleon of France had passed through. We, however, entrusted everything to God, and these are the buds, as mentioned above, that will not come to blossom.

And that is why Cornies said that [namely, that there will be beatings] for he knew well how he would force, oppress, and afflict us. For the wheat from 1844 we could get 20 roubles, but Cornies said that was too cheap because he insisted on knowing everything in advance. The wheat was calculated at 13 roubles, and from [18]45 we took away a monumental 29 *tchetvert* worth from my homestead. The *Schulzenamt* took this wheat by force.

[The Johannes Wipf Affair]

In 1846, a lad from Huttertal named Johannes Wipf had a fight with a Russian servant. The *Schulz* from Blumenort informed Cornies about Wipf, and Cornies immediately pronounced judgement and ordered the *Schulz* to beat Wipf. When the *Schulz* received the order, he immediately summoned his assistants and they beat Wipf. In doing so, Cornies, the *Schulz*, and the assistants neglected their religion, according to what Christ says in Mat-

thew 5:38–39, and [Christ] himself didn't use violence.

When elder Heinrich Wiens heard about this—that it was someone from his community [who gave the beating]—he put [the assistant *Schulz*] in the ban, separating and excluding him from the community [while] Bernhard [*Börn*] Fast[17] let Cornies and the *Schulz* go unpunished. When Cornies found out Wiens had put the assistant *Schulz* who beat [Johannes Wipf] into the ban, however, he became enraged and plotted what to do about it and devised a cunning scheme. Contrary to the pure gospel, he reached an agreement with Fast to accept the authorities among them [in their village].

Now just consider what arrogance and pride accomplish. Fast and Cornies forgot the lowliness of Christ and his birth. Dear reader, just consider the song, "*Es ist gewisslich an der Zeit.*"[18]

[Accepting Authority]

Cornies and Fast summoned all the ministers to a meeting. Daniel Janzen, David Hofer, and Jakob Hofer from Huttertal traveled to their area where they realized what Fast and Cornies' opinion [regarding local authorities] was. Fast revealed

---

17 Bernard Fast (1785–1861) was an ordained elder in the Molotschna Mennonite settlement. As a leader he was very progressive, supporting Johann Cornies' initiatives, promoting education, and a different, more open, way of understanding the Gospel and other Protestant groups. Although his progressiveness resulted in a schism, the objectives he promoted were generally and more widely accepted one or two generations later.

18 Bartholomäus Ringwaldt, 1586.

that [they thought] the authorities should be accepted among them because [he] accepted them. He put forward and pointed to the apostle Paul, Romans 13: Authorities are appointed by God for the protection of the faithful and for the punishment of the wicked, and whomever resists the authorities resists God's order.

That is true! We also accept what the Apostle Paul says, that it is from God, for "the authorities" do not bear the sword in vain. They bear it for vengeance because they are his avenger! says Paul. "'Do not avenge yourselves—vengeance is mine. I will repay!' says the Lord" (Romans 12:19).

Fast, however, in his blindness, prayed on his knees that God had revealed a middle way, and said, "I accept the authorities among us. Friedrick Lange [*Fritz Lang*][19] also accepted them, and if I were a governor, I could also be a Christian."

The schoolmaster Janzen from Huttertal also accepted [the authorities] and berated Elder Wiens to his face in a vile way: "He is certainly a true Christian in words alone, a true Free Mason,[20] and a *Walm Wieretz*."[21]

Cornies approached the two Hofers[22] and asked them to sign [the agreement as well]. They, how-ever, refused to do so because they feared the community. When they came from Halbstadt, from the [Molotschna Colony] district office, Hofer gathered the community in his house and advised that we should accept the authorities among us, like Fast and Lang.

Elder Jacob Walter and Jerg Waldner, however, admonished the community and said, "We cannot do that." David Hofer pressed hard and pointed to Fast and Lang, as reported above, and also to Fast's prayer.

When the assistant *Schulz*, Samuel Kleinsasser, heard this he stood up and said, "How can we recognize an authority among us? Christ teaches his disciples, Luke 22:25[–26], "The kings of the Gentiles lord it over them; and those in authority over them are called benefactors. But not so with you."

Then David Hofer attested, for the third time, that the Apostle Paul called the authorities God's servant and that we should sign our names [on the agreement]. It was easy to see that the two Hofers had joined themselves to the people of the world, to Cornies; David himself and Johann Cornies are pure world. "These are not followers of Christ" [*sic*].

---

19 Friedrich Wilhelm Lange (1800–1864) was a minister and elder in the Molotschna Mennonite Settlement. Favouring a warm piety, he actively promoted evangelism, missions, and music.

20 Anti-Masonry, surfacing here as a pejorative, was commonly grounded in the fact that they clung to the adage, "Loyalty to freedom overrides all other considerations." This meant that loyalty to country and local rulers were secondary considerations.

21 Meaning undetermined.

22 Jacob and David Hofer.

And then the assistant *Schulz* Samuel Kleinsasser said, "The apostle had no king, no prince, no law, and there should be no use of force. How can I take my brother by the neck, and he tear me down and beat me up? We cannot use violence against any person, raising our hand." Samuel Kleinsasser had explained himself correctly.

[The Elias Kleinsasser Affair]

[…] A young brother wanted to get married and became acquainted with a young sister, Susanna Hofer. The brother's name was Elias Kleinsasser. It became public in the middle of August, and they remained together until autumn or later in the year. Kleinsasser's relatives did not know he wanted to marry and subsequently permitted him to be hired by a master.[23] When autumn came, however, Elias was married according to Christian ordinance. When Cornies heard Elias had been married, he forced him to return to his master. Elias did return—but not for long. He returned to his wife a few times—up to three times. He was summoned by the *Schulzenamt*, but Elias refused go. The *Schulzenamt* wrote a report to Cornies [saying], "Elias does not want to obey." Cornies wrote in reply they should give him eight lashes.

When Elias heard he was to be flogged, he hid himself. Walter gathered the community wanting to address the community, and minister

David Hofer and the *Schulzenamt* pressed hard on the fact that he was to be bound and beaten, "according to Cornies' orders." The community, however, did not want to commit a sin and one of them admonished the assistant *Schulz* Samuel Kleinsasser that he should really think about what he was saying. As reported above he then said, "Surely this one can be beaten." Another exhorted him, "You said you could not stretch out your hand against anyone or use force." Kleinsasser maintained his position while Hofer argued with everyone. He began to count the people, up to 20, and said, "They are pure rebels."

It was cold by the time Elias was brought in. The *Schulz* took him under his authority and a meeting was held in the *Schulzenamt*. There [his beating] was again vehemently demanded, but the brothers responded as before: they would not lay a hand on him. The assistant *Schulz* Andreas Wollman stood up and banged on the table with his hand, thinking he would intimidate the brotherhood. [He] said he accepted the authorities and would obey them. The brothers said, "That is your choice."

The *Schulzenamt* realized they were not making any progress towards the flogging and wrote to their Lord God—to the worldly people, as minister David Hofer testified above, that Cornies was truly worldly. When Cornies received the report,

---

23 Master [*Meister*] is a remnant term from the old guild system.

he immediately came to Huttertal and the *Schulz* immediately filed a complaint. Cornies gave the *Schulz* instructions on what he should write, and Samuel Kleinsasser, "assistant *Schulz*," immediately bound the willows together. Now the *Disätnick*[24] was to do the flogging.

"No," said the *Disatnick*, "my faith does not permit it." Cornies asked, "Do you have a different faith from that of the *Schulz*?" "I don't know what faith the *Schulz* has," said the *Disatnick*. The *Disatnick's* name was Mattheus Waldner.

Cornies became enraged and threatened Waldner with a blow. Waldner, however, would not comply. [Cornies] threatened that he would throw him out of his farmstead [*Feuerstell*]. Waldner responded, "Do as you wish."

When Cornies saw that he was unable to proceed with the beating, he was enraged and sought horse and buggy to take Waldner away. Waldner, however, was not afraid because he wanted to remain God's friend, not Cornies' friend. The *Schulzenamt* and the two Hofers have bound themselves to the world. [...]

Jacob Hofer had a son who was watchman that day. He asked his father whether or not he should give the beating. The father did not give him an answer. This shows that he does not want to lose the favour of Cornies. Not only this one [i.e.,

Jacob Hofer], but they are all alike: the *Schulzamt* and also the minister David Hofer. They are very cold ministers who do not want to lose favour [*Freundschaft*] with Cornies. They were just like Pilate who washed his hands, and said, "I am innocent of this righteous man."[25] But the Jews cried, "If you release this man, you are no friend of the emperor" (John 19:12). When Pilate heard that he should lose the emperor's favour, he handed Jesus over to be put to death. This is also how it is with these ministers; they do not want to lose the favour of Cornies, which is why they were pressing so hard for the beating.

Because the beating did not happen, Cornies took Matthaeus Waldner on to his red *Toschenänk*[26] and locked him up in a dark hole until morning and pressured [*guelte*] him that he should give the beating. Waldner, however, would not listen [*machte dücke ohren*]. Cornies said, "If you do not want to do it, then hire someone for money." Waldner replied, "I have no money." Cornies replied, "I will lend you some." Waldner said, "I currently don't expect any [money to be able to pay you back]."

At that Cornies took his henchman and came to Huttertal. That day, Jerg Walter was watchman, and he was to take down Elias [for the beating]. "No," said Walter, "I will not do it." The assistant *Schulz*, Andreas Wollmann, walked around Walter

---

24 Meaning undetermined.
25 Matthew 27:24.
26 Meaning undetermined.

and said, "Walter, what kind of man are you? Take him down!" Cornies watched this and struck Walter a few times on the head so that he fell over. [Cornies] kicked Walter twice in the side with his foot and personally tore the clothes off his body. He pushed him down and trampled Elias on the back with his feet, while his henchman flayed him. Then he ordered Elias to return to Ohrloff to his *Boscher*[27] master. The beat-up Walter, who had not wanted to lay a hand on [Elias], his head swole up. After this [ordeal], he had to lie down [to recover] and then dig a ditch 15 fathoms long as a punishment because he did not want to lay hands on [Elias Kleinsasser], as reported above.

[In] Matthew 5:39, Christ himself says. "If anyone strikes you on the right cheek, turn the other also." Therefore, according to the Gospel, we cannot raise our hands [against somebody]. As reported above, Samuel Kleinsasser, assistant *Schulz*, gave false witness and testimony, but not for long.

[Elder Jacob Walter to be Imprisoned, Bribed]

And so further, dear reader, do not let it be a vexation to you [if I continue]. Cornies consulted with the *Schulzenamt*, and they agreed to put Elder Jacob Walter in prison at Ekaterinoslav [*Katrinasteb*].[28] Presumably the two ministers—the two Hofers—knew about this because they were so strongly and so firmly devoted to Cornies. Daniel Janzen had brought them to that point and led them astray in that they were so firm in their support of Cornies. [In] Jeremiah 17:[5],[29] the prophet Jeremiah said, "Cursed are those who trust in mere mortals [...] whose hearts turn away from the Lord."[30] The two ministers and Janzen have this judgement upon their head. The proverb says, "More learned, more perverted."

The highly enlightened Apostle Paul writes to the Galatians 6:7–8: "Do not be deceived; God is not mocked [...].[31] If you sow to your own flesh, you will reap corruption from the flesh; but if you sow to the Spirit, you will reap eternal life from the Spirit." We sing in a hymn, "Those who place their trust in God have built well; he will not be abandoned."[32] God has departed from the *Schulzenamt* because they rely on human strength [*Menschenarm*] and likewise the two ministers.

---

27   Meaning undetermined.
28   A local seat of government, later called Dnipropetrovsk.
29   The source erroneously cites verse 15.
30   The following is omitted: "and make mere flesh their strength."
31   Source omits: "…for you reap whatever you sow."
32   Similar to the conclusion to the first stanza of "*Was mein Gott will, das g'scheh allzeit*," by Albert of Prussia. This line is found verbatim in the so-called "Himmels-Brief/*Letter from Heaven*."

Johann Cornies
(1789–1848).
[Mennonite Library
and Archives, Bethel
College, North
Newton, Kansas:
2005–0101]

The *Schulzenamt* went to Elder Jacob Walter and informed him they were going to lead him into captivity in Ekaterinoslav. Assistant *Schulz* Wollman, however, with the arrogance of Cornies on whom he relies, said, "We must do this; we are sworn to it." They are God forsaken people, who have Cornies as their god. Now only consider, dear reader, now they have betrayed the elder—like Judas his master (Matthew 26). [...]

Cornies realized there would be no progress in sending the elder to prison because there had been no progress with the beating and brought along his henchman. Because of this, Cornies consulted with the *Schulzenamt*, asking if he should give Elder Jacob Walter money from his own [pocket] for support or sustenance if he, "the elder Jacob Walter," would not interfere anywhere. The assistant *Schulz*, Wollman, let this [detail] slip. Cornies wanted to bribe the old man with money, but it did not come to that.

[The Anna Hofer Affair]

[…] In 1846, a woman named Anna Hofer gave her child in service to a farmer in Ohrloff, Kornelius Wiens [*Knelswinz*]. Wiens treated the child very unfairly and beat it severely. When the mother heard this, she wanted to take the child away from Wiens. She went to Wiens who said, "Cornies gave me the child for fifteen years." The mother, however, sought an opportunity and took the child to Huttertal in 1847.

The *Schulzenamt* used great force and threatened to beat the mother. Thus, the mother had to lead her child into slavery with wet eyes. Now a believing Christian member can well imagine how that must have felt for this mother. As punishment, they put her on bread and water in the *Schulzenamt*. […]

[The Death of Mary Walter]

In 1848, Cornies had not yet taken a servant girl in his service. This was because of his good deeds.[33] Zacharias Walter had a daughter at home due to her health, and Cornies pressed hard for Walter to give his Maria into [his] service. Walter

excused himself, saying that she was not well. Cornies said, "He would be her doctor,"[34] and forced the girl [into service]. He took her [away] on his red *Taschenick*, and there she was always sick. The steward scolded Mary, saying, "Your grandfather has a large beard, that is why you spit blood." The father sought to free her because he took pity on her and went to Orloff twice to see Cornies. Cornies said he would come to treat her but did not come up to the time of his death. Maria came to church in Huttertal for Easter and her father would not let her return [to work].

The *Schulzenamt* and the two ministers attacked with vigour. They are all blowing into the same horn [and] Janzen was their advisor. The *Schulz* assembled the community, and the community said, "They should certainly not use such force with the sick girl." David Hofer said, "That is a disgrace [*wider Seligkeit*]; she must obey." The *Schulzenamt* proceeded with force and hired out the sick girl. The girl had to endure so much suffering. After 14 days the ill girl died. And furthermore, the *Schulzenamt* used great force and put Walter in prison in Halbstadt for eight days on bread and water to be considered a scoundrel as punishment.

[After Cornies]

After the death of Cornies [in 1848], the community was eager to make peace. They gathered, eager to come

---

33   Sarcasm?
34   As in original.

to an agreement. There was much discussion and debate. David Hofer and Jakob Hofer wanted to unify the two ministers and the *Schulzenamt* with the community. They wanted to establish terms [*Punkten*] but nothing came of it the first day. The next day, however, they came forward with the points. These were then read out and Daniel Janzen studied the points which the community was not willing to sign. The community said, "We have the gospel as instruction, we don't need these points." Because Elder Jacob Walter could not hear properly when the *Schulz* read them out, [he] took the points, intending to read them at home. David Hofer snatched them out of his hand saying, "You are not worthy to read this. You do not want to sign them, therefore, you do not need to read them."

Now consider, dear reader, the old covenant. To deal with the Lord's anointed with such force, whereas King David would not raise his hands [against Saul] and said to his men: "The Lord forbid that I should do this thing to my lord, the Lord's anointed, to raise my hand against him; for he is the Lord's anointed" (1 Sam 24:6). Hofer, however, though he could see [with his eyes], was blinded.

[...] The two Hofers, the *Schulzenamt*, and Daniel Janzen were not satisfied with this. In 1849 they wrote unfounded and misguided accusations [*Punkten*] to Philip Verein in Ohrloff. Philip wrote to Bernhard Fast, and Fast told Benjamin Ratzlaff [*Räzlauf*][35] and Peter Wedel [*Wädel*][36] they should come to Huttertal to investigate the points. They did come and had to fall silent [at what they found]. They had to listen to the deceit, false wiles, and the crimes "both Hofers" committed and wrought in Ukraine, each of which I will report its [proper] place. The elder, Walter, and his assistant, Jerg Waldner, explained themselves so poorly, that maybe the two Hofers and *Schulz* did what they did because of that. They thought Philip would depose the elder and Waldner, but it did not come to that.

[Concerns about Samuel Wipf]

Johannes Hofer took an apprentice, a boy named Samuel Wipf. Wipf worked diligently making spinning wheels and his master noticed Wipf's trustworthiness. Because of it, Hofer sent Wipf to the Molotschna with spinning wheels to sell. Wipf demonstrated and proved himself to be honest to his master, and the master was satisfied.

---

35 Benjamin Ratzlaff (1791–1874) was an elder of the Rudnerweide Mennonites in the Molotschna Mennonite Settlement. He was active during the time of revival and upheaval that lead to the formation of the Mennonite Brethren Conference. He was a proponent of migrating to North America and part of the first wave; becoming ill *en route*, he died several weeks after arriving at his destination in Kansas.

36 Peter Wedel (1792–1871) was the founding elder of the Alexanderwohl Mennonite village in the Molotschna Mennonite settlement. He was leader of a moderately progressive group that maintained contact with Moravians and promoted mission.

When Philip [Verein?] came to Huttertal, however, he summoned Johannes Hofer and also Wipf to the *Schulzenamt* and asked, "Why did you send Wipf to sell the spinning wheels in the Molotschna, where he would learn to drink [*saufen*] brandy?" Wipf replied, "Who can prove that for me?" Philip became furious and struck Wipf in the face. Presumably, Wipf must have responded to Philip too crassly since Philip considers himself an authority. […] Christ said, "The greatest among you must become like the youngest, and the leader like one who serves" (Luke 22:26). The pagans [*Heiden*] struck Christ in the face, and Philip does likewise; as the saying goes, "Birds of a feather flock together." […]

[The Crime of David Hofer]

Now I want to write about the crime of "minister" David Hofer. In 1823 he dared to exploit the crown's grain scale in Chernigov Governorate, in *Glokuffer Iüdß*[37] with a Jew named Aaron for big money. The Jew committed a great fraud with the scale. When buying grain, the Jew pushed the grain to the end [of the scale], and when [he] sold [grain], he pushed it back again. Thus, the Jew stole when he bought and also stole when he sold. […]

Now, where did the stolen grain end up[?] Nowhere else than with David Hofer […], who tampered [*verreckt*] with the crown scale. [He] began to

steal in 1823 and stole until 1849 and will continue to steal until the end of the world. […]

[Back to Authorities]

In 1847, Cornies wrote a letter to the *Schulzenamt* in Huttertal [which] Janzen read to [the community]. Janzen read a great deal about authority and police [and] that the *Schulz* was an authority. To this the community said, "That cannot be; you are contradicting the Gospel," and asked Janzen if the *Schulz* was also a brother [in the community]. Janzen replied, "Yes." The community asked how that could be possible. To that Janzen replied, "If there is a meeting with the *Schulz*, then he is not your brother; then the *Schulz* is an authority. When the meeting is over, then the *Schulz* is your brother again." That is a great aberration.

When Janzen came to Huttertal, that was the beginning of the disunity between the *Schulzenamt* and the ministers.

[The Crime of Jacob Hofer]

Jacob Hofer felled so much wood in the crown forest that it was not seemly for a minister. He also had to pay large fines three times. Walter admonished the minister, Jakob Hofer, in a Christian way before the community, that he should leave the crown forest in peace because [what he was doing] was nothing but theft. He would be scorned by God and

---

37 Unidentified.

man. But he disobeyed the elder, for he could not leave it be. As the cat cannot leave the mouse alone, neither could Hofer stop stealing.

He snuck back into the crown forest and did it so crudely that even he didn't realise what he was doing. [...] Because he had already paid a fine twice and was listed in a black book [...] a prominent nobleman gave him some advice: he should clear his name by sending his son to school. He would be able to clear his name because his son stole first.[38] That helped him and brought his son to the point that he was also written off as a thief in *Grälewiz* as he himself is. Then he stopped stealing because he realised what punishment was waiting for him, but the instruction and warning of the elders he did not heed. This is the crime of Jakob Hofer. [...]

[The Crime of Samuel Kleinsasser]

Now I want to mention the crime committed by the assistant *Schulz* Samuel Kleinsasser [in] about 1834—it could also be a year earlier or later because it only came to light in 1848—[at] the crown bridge in *Fataina-blüscher* Goverment[39] in Alexandrovsk.[40] Oh, how the *Pawirt*[41] went crazy. Like a thief and a scoundrel under the cover of darkness, Samuel Kleinsasser, the "assistant *Schulz*," forcibly broke

away or tore loose logs and lumber and hauled them away. [...] (At the same time, we heard that many innocent people were being marched to Siberia.)

Because the *Schulzenamt* used such force with him and berated Kleinsasser as a crown thief [*Krons Dieb*], and *Schulz* Christian Waldner as a lumber thief, David Hofer said, "The *Schulz* has been punished." "You fool," I thought to myself in my heart. *Schulz* Christian Waldner went around Huttertal with his assistant *Schulz* and *Disatnik* searching for the logs but could not find anything because the *Schulz* had stolen them at night and stashed them so that nobody could find them.

Cornies gave strict orders that the *Schulz* should find them, and that he would punish [whoever had them] severely. Because the *Schulz* could not find anything, however, Cornies imposed the fine on the entire village. Each farmstead [*Feuerstell*] had to pay a fine in roubles: there were 330 logs [*schläm*] stolen, one rouble for each log, and there were 30 households. The fine of 330 roubles was taken to the *Schulz*. Oh, what great deceit, what great folly!

In 1845 a schoolhouse was built in Huttertal, and the beams were stolen from the schoolhouse during the night. The *Schulzen* in Huttertal were fools such as this.

---

38 It remains unclear how this would have worked.
39 Unidentified.
40 Now Zaporizhzhia.
41 Meaning undetermined.

[Hiring Schoolteacher Daniel Janzen]

In 1849, the *Schulzenamt* used force and [with] the two Hofers hired [Daniel] Janzen [as a teacher] for four years, even though the community did not want him. The community wanted to have peace and quiet. The community met twice with the *Schulz* about Janzen, but the *Schulzenamt* and the two Hofer (ministers) pressed hard for the wayward Janzen. Then minister David Hofer forcibly had several brothers order the *Schulz* to complain to Philip [*Verein*] in writing.

That is when the *Schulzenamt* and the two communities of the church heard their pronouncement or verdict, [namely] that the community would not sign the contract. Then the five mighty men, the *Schulzenamt*, and the two ministers signed a contract with Janzen with-out the community; they signed it themselves and took by force the haylength from the village for Janzen to make hay and to plough. [...]

Afterwards, the community discovered that the *Schulz* had proceeded with cunning. When the community confronted the *Schulz* in the presence of Elder Jacob Walter in a meeting, the *Schulz* said. "We three are the entire community," and the assistant *Schulz* Andreas Wollman had also previously said, "We three are the entire community; what we do is well done."[42]

And then the *Schulzenamt* and the two Hofers forcibly hired Janzen as schoolmaster. That is, "Force in place of justice, says many a wretched servant." They granted Janzen 400 roubles and eight dessyatin[43] [*teßetin*] of land while the poor people had not yet paid the money due for 1848. [...]

[**Source:** Translated by Kenny Wollmann from a scanned copy found in the Mennonitische Forschungstelle, Weierhof. I am grateful to Glenn Penner, Winnipeg, MB, for helpful comments in identifying several place names and people.]

---

42   A play on the hymn, "*Was Gott tut, das ist wohlgetan.*"
43   2.70 acres.

UNKNOWN
Anfang unseren Schmieden Gemeinden /
The Origins of our Schmiedeleut
Community-of-Goods [in Russia], 1859

Michael Waldner's (aka, *Schmied-Michel*) dream that inspired the revival of communalism in the Molotschna is a pivotal moment in Hutterite history. It comes in the context of several failed attempts to re-establish community-of-goods as a way to address concerns over the administration of their villages and an overall crisis of identity. Readers may wish to compare this account with the accounts of the first baptism (71) and the initial establishment of community-of-goods (109).

A brief summary of the origins of Schmiedeleut community-of-goods. After true Christian community had been abandoned and fallen by the wayside, it was restored by divine intervention in 1859, according to the brief description given here:

With God's help and to the glory of God, I will hereby describe how the founders in Russia, through grace and the guidance of the Holy Spirit, once again gathered together in community-of-goods, according to the work of the Holy Spirit in the time of the Apostles. For it says, "All who believed were together and had all things in common; they would sell their possessions and goods and distribute the proceeds to all, as any had need" (Acts 2:44–45).

After the community had drifted apart for forty years and true Christian community had been abandoned, everyone lived in individual ownership. They still, however, elected servants of the Word and also attended church on Sundays. There were teachers [i.e., ministers] among them, but they did not have enough strength to restore true community.

Several families, together with teachers and servants of the Word, joined together twice intending to restore true community. It did not endure, however, and they parted ways again. Without doubt, they too will have prayed to God that he might accomplish his work—which is the establishment of the Holy Spirit—and help to restore and re-establish true community, because without God's will, help, and support, such a work cannot endure.

It so happened that in 1857, several servants of the Word were elected in Hutterdorf, South Russia [modern day Ukraine]. Among them were Michael Waldner and Jacob Hofer. After a time of testing, they were confirmed with the laying on of the elders' hands to be fully authorized in the service of the Word. All this took place while they were still living in individual ownership. However, when they preached the beautiful teachings put together by our dear forefathers on community-of-goods, and which many sealed with blood, they came to reflect deeply about how such beautiful teachings on community could not rightly and legitimately be upheld in private ownership; their way of life denied [these teachings] in many essential points and [their current life] could not accomplish and achieve what was being taught. They also prayed a great deal to God that he might help them and provide them with power from on high to achieve and accomplish this according to his divine will and good pleasure. And because

God had the desire to re-establish true community, he also found a means and a way to do so.

Several years before Michael Waldner was chosen as a servant of the Word, it happened that he fell very ill to the point that his relatives mourned him for dead because he had stopped breathing. They believed he had died. He was not dead, however, but merely in a trance, [in which] God revealed a great vision to him. Namely, a guide appeared to him and accompanied him. First, he showed him the holy host of many thousands of angels who sang indescribably beautiful praises to God; indeed, the singing was so beautiful to him that he could not forget it for the rest of his life.

Then his guide led him away from the beautiful singing and showed him hell and the multitude of the condemned, which was a dreadful sight to behold, namely the torment and agony that is in store there for the condemned which no human can imagine.

He then questioned his guide and said, "Where will my place be?" His guide replied, "Can you tell me if there was a single person at the time of the flood who was not drowned, apart from those in the ark?"[1] He said, "No one was rescued." Then his guide said: "That is how you can know where your place will be. The ark is the community of the Holy Spirit, which you no longer observe."

I   Cf. Gen 5.

He began to weep intensely. His guide told him to go back and establish a community like the one our forerunner Jesus Christ had with his disciples. "I myself," he said, "will be with you and will not abandon you until your death and will take you to myself again." With that, it felt like he was beginning to fly. His guide vanished from his sight, and he returned to consciousness.

When he opened his eyes, he saw his relatives standing around the bed and weeping. When they realized he had not died, their weeping turned to rejoicing and they thanked God he was still alive. He spoke to them and asked if they had not heard the sound and singing of the angels, because it was as if he could still hear them singing. With God's help, he soon recovered. But he then began to struggle, however, and plead with God that, if it might be his holy will, he would lead them in the right direction and not forsake them.

Soon after he was elected as a servant of the Word, as already mentioned. Now, even more than ever, he pleaded with God that, if it was his holy will, he should surely reveal to them the means and the way to establish the holy work of community.

He also shared what God had revealed to him with his colleagues, namely Jakob Hofer. He too fell into deep contemplation and began to pray earnestly to God.

Michael Waldner and Jakob Hofer often met together at a certain place to discuss and strengthen themselves with the Word of God. They fell on their knees and prayed fervently that God would fill them with power from on high so that he might advance his work through them, which is the work of the Holy Spirit, and that it might all be done to the praise, honour, and glory of his holy name. They no longer held counsel with flesh and blood, but with Almighty God, who knows the heart.[2] And he certainly did empower them from on high and strengthened them with his blessed Holy Spirit, so that they could carry out their intended purpose to the praise, honour, and glory of his holy name.

Finally, they came together again in one place to pray, and said to one another before the prayer, "Whoever finishes his prayer first, will stand up and receive the other into fellowship [*Gemeinschaft*] with the laying on of hands in the name of God the Father, and of the Son, and of the Holy Spirit." This was so because all things must be accomplished in accordance with Christian ordinances.

Then they fell on their knees and prayed fervently to God that he might help them and would grant them his mercy to fulfill this goal.

Jakob Hofer completed his prayer first, then rose and accepted Michael Waldner into fellowship [*Gemeinschaft*] with the laying on of his

---

2 Cf. Gal 1:16.

hands. After this Jakob Hofer knelt down and Michael Waldner rose and also accepted him into fellowship with the laying on his hands. All this was done with God's help and the support of our dear Lord and Saviour Jesus Christ—to him alone be the glory and the praise forever.

They also accepted [*einverleibet*] their spouses into fellowship [*Gemeinschaft*] and thus they began to observe community [*Gemeinschaft*] of the Holy Spirit. They pooled their goods and possessions together and organized themselves as a community.

They also went out to preach and teach the right way of true community, and God granted his blessing so that their community grew and increased.

Amen. To God alone be the praise and the glory.

And those who faithfully live in such a fellowship of saints here in this age and remains true, enduring to the end, will be part of the fellowship of saints in the age to come. Christ will declare, "Come, you who are blessed of my Father, inherit the kingdom prepared for you from the foundation of the world" (Mt. 25:34).[3]

This is the beginning of our Schmiedeleut community-of-goods in Russia in Hutterdorf [Huttertal Kutscherrof]. They lived there for several years until the order for military duty was issued, and all those summoned were to enlist without exception.

[**Source:** Translated by Kenny Wollmann from an original manuscript held in the Hutterian Brethen Book Centre Archive, MacGregor, MB. A published edition of the German is available: *Anfang von den Hutterischen Schmieden Gemeinden.* Hans Decker, editor. (Hawley: Spring Prairie Printing, 1986), and an alternative translation is found in *The Chronicle of the Hutterian Brethren*, Volume 2. Translated by the Hutterian Brethren (Ste. Agathe: Crystal Spring Colony, 1998), 661–664.]

---

3   This paragraph is quoted from Question 45 of the Hutterite catechism. *Im Weinstock treu bleiben: Hilfsquelle für hutterische Täuflinge / Abiding in the Vine: Resources for Hutterian Baptismal Candidates* (MacGregor: Hutterian Brethren Book Centre, 2018), 15.

John Lowe (1894–1918)
Letter to Delegation from Southern Russia, "*Privilegium*," 1873

In 1873, a delegation from the Molotschna (South Russia) including Hutterites Paul and Lorenz Tschetter travelled to North America to investigate the prospects of immigration.

In Canada, the delegation met with secretary of the Department of Agriculture, John Lowe, who responded in writing with a letter to the Mennonite members of the delegation assuring them that all their conditions for settlement would be met.

Although the Hutterites did not settle in Manitoba when they emigrated, the conditions defined in the *Privilegium* were extended to them in 1898 when the first community in Canada was established at Dominion City, and again in 1918 when the first six permanent communities were founded.

Department of Agriculture, Immigration Branch

Ottawa, 2nd July 1873

Messrs. David Klaassen, Jacob Peters, Heinrich Wiebe, Cornelius Toews, Mennonite Delegates from Southern Russia.

Gentlemen,

I have the honour under instruction of the Hon[ourable,] the Minister of Agriculture, to state to you in reply to your letter of this day's date the following facts relating to advantages offered to settlers, and to the immunities afforded to Mennonites, which are established by the Statute Law of Canada and by orders of His Excellency the Governor General in Council, for the information of German Mennonites having intention to emigrate to Canada via Hamburg.

1. An entire exemption from any Military Service is by law and Order in Council granted to the denomination of Christians called Mennonites.

2. An Order in Council was passed on the 3rd March last to reserve eight Townships in the Province of Manitoba for free grants on the condition of settlement, as provided in the Dominion Lands Act, that is to say "any person who is the head of a family, or has attained the age of 21 years, shall be entitled to be entered for one quarter section or a less quantity of unappropriated Dominion Lands, for the purpose of securing a homestead right in respect thereof."

3. The said reserve of eight Townships is for the exclusive use of the Mennonites, and the said free grants of on quarter section to consist of 160 acres each, as defined by the Act.

4. Should the Mennonite settlement extend beyond the eight Townships set aside by the Order in Council of March 3rd last, other Townships will be in the same way reserved to meet the full requirements of Mennonite immigration.

5. If next spring the Mennonite settlers in viewing the eight Townships set aside for their use, should prefer to exchange them for any other eight unoccupied Townships, such exchange will be allowed.

6. In addition to the free grant of a 1/4 section or 160 acres to every person over 21 years of age on the condition of settlement, the right to purchase the remaining 3/4 of the section at $1.00 per acre is granted by law so as to complete the whole section of 640 acres, which is the largest quantity of land the Government will grant a Patent for to one person.

7. The settler will receive a Patent, for a free grant, after three years residence, in accordance with the terms of the Dominion Lands Act.

8. In the event of the death of the settler the lawful heirs can claim the Patent for the Free Grant upon proof that settlement duties for three years have been performed.

9. From the moment of occupation, the settler acquires a "homestead right" in the land.

10. The fullest privilege of exercising their religious principles is by law afforded to the Mennonites, without any kind of molestation or restriction whatever; and the same privilege extends to the education of their children in schools.

11. The privilege of affirming instead of making [sworn] affidavits is afforded by law.

12. The Government of Canada will undertake to furnish passenger warrants [tickets] from Hamburg to Fort Garry for Mennonite families of good character, for the sum of $30.00 per adult person over the age of eight years; for persons under eight years, half-price, or $15.00; and for infants under one year, $3.00.

13. The Minister specially authorizes me to state that this arrangement as to price shall not be changed for the seasons 1874, 1875, and 1876.

14. I am further to state that if it is changed thereafter, the price shall not, up to the year 1882 exceed $40.00 per adult and children in proportion, subject to the approval of Parliament.

15. The immigrants will be provided with provisions on the portion of the journey between Liverpool and Collingwood; but during other portions of the journey they are to find their own provisions.

I have the honour to be, Gentlemen, your obedient Servant[,]

[SIGNED:] John Lowe

SECRETARY OF DEPARTMENT OF AGRICULTURE

John Lowe (1824–1913) is the namesake of the village of Lowe Farm, Manitoba.

[SOURCE: Chortitzer Mennonite Church Fonds, Volume 1417, Mennonite Heritage Archive, Winnipeg, MB.]

THE 20ᵀᴴ CENTURY

Peter Hofer (1885–1966), Joseph Kleinsasser (1890–1978), and Jacob Kleinsasser (1922–2017) Selected 19th and 20th-Century North American Schmiedeleut *Ordnungen*[1]

For most of the 19th and 20th centuries, *Ordnungen* were understood to be an important instrument for keeping 'the world' at bay and creating a shared identity. They regulated all facets of life, including clothing, home furnishings, sexual ethics, substance abuse, recreation, and more. While some *Ordnungen* prescribe ethical standards, others are intended as guidelines to ensure proper provisioning in contexts of neglect or excess.

For many Hutterites, adherence to the *Ordnung* was seen as a way to maintain unity through uniformity, and a means of avoiding assimilation into mainstream society. The place and purpose of the *Ordnungen* became a major source of tension in the Bruderhof-Hutterite relationship and in the 1992 Schmiedeleut Church Schism.

The *Ordnungen* are usually discussed and revised at an annual conference of Hutterite ministers presided over by the elder. For more discussion on the significance of Hutterite *Ordnungen*, see 111–112.

1884

1. Sending letters. It has been decided that no one should send letters unless they have been read by the elders. Also, no one should supply their own stamps, envelopes or postcards, but should get them from the *Haushalter*.[2]

---

1   The translator wishes to acknowledge that he benefited from comparing his work with the translation found in John Lehr and Yossi Katz, *Inside the Ark: The Hutterites in Canada and the United States*. University of Regina Press. 2014, 239–401.

2   This translation retains the original *Haushalter* because there is no satisfactory English equivalent. Common choices, such as "manager" and "steward" carry misleading modern connotations. Traditionally, the *Haushalter* was known as a *Diener der Notdurft*, servant of temporal needs, a formulation that nicely captures the spirit of the office but is wordy and inelegant. The term *Haushalter* captures something of

2. Opening mail. It was also recognized that nobody is allowed to open a letter not addressed to them.

3. Moustache or *Schnauzer*. It has been determined that no brother is permitted to grow a moustache, much less to twirl it.

4. Worldly clothing. When somebody returns to the community and brings along worldly clothing, they should be worn out as work clothes, and should not be spared. The clothing provided by the community should be used on Sundays.

1921

1. Hairstyles. Everyone should wear his hair as a brother is supposed to: parted in the middle. At the front and on the side, the hair should be even with the eyes and half the ear should be visible. No mop of hair is allowed, and layering is not permitted [*darf nicht geschindelt werden*]. Should a brother or son be disobedient, he should be punished and if necessary, even sent to another community.

2. Christmas trees may not be set up. The teacher, however, is permitted to give the children some candy or treat.

3. Making spirits, schnapps or wine for personal use should be completely stopped.

4. Aprons[3] with trim should not be tolerated, and those that are still in use should be worn inside out until they are worn out.

5. *Fleckenschuhe*[4] not permitted. A reminder was given that Fleckenschuhe should no longer be used or purchased.

6. Boots permitted. It has been discerned that boots may be purchased, but should be limited to rubber boots and purchased every three years.

1927

1. Annunciation should be observed as a holiday from now on.

2. Mail concerns. The incoming mail should be delivered to the *Haushalter*. Outgoing letters should

still—according to the Ordnung from 1884—be read by the minister. The unbaptized youth should not be permitted to send letters and mail. Mail sent to them should be

---

the broader original meaning of the term 'economy' as household management. The responsibilities of a *Haushalter* are many and may include bookkeeping, leading financial decision-making and reporting, purchasing groceries and dry goods, and overseeing requests for personal spending.

3   Apron translates the German *Fittich*. Although it resembles an apron, it served a different purpose. Initially it was used to cover the fly of a skirt that was wrapped around the body. In some circles, it took on an aura of holiness, as it came to be associated with the proper Hutterite *Trocht*.

4   It is not entirely clear what is meant by *Fleckenschuhe*, but likely it refers to shoes with some type of multi-coloured ornamentation.

censored by the *Prediger*, to prevent dishonest activities.

3. Chair ordinance. A family with six or more souls may have seven chairs; [a family] with 4–5 souls may have four chairs and [a family] with three or fewer souls, may have three chairs.

[**Note of Explanation or Encouragement:** The above ordinance, number three from 1884 (regarding moustaches) was presented to all communities in 1927 to vote on, and the majority, which was not expected, accepted it and validated it. And thus it is still in effect. We ministers would have preferred for it to be lifted because this is the most commonly violated ordinance. It is, however, still in effect.][5]

1931

1. Displaying dishes. No dishes may be displayed on the counter for ornamentation purposes. Only dishes that are in use may be displayed, such as one or two bowls. Everything else should be stored in cupboards or chests or elsewhere, where it is not visible.

2. *Hulba*[6] ban. All communities agreed that *Hulbas* should no longer take place when a couple is engaged. The youth may not sing or gather with the couple or anywhere else. Also, no alcohol is to be served, except what the couple offers to the parents and siblings that are present at the engagement ceremony.

February 12, 1956
Bon Homme Community

1. [Selecting a new minister.] At the annual ministers' conference held on February 12, 1956 at Bon Homme Community in Manitoba, the process for selecting ministers was discussed. Is it appropriate that a brother who was nominated in a previous election but was found to be unfit, be nominated again? Following lengthy consideration, it was unanimously agreed that he should not be nominated again in the next election. Those who nominate ministers should take note of this.

2. [Selecting a second minister.] It was also decided that when a community wants to buy land to establish a new *Hof*, the community in question should select a new minister at least one year beforehand, so

---

5   Not in the original; a later insert in an *Ordnung* compilation from the 1980s. Additions such as this point to the evolution of the Ordnungen and how they were implemented.

6   A Hulba is an engagement celebration that typically takes place at the bride's community a week before a wedding which takes place at the groom's community. The prospective bridegroom publicly requests permission from the prospective bride's parents, community elders, friends, and relatives who then ply the couple with words of wisdom. The couple is officially engaged and blessed at a special worship service.

that he has sufficient time to familiarize himself with his position, to prepare, learn, and gain experience. It is not right to delay selecting a second minister, which unfortunately happens too frequently.

3. [Hunting.] Because it is against the law,[7] and also unseemly for us as Christians, to hunt with guns [...], it was accepted that shooting moose, deer, and the like, should be totally stopped. It is proper that we who claim to be Christian are obedient to the authorities in all fitting things, [not] poachers and reckless lawbreakers [appearing] in a bad light before the world, which carefully watches us and does not expect this [type of behaviour] from us, when we are caught and found to be rascals and mischievous skulkers [*Wildschleicher*]. Our supporters [*Gönner*] can no longer step up to defend us by saying, "The Hutterites are loyal and law-abiding citizens." Conversely, we ought to pursue with zeal what Paul teaches us: "Do all things without[8] murmuring and arguing, so that you may be blameless and innocent, children of God without blemish in the midst of a crooked and perverse generation, in which you shine like stars in the world" (Phil. 2:[14–15][9]). Read also 1Peter 2:12–13 and Titus 3:1. Therefore, let us not be preoccupied with hunting [*Jägerlust*], so that we aren't descendants of Nimrod[10] whose greatest desire is hunting like the people of the world and carnal people.

Although guns have no place among us, a community may keep one to deter harmful predators. [This weapon] must be legally acquired, kept under supervision, and not used for hunting, as previously mentioned. People who hunt [*Jächtler*] generally tend to become feral [*verwildern*] like the reckless, carnal-minded Esau, and go on crooked paths, abandon their duties at home, becoming preoccupied with disorderly business which is detrimental to themselves and the community. Experience sufficiently proves this.

February 9, 1960
Waldheim Community

3. [Alcoholism.] In order to combat alcoholism, it was decided that each brother is allowed to drink one bottle of beer (the smallest one) once a day with a meal in a restaurant instead of going to a beer parlour or saloon. Everyone should completely stay away from beer parlours, saloons, or breweries. In small towns like Elie, Oakville, and so on, there

---

7   It appears that this Ordnung was developed in response to new legislation and repeated infractions by Hutterites of the new law.
8   As in the original.
9   Original incorrectly cites verses 12–13.
10   Gen 5.

is no need to go to a restaurant, because one is only there for a short while and should do one's work as quickly as possible and then return home. It is not in any way permissible to drink alcoholic beverages in unsanctioned, seedy places, because it has the same detrimental effect on alcoholics as [drinking in] parlours and saloons.

The reason for this long overdue ordinance is that a godless, disorderly life of alcoholism is being pursued by too many, and is done with the community's limited money, or perhaps with money that was stolen from the community or acquired dishonestly by the followers of Gehazi, who are already spiritually leprous and morally depraved and degenerate, and are governed, ruled, and possessed by the spirit of gluttony, and have thus fallen into various vices.[11]

Let us rescue those who are not yet bound with Satan's fetters of gluttony and debauchery, and let us do our job in accordance with sobriety, temperance, respectability, and self-control, and be a light of the world and salt of the earth. Let us strive with godly and persistent zeal against over-indulgence, extravagance, and excess, which are pursued in the drinking establishments, where the smokers, the blasphemers, the card players, the gamblers, and the godforsaken carousers, yes, the scum of humanity gather to amuse themselves like an eagle with carrion. We should be disgusted by what goes on there, and by how the frivolous among us run there and enter the way to hell by drinking with the mockers and the drunkards and becoming like them.

Also, all are warned against buying alcoholic beverages anywhere in order to drink them while driving in their trucks or vans, for this is strongly forbidden by the law. Only careless drinkers who cannot help themselves do this, and thus blindly stagger towards their ruin.

Let us all, especially ministers, *Haushalter*, and elders, unanimously work with God's assistance and with patience to enforce this long overdue ordinance, because drinking and drunkenness has become a cancer which brings lamentable consequences, which will be difficult—and perhaps not even possible—to eradicate completely. Let us no longer participate in the sins of others—which we have excused or justified until now—by allowing the debauched to go into taverns in order to carouse or to drink for pleasure. We and future generations will pay for it with impoverishment and immorality and we will have to give an answer for why we allowed our people to run wild, to decline spiritually, and to offer themselves up to gluttony and to the devil of drink. Our reputation is suffering. Let us blow the trumpets against this blatant sin and detestable gluttony, frivolity, and debauchery that so many pursue in the taverns.

11   2Kings 5:19–27.

4. [Projectors, Movies, Radios.] [Business] agents and others with film projectors, movies, radios, or musical instruments are not allowed to come into the community to show their products, wares, machines, etc., because this causes the young people to go that much more shamelessly into the cities and other places to [attend] movies, the theatre, and to watch television. On one hand, we do not want to introduce these devices into our schools because they have a harmful influence, yet on the other hand we allow them to be shown in our schools and churches, the very places where we teach and preach against them. What a contradiction!

5. [Driving around with Agents.] Our people are not allowed to drive around to communities or anywhere else with agents or related people, because that only breeds trouble and corrupts our people with worldly spirit, ideas, and habits, and tempts our people to participate in them. We must forcefully guard against such harmful influences, temptations, and impurities, and must do what we can to avoid

them. The spirit of worldliness is powerfully pressing upon us and will lead to our downfall and harm, and we ought to be frightened that the power of darkness is surrounding us and is coming ever nearer in order to blind us.

The above statement does not prohibit us from driving somewhere, with permission, with decent non-Hutterites, in order to survey some land or something else that the community has deemed useful.

6. [Nursing Mothers.] The ordinance that all of the communities received in 1959 regarding the dues for nursing mothers remains in effect, with the following changes: the two quarts of spirits are eliminated. In its place, 20 pounds of sugar or four pounds of coffee are to be given. Also, no more schnapps is to be given, as is the case in some communities. All communities and *Haushalter* are to take note of this.

This year the following [material] may be given: for men, one pair of pants and one jacket; for girls under 15, one dress and two aprons.

July 26, 1978
Woodland Community

1. [Mission]. Firstly, the matter of mission was discussed and it was recognized that we are failing the fulfill the Great Commission of Christ to go into all the world to preach the gospel to all nations and to baptize them in the name of the

Father, the Son, and the Holy Spirit, and to teach them to obey all that Christ commanded us. We need to wake up and try to do more, for the command of Christ remains as long as the world stands.

2. [**Committees.**] It was also decided that the committees[12] are not necessary and that matter should remain as they were before. But because the question was raised, in South Dakota things should remain as they are. Minister Joseph Wipf should be the contact person regarding the selection and confirmation of new ministers, and also regarding the purchase of land for a new community.

3. [**Refrigerators.**] Since there was a considerable amount of discussion both for and against coolers, it has been decided that each community may decide for itself which refrigerators it wants to allow, for such mundane [*äusserlichen*] matters do not belong among spiritual matters. Several other mundane matters will also be left up to each community to decide for itself.

July 2, 1981
[Location unspecified]

1. [**Probation for young people who return.**] If young people leave the community and get married while they are in the world, but then want to return to the community, they must demonstrate for a period of time that they are remorseful, and that they wish to change their ways. They must go to the community which they left and provide the community with an account of their monthly income and expenditures, and must behave sensibly in order to demonstrate that they have the community's interests in mind.

After that they are to be dealt with in good faith, as has been the custom for a long time. And if they have not been baptized, they must be baptized in the community that they left unless the ministers have been

consulted and an alternative course of action has been determined. They should not be accepted until they have demonstrated repentance, for the sacred ordinance of baptism should not be rushed into without consideration of a Christian witness.

Also, all those who return should sign a Power of Attorney document to make it possible to check the person's income tax status, and this must be done before the person can be accepted into the community.

2. [**Disruptions by young people who leave the community.**] It is a deplorable situation with the young people—both boys and the girls—who have run away. They are making a spectacle and an abomination of the community; their visits to their loved ones—whom they

---

12   Beginning with *Ältester* Joseph Kleinsasser (Milltown, 1934–1947), the Schmiedeleut senior elder resided in Manitoba. In order to deal with minor issues that arose in the American context in a more efficient manner, an assistant to the elder and a supporting committee were appointed in South Dakota. At the time of this ordinance, the American committee had overstepped its authority by installing a new assistant without consulting the senior elder in Manitoba.

abandoned—bring appalling mischief into the community: smoking, drinking, harlotry, fornication, unkempt hair and clothing, and cars at the doors of houses as if this were their world. During the major holidays—Christmas, Easter, and Pentecost—what is supposed to be a house of God is used as a place to party, and this is a big distraction from properly observing these important holy days.

In short, it cannot go on like this for much longer; rather, from now on it should no longer be tolerated unless it has been permitted by the minister and the leadership through a telephone conversation or through writing. And where parents or others are aware of such things, and they do not inform the leadership, then they are liable to also be questioned, and where necessary, disciplined.

3. [Romantic relationships with those who left the community.] If it occurs that young women or men who are in the world are in love with a young man or woman in our communities, it is not to be tolerated. And if parents turn a blind eye to it, then they are to be questioned as well and are liable to punishment.

Also, when young women and men go too far and fall into fornication, and where it is discovered that the parents have neglected their parental duty and did not pay close enough attention, and have allowed such disorderly running around,

and have allowed their children to get into such mischief, then such parents must apologize during the Sunday worship service and be disciplined.

4. [Foreign religious literature.] Also, more attention should be given to foreign religious literature arriving in the mail, whereby so much falsehood and confusion have infiltrated the church in the past year that it is barely possible to prevent it all. For example:

- One should be totally immersed during baptism
- Pentecostal miracles are a sign of the true church
- Foot washing, speaking in tongues, and baptism of the Holy Spirit, which is promoted by the Charismatics
- [The idea that] sick people are possessed by the devil
- Drinking grape juice during communion instead of wine
- Once saved, always saved
- Fasting
- The rapture
- Privately praying for the forgiveness of one's sins, and much more.

5. [Reporting debts.] From now on each community should try to accurately disclose its debts at the annual meeting for reporting income and expenditures. Where it is discovered that this has been neglected, the community will be fairly and properly investigated.

6. [Baptismal candidates.] If it arises that someone who is to be baptized is not behaving properly or has fallen into error and has not adequately demonstrated that they are prepared to stop during the probation period, then the baptism may be pushed back until Pentecost in order to give the person another probation period.

This should, however, be handled in a God-fearing manner and with the counsel of the senior elder.

Also, when baptismal candidates confess [their sins] before the baptism it should only be done before ordained ministers.

June 19–20, 1986
Crystal Spring Community

3. [Raising children.] To begin with, the conference report from June 25, 1985 was presented, expressing the need to put more care into raising our children. Yet, it remains the case that very few among us have taken this message to heart. Too few are committed to raising this treasure—our children—according to the example set by our forefathers, in order to protect them early on from self-interest and self-will, and in order to cultivate Christian virtues in them.

It was also announced that the worldly laws concerning childcare apply to us as well and serve to remind us that we are too negligent. Let us read the enclosed article about child abuse which clearly shows that the world takes the issue of childcare very seriously and will respond very strongly to neglect. It would be shameful if we were found to be in violation of the laws of the land.

It was decided that children should be cared for during the common mealtime. Older children should be given their food either before or after the mealtime so that they can care for the [younger] children while the adults are eating,

Also, in cases where mothers are working for most of the day, small children should all be brought together so that an older sister and a young girl can look after them until the mothers can care for them again. In comparison to our forefathers, child rearing is seriously lacking among us. Let us read and put into practice what it says in the Hutterite *Chronicle* and try harder to walk in the footsteps of our forefathers.

4. Tips. The ordinance from June 21, 1984 has still not borne fruit. Therefore, it has been decided that it is no longer acceptable to attend the large Hog Congress or any similar meetings involving feed companies or business people. Meetings with hospitality rooms or [other places] where alcohol is served should especially be avoided. These activities do more to serve the lust of the flesh than the welfare of the community.

Business people finance these meetings, and we become friends with them; yet they are more concerned about lining their own pocket than looking out for the welfare of the community. Our brothers cannot withstand the temptation and, as we know, disorder always arises when alcohol is involved. And how much more is there that we don't know about?

Therefore, accepting invitations from feed companies or other business people is no longer permitted.

If a business wants to offer a legitimate gift, it should go toward the community's account. If a meeting is needed, it should be held at a community.

And where it is necessary to research modern developments, it should occur at the community's expense, and be investigated by its leadership.

8. [**Donations.**] It was also decided that all of the Manitoba colonies should donate $100.00 to the Eden Hospital in Winkler, Manitoba. Send the money to Joseph Waldner (Blumengart), or to Michel Waldner (Rosedale Colony). They will deliver it to the hospital. This hospital operates solely through donations.

16. [**Curfew for young people.**] When a whole van full of young people visit a community, they must be gone by 11:00–11:30 because our young people do not behave reasonably and virtuously when they stay at another colony late into the night.

[**Source:** Translated by Jesse Hofer from originals held in the Hutterian Brethren Book Centre Archive, MacGregor, MB and [Jakob Kleinsasser,] *Schmiedeleut Ordnungen*, unpublished manuscript, 1982.]

Dora Maendel (1951–) and
Elsa Baer Maendel (1984–)
Hutterite-Indigenous Relations
in 20th Century Canada, 2021

In 1873, Canada's Minister of Agriculture John Lowe wrote a letter—popularly known as the *Privilegium*—to the Mennonites in South Russia, which granted Mennonite settlers broad religious freedoms and large tracts of land for settlement in south-eastern Manitoba (see Lowe, 379). Just two years earlier, the government had entered into a series of numbered treaties with Indigenous peoples to coexist on the land in a covenant or partnership of mutual trust and benefit, for "as long as the grass grows and the rivers flow." Without the signing of the treaties, the granting of land to immigrants under favourable conditions would not have been possible, or would have been significantly more complicated.

Like other settlers, Canadian Hutterites benefited from the land made available to settlers through the numbered treaties negotiated by the government of Canada with various First Nations groups. When the first Hutterite community was established near Dominion City in 1898 in anticipation of the Spanish-American War, Hutterites were able to secure similar rights as those granted to the Mennonites in 1873. The lands they bought to establish the original six communities in the RM of Cartier in 1918 were located on Treaty 1 territory. Although they paid significantly higher prices than the first wave of immigrants in the 1870s when they purchased the land from land speculators, the fact that it was available for settlement at all was due to the negotiation of the treaties half a century earlier. As such, learning about the history of First Nations peoples in Canada, the commitments made in the treaties, and the historical and ongoing injustices inflicted on Indigenous peoples is an essential aspect of honouring the treaty relationship and working toward a reconciled future.

While Canadian Mennonites have a strong tradition of advocating for Indigenous justice beginning in the latter half of the 20th century, Hutterites have been less attentive to these issues.[1] For most of the 20th century, Hutterites were content to be "the quiet in the land," favouring limited contact with non-Hutterites and generally avoiding public political engagement beyond their communities. However, Hutterites have been and are involved in another significant aspect of working toward understanding, goodwill, and mutual respect: forming friendships between settlers and Indigenous peoples.

The following accounts by Dora Maendel and Elsa Baer Maendel, the former written expressly for this publication, draw attention to the rich relationships that have existed between Hutterites and Indigenous peoples in Manitoba. Dora Maendel creatively combines elements of historical fiction with a more straightforward historical account of interactions between the Métis peoples at St. Eustache and Rosedale Hutterite Community following Hutterite settlement in the area in 1918, focusing on the pivotal role played by Joseph Maendel (1886–1937). Elsa Baer Maendel's piece describes the many ways her community of New Rosedale, established in 1944 as a daughter community of Rosedale, has been enriched by relations with the people of Long Plain Reserve (Ojibway). Her piece is an intimate tribute to Max Merrick, who was a close friend of her father.

Both stories testify to the power of friendship and relationship across cultural difference, of living peaceably with our neighbours, of sharing the land in a spirit of generosity and goodwill. It is not surprising that many of the people and communities in both accounts are connected by the legacy of Joseph Maendel.

Joseph Maendel of Rosedale
and the Métis[2] of St. Eustache

Dora Maendel

Except for Joseph and *Ona-Katrina*'s home, it's quiet and dark on a cool autumn evening at Rosedale Hutterite Community, Elie,

---

1   See Steve Heinrichs and Esther Epp-Tiessen, *Be it Resolved: Anabaptist and Partner Coalitions Advocate for Indigenous Justice, 1966–2020*. (Mennonite Central Committee and Mennonite Church Canada), 2020.

2   According to the *Canadian Encyclopedia*, "Métis are people of mixed European and Indigenous ancestry, and one of the three recognized Aboriginal peoples in Canada. [...] The term is used to describe communities of mixed European and Indigenous descent across Canada, and a specific community of people—defined as the Métis Nation—which originated largely in western Canada and emerged as a political force in the 19th century, radiating outwards from the Red River Settlement." (Adam Gaudry, "Métis," *The Canadian Encyclopedia*. Historica Canada. Article published January 07, 2009; last edited September 11, 2019. https://www.thecanadianencyclopedia.ca/en/article/metis).
     A History of the McKay Family of St. Eustache, Manitoba, 1846 to the Present by Raoul McKay, one of the few written sources describing the relationship between the Métis and the Hutterites at Rosedale, uses the older term, "Metif." For consistency, this article will use Métis.

Manitoba. Even upstairs a light is still on. Chuckles, banter, and laughter cavort through the open windows of the front room.

The passenger vehicle parked behind the two-storey clapboard house has South Dakota license plates. The Maendels are up late, enjoying their States visitors.

The oldest daughter, Katherina has just arrived with a pot of coffee and a jar of cream from the community kitchen. Through the open door a circle of chairs is visible. Joseph and his visiting brother sit across from each other at the large, oaken table.

Typically, an evening of visitors and visiting in the Maendel home is filled with a mixture of discussion, jokes, and, often, arguments. The four oldest sons, Joe, Jacob, Mike, and Paul are discussing the day's field work.

Katrina places the coffee pot and the cream beside the glass cups on the large table. From the vestibule out front, she brings a flowered metal cannister which she opens and sets on the table beside the kettle. Standing completely still, she looks at her Dad, who raises his hands and folds them in prayer. "*Komms beten*, [Let us pray]" he intones, glancing briefly around the room. In the silence he prays the familiar German table grace, "*Wir bitten dich, Herr Gott, himmlischer Vater, segne uns und*

A group of Hutterite men seining on the James River in South Dakota. Joseph Maendel is identified in the photo with a white • above his head. Photograph, ca. 1915. [courtesy of Tony Waldner]

diese, deine Gaben... [We ask thee, Lord God, heavenly Father, bless us and these, thy gifts...]."

As Katrina pours coffee, he offers his visitor a homemade fig bar and helps himself to one before passing the cannister to his cousin John. Again, the room fills with animated conversation.

"*Katrina, bring den krauchtn Fisch, wos sie gestn hobm getalt; mir sein hungrig!*"

As she moves toward the door to bring the smoked fish, there is a brief knock, but in the buzz of questions and talk, she is the only one who hears it.

Opening the door, she is greeted by a wiry Métis neighbour from St. Eustache. "Good Evening, Jaques!" she smiles.

"*Oui, Bonsoir!*" he grins, removing his toque. Looking around the room, he repeats, "*Bonsoir!*"

"*Oui, Jacques!*" Joseph responds warmly. "Come in and join us!" Fritz, the youngest son, rises from his chair and Joseph gestures for Jacques to sit. Then he passes him a fig bar and some smoked fish on a slice of homemade bread. "You're just in time Jacques," he adds, "we have visitors. My brother Michael from South Dakota."

Jacques nods at Michael and says, "South Dakota, eh? *Bien Venue au Manitoba!*"

Joseph hands him a cup of coffee and the visiting continues. Every-

one's eager to hear Michael *Vetter*'s news.

"When do you think you'll be able to begin moving?" his brother asks.

Michael sighs heavily. "I don't know why it's taking so long to find a buyer for our land, but I mean to stay until it's sold."

"And you not even well," Joseph says soberly. "It would certainly be better if you didn't have to travel so far to see Dr. Meindl in Winnipeg."

"Yes. We must be patient."

"*Bonsoir,* Madame!" Jacques greets *Ona-Katrina*, entering from the bedroom, where she's put the baby to sleep. She smiles and nods at him then sits beside her husband.

Reaching down, Michael pulls toward him the cardboard box beside his chair. "*Du, ich hob der wos mitgebrocht!*" He holds up two plastic bags of corn candy and hands them to his sister-in-law.

"Oh, Madame!" Jacques' eyes grow big and he grins widely. "Now you got sweets fer de little ones!"

"Look at this!" Michael continues. Tearing open a flat rectangular box, he pulls out a shiny bathroom scale. "At home they have these now. They say we older ones must not get too heavy and the young *Buben* compete to see who's strongest and heaviest!"

Placing it on the floor, he steps onto it. The numbers whirl by until finally 155 stops at the arrow.

"That fast," Joseph murmurs.

"That fast!" his brother responds. "Just step on it and your weight appears by the arrow in the little window. No nudging or readjusting a metal weight."

"You go first, Mike." Jacob pokes his younger brother. "You're the tallest." Mike obliges.

"Tall? Like fun!" Paul smirks triumphantly, "Muscle is what counts!" After Joe and Jacob, he steps on and indeed, he's heavier than both his older brothers.

"Your turn, Jacques," says Jacob, but Jacques shakes his head. "First Madame!" he says, "Mrs. Maendel!"

Smiling, she rises and says, "No, I want to put these away in my cupboard."

Giggles and gasps, groans and cheers fill the room as each in turn steps onto the inauspicious flat rectangle to watch the tell-tale number whizz instantly to the arrow and stop. John and Sam, the younger sons, Katrinna and Susanna, the daughters, cousin Maendel-Johnny and Sarah, his petite wife.

Turning to their youngest brother, Paul says, "Your turn, Fritz! So short and *krachzet*, d'you think it'll get to fifty?"

As Fritz steps off the scale, Paul gloats, "Let me try again, since I'm the only one who knows how!" He beams as the arrow indicates the desired number. "What's wrong,

Mike?" He teases. "You're taller, but I'm ten pounds heavier!"

"Who beat you at wrestling?" Mike asks calmly. "Up in the horse barn hayloft yesterday? Huh?"

Ona-Katrina returns from the bedroom, and Jacques repeats, "Madame, your turn now!" She shakes her head decisively and walks to the sideboard. Taking the *Tscheinik* from the hot plate, she offers everyone, including Jacques, more coffee. Then she returns to her chair beside her husband, picks up her knitting and starts studiously counting stitches.

A puzzled expression on his face, Jacques looks at her for several moments, then turns his attention to the conversation around him. Minutes later, he addresses her once more, "Madame, please! Your turn now to try de scale!"

Even amid the conversation hum, she hears. Glaring at him sternly, she places a forefinger on her lips and shakes her head.

He stares at her.

Her full, round face fiercely flushed, Madame keeps her eyes steadfastly on his. Then she moves the forefinger from her lips to shake it severely at him. Frozen-faced, he continues to stare as long moments pass.

Abruptly he hits his thigh so hard, the sound startles people to silence as Jacques bursts out laughing. "*Oh oui!*" he chortles. "**Now** I know why

Mrs. Maendel don't want to go on it de scale!" The room has gone quiet.

Slapping his forehead, he continues to laugh. "Madame **not go on** it de scale! She 'fraid she go on it de scale, she break it de scale!"

Nobody can resist laughing with him, not even Madame.

As a member of the Maendel clan living at New Rosedale Hutterite Community, south-west of Portage la Prairie from 1951 to 1959, I heard frequent references to and many stories of the years when my Dad and his family lived at Rosedale, north of Elie, Manitoba. As adolescents, the stories we heard from our uncles most often included examples of the interaction between Rosedale folk and their Métis neighbours from St. Eustache, particularly the McKay family. Before turning to some of these stories, I will provide a sketch of the circumstances surrounding settlement at Rosedale.

The first eight of Joseph and *Ona-Katrina*'s sixteen children were born in Rosedale, South Dakota, before the Hutterites immigrated to Canada in 1918; the other eight at Rosedale, Elie, MB. Their ninth child, Frederick, was the first baby born there—on October 7, 1918. Before the community branched out to establish New Rosedale in 1944, both parents had died: *Ona-Katrina* on June 25, 1932 at age 44, and Joseph on September 19, 1937 at age 51—in itself an unusually heartbreaking story.

We had goose bumps when our older cousins related to us that the baby, our Mary *Basel*, was only a year old when her mother died. On the morning of the funeral, the body was laid out in her home, surrounded by her grieving family and relatives. In the weary hush following the initial shocked hand-wringing and weeping, someone handed baby Mary to her dad sitting at the head. To everyone's amazement, she stretched out her arms, spoke the name "Mama" and began groping for a breast, where upon the whole room burst into sobs of empathy and grief.

As a result of harassment due to their refusal to participate in World War I, the Hutterites of South Dakota immigrated to Canada. The Dariusleut and Lehrerleut settled in the western Prairie Provinces, Alberta and Saskatchewan; the Schmiedeleut in Manitoba. Rosedale is one of the six oldest Hutterite communities in Manitoba, all of whom were established in 1918: Bon Homme, Huron, James Valley, Maxwell, Milltown, and Rosedale.

All six were established west of Winnipeg—three of them, Huron, Maxwell, and Rosedale, along the Assiniboine River; the other three, south of Elie. While all six branched out within the next ten years, Maxwell (Barickman, 1920) and Rosedale (Iberville, 1919) established their daughter communities also along the Assiniboine River. Huron established Poplar Point there, in

1938, and Maxwell founded Lakeside in 1946—a striking geographic contour from the air. Even today these six are referred to colloquially as *die Ribber Gmane*.

For the Rosedale families, it was a difficult beginning, with few completed buildings on the community proper, so the first to arrive went to a nearby place which they dubbed, es *Hefl*, the small yard, where there was little more than a grain shed. Even the flat landscape felt bare and foreign—a sharp difference from the gently rolling hills surrounding Rosedale in South Dakota.

Shortly after their arrival, *die Ona Katrina* went into labour, and that evening it began to rain. Fortunately, someone noticed a rolled-up piece of linoleum jutting from a wagonload of household goods. It was fetched, quickly unrolled and spread over the leaky part of the granary roof. Here, on October the 8th, 1918, *Ona Katrina* gave birth to the first baby born at Rosedale—her ninth child, the first to be Canadian-born. They named him Frederick and he became the beloved Fritz *Vetter* of his nieces and nephews; the Maendels of Windy Bay Community are his descendants.

Everybody worked hard, so that the move to Rosedale proper might be made as soon as possible. One milestone incident involves Joseph Maendel's daughters, Katrinna (11) and Susannah (9), both of whom dreadfully missed the natural beauty and familiarity of their birthplace. Their Dad was preoccupied with his *Hausholter-Omt* and their mother busy with the new baby, so they had to help even more than usual in the house and with their youngest brothers: John (1), Paul (3), and Michael (4).

One afternoon as they walked along Mill Creek, *Jokob Vetter* called to them. Crouching, he was digging in the creek bed with his bare hands, picking up gobs of mud. "*Su—sicht dess?*" he asked. "*Der poppiga Grunt is Gumbo!* Look, this sticky soil is gumbo!"

Following his instructions, they gathered up big balls of the clay and put them into his simple wooden cart. When it was full, he pushed it to a dry, flat spot a short distance from the kitchen beside some elm trees growing amid some low shrubbery and began to shape a round wall, using bits of straw to make it stickier as he patted each piece flat and added it to the circle.

From *die Schmittn*, the smithy, he brought a flat iron grate which he placed inside the hollow dome. Then he took them inside the kitchen to the baking area to a steel tub with a wheel on one side and some twisted irons inside. "*Do wenn mir Tag onriedn und knetn.*"

They watched as he set aside some warm water in an enamel bowl, gently stirred in some grayish granules and covered it with a cloth. Then he measured flour, water, lard.

and honey into the *Knet-Maschin*, turning the wheel to stir the mixture.

Finally, after adding more flour, while stirring the whole time, there was a mass of dough in the *Knet-Maschin*, and he covered it with a huge white dish towel.

"Come back later and you can watch us *Brot ausmochn*, shape loaves," he said.

That evening, they saw him pull the grate out of the oven and carefully remove the golden loaves. Wide-eyed, they breathed in the heavenly aroma of freshly baked bread—the first in Rosedale. A miracle! The homesick ache inside them grew less painful as they listened to the crackling whispers of the cooling loaves. Life at Rosedale could begin.

Later no one could remember when they first met their neighbours from St. Eustache, the Métis village a mile north of Rosedale. Dark-haired and olive-skinned, they were "offspring of European males, and Ojibway or Cree females, who, in the beginning grew up predominantly with their maternal relatives."[3]

It's not clear to what extent Joseph Maendel was familiar with the in-humane history of racism, coloniz-ation, and exploitation of the St. Eustache Métis, including the loss of their ancestral hunting lands due to incoming settlers, tyrannical gov-ernors at the Red River Settlement, ruthless land speculators, and finally, in the mid-1870s, the collapse of the buffalo hunt, which had been their main source of food, shelter and cash.[4]

It's similarly unclear whether he had heard about the 1873 encounter be-tween the Mennonite delegation—which included Hutterites Paul and Lorenz Tschetter, though they were not with the delegation at this time—and an angry Métis farmer who followed them, yelling, cursing, and threatening. The delegation had headed west of Winnipeg to check out the land for potential immigra-tion of Mennonite and Hutterite families from Russia.[5] The Hutter-ites subsequently settled in Dakota Territory, until harassment during WWI compelled them to immigrate to Canada in 1918.

Clear though, is the fact that Jo-seph Maendel, the *Housholter* at Rosedale was a strong leader and a man of gracious spirit. The German theologian and co-founder of the Bruderhof movement, Dr. Eberhard Arnold, who visited the Manitoba Hutterite communities in the years 1930–1931 describes him as "an ex-tremely capable steward."[6]

Another testimony to Joseph's char-acter is from his nephew, the late *Housholter*, Ben Maendel Sr., of Baker Community, who often spoke

3   Raoul McKay, "A History of the McKay Family of St. Eustache, Manitoba, 1846 to the
     Present," submitted to The Royal Commission on Aboriginal Peoples, 1994, 1.
4   Ibid., 20.
5   Ibid., 26.
6   Eberhard Arnold, *Brothers Unite*, (Rifton: Plough Publishing House, 1988), 146.

of Joseph Maendel (his paternal uncle) emphasizing how much he learned from him, because he, himself had no brother. "He showed me more kindness and patience than my own father (Joseph's brother John) did."

Joseph Maendel was decisive about being friendly to their Métis neighbours, making it clear that they were welcome on the community and in his own home or to join in for a meal in the *Essstubm*. Ben *Vetter* remembers his uncle's rationale for modeling and encouraging interaction with the Métis of St. Eustache. "*Se sein su wie mir—ausstussn*," he reasoned. "They too are different (from mainstream society) and like us, they are looked down on, even disdained. So, it's fitting that we work together and help each other."

He hired the Métis to help clear land and cut wood at which time it was understood that they would eat in the kitchen at Rosedale. "When the McKays, the St. Cyrs, and the Lussiers worked for the Hutterite farmers, they were generally gone for the whole week. They slept in bunk houses and ate with their employers."[7] The Métis enjoyed Hutterite food, and were especially fond of the home-baked bread spread with *Greipm-Schmolz*, cracklings and honey.

Another job where the Rosedale men worked side by side with their Métis neighbours was hay cutting. Under the Manitoba Act of 1870, the Métis had the privilege of grazing their livestock and cutting the hay of "the outer two miles" of land along the Assiniboine River. The McKay family, working alongside other Métis crews and Hutterites, would make up to a hundred twenty-foot, eight-ton stacks of hay per year.[8] This way of haying continued into the 1940s but was discontinued in the 1950s when balers were invented.[9]

During the decade known colloquially as the "Dirty Thirties" and historically as the Great Depression (1929–1939), the economy suffered and there was wide spread unemployment and hunger. The Métis of St. Eustache were particularly hard hit, finding it difficult to earn enough to feed their families. "Bob McKay and his sons cut wood for local farmers…and for several Hutterite colonies starting with Rosedale Colony, a mile away, Maxwell Colony, and finally Lakeside Colony."[10] Joseph Maendel let it be known that men who happened to be on the community at meal time, be invited to eat in the community kitchen, even when there was no work. He urged the women to offer them what left-over food could be packed up for taking home. *Borscht und Knedel* were ideal, because their flavour improved upon reheating.

---

7   McKay, "A History of the McKay Family of St. Eustache," 34.
8   Ibid., 28.
9   Ibid., 26.
10   Ibid., 33.

Seeing the dire need in St. Eustache, Joseph Maendel approached the municipality about a road-building project, using the gravel from the gravel pit on Rosedale's property to improve local roads starting with the one "from St. Eustache to Mill Creek in order to connect St. Eustache with the Elie Road running north and south a mile east of the village."[11]

The community would participate by providing horse-drawn scrapers, double-box wagons, and manpower. Thus, the cash-strapped, jobless Métis men had profitable work and a number of them continued working for the Highways Department for many years, later working "south of Elie to the American border and from Highway #13 East to Highway #75." A fortuitous enterprise, it provided these men with some income, while building up local roads and later, the "old" Trans-Canada Highway from Winnipeg to Portage la Prairie and beyond.[12]

It's impressive that for some of the Métis this project led to permanent work with the Highways Department, but also provided an opportunity for them and the Rosedale men to work collaboratively, shoulder to shoulder. Jonathan Maendel from Baker Hutterite Community remembers his grandfather, John (Hans) Maendel, Joseph Maendel's brother, telling them that he drove a

horse-drawn scraper. Others drove teams of horses to pull a *Duppel-Bax* of gravel to the construction site.

Eva Maendel Hofer from Airport Hutterite Community remembers accompanying her father, the late Jacob D. Maendel, senior minister of Fairholme, to Winnipeg for one of his final colon cancer treatments. Although he made the trip lying down, he asked them to let him know when they reach the old Trans-Canada Highway, the #26. At the designated site, they helped him to a sitting position. Gazing at the highway and the surrounding area, he told them wistfully, "*Ich hob e einiga Duppel-Bax Grebbel do her pfieht! Mit Ross, gonz derhahm von der Grebbel Pit bei Rosedale!*"

In addition to the mutual benefits of working and eating together, the relationship between Rosedale and the McKay family developed on two further levels: hockey playing and Christmas preparations. St. Eustache youth spent hours skating and tobogganing on Mill Creek. The McKay boys, however, always had their own hockey rink right outside their door, enabling the Rosedale *Buebm* to join them, even though skating was *verboten* for Hutterites.[13] "Every year Bob McKay would go to the Hutterites at Rosedale to purchase gifts and treats for the whole family. The Hutterites treated the family like one of their own and

---

11   Ibid., 35.
12   Ibid, 37.
13   Ibid., 63.

sold at cost things such as toys, fruit, and candies and gave them some of their home cooking goods and their home-made wine."[14]

This amicable interaction had some serendipitous, far-reaching effects. The first one involved language: "The program of studies in the St. Eustache School was difficult because the children began school speaking only French. The McKay children were somewhat more fortunate in that they learned English by associating with the Hutterites from Rosedale."[15]

Another effect involves the attitude toward Indigenous people. An incident involving amicable contact happened in Elm River, Rosedale's daughter community (1934). Over the summer, Jake Maendel noticed that someone or something was reducing the goose flock in one of his remote fields. One night he and his brother kept watch and accosted some Indigenous men. In the minister's house, while waiting for police, the men indicated that they helped themselves only to provide for their families. By the time police arrived, the *Hausholter*'s wife was serving sandwiches and coffee.

"Do you want to press charges?" the officer asked.

"No" the minister said, "These men are jobless, and their families are hungry."

"They robbed your goose flock, and you offer them food and coffee?"

"Yes! And we'll give them some provisions to take home."

"Well! I never saw anything like this before."

New Rosedale, another daughter community (1944) is only a mile south of Long Plain First Nation. Contact included trading food and clothing in exchange for handmade items such as bead work and braided rugs. Initially, they arrived in horse-drawn wagons.

In 1959, when New Rosedale established Fairholme, ten kilometers south, this contact continued. The *Hausholter*, John Maendel, and the minister, Jacob D. Maendel, sons of Joseph Maendel, offered land-clearing and other manual work to men of Long Plain, as well as carpenter work. They provided transportation to and from Fairholme, as well as meals and take-home foods.

One Long Plain woman became fondly known as *die Longclaws Ankela*, because she came so regularly, typically with several grandchildren in tow. Bright-eyed and gracious, she wore a babushka-style kerchief and always, always a skirt. Sometimes it was even a shortened Hutterite skirt.

"When I die," she told the Fairholme women, "I want to wear a Hutterite outfit. And would you come and sing at my wake and funeral?"

---

14   Ibid., 64.
15   Ibid., 48.

They promised and kept their word.

Two other examples of amicable contact between Hutterites and their First Nations neighbours, can be traced to the Rosedale-St. Eustache initiative. One involves the Sioux Valley First Nation community, north-west of Brandon, close to Deerboine Hutterite Community (1959) where two of Joseph Maendel's daughters lived. The second is at Windy Bay (1979) Fairholme's daughter community near Pilot Mound and the people of Swan Lake First Nation.

At both communities, assistance was mainly in the form of bartering or buying food. However, at Deerboine, nestled in the Brandon Hills, the Sioux people explained that some of the hills held special significance for them, because important battles had been fought there, buffalo hunted, and even chiefs buried. Sometimes men would accompany their women to the *Kuchel*, kitchen and ask for permission to climb the closest hill to engage in some commemorative spiritual activity.

A final incident occurred at Good Hope Hutterite Community (1989)

just five kilometres north-east of Long Plain. Eddie Wollmann, one of their young men, married Sandra Maendel of Fairholme, then registered in Brandon University's Bachelor of Education program. An avid outdoors-man and nature lover, he chose Long Plain School for one of his student-teaching practicum blocks—a successful experience, rich in cultural learning and mutual understanding.

Some time later, Eddie was gathering plants for herb tea in a field near Good Hope, when an ATV vehicle arrived and two men greeted him. "We're from Long Plain."

Upon learning what he was doing, they told him, "We have an elder with a great deal of knowledge about plants and medicinal herbs."

Smiling ruefully, Eddie said, "Yes, but he wouldn't be willing to share that knowledge with a white man, would he?"

"Maybe not," one of them said, "but we don't consider your people to be completely white."

Joseph Maendel would have agreed.

New Rosedale Hutterite Community and Long Plain First Nation (Ojibway): A tribute in loving memory of Max Merrick (December 28, 1924–February 24, 2009)

Elsa Baer Maendel

Recently, I took a trip to Long Plain First Nation with my aging

father. We needed to enquire about the birth date of my father's recently deceased friend, Max Merrick. I wanted to include it in a eulogy I'd written for him. We knocked on his daughter Helen's door and checked in at his son Jimmy's house, but couldn't find anyone home.

On the way back, my father commented: "Here's the Merrick graveyard. We'll probably find his birth date written here, no?" He pointed to a large area, with well-trimmed grass and a few trees around it. I slowed down and we drove in. As we walked up to the grave markers, my dad began reminiscing about preparing the area years ago. He drove his garden tractor and mulcher to Long Plain to help Max create the cemetery. Together, they planted grass and trees around it.

"Not all the trees made it," My dad stated, as he gazed around. Indeed, they seemed sparse. I had never heard this particular story before, or if I had, I had forgotten.

We stood there quietly, reminiscing over Max's grave. It had a beautiful large stone and the whole place had an aura of love and care. As we gazed at his headstone, I marvelled at their amazing friendship. They were just two neighbours helping each other out, in true Jesus-spirit—neither Jew nor Gentile, neither Indigenous nor Hutterite. Or perhaps one was fully Indigenous and the other fully Hutterite, and they enjoyed each other's differences as well as their common humanity.

During my childhood and *Diene* years in New Rosedale Hutterite Community, we had many positive interactions with the Indigenous people of the Long Plain First Nation (Ojibway). They were situated only one km from our community, about 20 km southwest of Portage la Prairie.

Residents from Long Plain frequently came to our community to buy milk, eggs, and leftover food. Our head cook, Rebecca Hofer, made many friends and frequently invited them to her home for coffee. She was an expert on weaving Fortrell rugs and loved to make them in the bright yellow, red, and blue colours that her Indigenous friends preferred. My mother shared her own brightest colours with Rebecca. I remember her saying, "We like earth tones better, and Rebecca likes Indigenous colours."

Our teacher, Hilda Maendel, took us to Christmas concerts at the Long Plain School, where our children's choir was invited to sing as well. She also invited Chief Angus Merrick to our school to show us his full headdress, regalia, and other artifacts such as smooth arrowheads and bead work. He drummed and sang for us. Years before we bought our own bus, we borrowed a yellow school bus from our friends at Long Plain for our school field trips.

In the 1970s, New Rosedale planned to build a hog barn but was short on *Buebm* to do the construction work. Under the leadership of Darius *Vetter*, New Rosedale hired approximately 15 Indigenous young men from Long Plain who worked alongside the community's *Diene*. The barn became famous for being built by *Diene* and natives.

Also in the 1970s, my dad's cousin Mary Baer Morrison, newly divorced from her Indigenous husband, came to our community from Ontario. With three toddlers to support, she needed a place to stay. At a small meeting of ministers, it was decided she could stay at New Rosedale for one year. Her children wore Hutterite clothes and attended the *Klanaschuel* and *Essenschuel*.

One day the chief's wife came to the New Rosedale kitchen to ask for leftovers. While she was there, she saw Mary's daughters wearing the Hutterite *Trocht*, their black braids sticking out of their *Mitzlen*. She must have been troubled by this, because the next morning her husband came to see the minister, Darius *Vetter*, enquiring about the children. Darius *Vetter* brought him to the school to see Mary, and asked her to explain. She laughed out loud when she was reminiscing about this with me. Mary and her children ended up staying for two school years. During the second year, she was hired to teach at New Rosedale School.

My dad was a big-hearted mechanic at New Rosedale who would fix anything for anyone! When the *Weiber* walked to his shop to have their lawn mowers fixed, he dropped everything to help and they received a rollicking good joke on the way out.

Indigenous people from Long Plain also regularly came to his shop to get their tires changed or a motor fixed. My dad often invited these friends home for coffee. Hutterites have a 3:00 coffee break where the table is loaded with pastries and snacks. Some of the names I remember are Ronnie Woods, Lloyd Woods, and especially Max Merrick. They all had such a wonderful sense of humour and our family had many laughs with them.

My parents had nine children. Some of them were married and already had children of their own when I was an adolescent. At my parent's snack table, all from the extended family were welcome, so you can imagine the scene. Everyone at the kitchen table was eating, talking, and visiting, and in particular, enjoying Max's entertaining stories.

Max came pretty much every day, and our fellow New Rosedalers took to dubbing him 'Max Baer' because of the strong friendship between him and my father. Max was an elder on the band council, and I remember him discussing with my father how best to spend the community's money. He complained about how the young members only wanted to spend, spend, spend, while he and the other elders were always struggling to save it.

Another way Max contributed to our family and community was to offer his services as a driver. In the 1980s and 90s, it wasn't easy for women who had married and moved to another community to find an opportunity to travel home to do some sewing during the winter. When my brother James' wife, Melinda, wanted to visit her parents in Rosedale Hutterite Community (near Elie, MB), Max willingly gave her a ride. When my sister Elaine needed a ride from Suncrest (near Kleefeld, MB) Max agreed to pick her up.

Elaine is well-known in our family for bringing a lot of baggage when she travels: sewing supplies, suitcases, and care packages. One time he delivered Elaine to our door with the usual huge pile of boxes, luggage, and car seats. We happily greeted her and her children and carried all her supplies into the house. Max turned to my father and asked, "Is she moving back home, Paul?"

Melinda and James were especially fond of Max and brought him traditional chicken broth during his final days in the hospital.

We often went to his house to watch television when there was an important event such as the Stanley Cup Finals or the 9/11 terrorist attacks. He came to Dad's shop every day, and freely offered to drive to Portage for parts if they were needed at the shop.

I remember Max telling us about going to residential school. He told us about watching some older boys who had tried to run away. They were brought back and received a terrible licking and it cured him of trying to leave.

Max may have seen worse things than "merciless lickings," but if he did, he never mentioned it to us. Maybe he was sparing us the traumatic details, or maybe it was simply too painful for him to speak of it. But even without him saying a word, I have read enough stories from survivors of residential schools to know how terribly commonplace abuse and neglect were.

Max told us his mother died while he was at school and he wasn't told until he came home for the summer and found her gone. He often told us this story and we could still sense his deep hurt. I cannot imagine the anticipation of seeing his mom for the first time in months, and then the pain of finding out she had died.

I never realized the far-reaching scope of residential schools and how many children were torn from their parents. What if it was my child? What if it wasn't what I wanted for my children's future? What if they were taken from my arms and beaten just for speaking German or *Hutterisch*? What must it have been like for countless children to lie awake in a strange dorm bed crying for their parents night after night? How horrible that when they were sick or unwell, they did not get the care and attention of a loving parent?

All of my father's Indigenous friends were about the same age he was. And while both my parents are alive and well at 78, all his Indigenous friends passed away a long time ago.

That is no accident. It's what trauma does to people. It drastically reduces their life span.

I am thankful my childhood Hutterite community, New Rosedale, fostered a strong relationship with Long Plain folk. I am deeply grateful for a father and family who interacted with Indigenous neighbours as if they were close relatives, honourable friends. Because that's what Max Merrick was to us—a loving uncle and friend. *Vielen lieben Dank*, Max Merrick Baer! And in your Ojibway language: *Miigwech*.

Michael A. Stahl (1894–1984)
Camp Funston Diary, 1917–1918

Following the passing of the Selective Services Act on May 18, 1917, fifty-five Hutterites aged 21–30 were drafted into the American army. Because there were no provisions for conscientious objectors in place at this time, and because Hutterite leaders could not get reliable information from government officials, the men reported to the military camps but refused to participate in the drills or perform any other duties. In many cases, this position of non-compliance drew the ire of the military personnel, and the men were subjected to a variety of torture and intimidation tactics. Michael A. Stahl from Tschetter Community in South Dakota spent 11.5 months at Camp Funston and Camp Dodge and 3.5 months on farm furlough. His diary provides a window into the experience at the camps.

It was the day we were supposed to leave, September 22nd, when we prepared for our journey to Parkston, South Dakota. We went to the Local Board where our names were all written down. In the evening all those who came from Hutchinson County assembled in the City Hall and sat in one row where we received our evening meal.

The first Hutterian brothers who were conscripted were Jakob Tschetter and Michael Stahl.

It was two o'clock in the morning when a special train arrived and we left about three o'clock. We travelled all night and arrived on September 23rd in Sioux City, Iowa. When the train stopped we all disembarked. At the depot was a cart with food which was our breakfast. It was ordered by the authorities and consisted of a cup of coffee, two pears and a little bit of meat. We stopped there for an hour. During that time some Red Cross nurses gave us some fruit for which we did not have to pay and then our train left. We arrived at 12 noon at Omaha, Nebraska, where we were given our midday meal which again was ordered by the authorities. We stayed in Nebraska for an hour and then our journey continued.

By six o'clock in the evening we arrived in Lincoln, Nebraska, where we were served our evening meal in a large hotel. During the time we ate, there was dancing and music on a stage to entertain the soldiers, to put them in a good mood and give them some fun. It was a whole train-load of soldiers; I don't know exactly how many there were. After our meal we all got back to our train where our beds were already prepared for the night. We were very tired and we went to sleep right away since we had not slept the night before. We travelled all night and on September 24th in the morning we arrived at Camp Funston, Kansas. I should mention that during our journey when we passed through the large cities there were always big bands playing and lots of singing going on.

When we arrived at Camp Funston we were greeted by our preachers who had waited for us already. There was my father, Paul Stahl, Minister Joseph Kleinsasser from Milltown, Minister Christian Waldner from Beadle and *Hausehalter* Jacob Tschetter. We were told before we left our homes to take only clothes which were not worth saving, since all our clothes would be burned as soon as we arrived at camp. This was done with all the clothes of the soldiers after they had received their uniforms. Everything was put in a large heap and burnt. They wanted to do the same with our clothes, but the preachers took everything back with them to Junction City, six miles from Camp Funston where they had taken lodgings.

When we had gone to our quarters and rested a bit we were measured for pants and shoes and in 15 minutes the uniforms arrived and we were told to put them on. We resisted because it was against our beliefs. They then called a captain and he read to us the laws which we had to follow and he told us to obey, if not we would be punished, but we still resisted. When they realized that they could not persuade us with words to put on these uniforms, they took us, both Michael Stahl and Jakob Tschetter, and dressed us by force. Then the captain arrived and ordered us to work in the Camp, at the warehouse or in the store. He did not want to send us to drill or march with the soldiers. But we refused this work since it was all connected with the war. They brought us a sack which we filled with straw and this was our bed. After we refused to work, they let us rest for one day. The next day our preachers visited us and the officer asked them what kind of people we were. The preachers explained to them where we came from, what our beliefs were, and told them that their requests were against everything we believed in. He then told the preachers that he would send a telegram to Washington to enquire what should be done with people like us; after that he would let us know.

The brothers from Rosedale, who were on the same train with us, lived only half a mile away, and also with the soldiers. Their names were Andreas Hofer and Zacharias Hofer. They were not forced to wear uniforms; they let them wear their own clothes. We visited them every day. One day when we came back from our visit we met our officer who told us that he had heard from Washington, and that we would be allowed to take our uniforms off. We let our preachers know about this right away. He also told us that he would put us together with the other brothers in a few days, which is what happened. We had our own house. In the next few weeks more Hutterian brothers arrived at Camp Funston; they were Paul Stahl, Peter Hofer, and Peter Tschetter from the Tschetter Colony, Joseph Waldner, Peter Entz, Joseph Entz, Paul Entz, and Paul Kleinsasser from New Elm. Now we were altogether twelve brothers.

One train carried 1,500 men; they came off the train like cattle. All together there were about 60,000 men here. All are trained in the art of murder and they are led to Satan. It is terrible to see with our own eyes how all their endeavours are directed towards teaching and training these young people to murder.

Our thoughts were with our loved ones, our wives and children, whom we had to leave behind, and we wrote to them with tears in our eyes. Our hearts were heavy when we thought about our lovely homes where we could sit quietly in the evening with our loved ones, where we could go to bed in peace in the evening and get up in the morning fresh and healthy and praise the Lord for it. Where we can go to our sermon and pray every Sunday. When one thinks about all this and then realizes how we are faring at the hands of these people who have no fear of God and how our Lord God could have let us get into their jaws, one could not help sighing and complaining in tears to God. As David has said: "God, have you forgotten all about us? How long are you hiding your face from us?"[1] But God let this not be the case; you will not let the righteous die with the godless.

Our preachers came to us in the morning for a visit from Junction City where they are staying. They came to us with many good and lovely words of comfort. They realized that it was time for us to fall to our knees before God and ask the Lord for comfort and help to relieve us from our sadness, so that we would not have to witness all this godless behaviour every hour of the day. They did this with us in tears and saddened hearts. We asked the Lord not to leave us, and help us to endure all this with patience.

When we had finished our prayers to God, the command came that all those who were not willing to serve in the war effort had to assemble outside. There a headcount was held, and both our men, the Mennonites and some others, amounted to 53. We were told to return to our houses. After about half an hour a sergeant

came to get us to appear before a higher authority about a mile away. We had to wait in some designated rooms there. We knew that our quiet hours had ended; it did not take too long. The same afternoon at one o'clock we were told to appear again so that the law could be explained to us again. They threatened us with severe punishment, if we did not obey the law; that was not a good omen, and it disturbed our good preachers when they heard about it. They admonished us to remain steadfast and true, and they were very happy to see that we, each of us one like the other, had decided not to sway to the right or left. Yes, we had decided not to take part in this war in any way; we would rather go to prison than stray from our vows and beliefs.

We were then called to have lunch, and after that we were told by an officer to get to the garbage trucks and help clean up all the refuse. When the trucks arrived, we were taken away four men at a time (also the Mennonites), to collect the garbage. But we refused again. We were brought back, four men at a time. The first four were Peter Entz, Paul Entz, Joseph Entz, and Jakob Tschetter. The godless people turned them over to six soldiers with rifles, each one had one slung over his shoulder. They then stood before the men with drawn rifles. Then they had to march very quickly, all four in one row, approximately two streets

[1]   Ps 13:1.

away, towards the prison. Behind them the soldiers with their rifles marched as if they were the greatest criminals in the world, passing large crowds of people. After that they were marched back, and the soldiers with the rifles again behind them, as if they had done something horrible. They were put onto the trucks again, driven around the camp, away from us where we could not see them.

The first four men who were treated like that were Peter Entz, Paul Entz, Joseph Entz, and Jakob Tschetter. After a little while four men who were taken away in the same manner, came back to the same place, where they had boarded the trucks. They were taken off the trucks and again put in one row. We thought now they would be treated in the same way, but it got worse. In our sadness we did not know what to do any more; we could barely endure watching. We only could sigh and ask God to help, which without doubt, he did.

The enemies of Christ soon stopped chasing us with their rifles, but we had to get onto the trucks again, and we were driven into the camp to be forced to work again. These four men were Paul Kleinsasser, Michael Stahl, Peter Hofer, and Andreas Hofer. Paul Stahl, Zacharias Hofer, Peter Tschetter, and Joseph Waldner occupied the third truck. You loved ones, it is a terrible thing to see all this and it wounds your innermost feelings. It is no surprise that someone watching this, and unable to

help, is wounded by this deeply, and cannot forget it.

Later we were led by another soldier into the house. We were made fun of, treated with contempt, and mistreated in many ways. The soldiers had rifles, revolvers and sticks and used them in a godless way with us. For our supper we received dry hard bread and water. We had to sleep on the floor in the middle of the rooms. The guards watched us from morning until the evening, the whole night with pointed rifles.

Dear brothers and sisters, we were in great fear and distress. Under these circumstances we were forced to pray to God and ask his help. We knelt down in front of these godless people with remorseful hearts, yes with fearful minds, and begged our almighty God not to forget us. We asked him in all humiliation to free us from the hands of these godless people. In such sadness and wretchedness we spent the night. We were not allowed to get up in the morning without permission. We knelt down and thanked the Lord for his help, which he gave us during the night. Although we did not sleep much, and we had to lie on a hard floor, we had lots to be thankful for. We also asked God wholeheartedly and fervently not to abandon us in the future, but to be with us in these sad times which had befallen us.

In the morning we had to stand up between several soldiers. We were teased and treated with contempt.

They pushed us from one house to the other, so that we almost broke down with sadness and distress. What evil thing they could think of, these children of Pilate and Herod did to us. But the Lord stood by us, and released us from their murderous hands. Without doubt our prayers and sighs were not unheard.

We were then returned to our rooms where we had been before. For this we thanked God who at this time came to our rescue again, and removed us from the hands of our tyrants.

Since Satan never rests, he planned a new plot and executed it through his servants to bring disaster to the believers. In the afternoon they came again and forced us onto the trucks, just to ride with them, not to work, so they said. But when we refused, they forced us to ride on the trucks all afternoon. But we remained steadfast in our promise, and did not do anything that was against our conscience. The next morning the servants of Satan returned to force us again onto their army trucks, but we refused again, and did not leave our rooms. Now they really got terribly hateful; they threatened us with the powers of the executioner. But we again prayed to God and begged Him not to try us too hard, not to heap more onto us than we could bear. We truly felt that God was with us, because finally these tyrants showed some feelings and became more friendly towards us and did not hurt us for five days.

But our dear preachers were told to leave; they could not visit us anymore. It was a hardship for us to be robbed of their comfort. But we stood with our God, our only helper, and reminded ourselves and each other to stay close to the Lord. We prepared ourselves for more temptations, which we knew would not be far away, so that we would, with the help of God, be secured against all sly attempts of the devil.

After this the seducers came back they wanted us to clean our house and the others too. We did this with great reluctance and in fear for our beliefs. We were not even half done when the godless hordes and henchmen came in great rage, and threw us with force onto the army trucks and war vehicles, brought us to a bath house, removed our clothes, and mistreated us unmercifully, and without any compassion. A stone would have been more merciful than these evil-minded people. There were about 30 of these dastardly soldiers. What one could not think of, the others could. After this mistreatment, when we were naked and bare, they did not give us back our clothes, but dressed us forcefully in blue pants. After that they shaved our heads and beards with great boldness and tyrannical force. Oh, what misery and distress; it is not possible to describe what we suffered under their evil hands. They made fun of our church and our beliefs; it was just terrible to listen to.

After they finally got tired of their tyranny, and they had cooled their evil mood they let us go back to our rooms, where we now had to stay. This all happened on October the 16th and 17th. It was truthfully a hard and strong temptation which these godless people submitted us to. Although it filled our hearts with sadness and hurt, we tried to encourage each other, and we told each other to be steadfast, and to trust God our Lord and Helper with more courage and enthusiasm and believe in his power and strength.

It was also a great comfort to be together with our twelve brothers in these times of temptation; we believed that it was a gift from God and were very thankful for it. Most of the evening and half the night we promised each other not to give in, that we would not deviate from our path neither to the right nor to the left, but to keep our promise which we made to God and his congregation.

On the morning of the 17th, the godless hordes did not rest any longer. They came and took three of the brothers away; they were Peter Entz, Joseph Entz, and Andreas Hofer. They forced them to work. But the three brothers behaved steadfastly and kept to their vows; without doubt God was there to give them support and comfort. Then they were severely punished, beaten with fists on their faces and heads, beaten on the back. But all this could not weaken them or force them to give up. After this they brought them back again. But the godless hordes returned to take the next three brothers, namely Paul Kleinsasser, Peter Tschetter, and Michael Stahl and mistreated us cruelly with beatings just as if the devil had advised them. They pushed us under water three times until we were breathless, which was done to scare us. They continued until they had cooled down their moods.

On that day we were so filled with sadness that we were not able to eat or drink. We were very concerned what else could happen to us. We sighed and prayed to God that he should stop the evil mood of these people. The other brothers were told that they would be separated, which made us fearful, and we continued to pray and beg God not to abandon us. There was no doubt that our pleading with God and our prayers did help. We noticed that the hearts of the godless softened, they became more lenient and stopped the separation of the brothers, which made us happy.

The next day we began to clean our house; we washed the dishes, we cleaned the floors and kept the wash-house clean. But only the houses which were occupied by the Mennonites who did not partake in military service.

Our preachers were again permitted to visit us. They asked us to write to them so that they could come. That is one of the reasons we started to work in the house with great fear and shuddering. We did not want to offend our God; we begged him with fearful hearts not to take it amiss, so that we would not fall in disgrace with him. We did not do these things because we wanted to, but only to show the authorities that it was not disobedience to the law but our innermost beliefs which made us disobey.

It was October 23rd when our preachers came to visit us again, we were full of joy and thanked God. With them came Johannes Entz and Zacharias Hofer, Jakob Hofer and Joseph Entz. They came every day for a visit. On the 27th we asked our officer in charge to allow us to leave the camp and go to Junction City which was located eight miles from

here. He gave his permission, and we thanked God for this. But before we left we had to finish our work.

We arrived there around ten o'clock, and we met our preachers. On the same Sunday afternoon Preacher Paul Stahl and Jacob Tschetter arrived and when we were all together, we started our sermon. Minister Zacharias Hofer gave the sermon from the 33rd Psalm; it was conducted with many tears and sighs. It was not as comforting as at home, but we gave our thanks and praise to God that we were able to have a sermon. The sermon gave us comfort and strength. The preliminary sermon was all about the christening and the promise we made to God. Around four o'clock we asked our preachers for prayers again.

[**SOURCE:** *Hutterite COs in World War I: Stories, Diaries, and other Accounts from the United States Military Camps* (Hawley: Spring Prairie Printing, 1997), 5–12. This edition reprints an earlier publication translated by Karl and Franziska Peter from 1982. Used by permission.]

Joseph Hofer (1894–1918)
Letter to Maria Hofer, 1918

This letter was written while traveling by train from Alcatraz to Fort Leavenworth. Joseph Hofer died on Nov. 29, 1918, shortly after his arrival at Fort Leavenworth and a few days before the death of his brother, Michael.

Nov. 17, 1918

To my dear wife and children:

Grace and the peace of God and our Lord Jesus be with you.

My precious, dear wife, Maria Hofer, because I have a bit of time and paper at the moment, I want to let you know how I am doing. I am in good health in body and soul, and on my way to Ft. Leavenworth. Do not know how we will fare there.

We are traveling the same way as we did to Alcatraz, but in the other direction. We will arrive there on Tuesday.

We may never see each other again. And the only way you can help us is by praying to God, who may deliver us from all evil, and give us strength to quench the fiery darts of the evil one.

My dear wife, even if we should never see each other in this sorrowful world, we will see each other yonder through the power of God. Thus, we must rest contentedly with what God permits upon us. And he will not burden us with more than we can bear with his strength.

And he knows it, and says that not a hair from our heads may fall without his will;[1] so we accept everything with patience.

And let us praise God that the bloodshed [of war] has come to an end, as we had hoped.

But this is now [a time of suffering]— as the Lord Jesus has taught us, that there will be such a time—as there has never been before as long as the world has existed, nor will ever be hereafter.[2]

---

1   1 Sam 14:45; Mt 10:30; Lk 12:7; 21:18.
2   Mt 24:21

This is the time to keep our eyes wide open, for it is possible that even the chosen ones may be deceived.[3]

As it was in the days of Noah and Lot, so shall it also be when the Son of Man comes[4]—and everything I say to you is his Word: keep watch!

And when you consider our scribbles, you can imagine how we are feeling and where we are: where the ocean waves are roaring, and in the time when the sea casts out its dead;[5] if you would only perceive this the right way.

That's all for this time, my dear wife. This is not a very good letter, because there is too much bumping and lurching.

In closing, my best wishes to you and our dear children, father and mother, and all brothers and sisters in faith.

Yet another greeting from me, your husband [*Eheteil*], to you.

[SIGNED:] Joseph Hofer

[**SOURCE:** Translated by Kenny Wollmann from an unattributed manuscript copy held in the Hutterian Brethen Book Centre Archive, MacGregor, MB.]

---

3   Mt 24:24.
4   Mt 24:37; Lk 17:26.
5   Rev 20:13.

Michael Hofer (1893–1918)
Letter to Maria Hofer, 1918

This letter was written while traveling by train from Alcatraz to Fort Leavenworth. Michael Hofer died on Dec. 2, 1918, shortly after his arrival at Fort Leavenworth and a few days after the death of his brother, Joseph. This was his last letter home.

November 17, 1918

To my dear wife [*Eheteil*], father, mother, brothers and sister in the faith—a heartfelt greeting from your afflicted brother.

Faith and peace be with you. I feel like writing to you now that we are on our way to Ft. Leavenworth, Kansas. We do not know, however, what we will encounter there. It is [only] known to God Almighty whether we will see each other in this world, for we go from one tribulation to another. Let us pray earnestly to God, for he has promised us that without his will not a hair will fall from our head.[1] And if we do not see each other here in this world, we shall see each other in the next.

Dear spouse, I received two letters from you, and one from dear brother Peter. As you can imagine, I wept when I read that you and our dear little daughter are ill. Do not rush out of the house. Keep yourself warm.

I am still healthy in body and soul and wish the same for you and all my brothers and sisters [in Christ]. That is the greatest treasure a person can obtain here on earth.

I will close now with a heartfelt greeting to all brothers and sisters in the community, especially dear David *Vetter*. May he remember us in his prayers. And remain your afflicted husband, Michael Y. Hofer, until death.

[Signed:] Michael Y. Hofer

[**Source:** Translated by Kenny Wollmann from an unattributed manuscript copy held in the Hutterian Brethen Book Centre Archive, MacGregor, MB.]

1   1Sam 14:45; Mt 10:30; Lk 12:7; 21:18.

UNKNOWN
Songs of Lament, 1920s–1930s

One of the great early challenges for Hutterites in Canada was paying off the substantial debt incurred from buying land at higher-than-average prices from land speculators. "*Verloren in Kanada*" and "Sweet Alberta Land" are two songs that give voice to the anxieties over economic uncertainty in a new country during the third decade of the 20th century.

[Despairing in Canada:] a lovely song to consider.
Written[1] by Kathrina J. Waldner, [ca. 1920]

Wir wollen euch jetzt vorsingen,	We want to sing to you now;
wir sind so sehr bekümmert	we are so very troubled
über unserm Zustand in diesem Land.	concerning our situation in this land.
Was wird die Zeit noch bringen?	What will the future bring?
Kamen von Vereinigten Staaten,	Came from the United States,
dort ist alles gut geraten.	where everything was going well.
Wo kommt es doch hin; wer gibt's uns im Sinn?	Where will it end up; who can make sense of it?
Verloren in Kanada!	Despairing in Canada!
Verloren in Kanada,	Despairing in Canada,
im lieben Manitoba.	in lovely Manitoba;
Wir schulden ja schon ein halb Million;	We already owe half a million;
ist das nicht über die Massen?	is that not over the top?
So weit sind wir gefallen,	We have fallen so far,
ist das nicht zu beklagen?	isn't that lamentable?

---

1   It is uncertain if this Kathrina Waldner from Rosedale Community, MB is the actual poet of these lyrics, or merely a copyist. Hutterite song collections use the designation "*geschrieben*" interchangeably. Additionally, the uneven nature of the metre make it difficult to determine which, if indeed any, tune was used to sing this text.

Die Alten gehn fort, hinterlassen den Ort	The old pass on, leaving the place
dem Jungen zu bezahlen.	for the young to pay.
Dem Armen zu bezahlen,	For the poor ones to pay,
wie ist ihr Gut verfallen!	how their wealth has been forfeited!
Sie erben nicht mehr als die Taschen ganz leer.	They inherit nothing but empty pockets.
Wie werden sie es bezahlen?	How will they pay for it?
Das nimmt noch viele Jahren.	That will still take many years.
Wer kann so viel ersparen,	Who can save so much
zu zahlen die Schuld, wer hat die Geduld?	to pay the debt—who has the patience?
Der Mut ist schier verfallen.	Endurance has nearly failed.
Es ist ja zu verzagen;	It is truly disheartening;
das Land kann's nicht ertragen,	the land cannot bear it,
den schrecklichen Lohn über ein halb Million.	the terrible burden of over half a million.
Wer hat dran ein Gefallen?	Who takes any pleasure in this?

[**SOURCE:** Prose translation by Kenny Wollmann from a transcript provided by Tony Waldner, Forest River Community, ND.]

Sweet Alberta Land

Possibly by a resident of
Sundale "Alsask" Community, SK, ca. 1930s

BEULAH LAND, 1879
John Robson Sweney (1837-1899), alt.

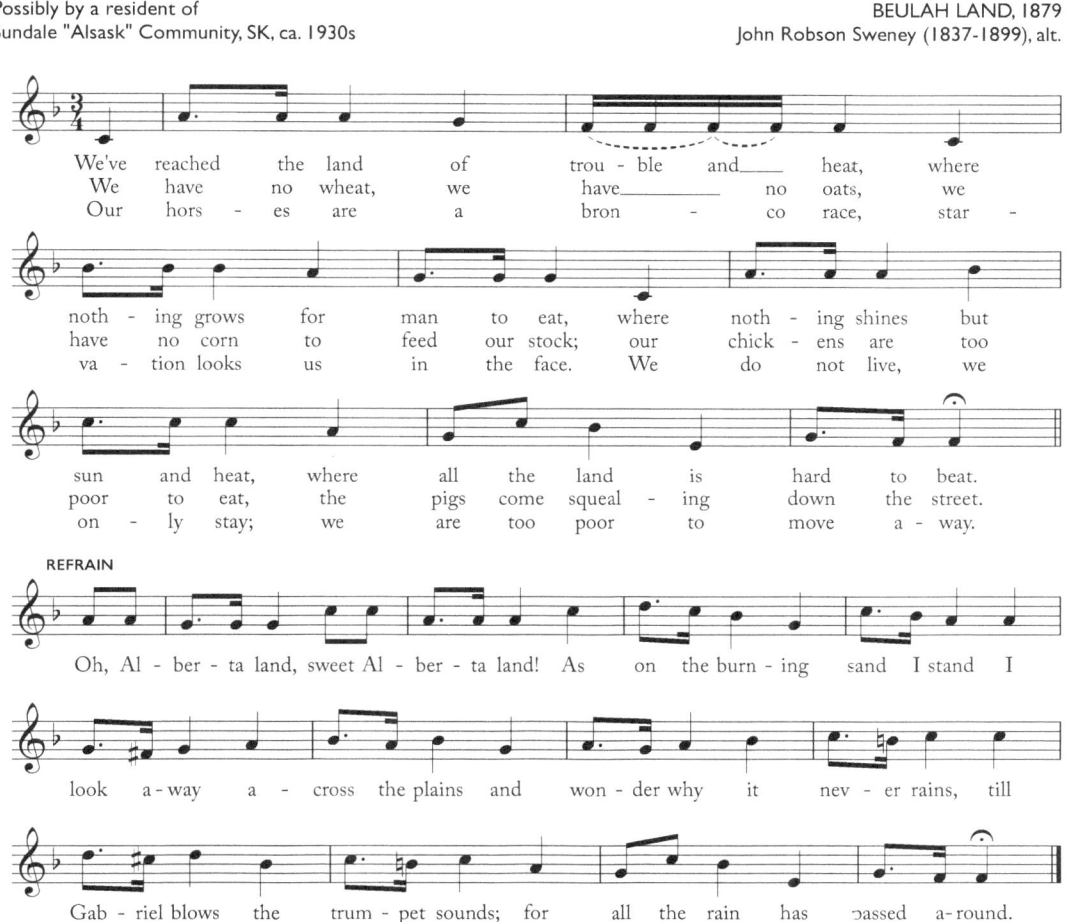

We've reached the land of trou-ble and heat, where
We have no wheat, we have no oats, we
Our hors-es are a bron-co race, star-

noth-ing grows for man to eat, where noth-ing shines but
have no corn to feed our stock; our chick-ens are too
va-tion looks us in the face. We do not live, we

sun and heat, where all the land is hard to beat.
poor to eat, the pigs come squeal-ing down the street.
on-ly stay; we are too poor to move a-way.

REFRAIN

Oh, Al-ber-ta land, sweet Al-ber-ta land! As on the burn-ing sand I stand I

look a-way a-cross the plains and won-der why it nev-er rains, till

Gab-riel blows the trum-pet sounds; for all the rain has passed a-round.

Mike Kleinsasser (1925–2007)
Account of CO Experience during WWII, 1944

By World War II both Canada and the United States had created programs that allowed conscientious objectors (COs) to perform alternative public service instead of enlisting for military service. Four hundred eighty-two Canadian Hutterites performed alternative service in national parks, at grain elevators and sawmills, and on farms. Before being cleared for alternative service, some of the men had to appear before a judge who assessed their convictions and motivations. Michael Kleinsasser's account focuses on the pressures faced by some young men during the recruitment process. The following is an oral history account of his experience.

We, the Hutterian Church, are pacifists—conscientious objectors to war. We believe that we can't love our enemies by shooting them as it is not in accordance with the teaching of Jesus. It was pretty hard for us to take up that position when all our neighbours' boys were going to fight for their country. The latter thought it to be patriotism. At eighteen and a half years old, we were drafted into military service. At sixteen years the boys had to register. When they were eighteen and a half years old, they received a registered letter asking them to appear at the military camp. Our young boys were not drafted until 1944; until then they could volunteer. The boys got the call to go up to their own private medical doctor for a certificate. Coincidentally we were friends with our doctors, so they got a very agreeable discharge but not for long. There were too many Hutterites that failed the medical exam: the military decided that as farmers they couldn't be so bad. A new law was passed that they should go to the military barracks for medical examination and also to take IQ exams to find out what jobs they could do. So in July 1944, I got a registered letter to appear at the military barracks in Winnipeg where they train three to five thousand soldiers at a time. Our neighbours' boys in Manitoba had to go, and quite a number of those we had known had left in advance for the Air Force and for the Navy.

The world could not accept that we stay at home to enjoy the freedoms and privileges of Canada while their boys had to go out and fight the war. So it was that I eventually received a letter asking me to appear at the Osborne Barracks in Winnipeg.

Samuel Kleinsasser, an old minister from Sturgeon Creek Colony came to me and said, "Mike, I want you to go to the military barracks. You are the second Hutterite that has been called there. It's true that the school board complains that the Hutterites who also wrote exams and filled out papers have a low IQ rating, and it's going to backfire in our schools. Everyone was playing it dumb, not only sick. I want you to do your best. You are one of my star pupils in school. I trust you will be what you are; anyway, do your best! Make as high grades as possible."

And so it was that I, along with my dad, left for Winnipeg. I had received a prepaid bus ticket to the Osborne Barracks which stops about 100 ft. from the entry to the military camp.

When they saw us coming, the two soldiers crossed their bayonets so that we couldn't walk through the gate. When I showed my pass, I walked through. When I looked back I saw two bayonets were thrust onto my father's chest. He had walked straight into them.

"Where are you going?" they asked. "With him," said my dad.

"Where is your pass?" He didn't have one.

"No one is getting in here without one. So you are not coming in."

"Can I give you his handbag?" dad asked.

"No! Nothing goes through that doesn't go with him," they responded.

So I had to go out and in again to get my handbag. It was war time, so they were very strict. I said goodbye to dad and went in.

When you join the army, you are suddenly not much of a human being. A soldier came up, asked my name and I showed him my card.

He said, "Your name was called twenty minutes ago."

"No, that can't be; I still have ten minutes to go."

A soldier called out, "Mike Kleinsasser!" I was surprised that he pronounced my name so clearly. There are so many different names, but he had it right on, which happened very seldom! Up above him the announcement read: Come over here and take a number. He said, "Here is a button with your number. Tie it around your neck. From now on you are a number. You are no longer a Kleinsasser. For four days, you are no longer Mike! You are strictly a number."

They call it a cog in the wheel. So then they took us to school; they waited until there were forty. There was a reason for this number, because the Canadian Army platoon has forty people, so we started to work with forty. They told us that the whole platoon is only as strong as the weakest link, as the one individual or the one cog in the wheel.

"You are forever a unit now!" they yelled. That's the way they indoctrinate you!

So we went to school for four days; to the medical doctor for one hour, wrote exams, more exams and some more exams, and saw some more doctors. For four days we ran obstacle courses inside buildings a couple of thousand feet long. We had to climb ropes and poles and jump off obstacles. At the end of each thousand-foot run, the male nurse felt one's pulse to see how each individual was doing.

There were eight farmers in my platoon. The rest were university students, from the city universities. There was such a big difference between the farmers and the university boys, that soon eight farmers had to run back again as the examiners could not believe the farmers were that tough. The city boys were puffing away around that course. When they came around a second time, I was left alone. I had to run back the third time, running and jumping through the bars.

"What are you doing anyway? your heart hasn't even started beating!"

They were a bit stunned that we were stronger than the city boys. Harvesting in the fresh air on the farm made us stronger.

I wasn't aware at the time, but later I caught on why I had to run the obstacle course three times. They weren't just testing my stamina. In the first hour of school, there was a questionnaire. (It pays to stick to the truth! Sometimes you think a little white lie is passable.) The question was, "Do you have any scars on your body? Some day when you might be a dead soldier, you might need to be identified!"

From the very start they give you the facts! "This is a killing machine! Some soldiers die. Your training is to prepare you to fight and possibly to die for your country." They tell you so.

On the form, I indicated that I had a scar on my body for identification. Five minutes later they gave those who said, "Yes" another form to fill out. "Does the scar ever bother you?" I wrote a very small "yes" instead of a "no." It cost me dearly! I had to run that obstacle course a third time to see if that scar would bother me or not. So much for that; I had to strike out the "yes" and mark a "no." They don't let you get away with it!

I saw some Mennonite friends who made out papers indicating that they didn't hear very well. They pretended to be partially deaf. They were caught so quick, it wasn't even funny! One of them said to me, "Here one must speak the truth, here one can't lie; they find out anyway."

They showed us films and meanwhile we had three teachers: an Air Force teacher, an Army teacher and a Navy teacher. They give the exams and put the highest and lowest marks on the board after every five-minute session.

Soon the five farmers start showing their colours again. The city boys with the higher education were no comparison to our ninth and tenth grades plus our experience on the farm. Our education had given us a wider range of education so that we could answer the questions far better.

"Now what job would you like to have?" was asked a hundred times a day. Of course I wrote, "I am a conscientious objector to military service." That was disregarded as if I hadn't written it. One kept on moving down the line; it would take a week to describe all one did in those four days.

Finally, the Commanding Officer said, "Wait a while; we have a job for you." On the third day, he said, "You are wasting your time here in the barracks; the camp officers have a job for you."

All the university men were signing up as officers and the kind of jobs they liked to have, but I don't think many of them got it because they were as low as 46% averages in a day and in the exams. The farm boys were in the 80% and 90% zone. That was the difference between the university students and the farm boys.

In my group, there were several of our French neighbourhood farm boys from near Milltown colony. They knew the Hutterites. I told them, "It doesn't matter what they offer me, I can't accept it." They didn't accept that either.

We ate at the barracks, but didn't sleep there. We went up town in a bus. It cost 25 cents to sleep in a place in Winnipeg in 1944. We did this for four days and then we all lined up and waited for our number to appear. There were three desks in front, and the soldiers sorted the papers and stamped them and you went forward to get them. There was a French boy from Elie who had four brothers in Italy fighting in the war. He had very thick glasses and couldn't see very far and he stumbled wherever he went.

He wanted to join the Army but was not wanted. He started to cry. I took out my papers and said, "Let's trade, if you want to stop a bullet. I'm not going anywhere; you are only a number, not a man."

He answered, "They would catch up before I was half way out of the building."

When I went forward to the desk, there was a Mennonite boy in uniform who said to me, "According to your papers, they are going to make a good soldier out of you."

"No, they are not going to make a good soldier out of me," I said.

He answered, "They are going to try hard."

"But" I said, "What are you doing behind that desk encouraging an 18-year-old boy like me? Your church is teaching exactly the same Testament as ours. We all profess to be Christians! What are you doing in that uniform behind that desk?"

"Oh, I made a deal with the armed forces and that is as far as I'll go. Not one step past this desk or out of Canada either. I'm not fighting nor do I carry a gun."

"Did you try one on when you trained?" I asked.

"No. I refused to; I went under that condition and they let me have this job behind this desk." So there were some allowances made for some of them.

Then he told me, "Well, there is something exceptional here in your papers. Do you see those two military policemen at the back there on each side of those forty boys?" Sure enough it was true.

"They are waiting for you! It looks like our commanding officer likes the passing marks that you have here; he's not going to let you go so easily; they have to take you, according to these papers."

The hair on my arms lifted up a bit! The boy at the desk said, "I've never seen this happen before." He added, "Because this is a civilian building, those soldiers aren't allowed to talk with you until you are outside! Not even on the steps!"

The next thing I knew, I was standing between these two soldiers. They did not touch me or attempt to talk. I looked first at this one and then at that one as I walked towards the door. They walked so close to me that I couldn't go to the right or the left until I was outside. I decided they would talk first so I just kept looking at them until they got red in the face. I felt sorry for them as it was not their fault they had to escort me in that manner.

One of them said "This is an escort, not an arrest. Our commanding officer gave us orders that you are to be brought to him before you leave. He wants to talk with you."

It was a 3/4 mile walk, so we walked sometimes slowly and sometimes faster until we came up to the building and walked inside. A soldier was standing there, and he was given my papers.

"Here's the 'Cowboy' you were waiting for."

I was told to hang up my hat; "Now we are going to take you in to see not just an ordinary man; he is the highest class officer in the Canadian

Army. At this moment he wants to speak to you. Don't say 'Hello' to him; he will say, 'Good day, sir' and you must address him as 'sir.' You say 'yes, sir' and 'no, sir.' Do everything just right."

The door was opened, and I was pushed in. It was a large room. I had never seen so much wealth except in pictures. There was so much gleaming brass and glitter that it was kind of scary being shut in with this powerful man. But, he stood up and reached across the table with both hands and said "Good day, sir."

I responded, "Good day, sir." To my astonishment he said "I wish the world would be full of people like you, then there would be no war to fight." He had seen the two hundred times I'd said I was a CO.

I said, "You wouldn't have a job, sir." He answered, "I'd gladly relinquish my job not to have this war, but we have to fight. We need your help; we need young people like you. Are you serious with what you've applied for here? Did they give you a ticket to a certain camp in Ontario?"

"Yes, I have a ticket."

He said, "Come tomorrow with your graduation papers. Will you accept it?"

"At the present time, I don't think so." I answered.

"Will you promise to consider it?" he responded. "We need people like you! We are at war!"

"I'm afraid you are not getting this one!" was my reply.

He wouldn't give up. "Will you promise to reconsider?"

"I can promise you anything, but I am pretty positive I am not using that ticket," I said again.

The commanding officer also tried to tempt me. He said, "If you want, I can arrange for a taxi to pick you up right now, and we can have you on a flight to Ontario in four hours. You won't have to go home to your parents and minister." I just looked at him and then answered, "I didn't say my parents or minister were Conscientious Objectors to military service. I said I am a Conscientious Objector to military service."

He sat silently for a little while and then he said, "I hope you will seriously reconsider, but if you are serious, I, for my part, promise you will be granted your rights as a CO. Here is a form, take it home and consider it for fourteen days and if you are still undecided, fill out this form and return it in the mail. In 24 hours you will get notice where to appear next."

The reason why the officer was so disappointed with me was because I had refused to take a position that he had offered me. This came about because during our time of testing at the barracks, they discovered that I had exceptional eyesight. They wanted me to become a spotter and a sniper. However, I refused. They then offered me another job in which

I would be working on what was at the time a military secret. You see, at that time, the Japanese were releasing fire balloons into the jet stream. These balloons would drift across the Pacific Ocean and were supposed to explode when they landed in the North American interior. The army wanted me to agree to help spot and shoot down these balloons before they came to the mainland. Of course, at the time, I was warned not to tell anyone of these balloons. They didn't want people getting scared, but also, they didn't want the Japanese to hear that their balloons were successfully landing in North America. Even today, people are still finding these bombs in the forests in BC. Only a few years ago, a family found one and when they touched it, it exploded, killing them all.

During the war, the existence of these fire balloons were kept secret by both the Canadian and the United States military. Eventually, the Japanese stopped releasing them into the jet stream as they thought they were not landing in North America but were all crashing into the ocean. After the war, literally thousands of these bombs, manufactured by Japanese children, were discovered in Japanese warehouses, ready to be sent to North America as soon as word came that they were reaching their intended targets.

This wasn't a bad job! I wouldn't actually have had to kill anybody. However, I was suspicious of their motives. I asked the officer whether I would be required to wear a uniform.

"Yes, of course," was his reply.

To which I answered, "When I was first brought into the barracks, I was told that once I wore the uniform and worked for the army, I become a cog in the wheel, a link in the chain. After this job is finished, I would have to do as I'm told, even if it meant fighting and killing which are both against my conscience and faith."

So I went home, but I could not sleep. I told my dad what happened. I was still fighting within myself. It was a good job which the officer had offered me and being a young, adventurous person, I seriously considered taking the position. But I fought with my conscience day and night. I read my Testament and re-read Jesus' teaching. I saw no loophole that would give me any rope to take up that job. It took me fourteen days to decide. On that fourteenth day, I stood by my upstairs window looking outside where a strong wind was blowing. I looked at my ticket and slowly tore it up into tiny shreds and threw them into the wind. My battle was over, but it was not an easy victory. My mother had felt there was something wrong; so she came to me every day and said, "Make the right decision, Mike." Finally, the right decision was made! Twenty-four hours later another letter came asking me to appear before a judge in Winnipeg who would ultimately decide if I received CO status or not.

So, once more my dad and I drove to Winnipeg for my hearing at the civil court. I was ushered into a courtroom where I stood before five judges. There was a box on the table filled with cards. I took out my card and read my name aloud.

This judge was a very scary judge. All the Hutterites were afraid of him because he was so stern and rough. He usually gave COs a good verbal beating. There was no other choice or alternative. You had to face him and that was that. I was warned that my card was bad. "You'd better watch what you say," somebody warned me. "He knows all the weak points of every young man. He has all the records of all the COs for the last three years and some were not good."

I told dad that I had torn up my ticket once and for all, so it didn't matter what kind of a judge I had to face.

The judges usually worked the case before your turn began. They would study your weaknesses and plan what to say. The COs, however, were new to this and hardly knew what to do, so they had people there giving you instructions on how to conduct yourself. For instance, we were told that it was our right to stand to the left side of the courtroom and listen to the case being tried before you. You must witness one court procedure before your turn, this way they

didn't have to do a lot of explaining. You just watched and learned.

When I entered the courtroom, there was a young 18-and-a-half-year-old Ukrainian boy who was facing the judge. The judge said, "Johnny, you stand over there and swear on the bible that you will speak the truth." The young man did as he was told.

"Our boys go to war and you want to sit at home and enjoy the benefits of this country."

Johnny said, "I have not said I am not going."

"But your papers say you have applied for CO status. What does it mean?"

Johnny answered: "My mother will not let me go."

"Where is she? Go and get her."

He walked outside the courtroom and called his mother. She was asked to stand in the witness place.

"Your son says you won't let him go to war. Why? Don't you know there is a great war going on? Do you think he is better than any of us?"

She answered: "Because it's not our war! Let them fight their own war! You don't know what war is! War is killing! Houses are burned and lands are ruined! War is seeing your sons murdered, your daughters raped, butchered, slaughtered. That's what war is. You don't know any better because you have never been in a war. I have been through a revolution and a war. If war comes here, I'll fight! I've killed more people with a pitchfork than you would believe. I fought until my husband was killed. I killed Cossack soldiers with my pitchfork."

The judge said, "I believe nearly all you said. War is hell! War is all that! Wouldn't it be better to go to Europe and fight them in their own country? Why let them come here? Isn't it better to go there?"

Johnny's mother agreed and gave permission for her son to enlist.

Then it was my turn. Dad had to go stand in the witness box. I was told to swear on the Bible that I would speak the truth and nothing but the truth.

I said: "Your Honour, we do not believe in swearing on the Bible, but I promise to speak the truth." The lady at the desk told the judge that I will affirm.

The judge said: "You have just heard the unique case which was tried before you. But, coming back to all seriousness; do you Hutterites think you are taking the right stand in refusing to fight in the war? I have four boys in the Armed Forces. Two are already dead, killed in Italy, and I have two more that are fighting in the war. You, however, want to live here in this country and not do anything while we sacrifice our young people's lives!"

He talked on, saying how patriotic his sons were. "One even lied and said he was 18 and a half but he was only 17 and a half years old." He kept on talking about how patriotic his sons were and all the other boys who signed up to fight. Finally, I raised my hand indicating that I wanted to speak.

"You may speak in your defense," said the judge, "but you Hutterites are absolutely wrong. It is not right what you are doing."

I faced right up to him and said, "I think there is a big generation gap here. I'm also 18 and a half years old, just like your sons and many others who choose to go to war. But I dare to correct you, your Honour. My generation is very adventuresome, but we are not patriotic. I don't believe your sons are fighting in Europe because they are any more patriotic then I am! They are fighting in Europe because they thought it would be a great adventure. I tore up my ticket to the training camp 48 hours ago and do you know what made me keep it for 14 days? It was my longing for adventure which kept me from tearing it up before then. I too love adventure and like your boys, I too would love to see the world but my conscience will not allow me to go and become a part of this killing machine. The New Testament, on which you wanted me to swear, does not allow me to kill another human being."

"We are not asking you to kill," he answered.

"Yes, you are," I responded. This job you are offering me is a sort of killing machine. I will not drop a bomb on anyone."

"No, we don't expect that either," he answered. "You know better than that." He wanted to be extra civil about what the job called for.

"I have studied for 14 days what this New Testament says and I cannot kill or drop bombs on innocent children and people."

We hadn't quite finished when there was a knock on the door. A city messenger boy brought in a letter and laid it in front of the judge. I was shocked to see the letter because I recognized what it was. A black striped letter could only be issued by the government and was always a notification that a somebody had been killed in action. I had seen similar letter which some of our neighbours had received when their sons were killed while fighting overseas. The judge sat there for some minutes and wouldn't speak. That letter was for him. His 17-and-a-half-year-old son had been killed while serving in England. He stood up and went into his office. When he came out again, his face was wet with tears. He told the lady clerk that he could take no more cases that day. He had to go home. But then he turned on me and my dad and hammered at us right and left. It was terrible to hear. He used very rough language, and he hammered away at us; there was no stopping him.

Just try to imagine this situation. Here I was with my father asking to be excused from war. There he sat: a father whose three sons had died in a war fighting for their country.

He said, "I have to go home and tell his mother that her sons are dead while you get to live on here in this country and have all the privilege of living in a free nation. Yet, you are not willing to do anything to defend this nation. This is just not right! It has to end somewhere! I've only one more son left and he is fighting in Italy and could be gone tomorrow, and still you don't do anything." He kept on hammering at us. When he stopped, I raised my hand and he said "Yes, you may speak."

I said, "First of all, I want to offer my sincere sympathy, your Honour. But at the same time, I want to point out that I too am an adventurous boy, just like your sons. I would love to have taken the job you offered, but this Testament doesn't allow me to do so. How can I love my enemy by killing him? Take this Testament, your honour, and prove it to me. How can I do good to my enemy by killing them? You have the Holy Word in front of you, too. Show me where it says that I can kill my enemies, and I will kill. During my time at the Osborne Barracks, they showed me war films in which they kept repeating, 'You must defend your partner.' If I had been standing beside your son yesterday, I could not have defended him as I cannot kill another man. I can't! So what sort of soldier would I be?"

He said: "Okay, that's enough; I'll make a deal with you." He walked to his office and came back with a booklet and said to my dad, "I need a witness for this. He has to read this booklet tonight." He then turned to me and handed me the booklet and a paper and said, "If you are still convinced you cannot be a soldier even after your government asks this of you, then mail in this form. All it needs is my signature, and you will be accepted as a CO."

The title of the booklet was, *Killing in Battle—Is it Murder?*, written by Samuel Logan Brengle of the Salvation Army. The preface read: "The letter is not written in defence of murder but to quiet a soldier's conscience."[1]

Both my father and I had to promise that I would read it that night and so I did.

The author wrote, "This is the Word of God. Not one word has been added."

What it didn't say was, "Not one word has been taken away." The author quickly went through the New Testament adding quotes from here and there but leaving out others that contradicted the points he wanted to make. It would have fooled most of the young soldiers who were not familiar with the Bible texts. Many young soldier on the front lines relied on this booklet to still their conscience. It was just terrible!

At the time, my grandfather from Milltown, the Elder Joseph Kleinsasser, came to Sturgeon Creek Colony to see how things had gone in court. Grandfather and three other ministers were overseers who were to help the Hutterite CO boys. Because I was one of the first boys to go to the barracks in Winnipeg, my grandfather wanted to see how the judges were going to treat us. When he came in the evening, he asked my dad, "You were in court today with Mike; were there any new developments?"

Dad explained that it had been a very rough and unique experience. Grandfather asked where I was, as he wanted to hear from me personally what had happened. Father told him that I was still upstairs reading the Judge's booklet which I had promised to read. It took me about an hour and a half to read the book. When I came downstairs, I greeted

---

1   Ken Reddig states that, "[Judge Adamson was] continually on the lookout for material to advance his position against conscientious objectors [and] circulated a three-page letter written by Samuel Logan Brengle of the Salvation Army. [...] He quotes one paragraph to sum up Brengle's thesis: "So a soldier, fighting not with any thought of personal vengeance but only in the interests of humanity and the sacred, inalienable rights of men, does not murder when he kills, but is God's minister and is doing an awful but a righteous service." The judge wrote the following note on the back of the letter: "All those applying for postponement as conscientious objectors must read this article prior to appearing before the board." Ken Reddig, "Judge Adamson Versus the Mennonites of Manitoba during World War II," *Journal of Mennonite Studies* 7 (1989), 65.

Chief Justice John Adamson (1884–1961). [Manitoba Historical Society, *Memorable Manitobans*]

er stove and tore each page out separately and burned it in the wood stove.

He said, "The devil has written this book! And if not, he surely must have guided the hand of the writer from the very first letter to the last period." He kept repeating those words while he tore each page and burnt it.

So the next day I mailed back the form which the judge had given me. In a week I received a notice which notified me to which camp I was to be sent to along with 55 other Hutterite boys.

During this time, Reverend Johannes Hofer from Blumengart came on a visit. He told about visiting some of the CO boys at Fort William in Ontario. He was very disappointed with some of the COs, as some of them wore worldly cloths, took local girls to watch movies, and came back at two or three o'clock a.m. on weekends.

my grandfather and then gave him the booklet. He took the book and retired to a back room where he also read it. When he emerged from the back room he asked me, "Did you actually read this booklet?"

"Yes, I did," I answered.

"Well, you shouldn't have," he responded.

Dad answered and said, "He had to read it. We both had to promise the judge that he would."

"Well no one else will ever read this book again," said grandfather. He walked over and opened the Book-

This report bothered me some, so when I went to see the Alternative Service officer, Mr. Davis, who also told me about how some of the boys were behaving. I stood my ground and refused to go to Fort Williams. As it was harvest time, I was allowed to stay at home and help with the harvest. After the harvest, I received a registered letter informing me that I was to report to National Mills with 55 other Hutterites. After working with these boys, most of whom had been at Fort Williams, I discovered that they weren't really as bad as the reports had said. In general, they were decent young people who took their stand as COs seriously.

I wasn't the only one from my family to be conscripted by the government. My two older brothers were also conscripted. Jake, my oldest brother, was twice granted leave by the judge as he was the head carpenter at home and also had to take care of our mother, who was recovering from a big surgery. Joseph, my second oldest brother was hurt while working in the work camps. A tree fell down and hit him in the face, and he was sent home.

Each day, we had to walk six miles inland and chop down trees all day. At the end of the day, we walked the six miles back to camp. After doing this for weeks on end, we became hardened and tough, and we learned to survive in the harsh temperatures that we were called on to face. Some days the temperature would drop close to minus 50. You had to eat your food really fast otherwise it froze to your plate. The tea that they served was so strong that it caused the skin inside your mouth to peel off.

Even though the government insisted on paying us wages, we refused to keep the money. Instead, we handed it over to the Canadian Red Cross. However, we added one stipulation that it not be used directly for soldier's packages or any other war packages.

Our group of COs consisted of 55 Hutterites and two Hutterite ministers. However, there were also some outsiders [non-Hutterites] at this camp. We thought they were COs too and were in camp because their faith did not allow them to kill anyone. But later, while working with them, we discovered that they were COs, but that they didn't believe in God. They were COs on humanitarian grounds only.

"How come you are here?" I asked one of them. He responded, "I'm not killing anybody for anyone." The wickedest person I ever met was one of these men. He said he would never kill anybody. He was also an atheist in every way and form. A very wicked one too.

We really do have special privileges here in this country, but our faith requires us to take a stand against killing and war. This is a decision that our generation and others had to make. But a time like this may come again tomorrow.

When we look at the world and our neighbours, we do ask a lot from them in that we ask them to respect our beliefs and ask that they let us live here in this free country. Our forefathers left Russia because the government told them that in 10 years military exemption would be taken away, and they would all have to serve time in the military. And so our forefathers moved to America and later to Canada. They moved from one country to another until they ended up here in Canada where we have been granted freedom to live in accordance with our conscience. Here we are tolerated and protected to such an extent just like the army officer said: "I stand on this side of the desk and I, for my part, promise you will be granted your rights as a CO." This is what makes both Canada and America great in that they grant people like us religious freedom. I wish I could say that our COs all made a good stand, but sad to say, many of them did not represent their faith very well.

During these hard and trying years, I was never alone for the God that we serve was always at my side and is still with us today.

[**Source:** Ian Kleinsasser, *Hutterite Conscientious Objectors in World War Two* ([Ste. Agathe], Crystal Spring Colony, [2011], 4–11. Used by permission.]

EBERHARD ARNOLD (1883–1935)
Letter to *Ältester* Elias Walter, 1931

Eberhard Arnold, his wife, Emmy, his sister-in-law, Else von Hollander, and other like-minded Christians established communal living in 1920 at Sannerz, Germany. When Eberhard Arnold learned from J.G. Ewert, a professor at Tabor College in Hillsboro, Kansas, that descendants of the 16th century Hutterites were living in North America, he contacted Elias Walter, a Dariusleut minister, in 1926 to arrange a visit. Following a trans-national tour of all contemporary Hutterite communities in the United States and Canada, Elias Walter later presided over his baptism and incorporation at Standoff, Alberta, in December of 1930. In the course of his journey, Arnold visited the three remaining American communities (Bonhomme, Rockport, Wolf Creek—one from each *Leut*) and all thirty of the Canadian communities, including a second visit to the twenty Alberta communities following his incorporation. When Arnold returned to Germany, he sent Walter a letter in which he lists a number of problems or weaknesses he saw among the Hutterites he visited.

RHÖN BRUDERHOF, June 15, 1931

My beloved Elias [Walter] *Vetter*,

U nfortunately, I did not manage to write to you on the ship as I had planned. I was not seasick, as I am not inclined to be so, but my other ailments were very troublesome. Now at home both my eyes are bad again, even the better one, and this is very unpleasant. Then on the ship many people came to me even when I was in bed, sharing their needs, confessing their sins, and asking me about true faith and true community. In Germany I have been accustomed to this ready inner contact with people who are deeply disturbed, though not yet Christian. But I did not encounter it in American cities. Now I met it again the moment I stepped on board a German ship, though I was not yet on German soil.

When I reached home, I had the great joy of being greeted and welcomed by the whole Bruderhof in deep gratitude to God and in the strength of complete unity of heart

Eberhard Arnold before establishing contact with North American Hutterites, photograph, ca. 1920.

know and we will forward more to you.

Once again I was surprised by the inner life of our Bruderhof with its glowing first love and its burning enthusiasm for total dedication, self-surrender, unity, and community. On the other hand, after a whole year's absence and a deep insight into the dignified, serene, and peaceful atmosphere among you, our Bruderhof strikes me as rather passionate, youthful, and impetuous, and in need of your maturity and long experience.

Since I need to rest so much because of my eye, I have thought a lot about how I can best repay the great love you showed me during my journey. I am thinking of the general situation of your communities and of all brothers and sisters. Later maybe, if and when a request comes from someone over there, I would like to share in detail with all the elders what I see as your strength and as your weakness, and how the great strength given you by God can overcome the great danger presented by your weaknesses. To you, my beloved and deeply respected Elias *Vetter*, I can already touch upon these things briefly in this letter and tell you a little of my thinking. But I want to do this quite confidentially, that is, in the deepest trust between you and me only.

First, leadership through the Word should be represented more strongly and firmly in the service of the

and mind in the spirit of Jesus Christ. To our great joy, the well-packed sacks that you and yours took so much trouble over have now arrived in Fulda. The contents of the first packing case, which came with me on the ship, had been shared earlier among the brothers and sisters, among jubilant thanks. You will learn of outward events in our common life from our steward's report and from the enclosed copies of my letters to other brothers. I ask you to read Hans Zumpe's letter with particular care. If you do not have enough copies of any of these, let us

Word, particularly by the older brothers.

Second, those who serve through leadership should act in all things in full accord and innermost unity with all brothers.

Third, this is possible only if the gifts of bringing to belief, of warm encouragement, of speaking from heart to heart through the Spirit in great love are living among the servants of the Word in the strongest possible way.

Fourth, every trace of personal property and private money ought to be completely done away with.

Fifth, the grave disorder of having small communities made up of a few related families must be completely stopped. In any case, family ties must never be placed above the spiritual community.

Sixth, then all evil gossip can be sharply fought and abolished. (Such evil gossip helped lead to the ending of the first great period of the church after the death of Andreas Ehrenpreis and Hans Friedrich Küntsche.) Furthermore, the differences between the three groups (Schmiedeleut, Dariusleut, and Lehrerleut) with their friendships among closely related families would not cause separation.

Seventh, instead, the uniting of all Bruderhofs in faithful obedience and innermost unanimity under one elder would be possible. This can happen only if the easily influenced brothers always submit to the firmer ones.

Eighth, I firmly believe that these seven goals, which seem almost unreachable, are in fact one goal and can be reached. For I have seen among you, in particular with you, dear Elias *Vetter*, that there is a great love coming from all brothers in all these closely knit groups. This love, rooted in pure and genuine faith, is coupled with the sharp teaching of truth and, in some places, with discipline still kept in its original force. Only when love keeps its salt

Eberhard Arnold as Hutterite minister, photograph, ca. 1935.

Youth Movement Conference in Germany, 1920. [*WikiCommons*]

and when salt keeps its love can true community be preserved. Then we will have the strength to show and maintain this love which never loses its salt, even towards the weakest brothers and those not always moved by the spirit, yet without taking sides.

Ninth, then the most serious danger to your present-day communities will be overcome in the following way: in the future a Bruderhof made up of closely knit families, an individual Hutterian community, will no longer consider itself the legal owner of its property, goods, fields, income, and harvests. Instead, in the obedience of faith and total surrender, the community will see itself as the steward of its goods and possessions, its livestock and fixtures, in the name of the whole church of God under the authority of the main elder. Only when the church is integrated and united in this clear way will we be able to withstand all the

dangers with which the devil threatens us.

Tenth, therefore, I wish for all our church communities an Andreas Ehrenpreis for the present year 1931, who will bear a different name today but will reestablish the unity and the harmonious working together within the church with the same love, the same inner clarity, and the same well-defined order and strict discipline that he used. Without Andreas Ehrenpreis and such clear, firm co-servants as Hans Friedrich Küntsche in Kesselsdorf, the community would have collapsed long before 1699. That collapse would have occurred around 1650 or 1660 in the wake of all the terrible weakening and brutalizing effects of immorality brought about by the Thirty Years' War and the Turkish invasions.

I do not believe that the habit of communal living can prevent the collapse of the community. Only the fact of daily asking for the Holy Spirit and the reality of the daily strength of this Holy Spirit in the proclamation of the Word and in the communal work can keep us in truly full community. Therefore, we are with you daily in our prayers, especially when, united with you in the Spirit, we bend our knees before God and raise our hands to him.

In the future we must find a way to send simpler greetings from time to time, so that you do not have to wait as long as you did this time for our detailed explanations and letters. It is very difficult that our best secretary, the one whose lettering you have so often admired, is now seriously ill with tuberculosis. Like my terribly thin daughter, Emy-Margret, whose marriage is planned for July 26, Else has spent several months with friends in the mountains of Switzerland. Otherwise she would certainly have lost her life.

The troubles facing me here were and are such a heavy burden, and the main facts are so well known to you, that I would rather not go into other details. Since your laying on of hands, I feel much more acutely the weight of responsibility for the right life for our seventy people, and this care and anxiety are agonizing.

We must provide rooms with bare necessities, yet fitting, for our six newly-married couples and receive the earnest and believing people who request to visit us. This is absolutely impossible, but we must nevertheless prove it possible through faith. For instance, there is the question of inviting a fifty-year-old tailor from Frankfurt. At the same time you, too, have many worries, which weigh on me also.

I should not actually have come home without the means needed for our sound building up. In spite of all your loving care, the journey through South Dakota, Manitoba, and especially through Alberta has been such a strain on me, both in body and in soul, that I have come home exhausted and will hardly be able to undertake such a long journey again.

All the more, we hope for a visit from our brothers and particularly from you, beloved Elias *Vetter*. We, your brothers and sisters who love you with all our hearts, plead for this once again. And especially I, your brother who loves you from the bottom of his heart and embraces you in trust and respect,

[SIGNED:] Eberhard Arnold

[**Source:** *Brothers Unite: An Account of the Uniting of Eberhard Arnold and the Rhön Bruderhof with the Hutterian Church.* Translated and edited by the Hutterian Brethren (Ulster Park: Plough Publishing House, 1988), 259–263. Used by permission.]

Michael Waldner and David Hofer in Europe, 1937. [Treasures of Time Collection, Hutterian Brethen Book Centre Archive.]

David Hofer (1877–1941)
Visit to Rhön Bruderhof Travelogue, 1937

When Eberhard Arnold and the Bruderhof were officially accepted by the Hutterites in North America, the Hutterites promised to send a delegation to visit and support them. To honour this commitment, David Hofer (James Valley Community, MB) and Michael Waldner (Bon Homme Community, SD) were sent first to the Cotswold Bruderhof in England then to the Rhön Bruderhof in Germany in 1937.

By this time, Eberhard Arnold had died (November 22, 1935) and the Bruderhof movement had three communities: the Rhön Bruderhof in Germany, the Alm Bruderhof in Liechtenstein (a small landlocked country bordered by Switzerland and Austria), and the Cotswold Bruderhof in England. The Alm Bruderhof was established in 1934 due to restrictions imposed by the Nazis, and the Cotswold Bruderhof was established in 1936.

At the Rhön Bruderhof the two North American Hutterites were to help negotiate an exemption for the young men who were required to serve in the military. Only days after they arrived, the community was raided by the Gestapo. Their property and money were confiscated, several of the leaders were imprisoned, and its members were forced to flee to Liechtenstein and England. The presence of the two Hutterite brothers from North America was providential because it gave the community more legitimacy in the eyes of the government, who did not want to provoke foreign powers. They were able to intervene to delay the dissolution and give the community time to prepare for the exodus. In his travelogue David Hofer recounts this dramatic experience.

David Hofer and Michael Waldner were the first North American Hutterites to tour the sites in Europe related to Hutterite history.

On April the 7th, we received news from the Rhön Bruderhof in Germany that the situation was becoming very bad there. Wicked people had set various places on fire, but they were extinguished again by the brothers. And since some of the brothers were to be conscripted into

447

military service again, the situation for the community in Germany had become quite precarious.

For this reason, we held council [at the Cotswold Bruderhof, England] and concluded that we, Michael *Vetter* and I, should prepare to travel to Germany to the Rhön Bruderhof; perhaps we could mediate in some way, because we were foreigners.

[From April 8–13, David Hofer describes their journey from the Cotswold Bruderhof to the Rhön Bruderhof in Germany. They traveled through London, the Hook of Holland, and several German towns, where he carefully noted the scenery and local life. Upon arrival, they were warmly greeted by Bruderhof members and witnessed the Bruderhof's preparations for potential government action against them. Their discussions highlighted the urgency of relocating and selling possessions due to increased scrutiny and the possible forced sale of their property.]

On April the 14th, Michael *Vetter* and I were in Eberhard *Vetter*'s study at about 10 o'clock forenoon, writing letters and other things, when Hans Meier opened the door and said to us, "Brothers, brace yourselves! I am just coming from up the hill, and I saw a large troupe of officers behind the woods. They may come to the *Hof*, but they cannot do anything to you." [With that] he closed the door and went off to his office to tidy up.

By then 25 officers were already at the door. One shouted at me, "Where is Hans Meier?"

I replied very calmly, "Without a doubt, in the house."

"Call him out," was the command.

When I came to Hans Meier's room, he was already coming towards me and presented himself to the officers, quite calmly and without fear. Then the chief officer [*Oberste*] read the order to Hans Meier: "I hereby inform you that the Rhön Bruderhof is now dissolved by the state and no longer exists. From now on it shall be called Sparhof. And since you are the leader of the *Hof*, I require from you the books and all the keys. I also inform you that everyone must vacate the *Hof* within 24 hours."

He then went directly to the office or study with Hans Meier. The other officers surrounded the entire *Hof* and herded all the brothers and sisters, young and old, into the dining room. There they were guarded by two officers, and no one was allowed in or out.

In the meantime, the others searched all the rooms, carrying off everything they wished to their cars.

Finally, we were also ordered to join the rest of them in the dining room. As foreigners, we objected, but we were told, "You are here now, and you must obey! No harm will come to you."

Thus we very calmly and confidently went downstairs to join the rest of the brothers and sisters and found them quite disheartened and discouraged. We encouraged and reassured them as best we could, urging them not to lose heart.

Then two officials entered, one carrying a typewriter, the other a packet of paper. They seated themselves and then called each one by name, and everyone had to answer what they were asked. When it was over, the completed document was signed, but it was only a notice of conscription [*Verkündigung wegen der Musterung*]. We carefully examined the document ourselves before it was signed.

In the meantime, we saw through the window how they ransacked all the rooms and carried off whatever they wanted. When I realized that it would soon be our room's turn, I wanted to leave and go to our room, but I was stopped at the door and sent back to the dining room.

I said, "I want to go to my room; we are foreigners after all, and I don't want our belongings inspected and carried off."

He said, "I am not permitted to let anyone leave. If you want to leave, you must first get permission from the chief officer [*Obersten*] and bring it to me."

I asked, "Where is he?"

He replied, "Upstairs in the study."

I went back and approached the esteemed gentleman in the study, who was dealing with Hans Meier at the moment, and requested permission to go up to my room, which he granted me.

Also worth mentioning: when I tried to go out of our room earlier, one of them came toward me all agitated and angry, drew his sabre from its sheath saying, "Not another step!"

That's when I realized the gravity [of the situation].

Once I had permission, I summoned Michael *Vetter*, and we went to our room together. [The officer at the door] let us leave unhindered when I gave him the note: "Now you can go."

It wasn't long, however, before our house guests were in our room. They immediately asked, "What are you doing here? Why aren't you in the dining room?" We explained to them that we were foreigners, and German nationals/aliens at that, and didn't want our belongings searched. They asked us what attracted us to these people. We replied, "These people are our brothers to whom we have already sent a great deal of aid from America for the establishment of this Bruderhof. [We] are therefore also keenly interested in what might happen here at this point, and how things will now proceed with them."

We noticed immediately that we were not welcome here and stood in their way. We pleaded with them to let us remain here for several days, but they refused and said they had no say in the matter.

By this time, the brothers and sisters had all finished signing the papers. It was three o'clock in the afternoon by the time they finished with that. Only then were the brothers and sisters permitted to eat. Our food had been brought to us earlier, so we had already eaten.

The officers remained standing outside in front of the dining room talking to one another, so I went over to speak with them about this incident. I told them that what we are experiencing here today was quite unprecedented and that I would never have expected anything of the sort from Germany. "I always thought that they would treat their citizens and peasants [*Bauern*] better than what we are witnessing and experiencing today." Then I told them they were worse than the Americans.

They asked, "How so?"

I told them that we as Germans were drafted for military service against Germany in the last World War. "We objected and flatly refused, just like these brothers of ours here."

They said, "Yeah, we could not accept that."

From the American government we had requested that, because we could not comply with war and military service, they should let us freely leave the country for a country where we would not be drafted or required to do military service.

We asked to sell all our property and leave nothing behind, which the government did not refuse us, and we were permitted to freely emigrate to Canada during the war. The government even protected us, so no harm came to us. I asked them why they couldn't treat this community the same way?

In response they said, "Why can't you show your loyalty to the government like other people and obey?"

I told them we highly respect and appreciate the government, but we cannot obey what is asked of us if it is contrary to our conscience.

Then he asked, "What do you mean?"

I replied, "The Word of God says I must love my neighbour and not kill them, and therefore we cannot comply with the government and be obedient." Then another spoke up and said, "Friend, have you not yet read that our saviour said, 'I haven't come to bring peace but a sword,'[1] and that he instructed his disciples to buy swords?[2] Why don't you believe these Scripture passages?"

I shared with him how I understood those passages.

He replied that my interpretation was wrong. He then went on to say, "If the whole world were full of angels like you, then there would be no need for war, but you know that people are not all like that."

---

1   Mt 10:34b.
2   Lk 22:26b.

Children's House at the Rhön Bruderhof, ca. 1932. [GAMEO]

"We don't want war either," they claimed. "We only want to make ourselves strong because everyone fears the mighty. If we are weak, everyone will attack us; if we are strong, however, they will fear us. That's why we prepare for war, and not because we like war."

The others thought the brothers and sisters were taking too long to eat and asked if they were consuming an entire ox given it was taking so long.

After the meal they ordered the entire community out into the *Hof* on the doorstep. Michael *Vetter* and I were also summoned, as thought they had an order to read out. I soon realized, however, that they merely wanted to take photographs. I stepped out of the line and said to Michael *Vetter*, "Come into the house." and to them I said, "This is not necessary."

At this point, he read the order to them stating that the Bruderhof was now dissolved and that there was no longer a Bruderhof in Germany. None of them were to dare take anything belonging to the farm or the property of the community that was not their own personal possession, such as household items or precious valuables; if anyone attempted to take anything other than their clothes and the like the result would be serious investigations, and they would be harshly punished.

With this order they all left the *Hof*.

But we, together with the entire community, gathered for prayer with very heavy hearts. We poured out our distress and sorrow to our dear and faithful God, earnestly implored and asked him not to abandon us in this difficult hour and situation, but to give us the necessary understanding and wisdom, to lead and guide us according to his divine counsel, and to keep us together as his dear children. Indeed, may he himself be our counsellor and leader [*Führer*] and not forsake us.

Following the prayer, we deliberated on how everything should proceed and how we could ensure that the entire community remained together, because the godless lot intended to scatter all the brothers and sisters in Germany among their relatives.

We also desperately wanted to notify the communities in England and Liechtenstein about what had happened here on the Rhön Bruderhof.

So it was first decided to send Arno Martin—steward of Liechtenstein, who was present at the time—to Liechtenstein to report to Hans Zumpe,[3] and also to send this report to the community in England as soon as he was across the German border. But how [were we] to send anyone, since the officers had robbed and seized all the money, which was more than 400 marks. Thus, not a cent or penny remained in the hands of the community, because everything had been stolen and confiscated—all the keys and books; all the rooms and communal storerooms were sealed off. It was therefore necessary to share some of our travel funds with the community.

And so, as we had decided, Hans Meier, Arno Martin, and I drove to Schlüchtern. Arriving there at 12 o'clock midnight, we bought him a ticket and sent him off to convey this message to the other communities from Holland.

We returned to the community with heavy hearts and found them all still up and waiting for us; we went to bed, but there was little sleep.

[**Source:** Translated by Kenny Wollmann from David Hofer's original manuscript held in a private collection.]

---

3   Zumpe, Eberhard Arnold's son-in-law, succeeded Eberhard Arnold as the leader of the Bruderhof.

Joseph Kleinsasser (1890–1978) and David Hofer (1877–1941)
Letter to Georg Barth and Hardy Arnold, 1937

When David Hofer and Michael Waldner returned from their trip to the Bruderhof communities in Europe, they reported a number of violations of the Hutterite *Ordnungen*. In response, *Ältester* Joseph Kleinsasser and David Hofer wrote a letter to the Bruderhof elders in which they identified eight "differences between you and us [that] should not be." The letter sheds light on the cultural and theological differences between the two groups and the ongoing tensions surrounding their merger.

Benard, Manitoba
November 1937

May the grace of God, the love of Jesus Christ, and the community of the Holy Spirit be with you and us all. Amen.

Dear and beloved brothers: As we were with you on our visit and talked together many times about the differences between you and us, so I want, now that under God's protection I am safely at home again, to remind you of these things once again, because I, and our church communities, hold that these differences between you and us should not be.

First about the fact that you do not have a communal thanksgiving (or grace) at mealtimes, but that each one of you prays and gives thanks by himself for the gifts of God. We hold that you should change this. It does not seem communal to use a private and individual thanksgiving at the common table for the gifts of God which we enjoy communally and for which we have communally worked together. We think it is completely unfitting and not at all proper or suitable that we should live in community and not use a communal thanksgiving at mealtimes. For Jesus, our dear Lord and Saviour, who is our example and pattern in all things, has certainly not used private thanksgiving when he enjoyed food with his disciples or followers. Because every time when

453

we read that he partook of food with his disciples or followers his thanking is always included. And it is not to be thought or believed that this was a private thanking. Much rather we hold to it and believe that Jesus thanked communally and aloud before them. It would seem to us so improper and unseemly, as if a father prayed with his family at mealtimes, and every member of his family would thank by himself and not praise and thank God with all the other family members together. It is our united opinion and recognition that you should change this and introduce and use a communal thanksgiving as is used by all Hutterian communities.

SECOND: That you have the women in the council when you are dealing with church matters. From the beginning God has so ordered it that for the sake of the woman she should be subject to the man, and the man should be her lord, as God ordered it she should remain in her condition and adorn herself with good deeds and all submissiveness according to Paul's teaching 1 Timothy 2:9–15. And in Ephesians 5, Paul teaches: "Wives be subject to your husbands as to the Lord. For the husband is the head of the wife." The head (the man) should rule, and the woman should allow herself to be ruled, and not want to rule herself and involve herself in government. Only read the teaching of our forefathers on Ephesians 5, verses 22–23 and you will see how

they held it with regard to the position of the woman. For, although it is the duty of the husbands to love their wives as themselves, to care for them, and to honour them as the weaker vessels, nevertheless God's order remains in the Old and the New Testament, that the husband should rule the wife and the wife be subject to the husband. And therefore the women do not belong to the council when the men consider matters and things of the church. So that all remains as God has ordered it.

THIRD: We also do not find it good that you do not allow the new members or novices as you call them to come to the communal worship. Because our worship of God is two things: it is a thanksgiving to God and also an instruction and teaching out of the Word of God, how one should live and conduct oneself in the house of God. And this teaching and instruction is very valuable for the new members and they should receive it. Jesus our predecessor and master gave his sermons about the kingdom of God not only to his disciples but to all those who followed him together with his disciples. Also after him his apostles taught all those who came to them to listen. And we read nowhere that they made any distinction. In 1 Corinthians 14, Paul speaks about speaking in tongues and prophesying, teaching and exhorting and maintains that the outsiders who are there say "Amen" to the thanksgiving. And in verse 24 he says: "But if all prophesy, and an unbeliever or outsider enters, he is convicted by all, he is called to account by all, the secrets of his heart are disclosed; and so falling on his face, he will worship God and declare that God is really among you." But if a new member is not allowed to come to the teaching and exhortation how can he be convinced or called to account. How can an unbeliever be struck in his heart without hearing the Word of God? It is quite clear from the Acts of the Apostles and the letters of Paul that such a separation of the new members from the exhortation was not done by them. All may come to our meetings and exhortations out of the Word of God: believers, unbelievers, and novices, everyone has free entry.

FOURTH: We have seen that you do not have Sunday school as is the custom in all our communities. Every Sunday and [holi-]day for two hours in the afternoon, the unbaptized young people are instructed in the Word of God and in matters of faith by a [male] teacher who has the oversight over the unbaptized young people. He gives them passages out of the Bible and questions about our faith to learn, so that from their youth up they know the Word of God and are instructed in our faith. Such a teacher is also asked to punish such young people as are naughty and not well behaved so that they may be instructed and otherwise to punish when necessary.

We regard this Sunday school as necessary for the young people and hold that you should do the same.

FIFTH: In our communities the services in the church are appointed in no other way than by a majority of votes of the male members (with the exception of an election to the service of the Word.) No one is proposed, but every individual member gives his choice to the preacher for the service in question, so that no one but the preacher knows who he has chosen. And he who has the most votes for the service in question has this service commended and laid upon him in the presence of all the male members. This is done whether the office or service is for a male or female member. He who is chosen for such a service must stand up and in the presence of the brothers gathered together show his obedience, and take upon himself the office or service in question and promise to perform this service faithfully, honestly and industriously according to his ability. At the same time he is exhorted by the Word leader or the oldest servant of the Word to undertake this service. It is also not conducted in any other way if a sister is chosen for an office or service. She must accept the service exactly like a brother. And it is not conducted in any other way than with a brother except that she has not taken part in the election. All services (except that of preacher) are chosen by us in this way.

SIXTH: We regard the custom as you have it with those engaged to be married as much too worldly. That such an engaged couple may, as it is in the world, go around with one another in the woods, in the fields and to neighbours whereby they are exposed to much too great a temptation. With us, such an engaged couple would be married after a few days or weeks. They would not be left in such an engaged situation for so many months so that they might not be misled by the evil enemy.

SEVENTH: With us the mealtimes such as breakfast, the midday and evening meals are all taken in the communal dining room, at which the men sit separately and the sisters and women also sit separately and not men and women together as it is with you. We consider that the sisters would rather have it and that it is more pleasant for them to sit in this way.

EIGHTH: We consider that hair and beard styles should be the same for everyone.

Your humble and well-meaning coworkers,

[SIGNED:] Joseph Kleinsasser and David Hofer

[SOURCE: Bruderhof Archives, Walden, NY. Used by permission.]

Tony Waldner (1957–)
The History of Forest River Community, 1990

In February of 1956, the Hutterites excommunicated the Bruderhof over a conflict that played out at the Schmiedeleut community of Forest River, North Dakota, but had deeper roots. Forest River had close ties to the Bruderhof; for example, two of the five-person carpenter crew sent to Woodcrest in 1955 were from Forest River.

Without consulting their senior minister, Andreas Hofer, or church leaders, the majority of members at Forest River attempted to align more closely with the Bruderhof by inviting some of their ministers and several families to come to live at Forest River. The delegation of 11 Hutterite ministers sent to deal with the situation were treated with disrespect by the group that supported the Bruderhof, and the community was eventually excommunicated. The 43 members who did not support the Bruderhof moved to New Rosedale Community, MB.

In the following excerpt from his history of Forest River, Tony Waldner describes the context in which these conflicts unfolded.

In the background to the break is the 1950 visit to the Bruderhof communities in Paraguay by ministers Samuel Kleinsasser (Sturgeon Creek, Manitoba) and John R. Wipf (Spink, South Dakota), where they encountered a number of practices—such as smoking, dancing, and playing musical instruments—that they deemed were not in line with the Hutterite *Ordnungen*. There was widespread concern over these issues within the Hutterite world.

Reaching Out

In May of 1954, business manager John Maendel was elected junior minister; Allan Baer was then elected business manager. This same year the Colony decided to reach out to other non-Hutterite communities as a part of our missionary duty.

The first group Forest River had contact with was Koinonia Community Farm in southern Georgia. This community was started in

457

the late forties by Clarence Jordan, a Baptist minister. Koinonia was open to anyone seeking to live out the teachings of Jesus' Sermon on the Mount. (This included [Blacks], which caused a lot controversy from the beginning and through the sixties.) In 1955 Forest River requested a school teacher from Koinonia. Claude and Billie Nelson moved to Forest River in exchange for John Maendel, who temporally moved to Koinonia with part of his family in July of 1955.

Forest River also began to associate with the Society of Brothers in 1955. A brief history and introduction of this communal group is in order here.

In the 1920s a small group of Christians in Germany started living together in community with Eberhard Arnold as their leader and founder. After hearing of the Hutterites and agreeing with their doctrines, Eberhard came to America in 1930 and visited every Hutterite colony. During his stay he was ordained as a Hutterite minister to witness for the cause of communal living, as the Apostles practiced it, in Europe. The Society of Brothers, or Bruderhof, was thus united with the Hutterian Church. In 1937 the Nazis expelled the Bruderhof and by 1938 they had fled to England. With the beginning of WW II and the anti-German fury in England, the Bruderhof was again forced to move. They then estab-

lished some communities in South America, particularly Paraguay. In 1954 the Society of Brothers established Woodcrest near Rifton, New York.

During the spring of 1955 Paul Walter from Spring Creek, MT, began a trip to Koinonia. On his way through North Dakota he picked up John Maendel and Edna Baer from Forest River and John R. Hofer from Riverside Colony, Manitoba. They visited Koinonia and on the way back also visited Woodcrest. They saw their need of help with various building projects, thus the following carpenters were sent to Woodcrest to help build a house: Paul Maendel (Forest River), Darius Maendel (Forest River), Dave Waldner (Milltown), Sam Hofer (Riverside), and Fred Kleinsasser (Crystal Spring).

The carpenters left in May and came back in July.[1] That spring John Maendel and Allan Baer met with some representatives from Woodcrest in Chicago.[2] At this meeting John and Allan invited some Bruderhof ministers to come to Forest River so there might be better unity and contact between Forest River and the Bruderhof. The majority of Forest River members were in favour of closer ties with the Society of Brothers, but this was done without consulting the senior minister, Andreas Hofer, and the other members of the Hutterite Church in Manitoba.

---

1   The carpenters were in Woodcrest from June 3–30.
2   The meeting occurred on July 11.

Issues and Conflict

When the five carpenters returned home, they were asked to give a report of their stay in Woodcrest. The carpenters were generally impressed with the Bruderhof's way of life, but also had to report that some Hutterite ordinances were not kept. On August 21, 1955, a ministers' conference was held in James Valley, MB. Representatives from the Society of Brothers were invited to explain their position on various issues.

After this conference John Maendel was also called to Manitoba for a meeting with Elder Peter Hofer. Refusing to come to a meeting, John Maendel was dismissed from his ministerial duties and excluded as a member on August 28. The next day Peter Hofer and ten other ministers came to Forest River for a hearing. The representatives from Woodcrest—Hans Meier, Heini Arnold, Bruce Sumner and Arnold Mason—were also in Forest River. These representatives, as well as other Forest River members, didn't like the way the ministers from Manitoba chose to conduct this hearing. They did not cooperate with the wishes of the ministers, for which the ministers partly blamed the Bruderhof representatives. Elder Peter Hofer felt they were interfering in the affairs of Forest River.

The main issue was that if the Society of Brothers wanted to remain united with the Hutterian Church they would have to abide by their rules and regulations—or at least compromise more. Smoking, folk dancing, musical instruments, and women not wearing a head covering, etc., were serious offences to the Hutterites. Forest River members who sided with the Society maintained that these were minor offences and instead emphasized that the Bruderhof members were living more zealous Christian lives within community. Their child-rearing program and missionary outreach were also sighted as being ahead of the Hutterites.

The Break of 1955

The ministers decided that the Forest River members who wanted to remain with the Hutterian Church should move back to New Rosedale. The others were excommunicated from the Hutterites. Sixty-six people stayed at Forest River and 43 moved back to New Rosedale. This is referred to as "The Break of 1955." This break in relations also resulted in the excommunication of the Society of Brothers in February of 1956—a situation which was not resolved for almost two decades.

However, the relationship between Forest River and the Society continued.[3] In the fall of 1955, Bruderhof families started to move to Forest River from Woodcrest and South

---

3   From September 1, 1955 to 1957, Forest River was excommunicated from the Hutterian Church and aligned with Woodcrest and the Bruderhof movement—in other words, in this period they self-identified as a Bruderhof.

America. In 1956 several Forest River families also moved to Woodcrest. The 1957 census shows 28 Bruderhof members living at Forest River. Soon after their move to North Dakota, however, it became apparent that they did not want to become farmers. Instead they chose manufacturing as their livelihood.

By the fall of 1956 the leadership of Forest River was mostly in the hands of the Society of Brothers. That fall it was decided to sell Forest River and relocate to Farmington, Pennsylvania. An auction was held in the spring of 1957, but the land could not be sold. Most members of Forest River were in favour of this relocation; however Joe Maendel Jr., and Allan Baer very much opposed this decision. Joe and Allan wanted to remain in the farming business and had also become dissatisfied with some aspects of the Society leadership, especially the decision-making process.

In the beginning of June 1957, when a lot of families had already left and the livestock was ready to be sold, Allan Baer, Joe Maendel Sr., Joe Maendel Jr., and Paul Waldner forcibly took over Forest River. This resulted in another break of relations with the Society of Brothers. By the end of June all but the four above-named members and their families had gone to Oak Lake, near Farmington, PA. Forest River was now in serious financial trouble. Receivership status had been filed in the spring of 1957 in an attempt to re-

gain financial stability. In two years the financial situation had improved considerable.

Beginning Again

[…] In 1958 business manager Allan Baer and family left Forest River and moved to Koinonia. From there he moved to Oak Lake, PA, for the next year and a half. After this stay at Oak Lake they moved back to the Midwest, eventually settling near Lake Park, Minnesota.

With only three families left, Forest River appealed to Koinonia, Reba Place Fellowship in Evanston, Ill, and other communities for help. During the next several years the following persons were among those who came to Forest River for various lengths of time. John Gabor (Community Farm of the Brethren), Paul Goodman with two children, Sammy Maendel (Sturgeon Creek, MB), Al and Ann Zook with two children (Reba Place), Ben Chic (Community Farm of the Brethren), Will and Margaret Wittkemper with three children (Koinonia), Gorden Bindernagel with daughter (Ontario), Fred Kemp (Community Farm of the Brethren), Ted Hartsaugh (Reba Place), Leonard and Joan Pavitt with four children (Bruderhof), and Simon Britts (Bruderhof).

Reconciliation

In 1957 Forest River had begun associating with Reba Place Fellowship, founded that year. John Miller, an early Reba Place leader, encouraged both Forest River and the Society of Brothers to reconcile with each other. Reba Place also encouraged Forest River to reconcile with New Rosedale Colony and the Hutterian Church. Many letters were written over several years, but eventually there were results.

On Dec. 4, 1960, Forest River wrote to New Rosedale to ask for forgiveness for the 1955 break and also requested some families and a minister. The elders of the church were consulted and their condition was that all families not originally from Forest River would have to leave before a settlement could be made. This condition was received very reluctantly and with much pain. But Forest River had a longing to be reunited with the Hutterian Church, so by the spring of 1962 only the Joe Maendel Sr., family and the Joe Maendel Jr., family were left at Forest River.

Before Easter of 1962 Joe Sr., and Mary Maendel and Joe Jr., and Rachel Maendel went to New Rosedale to reconcile with the Hutterian Church.

It was decided that families would move to Forest River after the election of a minister. Paul Maendel was chosen to be minister on March 4, 1963. He temporally moved to Forest River to repair buildings and to reorganize after the years of financial crisis. Paul Maendel felt he had been chosen to be the minister for Forest River but the older ministers felt Andrew Hofer and a few families should move to Forest River instead. After much debate, Andrew Hofer, Eddie Maendel and Dan Maendel with their families moved to Forest River in July of 1964. Andrew Hofer was the minister; Eddie was in charge of the geese; and Dan took charge of the chicken business. Joe Maendel Sr., was officially elected business manager, and Joe Jr., was elected farm manager.

[**Source:** Tony Waldner, *The History of Forest River Community* (Fordville: Forest River Community, 1990), 16–24. Used by permission.]

Merrill Mow (1928–1987)
Of One Mind, 1989

A decade before the 1974 reuniting, Heini Arnold visited *Ältester* Peter Hofer and other senior ministers to apologize for his role in the 1955–56 division. Bruderhof Servant of the Word Merrill Mow uses the format of a dialogue—based on recordings of key meetings, interspersed with his own commentary—to describe the context and circumstances that led to the reuniting between the Hutterites and the Bruderhof in 1974.

Until 1973 there seemed to be no possibility of mending our relationship with the brothers in the West, broken in 1955 through sin and wrongdoing on our part. […] In 1973 God stepped in more decisively, and we were able to listen more. What happened becomes most vivid through what was reported at the time. I quote first from two servants of the Word:

> **Don Alexander:** Heini had a burning longing in his heart for reconciliation with the Brothers and for the reestablishment of the bond that had been made in 1930 by his father, our Word leader Eberhard Arnold. […] In our brotherhood circle in the Easter time of 1973, we considered the question of dress and the meaning of the head covering. We turned again to the New Testament and felt together to adopt a head covering for *Gemeindestunde*, brotherhood meetings, and celebrations of the Lord's Supper, out of respect for what the apostle Paul writes concerning this. God was leading us to a renewed relationship with our brothers in the West, although we were not aware of it at the time. […]
>
> Dwight [Blough] had come to Darvell with Heini, and they returned together in March. I still remember the phone call Dwight made from Woodcrest to Darvell after their return. He told about the lovemeal welcoming them back, and I could almost think we were present. The doors opened, and there stood two brothers from

the West, Jacob Kleinsasser *Vetter* (Jake *Vetter*) from Crystal Spring and Jacob Hofer *Vetter* from Elm River, completely unexpected. They simply walked into the middle of the lovemeal on a surprise visit. Heini and Dwight each said that as soon as they saw those two brothers, they felt it was an important and historic moment.

Glenn Swinger: We had no idea that a Hutterian brother would be within a thousand miles. They hadn't come straight to the dining room. They had first stopped at the Primavera House and met Sibyl and Jeanette, who were the children's watches over supper. Sibyl told us later that when she found out who they were, she spoke right out, "You will be very happy to hear that we've all quit smoking," but she noticed it didn't seem to impress them too much. The brothers had been somewhat fearful of coming, but they found Sibyl and Jeanette very friendly, and that encouraged them. They had been in Ottawa on business, and at a certain point in their travels had simply felt led to turn in our direction and come to Woodcrest. We later heard from Jake *Vetter* that on the way home they said to each other, "We have to go to work for a reuniting." And they really did.

In May 1973 at a joint conference in Woodcrest with all three brotherhoods, we read "The Darmstadt Report," the report by Emmy [Arnold] of the last days of Eberhard. It contained his hope that each one in the circle could answer the question, "Why do I love Christ?" Heini brought this same question to us at that conference.

Then there was a two-week interval, during which our beloved brother Fred Goodwin was very suddenly called into eternity. The brotherhoods gathered again for a second conference to fight through inner concerns and to consider the possibility of a meeting with the Brothers. Four days after the brotherhoods returned home, came the next important visit toward the reuniting: three Dariusleut ministers arrived in Woodcrest on June 6, 1973. They came specially to see Heini. After they left, he wrote a short report:

In the early afternoon of Wednesday, June 6, Annemarie came to me and said she saw three men with black hats and suspenders and one man in ordinary clothes walking toward the dining room. Since no one had told me that Hutterites had arrived, I thought they might be Jewish rabbis or Amish people. In about fifteen minutes my son Christoph came to tell me that there were three Dariusleut preachers from Alberta, Canada in the lounge with a Mennonite sociologist, John Hostetler. We invited them home for tea.

I waited for them at the door of our living room. First came the oldest man with white hair and a white beard, Peter Tschetter *Vetter*. He stretched out his hands to me, and I embraced and kissed him. We all went in and sat down. When he saw my mother, Peter *Vetter* jubilated; he would never have believed he would lay his eyes on "Emma *Basl*." He was very warm. At this teatime there were, besides Annemarie and myself and our children, Merrill, John and Sarah Maendel, and later Hardy and Doug. I think I never experienced Hutterites so warm and loving as these three brothers were. (I heard later that several sisters had greeted them by saying, "I am a Hutterian sister," and that Peter *Vetter* had replied, "*Sehr gut, sehr gut* / Very good, very good.")

Peter Tschetter *Vetter* had been present at the baptism and ordination of my father, Eberhard Arnold. He said that it was the greatest event for the Hutterites in America. He witnessed that Eberhard Arnold was not just a preacher but an apostle. The three brothers spoke of him with warmest love. When they saw the picture of my parents on the wall, they were very animated and could hardly believe that my mother was so young at that time. Christoph pointed out that his grandfather wore a Lehrerleut jacket with buttons. Peter *Vetter* said with fiery love, "Arnold *Vetter* did everything. When he came to the Dariusleut, he wore hooks and eyes; when he was with the Lehrerleut, he wore buttons. That is just how he was."

You all know that Annemarie had a certain worry that we might become narrow and accept human laws. But when we were among ourselves, she said she too was willing to do anything out of love, and we agreed that the only hindrance lay in making it a condition of discipleship of Christ to accept certain rules and regulations. These brothers were in Woodcrest for about two hours and left very enthusiastic, saying again and again that John Hostetler was witness to this meeting.

When Jake *Vetter* and Jacob Hofer *Vetter* had made their surprise visit in March, we had been reading in the brotherhood some of Eberhard and Emmy's engagement letters. To indicate how Eberhard had been called by God many years before the first uniting in 1930 with the Hutterian Brethren, and how his life with Emmy and Else had been used, Heini had wanted very much to write a *Sendbrief* to all Hutterians. We had just finished assembling most of the materials for printing this *Sendbrief* when these three Darius brothers arrived on June 6. It was a pretty fat book when typed up. One copy was given to the brothers and John Hostetler, and they read it in the car on the way back to John's house near Philadelphia. [...]

My own memory of this visit was that it was a very hot, muggy day. Soon Christoph came, all out of breath, barefoot, very hot, and in a T-shirt. [...] When we went over to the Forest River House, we were astounded by the respect and love these brothers showed, and by the reverence that came from them toward Heini, and especially toward "Emma *Basel*."

Peter Tschetter *Vetter* was deeply moved by the experience. He was a very close and dear friend of Sam Kleinsasser *Vetter* of Sturgeon Creek, the son of Samuel Kleinsasser *Vetter* who had visited Primavera in 1950 with John Wipf *Vetter*. (I have told how Primavera had not treated them then with the right respect at all and how Fred Goodwin had expressed sorrow at the disrespect we had shown them in Paraguay.) Well, Sam Kleinsasser *Vetter* the son, knowing about this and the affair in Forest River, was one of those who found the idea of a reuniting very hard. All of those brothers who before 1974 were in opposition to reuniting had experienced difficult and wrong things from us. We should not be surprised that there

was in some a resistance and a feeling of "No, not again!" And Sam *Vetter* was one of those. Now he was a very dear friend of Peter S. Tschetter *Vetter*, and we are quite sure that during the months before the final meeting at Sturgeon Creek, Peter Tschetter's visit to us had a certain effect on Sam *Vetter*. Peter *Vetter* was also one of the Darius ministers who was there on January 7, 1974; he was a part of that meeting and wrote a very moving letter to Sam *Vetter* afterwards, referring to it as the "Year of Jubilee." All these different events fit together in a wonderful pattern.

On June 21, 1973, a letter came to Heini from Jake [Kleinsasser] *Vetter*, requesting that Heini and two servants who had not been involved in the Forest River crisis come to Manitoba soon to speak with the Brothers. That did not happen then, as we know. The way had not yet been rightly prepared in our hearts. God had a different time in mind.

As background to the uniting, I quote from what Heini wrote afterwards to his son Christoph and to the brotherhood about his concern for unity amongst the Hutterian Brethren after the break:

> It has been a real torment to me ever since 1963, when I realized that the whole Forest River action in 1955 was wrong and sinful— we as a Bruderhof were unfaithful to Jesus. I saw no way of putting this sinful and disastrous state of affairs in order again before my death. We were too much used to unpeace before 1963; and because the brothers and sisters who joined us from there seemed

so genuine, I at first believed that the Hutterites were more in the wrong than we. Since the Brothers demanded in the first place the return of all their baptized members, I knew no way to find a solution. If I had suggested sending those brothers and sisters back to Forest River, I would have felt I was committing a grave sin and betraying them. I beseeched God in deep prayer to open up a way, and God heard my prayer. In the end he gave me much more than I would have dared to think or hope. I now see the coming and the influence of the brothers and sisters from the Hutterites as a very special gift from God.

Heini then speaks of specific questions and struggles that came about in our circle because a few were afraid of the Hutterites, fearful lest we would have to wear different clothes and so on. Heini said: "I for my part want by no means to force anything, but the brothers in the West simply won't understand it if we are not willing to yield to them on some points out of love."

Several times in reasserting that he would never force anything, Heini would also add, "Out of love to the Brothers I would gladly wear five hats! It will of course get more difficult if ever anything is required of us that would bring narrowness or anything oppressive into our church life. On this point you must persist in prayer to God and listen to the brotherhood, and take great care that it never again comes to a break."

At the beginning of October 1973 we decided which brothers would go with Heini to the West. At the end of November the elders of the Schmiedeleut had a meeting in Sunnyside Colony looking toward the uniting. On the way home from that meeting Jake *Vetter* was involved in a bad accident. He had broken ribs and was in the hospital. He said later he didn't mind about the ribs, but he was afraid lest anything might stand in the way of the coming together with the brothers in the East—his heart was really set on that. Two days after this accident Mike Waldner *Vetter* and Dave Waldner of Milltown arrived at Woodcrest, as they were in eastern Canada. It wasn't a long visit, but it was a wonderful and important one. I am certain that when those two brothers returned home, they did everything they could to help along the cause of the reuniting.

For the further telling of the reuniting story, I next quote [...] Glenn Swinger: [...]

Glenn: We received a warm welcome when we got to Crystal Spring. Grandmother Katharina *Basel* had very lovingly given us her house while we were there. That allowed us younger brothers to live upstairs. A living room downstairs adjoined a bedroom where Heini could withdraw, as the living room was never empty.

On Saturday, January 5, we toured the hof at Crystal Spring. Jake *Vetter* had gone away to a ministers' meeting, which we found out later was very difficult. He was so discouraged he even considered cancelling the meeting on January 7. But he couldn't let Heini come all that distance in his condition and not go through with it. Crystal Spring very lovingly provided us with jackets like theirs because we, although simply dressed, were not uniformly dressed. They had no jacket that would fit Heini, so they went to work and made him one. In the afternoon of Sunday, January 6, Jake *Vetter* said to Heini that he would like to propose that two of our brothers meet with ministers at Poplar Point, who had questions they wanted to ask us. Heini and Jake *Vetter* asked Dwight and me to go, and Mike Kleinsasser took us. Fritz *Vetter* of Poplar Point was present with his brothers Mike Waldner *Vetter* from Pearl Creek and Jake Waldner *Vetter* (mostly called Uli *Vetter*) from Huron. Glanzer *Vetter* from Huron was also present. They had many questions to us. Some of the main ones were about children's education, our young people, baptism, engagements, and weddings. Dwight led in answering, and in the end we felt very close to them all. It went well past midnight, so we were invited to spend the night with Fritz *Vetter*.

The evening after the reuniting, Heini wrote to Annemarie and the brothers and sisters at home. It is a very complete record except that Heini did not report about himself. Later the same evening Dwight and the others of us put together a report about how we experienced Heini in those meetings. To make one full story, I will alternate quotes from Heini's letters, from the other four servants' reports, and from a letter of Peter S. Tschetter *Vetter* of Mixburn Colony, Alberta:

Heini Arnold: I would like to give you a report about the historic events of today—a day that still leaves me completely overwhelmed. We only asked for forgiveness for our guilt. [...]
This morning, January 7, we were driven to Sturgeon Creek, where there was a meeting of a large number of preachers (seventy servants of the Word, I believe). Many of them shook hands with me warmly, but one said, "I am not shaking hands with you. We are not united." I heard later that he was a Darius brother. The Lehrerleut (I had never before seen a Lehrerleut preacher) were extremely warm and friendly, and I was able to recognize them immediately because they are the only ones with buttons on their jackets.
We were called into the meeting, and Jacob Kleinsasser *Vetter* (Jake *Vetter*) read to the elders an English translation of my letter (well known to the brotherhood). Then the elder, Joseph Kleinsasser *Vet-*

ter (Jake *Vetter*'s uncle), stood up and read the same letter in German. Then each one of us was asked to speak. I stood up first and asked for forgiveness for everything that happened in Forest River.

Dwight Blough: Jake *Vetter* asked Heini to tell the meeting what he had come for, which Heini did in a very moving and humble way. He promised he would accept whatever the brothers would decide. It was painful for us to hear Heini laying his life and his service completely and absolutely in their hands. We had no idea what they would decide. […] Then Jake *Vetter* said each of us others should speak. We tried to share how Heini had grieved over this question, had sought forgiveness again and again (long before his trip to Manitoba in 1964), and how he had suffered all through the years in fighting for what his father had established. […]

They asked Heini what Peter Hofer *Vetter* had said to him in 1964 at Milltown, because no one there could remember what had been accomplished in that meeting. Nobody had notes, nobody had any memory, even though there were people present who had been there. This put them in a dilemma, because Heini had not asked for only personal forgiveness from Peter *Vetter*, but forgiveness for all that had happened in Forest River. Yet Heini had been told that only he personally was forgiven, and the Bruderhof was not given the handshake or invited to the common table. Their dilemma was that they felt, on the one hand, they could not exclude Heini if that had been spoken out to him as forgiveness, and on the other hand, how could they give church forgiveness without exclusion? This went on—back and forth. Several times they asked Heini to say again both in English and in German what he had asked for in that meeting and what he had said to the preachers and to Peter *Vetter* in 1964.

Finally it was clear that it was not only personal forgiveness from Peter Hofer *Vetter* to Heini that had been accomplished with Peter *Vetter* alone at James Valley before the meeting. For when Peter *Vetter* had called the meeting at Milltown, it could no longer have been just for personal forgiveness between two men, because it had thus been brought to the church.

Dwight: After this point had been made as clear as seemed possible, Heini was asked by Joseph Waldner *Vetter* from South Dakota about the financial settlement at Forest River. (We learned later that Joseph *Vetter* was one of the very outspoken brothers from South Dakota who had stood very much against our request, especially on

Saturday at the pre-meeting.) Joseph *Vetter* asked three questions: about the auction in Forest River, about the settlement of the debts, and about who took over the property. (This referred to 1957, when the Bruderhof moved back East from Forest River and began the Oak Lake community.) Joseph *Vetter* was completely satisfied with every answer Heini gave.

Jake *Vetter* said to the meeting that if anyone had questions about other points, they should be addressed to him as chairman of the meeting. "Otherwise we want to consider only this main question about Heini *Vetter* and the forgiveness." We were asked to leave the meeting and were taken to the living room of Samuel Kleinsasser *Vetter*, the servant in Sturgeon Creek. We were escorted there by Dave Waldner, who stayed very much by our side, also by Mike Kleinsasser, who is a dearly beloved brother and friend. And Joseph Waldner *Vetter* from White Rock in South Dakota came with us. […]

Heini: […] Suddenly Joseph *Vetter* was fetched away, and the rumour went around that I would have to be excluded. Then Jake *Vetter* came in, and Mike told him of the rumour. Jake *Vetter* said he was not really supposed to give anything away, since the matter was not settled. He would only say this much, that they had decided that I was not to be excluded. After supper we were told please to wait patiently; they would decide now what should happen.

Dwight: After supper they met for about an hour and a half. Then Jake *Vetter* and Joseph Waldner *Vetter* came back to Samuel *Vetter*'s house and told us their decision: Heini *Vetter* should shake hands personally with all those preachers who sat on the front bench and ask for forgiveness; there were sixteen of them. Then he was to turn to the whole meeting and apologize. They had decided to close the matter with that. Jacob Hofer *Vetter* of Woodland (the other assistant to Joseph Kleinsasser *Vetter*) would speak out the forgiveness of the Church. We were to sit at the back of the room during this time. Heini then went in and spoke to each elder. He had been told to say simply, "Beloved brother, I ask you for forgiveness," but Heini spoke in a very moving way and humbled himself to each brother.

Heini: I can only tell you that it was a very moving moment. I went to the first one and asked for forgiveness. How lovingly most of them took my hand in both of theirs and said how gladly they forgave me and what a joy it was that I humbled myself so, and how much they loved my father, and I should please never again do anything like we had done at Forest River. Some things were especially moving: how Joseph Glanzer *Vetter* of Huron spoke to me, how the Elder Joseph Kleinsasser *Vetter* took both my hands—what a dear little man—and said, "How glad I am to forgive you. How glad! What a joy that you have come." [...]

There was complete silence in the whole room, an atmosphere of reverence and complete forgiveness. It was an hour of God. [...]

Heini: When our apology was over, we were informed [...] that they had decided that all those who had been baptized by them were to be placed in exclusion for a time because of having marched into the church and having moved East without permission. We were then also told that two [later this was changed to five] preachers would be asked to come to Woodcrest and Evergreen to carry out the exclusions and the church forgiveness and that this would make us Hutterian Brothers. That was a tremendous surprise for us. We had no opportunity to talk together alone, but we all felt that it was God's leading and that we had nothing to say. It would have been a second Forest River-type sin if we had said we couldn't do that without asking at home first. If you had experienced that atmosphere of love and embracing, you would understand. [...]

Don: Jake *Vetter* then led Heini down the aisle out of the church building with several of the other elders, and we joined them in leaving the building. We felt a great joy and thankfulness as we went out and gathered again in Samuel *Vetter*'s living room. We sat around in a large gathering with many brothers.

Merrill: There was a great press in the house; at least twenty came up to Heini one after another and embraced him, shook his hand, and expressed their love in a very moving way. This included Dariusleut and Lehrerleut representatives.

Dwight: There were at least three ministers who said to me that now Heini *Vetter* takes up the task where Eberhard *Vetter* left off. With the rift healed, they see Heini as fulfilling the task of an apostle. No one spoke about points or criticisms or questions. How love came from these brothers to Heini especially, but to each one of us! Earlier, there had been reserve in many of the ministers; now they were warm and loving, praising God that this could come about. [...]

Heini: [...] Fred Kleinsasser of Crystal, who is known in Woodcrest as one of the five carpenters, enquired of Jake *Vetter* in my presence about the "points" of their traditional rules. Jake *Vetter* told him that he and the elder had quite intentionally not brought up the points so as not to bring dissension. Unfortunately, I cannot foresee what this will mean for us in the future. […]

The delegation of five ministers to make suggestions for corrections and improvements arrived in Woodcrest on the 27th of January. They visited our three places in the States. It was an experience of great love, especially the exclusions. There had been a lot of fear and trembling from different ones of us. Afterward everyone wondered what the fear was all about. In Woodcrest in 1986 Jake [Kleinsasser] *Vetter* (one of the five) shared about this visit:

Five brothers were to come to Woodcrest to work out the suggestions agreed on at the reuniting. This was all thoroughly dealt with. Then Heini *Vetter* experienced another great astonishment in how these five brothers led in a wonderful reconciliation. I don't know where that power came from, and all that wisdom. Nothing was left undone; they did everything.

Artist's rendition of 1974 uniting, 1989, pencil.

Who got rid of all the fear of rules among you? I didn't. None of us can say we did. But God knew the uniting Spirit was there, making us all of one mind and one heart like the early church. Then even a united dress fell into place. Wanting to be different disappears when God sends the spirit of unity. In John 17 Jesus prayed, "Father, make my disciples one as we are one." This Spirit is what we need. This is why at Pentecost they were all of one heart, one mind, one soul, and one accord. The Spirit did it. I still marvel at the real, true, honest forgiveness from our wonderful God. Before, we could have written a thick book about accusations and guilt. Now they are all gone. The Christ-like spirit brought us together and made us forgive each other and bear each other. I thank God all the time. [...]

[**Source:** Text and image, from Merrill Mow, *Torches Rekindled: The Bruderhof's Struggle for Renewal* (Rifton: Plough Publishing House, 1989), 200–230. Used by permission.]

John "Hons" Decker (1928–1990)
Orthodoxy doesn't result in faithfulness, 1985

Hans Decker (1928–1990), aka "Philosopher," was a *Prediger* from Wolf Creek Community, South Dakota. Decker is one of the few Hutterites of that era who wrote critically about educational practices, a legalistic approach to faith, and growing materialism.

Orthodoxy[1] occurs when a person or people seek to fill a spiritual void with material or concrete things. It may maintain the church, but it does not lead to faithfulness. [A faithful church] must simultaneously encompass both the spiritual and secular realms; where this is not the case, it is more damaging than beneficial.

If one segment of an organization remains under the power of orthodoxy and another is permitted to change according to personal discretion, then orthodoxy is harmful.

Since there are no regulations for the modern acquisition of goods, this segment [of society] is rushing toward disaster like a wild horse—unhindered and unstoppable. The system is unbalanced.

Orthodoxy is an impotent ideology because it is founded on ruined [*explodierte*] human statutes. [In comparison,] Capitalism is a powerful ideology because its driving force [*Verwalter*] is individualism. It is therefore futile to attempt to control the spirit of capitalism with orthodoxy [i.e., traditionalism].

Orthodoxy seeks to compensate for spiritual deficiency by material means in order to imitate spirituality. [...] An orthodox mentality senses its spiritual shortcomings, but because it can prop itself up materially—that is, through external appearance—it does not realize that it is already spiritually dead.

---

1 Gr. ὀρθόδ/*orthos* = right or correct; gr. δοξη/*doxá* = opinion, faith. In intellectual history, 'orthodoxy' refers to holding on to traditional faith, thought, and inherited structures or 'way of doing things.' Decker has a very specific understanding of this word, namely one that is concerned with religious conservatism or narrow traditionalism expressed in such things as rigid clothing guidelines and strict policing of customs.

Hutterianism is a social system intended to be a stewardess of the knowledge of Christ with the objective of bringing people under the grace of God so that they might gain salvation. The Jewish kibbutzim are a similarly organized system, but with the goal of establishing a [Jewish] homeland. While Hutterianism seeks a spiritual home, the Kibbutzim seeks an earthly one.[2] Hutterianism was established through the leading of God's spirit. The Kibbutzim was established based on a human desire for earthly gain.

Both systems are thus subject to a higher authority; so long as they remain subject to their master, they will achieve their goals.

Through [the example of] the Kibbutzim we are convinced that it is possible to have community-of-goods without the Spirit of God. Just as the Kibbutzim is driven by an earthly spirit, so can the Hutterian system be led by the same [worldly] spirit. The goal of Hutterianism is far from accomplished and it cannot be achieved if the Spirit of God is not the motivating force.

The following accepted practices and traditions will most certainly not bring us eternal blessedness:
• living in community
• living in isolation
• aggressively pursuing our livelihood
• the traditional mores and customs
• nor the incessant crying of "Lord! Lord!" […]

The dress code and traditions of our fore-parents [*Alten*] are good and useful, but these alone will not make anybody fit for the kingdom of God.

Since we know we lack spiritual substance, we seek to maintain the appearances of holiness through orthodoxy, but only insofar as it does not make any demands of the flesh. In fact, seeking every comfort and luxury for the flesh is progressing full speed ahead.

When will we awaken from our deep slumber, for it is evident that Hutterianism is soundly asleep.

[POSTSCRIPT:] This orthodoxy is present in Hutterianism today. It is a hindrance to important changes within the church in the area of education [*Kinderzucht*] and mission; these changes are crucial if we hope to preserve our heritage.

[**SOURCE:** Translated by Kenny Wollmann from a photocopy of an edition prepared by Lothar Korff held in the Hutterian Brethren Book Centre Archive, MacGregor, MB.]

---

2   In addition to the secular kibbutzim, there are also some that are religious. Decker appears to be unaware of this.

WILHELM EGGER (1940–2008) &
MANFRED SCHEUER (1955–)
Letter of Reconciliation, 2008

Since 2006, members of the *Hutterer Arbeitskreis von Tirol und Südtirol* have worked tirelessly to draw attention to the dark history relating to the 16th century Anabaptists in the region where many early Hutterites once called home. They have toured and hosted dozens of Hutterite guests in the region and organized numerous events to commemorate the sacrifices and legacy of a persecuted religious minority. The committee is composed of individuals—both scholars and laypeople—who have been inspired by the witness of the 16th century Anabaptists and Hutterites.

In 2007 the *Arbeitskreis* organized an exchange visit to initiate a process of reconciliation in acknowledgement of the 16th century Catholic Church's persecution of Anabaptists and Hutterites. This involved a visit to Tyrol and South Tyrol by a Hutterite delegation as well as a return visit by a delegation from the *Arbeitskreis*. As part of this initiative, the Roman Catholic bishops of Innsbruck and Bozen-Brixen wrote to the Hutterite elders acknowledging the great injustice suffered by their forefathers which had been carried out in the name of the church. The State Governors of Tyrol and South Tyrol have expressed their profound sadness about what happened and emphasized the importance of learning from history.

> To the highly respected
> Elders of the Hutterian Brethren
> and Hutterite Communities in North America

> **May 2008**

> Dear brothers in the Lord,

> In the past year and for the first time ever, representatives of your communities met with us, the Roman Catholic bishops of Innsbruck and Bozen-Brixen. We learned about your life, and your

people got to know us and encounter the culture of the lands from which your ancestors fled.

These encounters were an opportunity for many people in our countries, and also for us as representatives of the church, to re-member the unfortunate events which led to the exodus of your ancestors. Through the members of the *Hutterer Arbeitskreis von Tirol und Südtirol*, we wish to send you the following message:

We recognize today that the persecution, torture, and execution of your foreparents in the 16th century was a great injustice. The Catholic Church of that day carried a great share of the responsib-ility for this injustice. We deeply regret the decisions and actions of that time, and the many forms of suffering that resulted from them. We pray to the Holy Spirit, that he might lead us into a future of mutual understanding and trust, so that the memory of the disdain, contempt, and hate of the previous centuries may be absolved and that through our common faith in the sacrificial death of Christ, a vicarious [*stellvertretende*] apology may be possible.

[SIGNED:] Dr. Wilhelm Egger
BISHOP OF BOZEN-BRIXEN

Dr. Manfred Scheuer
BISHOP OF INNSBRUCK

[**SOURCE:** Translated by Jesse Hofer from copies held in the Hutterian Brethen Book Centre Archive, MacGregor, MB.]

Edward Kleinsasser (1947–)
Huttererpark Grand Opening Speech, 2015

In 2015, after years of planning and building on the exchanges in 2007, the *Hutterer Arbeitskreis* committee invited representatives of the major denominations (Catholic, Lutheran, Free Church, and Hutterite) to attend the opening of *Huttererpark*, a memorial situated along the Inn River in Innsbruck where the legacy of the Anabaptists is celebrated in a circle of twelve boulders each bearing witness to the life of an Anabaptist martyr. Edward and Judith Kleinsasser (Crystal Spring, Manitoba) and Jack and Margaret Waldner (Decker, Manitoba) represented the Hutterites at this occasion. The organizers were motivated not only by the Anabaptist witness for religious freedom, peace, and social justice, but also by their concern for the injustices Muslims and other minority groups face in Europe and across the world today.

Innsbruck, October 16, 2015

[…]

The boulders in this park should not only be a reminder of this dark past, but should point to the future. We must not forget the words inscribed on a plaque here in Huttererpark, [to show] "tolerance and respect towards other religious groups and people who think differently." […]

Hutterites are very proud of and grateful for the faithful witness of the persecuted martyrs of this time, and draw encouragement from the steadfast Christian faith shown by their Anabaptist ancestors. To carry on this simple spirit and to live out this calling is the greatest challenge for us today, as is suggested by the text from Sacharja: "for like the jewels of a crown / they shall shine on his land." (9:16). Our ancestors shone to the extent that they followed after Jesus, expressed love of neighbour through a life of fellowship, and were prepared to suffer martyrdom for the sake of their Christian faith. […]

Today's Hutterites do not bear a grudge over the terrible events of the past. They accept that the people

Edward Kleinsasser delivering address at the opening of Huttererpark, 2015, photograph.

The danger that creeps in through a life of luxury and materialism is expressed in an old proverb: "Good days don't produce good Christians." Although Hutterites have tried to distance themselves from mainstream society, they have still been impacted by the rapid changes in the modern world. These changes lead to tensions between the thinking of the young and the old. The various perspectives on capitalism, tradition, acculturation, and culture among the four *Leut* have put Hutterites to a hard test. [Striking a] balance between preserving tradition on one hand and the dangers resulting from the negative effects of acculturation on the other, is a challenge. How much value does one put on one or the other? What has the actual essence of Hutterite faith become? How long and how intensely should one cling to outdated customs? Those are questions which we Hutterites have to answer ourselves!

[…]

in the past are responsible for what they did in their time, just like we are responsible for what we contribute to society today. They hold to what God teaches us through Paul's letter to the Romans: "Vengeance is mine; I will repay" (12:19). [...]

[**Source:** Translated by Jesse Hofer. Used by permission.]

Denn Steine an seinem Diadem sind sie, die über seinem Land funkeln.

For like jewels on his crown they shall shine on his land.

The opening event of Huttererpark, 2015, photographs.

481

A Selected Bibliography

The following list of titles does not attempt to be exhaustive. Instead, this list is intended as a starting point for further reading or student research in the area of Hutterite Studies. Where possible, we have tried to choose general or seminal texts rather than specialist volumes.

Reformation

Bainton, Roland H. *Here I Stand: A Life of Martin Luther*. Nashville: Abingdon, 1995.

Eire, Carlos M.N. *Reformations: The Early Modern World, 1450–1650*. New Haven: Yale University Press, 2016.

Gordon, F. Bruce. *Zwingli: God's Armed Prophet*. New Haven: Yale University Press, 2023.

Gregory, Brad S. *Salvation at Stake: Christian Martyrdom in Early Modern Christianity*. Cambridge: Harvard University Press, 1999.

Lindberg, Carter. *European Reformations*. 3rd Edition. Oxford: Wiley-Blackwell, 2021.

MacCulloch, Diarmaid. *The Reformation: A History*. New York: Viking, 2003.

Anabaptism

Brewer, Brian C., ed. *T&T Clark Handbook of Anabaptism*. New York: T&T Clark: Bloomsbury Publishing, 2022.

Osborne, Troy. *Radicals and Reformers: A Survey of Global Anabaptist History*. Harrisonburg: Herald Press, 2024.

Packull, Werner O. *Mysticism and the Early South German-Austrian Anabaptist Movement, 1525–1531*. Scottdale: Herald Press, 1977.

Snyder, C. Arnold. *Anabaptist History and Theology: An Introduction*. Kitchener: Pandora Press, 1995.

_____. *From Anabaptist Seed: The Historical Core of Anabaptist-Related Identity*. Kitchener: Pandora Press, 2007.

Snyder, C. Arnold and Linda A. Huebert Hecht. *Profiles of Anabaptist Women Sixteenth-Century Reforming Pioneers*. Waterloo: Wilfrid Laurier University Press, 1996.

Steinmetz, David C. *Reformers in the Wings: From Geiler von Kaysersberg to Theodore Beza*. 2nd Edition. Oxford: Oxford University Press, 2007.

Williams, George Huntston. *The Radical Reformation*. 3rd Edition. Pennsylvania: Penn State University Press, 1992.

Anabaptist Primary Sources[1]

Klassen, Walter, ed. *Anabaptism in Outline: Selected Primary Sources*. Walden: Plough Publishing House, 2019.

Leland Harder, ed. *The Sources Of Swiss Anabaptism: The Grebel Letters and Related Documents*. Walden: Plough Publishing House, 2019.

Snyder, C. Arnold, ed. *Sources of South German/Austrian Anabaptism*. Translated by Walter Klassen, Frank Friesen, and Werner O. Packull. Kitchener: Pandora Press, 2001.

Hutterite Historical Overviews

Hofer, John. *The History of the Hutterites*. Rev. ed. Altona: D.W. Friesen & Sons, 1988.

Hostetler, John, A. *Hutterite Society*. Baltimore: Johns Hopkins University Press, 1974.

von Schlachta, Astrid. *"Holding Fast to What is Good?" Tradition and Renewal in Hutterite History*. Translated by Jesse Hofer. MacGregor: Hutterian Brethren Book Centre, 2020.

_____. *From the Tyrol to North America: The Hutterite Story through the Centuries*. Translated by Werner and Karin Packull. Kitchener: Pandora Press, 2008.

Hutterite Primary Sources

Barth Maendel, Emmy and Jonathan Seiling, trans. and ed. *Jakob Hutter: His Life and Letters*. Walden: Plough Publishing House, 2024.

---

[1]   The *Classics of the Radical Reformation* series contains a number of important early Anabaptist texts. The three books in this section are all from that series.

The Chronicle of the Hutterian Brethren. Vol. 1. Rifton: Plough Publishing House, 1986.

The Chronicle of the Hutterian Brethren. Vol. 2. Ste. Agathe: Crystal Spring Colony, 1998.

Hostetler, John, et al. *Selected Hutterian Documents in Translation, 1542–1654.* MacGregor: Hutterian Brethren Book Centre, 2013.

Die Hutterischen Episteln, 1527–1763. 4 Vols. Elie: James Valley Book Centre, 1986–1991.

Im Weinstock treu bleiben: Hilfsquelle für hutterische Täuflinge/Abiding in the Vine: Resources for Hutterian Baptismal Candidates. MacGregor: Hutterian Brethren Book Centre, 2018.

Rauert, Matthias H., Martin Rothkegel, and Gottfried Seebass, eds. *Katalog der Hutterischen Handschriften und der Drucke aus hutterischem Besitz in Europa.* 2 Vols. Gütersloh: Gütersloher Verlagshaus, 2011.

Riedemann, Peter. *Peter Riedemann's Hutterite Confession of Faith.* Edited and translated by John J. Friesen. Walden: Plough Publishing House, 2019.

Zapff, Hauprecht. *Johannes der Evangelist über alle Kapitel erklärt: Ein täuferischer Bibelkommentar von 1597.* Edited by Martin Rothkegel. MacGregor: Hutterian Brethren Book Centre, 2017.

Beginnings in Europe and Russia

Friedmann, Robert. *Hutterite Studies: Celebrating the Life and Work of an Anabaptist Scholar.* MacGregor: Hutterian Brethren Book Centre, 2010.

Gross, Leonard. *The Golden Years of the Hutterites: The Witness and Thought of the Communal Moravian Anabaptists During the Walpot Era, 1565–1578.* Kitchener: Pandora Press, 1998.

Harrison, Wes. *Andreas Ehrenpreis and Hutterite Faith and Practice.* Kitchener: Pandora Press, 1997.

Packull, Werner O. *Hutterite Beginnings: Communitarian Experiments During the Reformation.* Baltimore: Johns Hopkins University Press, 1995.

———. *Peter Riedemann: Shaper of the Hutterite Tradition.* Kitchener: Pandora Press, 2007.

Staples, John R. *Johann Cornies, the Mennonites, and Russian Colonialism in Southern Ukraine.* Toronto: Toronto of University Press, 2024.

Stayer, James M. *The German Peasants' War and Anabaptist Community of Goods*. Montreal: McGill Queen's University Press, 1991.

Robertshaw, Eileen, comp. *Over the Mountains: A Story Based on the Second Chronicle of the Hutterian Brethren and other Contemporary Records*. Plough Publishing House, 2012.

North America

Hofer, Arnold M., ed. *A History of the Hutterite-Mennonites*. Freeman: Hutterian Centennial Committee, 1974.

Janzen, Rod. *The Prairie People: Forgotten Anabaptists*. Hanover: University Press of New England, 1999.

Kleinsasser, Ian. *Blessings and Burdens: 100 Years of Hutterites in Manitoba*. MacGregor: Hutterian Brethren Book Centre, 2019.

Stoltzfus, Duane C.S. *Pacifists in Chains: The Persecution of Hutterite during the Great War*. Baltimore: Johns Hopkins University Press, 2013.

Treasures of Time: the Rural Municipality of Cartier, 1914–1984. Elie: RM of Cartier, 1985.

Wollmann, Kenny, ed. *Navigating Tradition and Innovation: Essays Commemorating the Permanent Settlement of Hutterites in Manitoba*. MacGregor: Hutterian Brethren Book Centre, 2024.

Bruderhof

Arnold, Eberhard. *Selected Writings*. Edited by Johann Christoph Arnold. Maryknoll: Orbis Books, 2000.

Arnold, Emmy. *Torches Together: The Story of the Bruderhof Communities*. Rifton: Plough Publishing House, 1964.

Barth, Emmy. *An Embassy Besieged: The Story of a Christian Community in Nazi Germany*. Eugene: Cascade Books; Rifton: Plough Publishing House, 2010.

Baum, Marcus. *Against the Wind: Eberhard Arnold and the Bruderhof*. Rifton: Plough Publishing House, 2002.

Brothers Unite: An Account of the Uniting of Eberhard Arnold and the Rhön Bruderhof with the Hutterian Church. Ulster Park: Plough Publishing House, 1988.

Janzen, Rod. "The Hutterites and the Bruderhof: The Relationship Between an Old Older Religious Society and a Twentieth-Century Communal Group." *Mennonite Quarterly Review* 79, no. 4 (2005): 505–544.

Mow, Merrill. *Torches Rekindled: The Bruderhof's Struggle for Renewal.* Ulster Park: Plough Publishing House, 1989.

Hutterite Sociology and Anthropology

Janzen, Rod and Max Stanton. *The Hutterites in North America.* Baltimore: Johns Hopkins University Press, 2010.

Katz, Yossi and John Lehr. *Inside the Ark: The Hutterites in Canada and the United States.* Revised Edition. Regina: Canadian Plains Research Centre Press, 2014.

Peter, Karl. *The Dynamics of Hutterite Society: An Analytical Approach.* Edmonton: University of Alberta Press, 1987.

Peters, Victor. *All Things Common: The Hutterian Way of Life.* Minneapolis: University of Minnesota Press, 1965.

Personal Accounts

Holzach, Michael. *The Forgotten People: A Year Among the Hutterites.* Translated by Stephan Lhotzky. Sioux Falls: Ex Machina Publishing Company, 1993.

Kirkby, Maryanne. *I Am Hutterite: The Fascinating True Story of a Young Woman's Journey to Reclaim her Heritage.* Nashville: Thomas Nelson, 2010.

Maendel, Linda. *Hutterite Diaries: Wisdom from my Prairie Community.* Harrisonburg: Herald Press, 2015.

Rhodes, Robert. *Nightwatch: An Inquiry into Solitude.* Intercourse: Good Books, 2009.

Stahl, Lisa Marie. *My Hutterite Life.* Helena: Farcountry Press, 2003.

Internet Sources

Eberhard Arnold Archives: https://www.eberhardarnold.com.

Global Anabaptist Mennonite Encyclopedia Online (GAMEO): https://gameo.org.

Hutterian Brethren website: https://hutterites.org.

Jacob D. Maendel Lectures website: https://www.jdmlectures.org.

www.ingramcontent.com/pod-product-compliance
Lightning Source LLC
Chambersburg PA
CBHW080943120626
46546CB00010B/2823